MEMOIRS OF THE SPIRIT

MEMOIRS OF THE SPIRIT

*American Religious Autobiography
from Jonathan Edwards to Maya Angelou*

Edited by

EDWIN S. GAUSTAD

WILLIAM B. EERDMANS PUBLISHING COMPANY
GRAND RAPIDS, MICHIGAN / CAMBRIDGE, U.K.

© 1999 Wm. B. Eerdmans Publishing Co.
255 Jefferson Ave. S.E., Grand Rapids, Michigan 49503 /
P.O. Box 163, Cambridge CB3 9PU U.K.

Paperback edition 2001

Printed in the United States of America

06 05 04 03 02 01   7 6 5 4 3 2

Library of Congress Cataloging-in-Publication Data

Memoirs of the spirit / edited [i.e. compiled] by Edwin S. Gaustad.
p.   cm.
Includes bibliographical references.
ISBN 0-8028-4996-2 (pbk : alk. paper)
1. Religious autobiography — United States.
I. Gaustad, Edwin S. (Edwin Scott)
BL2525.M455 1999
200′.92′273 — dc21
[B]   99-32614
CIP

For Charles Van Hof

for twenty years my editor —
superb and unflappable

CONTENTS

CONTENTS

ACKNOWLEDGMENTS

Grateful acknowledgment is extended to the following publishers or agencies for permission to use materials for which they hold the rights.

Mary Rowlandson. *The Sovereignty and Goodness of God.* Copyright © 4/98 by St. Martin's Press, Inc. Reprinted with permission of Bedford/ St. Martin's Press, Inc.

Jonathan Edwards. *A Jonathan Edwards Reader.* Edited by John E. Smith et al. Yale University Press, copyright © 1995. Used by permission of the publisher.

Benjamin Rush. *The Autobiography of Benjamin Rush.* Copyright © 1948 by Princeton University Press. Reprinted by permission of Princeton University Press.

Richard Allen. *The Life Experience and Gospel Labors of the Rt. Rev. Richard Allen.* Copyright © 1960 by Abingdon Press. Used by permission of Abingdon Press.

Peter Cartwright. *Autobiography of Peter Cartwright.* Copyright © 1956, 1984 by Abingdon Press. Used by permission of Abingdon Press.

Frederick Douglass. *Narrative of the Life of Frederick Douglass, An American Slave, Written by Himself,* edited by Benjamin Quarles. The Belknap Press of Harvard University Press. Copyright © 1960 by the President and Fellows of Harvard College. Reprinted by permission.

Black Elk. *Black Elk Speaks* by John G. Neihardt. Copyright 1932, 1959,

1972 by John G. Neihardt. Copyright © 1961 by the John G. Neihardt Trust. Used by permission of University of Nebraska Press.

Harry E. Fosdick. *The Living of These Days: An Autobiography*. Copyright © 1956 by Harper & Row; renewed 1984 by Dorothy Fosdick and Elinor F. Downs. Reprinted by permission of HarperCollins Publishers, Inc.

John La Farge, S.J. "Hoisting a Visible Sign" in *The Manner Is Ordinary*. Copyright © 1954 and renewed 1982 by John La Farge, reprinted by permission of Harcourt, Brace & Co.

Reinhold Niebuhr. *Leaves from the Notebook of a Tamed Cynic*. Copyright © 1929; renewed by Reinhold Niebuhr, 1957; by Harper & Row, 1980. Used by permission of Westminster John Knox Press.

Paramahansa Yogananda. *Autobiography of a Yogi*. Published by Self-Realization Fellowship, Los Angeles. Copyright © 1946; renewed 1974, 1981, 1993. Used by permission of the Self-Realization Fellowship.

Dorothy Day. "War Is the Health of the State," from *The Long Loneliness*. Copyright © 1952 by Harper & Row, Publishers, Inc. Copyright renewed © 1982 by Tamar Teresa Hennessy. Reprinted by permission of HarperCollins Publishers, Inc.

Mary McCarthy. "The Blackguard," from *Memories of a Catholic Girlhood*. Copyright © 1974 by Mary McCarthy. Reprinted by permission of Harcourt, Brace & Co.

Virginia Sorensen. *Where Nothing Is Long Ago*. First published by Harcourt, Brace & Co. Copyright © 1955, 1960, 1963 by Virginia Sorensen. Used by permission of Curtis Brown, Ltd., and of Signature Books.

Thomas Merton. *The Seven Storey Mountain*. Copyright © 1948 by Harcourt, Inc.; renewed 1976 by the Trustees of the Merton Legacy Trust. Used by permission of Harcourt, Brace & Co.

Alan Watts. *In My Own Way: An Autobiography*. Pantheon Books. Copyright © 1972 by Alan Watts. Used by permission of Russell & Volkening, agents for the author.

Billy Graham. *Just As I Am*. Copyright © 1997 by the Billy Graham Evangelistic Association. Used by permission of HarperCollins Publishers, Inc.

Jimmy Carter. *Living Faith*. Copyright © 1996 by Jimmy Carter. Used by permission of Times Books, a division of Random House, Inc.

William F. Buckley Jr. *Nearer My God: An Autobiography of Faith*. Copyright © 1997 by William F. Buckley, Jr. Used by permission of Doubleday, a division of Random House, Inc.

Maya Angelou. *I Know Why the Caged Bird Sings.* Copyright © 1969; renewed 1997 by Maya Angelou. Used by permission of Random House, Inc.

Barbara G. Harrison. *Visions of Glory: A History and a Memory of Jehovah's Witnesses.* New York: Simon and Schuster, 1978. Copyright © 1978 by Barbara Grizzuti Harrison. Used by permission of Georges Borchardt, Inc., agents for the author.

Richard Rodriguez. *Hunger of Memory: The Education of Richard Rodriguez.* Copyright © 1982 by Richard Rodriguez. Used by permission of David R. Godine, Publisher, Inc.

I also acknowledge the following for their assistance with the illustrations.

Mary Rowlandson. Title page of *The Sovereignty and Goodness of God.* Courtesy of the Boston Public Library.

Jonathan Edwards. Portrait by John F. Weir, 1910, after an unknown artist. Courtesy of the Yale University Art Gallery.

Benjamin Rush. Portrait by Edward Savage, 1800. Courtesy of The National Portrait Gallery, Smithsonian Institution.

Richard Allen. Portrait by P. S. Duval, c. 1840. Courtesy of The National Portrait Gallery, Smithsonian Institution.

Peter Cartwright. Photo undated. Courtesy of the McLean County Historical Society, Illinois.

Orestes Brownson. Portrait by P. A. Healy, 1863. Courtesy of The National Portrait Gallery, Smithsonian Institution.

Frederick Douglass. Photo by George K. Warren, c. 1879. Courtesy of The National Portrait Gallery, Smithsonian Institution.

Isaac Mayer Wise. Portrait by Michael Goldstein, undated. Courtesy of The National Portrait Gallery, Smithsonian Institution.

Black Elk. Photo by John Neihardt, 1931. Courtesy of Hilda Neihardt.

Harry Emerson Fosdick. Portrait by S. J. Woolf, 1930. Courtesy of The National Portrait Gallery, Smithsonian Institution.

John La Farge, S.J. Photo courtesy of *America: The National Catholic Weekly.*

Mary Antin. From Mary H. Wade, *Pilgrims of Today* (1916). Courtesy of The Library of Congress.

ACKNOWLEDGMENTS

Reinhold Niebuhr. Photo, undated. Courtesy of Union Theological Seminary, New York City.

Paramahansa Yogananda. "The Last Smile," 1952. Courtesy of The Self-Realization Fellowship, Los Angeles.

Benjamin E. Mays. Photo by G. J. Davis, 1949. Courtesy of The National Portrait Gallery, Smithsonian Institution.

Dorothy Day. Photo by Vivian Cherry, © 1955. Courtesy of The National Portrait Gallery, Smithsonian Institution.

Mary McCarthy, photographed in Portugal, c. 1961. Courtesy of the Vassar College Libraries.

Virginia Sorensen. Photograph courtesy of Beth Hepburn and Fred Sorensen.

Thomas Merton. Photo by R. E. Meatyard, 1966. Courtesy of The National Portrait Gallery, Smithsonian Institution.

Alan Watts. Courtesy of the Alan Watts Electronic University.

Billy Graham. Courtesy of the Billy Graham Evangelistic Association.

Jimmy Carter. Photo by Rick Diamond. Courtesy of the Carter Center, Atlanta, Georgia.

William F. Buckley Jr. Courtesy of Frances Bronson and *The National Review.*

Maya Angelou. Photo by Steve Dunwell. Courtesy of Wake Forest University.

Barbara G. Harrison. Courtesy of Barbara G. Harrison and Georges Borchardt, Inc.

Richard Rodriguez. Courtesy of Georges Borchardt, Inc.

INTRODUCTION

Memory is always fallible, and history is always partial. Yet these two weak reeds do lean upon each other, do inevitably depend on each other. Memory provides the initial impetus for history, while history becomes a reinforcement, possibly even a validation, of memory. Like wounded warriors, the two support each other as they make their way toward a brighter light. "Critical history," said Carl Becker, "is simply the instinctive and necessary exercise of memory, but of memory tested and fortified by reliable sources."[1]

Memory is notoriously imprecise: it is faulty, failing, selective, and often self-serving. And "critical history," or even "scientific history" for a time seemed the unfailing corrective to the sins of memory. But then we came to see that history also has its failures: incapable of total objectivity, thesis riven and driven, impressionistic and spotty. And yet one author, seizing both horns of the dilemma, writes of *History as an Art of Memory*.[2] Another, Jill Ker Conway, in her book *When Memory Speaks: Reflections on Autobiography*, asks whether autobiography is merely the "most popular

---

1. Quoted in Michael Kammen, *Selvages & Biases: The Fabric of History in American Culture* (Ithaca, N.Y.: Cornell University Press, 1987), pp. 97-98. On the relationships between memory and history, see also Kammen's *A Season of Youth: The American Revolution and the Historical Imagination* (Ithaca, N.Y.: Cornell University Press, 1978).

2. Patrick H. Hutton, University Press of New England, 1993. Also see "The Uses of Memory: A Round Table," *Journal of American History* 85:2 (September 1998): 409-65.

form of fiction." But she responds that autobiography does have to pay attention to the "hard angularity" of facts. It does so in such a way, however, as to enable the reader "to try on the experience of another, just as one would try on a dress or a suit of clothes, to see what the image in the mirror then looks like." When a "convincing narrative" lets us inside another person's life, the result is "deeply satisfying."[3]

At first glance, autobiography might seem to offer us the worst of all possible worlds so far as the potential virtues of memory and history are concerned. Surely here, if anywhere, memory is least likely to be trusted, while history is reduced to a subservient role: a Greek chorus offering "backup" for the solo voice. Is every autobiography of necessity a hopelessly egocentric *Song of Myself,* to cite Walt Whitman, or unseemly *Advertisements for Myself,* to name Norman Mailer? Or is the self-centeredness illusory? Is Whitman perhaps speaking for a young nation, and Mailer for a sorely tried generation? Collective autobiography may, of course, be as suspect as the private kind, but it may also transmute itself into the necessary myths by which peoples and nations live.

Arthur R. Gold, for example, argues that the Bible itself, the Book of Exodus in particular, cannot be properly appreciated until its autobiographical character is well understood. The Hebrew scriptures in particular, Gold writes, are "a people's description of itself, a national autobiography, in which a people investigates, affirms, and perpetuates its own complex identity."[4] Similarly, many American autobiographers blend their own story with that of their society and their nation. An inner, private history becomes a window through which to see more clearly the complexities and ironies of the modern world. Such writers, as Robert F. Sayre has noted, "have made their personal dreams and nightmares a part of the public discourse."[5]

Of course, the interests are not always that broad. Some write not so much to reveal themselves as to discover themselves. Alfred Kazin writes for himself, he admits, for he believes that he has been "saved by language." An autobiography is not raw memory, but a sifting and shifting of memory and, therefore, of one's life. "By the time experience is distilled enough," Kazin writes, "to set some particular thing down on paper, so much unconscious reordering has gone on that even the

---

3. Published by Alfred Knopf, 1998; quotations from pp. 3, 6. Her book (and her bibliography) give special attention to female autobiographies.

4. *Commentary* 43:5 (May 1967): 46.

5. *American Quarterly* 29:3 (1977): 258. Also see the bibliography herein, pp. 258-62.

naïve wish to be wholly 'truthful' fades before the intoxication of line, pattern, form."[6] Other writers reach more for poetry than for truth, while still others find refuge in generalizations that obscure or omit all startling or illuminating detail.

And then there are those who, like Mark Twain, undertake their autobiographical mission with a maddening casualness. After much reflection on the proper technique, Twain reports that at last "I hit upon the right way to do an Autobiography." That right way is as follows:

> Start at no particular time of your life; wander at your free will all over your life; talk about the only things which interest you for the moment; drop it the moment its interests threaten to pale, and turn your talk upon the new and more interesting thing that has intruded itself into your mind meantime.[7]

Yet, Twain, with supreme self-confidence, saw his work "as a model for all future autobiographies" just because it mixed past and present together so freely. For by this method, the reader would have his interest constantly fired up "all along like contact of flint with steel." Facts, he noted, sometimes get in the way of fancy, and that should never be allowed to happen.[8]

Religious autobiography may take the facts more seriously, but here, too, larger purposes must often be served. The classic model, Augustine's *Confessions,* made its goal clear: "Let me know Thee who knowest me," he wrote, adding from Paul's words to the Corinthians, "let me know Thee even as I am known." One seeks to know the self better in order to know God better. And confession is the way to achieve both — confession which, at least in Augustine's case, took the form of a full-blown autobiography. The remaining purpose for him was to help others follow a similar path of liberation and salvation. "I, O Lord, confess to You that men may hear."[9] The confession is to God; the testimony is in behalf of all humankind.

Similarly, in America the case of John Woolman demonstrates

6. Quotations are from Joyce Carol Oates's review of *Telling Lives: The Biographer's Art,* in the *New York Times Book Review,* May 13, 1979, pp. 3, 29.

7. In Charles Neider's Introduction to *The Autobiography of Mark Twain* (New York: Washington Square Press, 1961), p. xi.

8. *The Autobiography of Mark Twain,* pp. xii, xiii.

9. See Brooke Hopkins, "Reading, and Believing in, Autobiography," *Soundings* 64:1 (Spring, 1981): 95-96.

that religious autobiography can be understood more as an instance of self-effacement than of self-aggrandizement. "I have often felt a notion of Love," Woolman wrote, "to leave some hints of my experience of the Goodness of God."[10] The self is diminished, so that the goodness of God may be enlarged. Or, as John the Baptist is recorded as saying of Jesus, "He must increase, but I must decrease."[11] Woolman's identification with the Indian and the slave was, moreover, autobiographical rather than theoretical. He reached them by walking, "that by so Traveling I might have a more lively feeling of the condition of the Oppressed Slaves"; and, in the case of the Indians, "a Concern arose to Spend Some time with [them], that I might feel and understand their life."[12]

Some have pointed out that the conversion narrative is at the root of autobiography. Robert F. Sayre quotes Roy Pascal to the effect that genuine autobiography "imposes a pattern on a life, constructs out of it a coherent story." Sayre adds that the conversion narrative does precisely that and is, from this point of view, "the major precursor of modern autobiography." Such narrators look "back from a single organizing perspective and [tell] a fairly coherent story of a sizeable portion of their lives."[13] In the present volume, Jonathan Edwards's *Personal Narrative* best represents this classic form. In telling what God had done for him, Edwards would have a wider public know what God may, in turn, do for them. And, to some degree, every autobiography — religious or no — offers the reader an enlargement, or perhaps a confirmation, of his or her own experience.

In Benjamin Franklin's *Autobiography*[14] many see the transition from a salvation story to a secular one. Yet, Franklin's immensely popular memoir can be regarded as but an adaptation of the more explicitly spiritual "pilgrim's progress." Franklin tells of another kind of salvation: from obscurity and poverty to fame and an agreeable station in life, from ignorance to illumination, and from intense activity to calm reflection — "the Thing most like living one's Life over again." Though the word "autobiography" had not yet been invented, Franklin none-

10. See Daniel B. Shea, Jr., *Spiritual Autobiography in Early America* (Princeton, N.J.: Princeton University Press, 1968), p. 46ff.

11. John 3:30.

12. Shea, *Spiritual Autobiography,* pp. 52, 53.

13. *American Quarterly* 29:3 (1977): 243.

14. First published in 1791. The most useful modern edition is that edited by J. A. Leo Lamay and P. M. Zall, and published by W. W. Norton in 1986.

theless gave the genre an ever enlarging place in American letters. And however skeptical or doggedly practical his tone, he did not drive religion from the field.

Indeed, Alfred Kazin has argued in *God and the American Writer* that much of our literature does not escape that "Hound of Heaven" that Francis Thompson identified. The American writer may well avoid a public religion often so "vehement, politicized, and censorious." But there is another kind of religion, Kazin notes, that envelops: a heritage, a teaching, a company, a safety. This religion "is where we are most at home and is always there when we need to go home again."[15] And Thornton Wilder saw the ephemeral ("adulteries of dentists") as unworthy of the attention of the serious writer. "I am interested," he noted, "in those things that repeat and repeat and repeat in the lives of millions" — in other words, in the human heartbeats and the spiritual searches.[16] Autobiographers do not trivialize history: they embody it.

In this book, many of the authors do not see themselves as writing a religious autobiography. Mary Rowlandson (ch. 1) concentrates on a single episode of her life, though certainly a traumatic and transforming one. Jonathan Edwards (ch. 2) tells a quite limited story, though some of his other expansive writings illuminate his short "personal narrative." In the crowded canvas of the American Revolution and its aftermath, Benjamin Rush (ch. 3) hardly has time for a full unfolding of his religious views. But in Chapters 4, 5, and 6 (Richard Allen, Peter Cartwright, and Orestes Brownson), the reader is exposed to a more nearly complete autobiographical statement, though only portions of each are offered here.

With the famous abolitionist, Frederick Douglass (ch. 7), one encounters for the first time an autobiographer who is essentially unfriendly to religion, at least to the Christianity that he saw being practiced all around him. Rabbi Isaac Mayer Wise (ch. 8) provides "reminiscences" as valuable for their insight into nineteenth-century American Judaism as into the reason and passion of Wise himself. In Chapter 9, one garners some insight into the religion of a Native American, though one who at this point in the nation's history has not been

15. Published by Alfred Knopf in 1997; quotation from p. 258.
16. Quoted in J. D. McCatchy, "Wilder and the Marvels of the Heart," *New York Times Book Review*, April 13, 1997, p. 35.

impervious to the influence of Christianity. Harry Emerson Fosdick (ch. 10) was so totally immersed in the strong and contrary currents of American religion in the first half of the twentieth century that his autobiographical prism is inevitably of unique value.

Orestes Brownson had introduced one kind of Roman Catholicism to a largely hostile, even more largely ignorant, American audience, but the sophisticated and literate Jesuit, John LaFarge (ch. 11) seized many more opportunities to exercise influence at another level. And if Rabbi Wise represented one kind of official Judaism, Mary Antin (ch. 12) speaks for the operational force of Judaism at a less formal level. For a time, Reinhold Niebuhr (ch. 13) stood in danger of becoming everyone's favorite Protestant theologian: of the politicians, the journalists, the philosophers, and even other theologians. On the other hand, if the American public knew the name of any spokesman for the Hindu tradition — apart from Gandhi — that name was likely to be Yogananda (ch. 14).

Martin Luther King is surely the best known African American voice in the twentieth century, but he would be glad to share a small portion of his fame with his good friend and mentor, Benjamin Mays (ch. 15). Few if any in this book would think of themselves as even remotely related to the notion of sainthood; Dorothy Day (ch. 16), however, has actually been proposed, informally, for this exalted status. Mary McCarthy (ch. 17) was a different kind of Catholic and a different kind of writer, her presence here helping to illustrate the breadth of that ancient tradition. On behalf of a much newer tradition, Virginia Sorensen (ch. 18) movingly re-creates the Mormonism of her childhood. Roman Catholic breadth is further revealed in the abundant writings of America's "favorite monk," Thomas Merton (ch. 19).

The awareness of, or admission of, pluralism in America took a major step forward via the facile pen of Alan Watts (ch. 20), while the "old-time religion" found a powerful spokesman in the person of Billy Graham (ch. 21). Former president Jimmy Carter (ch. 22) managed to give religion, and especially the good works presumably associated therewith, a good name. In the late twentieth century, Catholicism could take pleasure in another eloquent spokesman and loyal churchman: William Buckley (ch. 23). If Benjamin Mays revealed the social force of black religion, Maya Angelou (ch. 24) recalled the power of its passion. Alone among the twenty-six authors, Barbara G. Harrison (ch. 25) writes of a religious identification wholly rejected and abandoned. Also alone among these twenty-six, Richard Rodriguez (ch. 26) shares the warmth and the strength of a family Catholicism that was Hispanic.

Introduction

Why these twenty-six and not others? No easy answer can ever be given to justify or fully explain the selectivity that operates, generally more subtly, in any historical undertaking. In a collection of this sort, readers will be tempted to offer replacements or additions. This is both appropriate and healthy. My own choices respond to two uneven desires: first, to include some favorites; and, second, to give the bright tapestry that is American religion a fair (though it can never be full) representation. *Memoirs of the Spirit* invites one to walk through a variety of corridors and rooms that reveal something of the nation's rich religious past. It may even invite a few to indulge in autobiographical reflections of their own.

Such reflection need not be lengthy. My own, for example, is quite short. It echoes the anxiety of the father of the epileptic child, as recorded in the Gospel of Mark (and expressed in the King James Version with which I grew up and from which I have never wholly escaped): "Lord, I believe; help, Thou, mine unbelief."

E.S.G.
Santa Fe, New Mexico

MEMOIRS OF THE SPIRIT

THE

Soveraignty & Goodness

OF

GOD,

Together,

With the Faithsulness of His Promises
Displayed;
Being a

NARRATIVE

Of the Captivity and Restauration of

Mrs. Mary Rowlandson.

Commended by her, to all that desires to
know the Lords doings to, and
dealings with Her.

Especially to her dear Children and Relations,

The second Addition Corrected and amended.

Written by Her own Hand for Her private Use, and now
made Publick at the earnest Desire of some Friends,
and for the benefit of the Afflicted.

Deut. 32. 29, *See now that I, even I am he, and there is no
God with me: I kill and I make alive, I wound and I heal
neither is there any can deliver out of my hand.*

CAMBRIDGE,
Printed by Samuel Green, 1 6 8 2.

THE CAPTIVE

Mary Rowlandson

(C. 1637-1711)

In 1676 a Massachusetts wife and mother was captured by Indians in the midst of King Philip's [Metacom's] War. Wrenched from home and family, wounded and forced to watch one daughter die, she suffered deprivation and deepest anxieties for four months of captivity. When, after her release, she wrote of her experience, Mary Rowlandson gave her narrative a perhaps surprising title: *The Sovereignty and Goodness of God* (1682). This first account set a pattern not only for the great many captivity narratives that would follow, but also served as a type of the Christian life: captivity (to sin), redemption (by God).

King Philip's War, launched in 1675, represented a last great effort by Indian tribes in New England to stem the steady encroachment of the English settlers upon their lands and their culture. Not all Indians joined in the battle: some actually fought alongside the English while others remained neutral. But enough of them followed Philip to wreak havoc of unprecedented magnitude on the immigrants from England, now in their second or third generation of settlement. In terms of percentages of lives lost (both Indian and Europeans), King Philip's War remains America's costliest war ever.

Mary White, born in England, emigrated as a very young child to Massachusetts in 1639. Her family moved to Lancaster, Massachusetts, in 1653 and, about three years later, she married Joseph Rowlandson, Lancaster's first minister (Congregational). By the time of the Indian attack on the frontier town in February 1676, the couple had three children, ages fifteen, eleven, and seven. The attack came while Joseph Rowlandson joined with other men to go back to Boston to plead for troops to help defend their small town. But by the time the first troops arrived, the Rowlandson house was already aflame, fourteen of Lancaster's citizens lay dead, and twenty-three had been captured. Mary Rowlandson's own words cannot be improved on for portraying the horror and terror of her capture — and her captivity.

Complicated negotiations for her release took some time, and she describes in detail her reflections on the change of fortune. Filled with biblical imagery and with Puritan theology, she writes most naturally of how every hardship only made her realize more fully her dependence on God and "how good the Lord is, to enquire with David, *What shall I render to the Lord, for all his benefits to me? Psal. 116. 12.*"

[See the excellent introduction and notes by Neal Salisbury in his edition of Mary Rowlandson's narrative (Boston: Bedford Books, 1997).]

At length they came and beset our own house, and quickly it was the dolefullest day that ever mine eyes saw. The House stood upon the edge of a hill; some of the *Indians* got behind the hill, others into the Barn, and others behind any thing that could shelter them; from all which places they shot against the House, so that the Bullets seemed to fly like hail; and quickly they wounded one man among us, then another, and then a third. About two hours (according to my observation, in that amazing time) they had been about the house before they prevailed to fire it (which they did with Flax and Hemp, which they brought out of the Barn, and there being no defence about the House, only two Flankers at two opposite corners, and one of them not finished) they fired it once and one ventured out and quenched it but they quickly fired again, and that took. Now is that dreadfull hour come, that I have often heard of (in time of War, as it was the case of others) but now mine eyes see it. Some in our house were fighting for their lives. others wallowing in their blood, the House on fire over our heads, and the bloody Heathen ready to knock us on the head, if we stirred out. Now might we hear Mothers & Children crying out for themselves, and one another, *Lord, What shall we do?* Then I took my Children (and one of my sisters, hers) to go forth and leave the

Source: Neal Salisbury, ed., *The Sovereignty and Goodness of God* [1682] (Boston: Bedford Books, 1997), pp. 68-70; 104-12.

house: but as soon as we came to the door and appeared, the *Indians* shot so thick that the bullets rattled against the House, as if one had taken an handfull of stones and threw them, so that we were fain to give back. We had six stout Dogs belonging to our Garrison, but none of them wou'd stir, though another time, if any *Indian* had came to the door, they were ready to fly upon him and tear him down. The Lord hereby would make us the more to acknowledge his hand, and to see that our help is alwayes in him. But out we must go, the fire increasing, and coming along behind us, roaring, and the Indians gaping before us with their Guns, Spears and Hatchets to devour us. No sooner were we out of the House, but my Brother in Law (being before wounded, in defending the house, in or near the throat) fell down dead, whereat the *Indians* scornfully shouted, and hallowed, and were presently upon him, shipping off his cloaths, the bulletts flying thick, one went through my side, and the same (as would seem) through the bowels and hand of my dear Child in my arms.* One of my elder Sisters Children, named *William,* had then his Leg broken, which the *Indians* perceiving, they knockt him on head. Thus were we butchered by those merciless Heathen, standing amazed, with the blood running down to our heels. My eldest Sister being yet in the House, and seeing those wofull sights, the Infidels haling Mothers one way, and Children another, and some wallowing in their blood: and her elder Son telling her that her Son *William* was dead, and my self was wounded, she said, And, *Lord, let me dy with them;* which was no sooner said, but she was struck with a Bullet and fell down dead over the threshold. I hope she is reaping the fruit of her good labours, being faithfull to the service of God in her place. In her younger years she lay under much trouble upon spiritual accounts, till it pleased God to make that precious scripture take hold of her heart, *2 Cor.* 12.9. *And he said unto me, my grace is sufficient for thee.* More than twenty years after I have heard her tell how sweet and comfortable that place was to her. But to return: the *Indians* laid hold of us, pulling me one way, and the Children another, and said, *Come go along with us;* I told them they would kill me: they answered, *If I were willing to go along with them, they would not hurt me.*

Oh the dolefull sight that now was to behold at this House! *Come, behold the works of the Lord, what desolations he has made in the Earth.* Of thirty seven persons who were in this one House, none escaped either present death, or a bitter captivity, save only one, who might say as he, *Job* 1. 15.

* Mary's youngest child, Sarah, age seven. (ed.)

And I only am escaped alone to tell the News. There were twelve killed, some shot, some stab'd with their Spears, some knock'd down with their Hatchets. When we are in prosperity, Oh the little that we think of such dreadfull sights, and to see our dear Friends, and Relations ly bleeding out their heart-blood upon the ground. There was one who was chopt into the head with a Hatchet, and stripped naked, and yet was crawling up and down. It is a solemn sight to see so many Christians lying in their blood, some here, and some there, like a company of Sheep torn by Wolves. All of them stript naked by a company of hell-hounds, roaring, singing, ranting and insulting, as if they would have torn our very hearts out; yet the Lord by his Almighty power preserved a number of us from death, for there were twenty-four of us taken alive and carried captive.

I had often before this said, that if the *Indians* should come, I should chuse rather to be killed by them than be taken alive, but when it came to the tryal my mind changed; their glittering weapons so daunted my spirit, that I chose rather to go along with those (as I may say) ravenous Beasts, than that moment to end my dayes; and that I may the better declare what happened to me during that grievous Captivity, I shall particularly speak of the severall Removes we had up and down the Wilderness.

❧

But before I go any further, I would take leave to mention a few remarkable passages of providence, which I took special notice of in my afflicted time.

1. *Of the fair opportunity lost in the long March, a little after the* Fortfight, *when our* English Army *was so numerous, and in pursuit of the* Enemy, *and so near as to take several and destroy them: and the* Enemy *in such distress for food, that our men might track them by their rooting in the earth for Ground-nuts whilest they were flying for their lives.* I say, that then our Army should want Provision, and be forced to leave their pursuit and return homeward: and the very next week the *Enemy* came upon our *Town*, like Bears bereft of their whelps, or so many ravenous Wolves, rending us and our Lambs to death. But what shall I say? God seemed to leave His People to themselves, and order all things for His own holy ends. *Shall there be evil in the City and the Lord hath not done it? They are not grieved for the affliction of* Joseph, *therefore shall they go Captive, with the first that go Captive. It is the Lords doing, and it should be marvelous in our eyes.*

2. I cannot but remember how the Indians *derided the slowness, and dulness of the* English *Army, in its setting out.* For after the desolations at *Lancaster* and *Medfield,* as I went along with them, they asked me when I thought the *English* Army would come after them? I told them I could not tell: It may be they will come in *May,* said they. Thus did they scoffe at us, as if the *English* would be a quarter of a year getting ready.

3. Which also I have hinted before, when the English *Army with new supplies were sent forth to pursue after the enemy, and they understanding it, fled before them till they came to* Baquaug *River, where they forthwith went over safely: that that River should be impassable to the* English. I can but admire to see the wonderfull providence of God in preserving the heathen for farther affliction to our poor Countrey. They could go in great numbers over, but the *English* must stop: God had an over-ruling hand in all those things.

4. It was thought, if their corn were cut down, they would starve and dy with hunger: and all their Corn that could be found, was destroyed, and they driven from that little they had in store, into the Woods in the midst of Winter; and yet how to admiration did the Lord preserve them for his Holy ends, and the destruction of many still amongst the *English!* Strangely did the Lord provide for them; that I did not see (all the time I was among them) one Man, Woman, or Child, die with hunger.

Though many times they would eat that, that a Hog or a Dog would hardly touch; yet by that God strengthened them to be a scourge to His People.

The chief and commonest food was Ground-nuts: They eat also Nuts and Acorns, Harty-choaks, Lilly roots, Ground-beans, and several other weeds and roots, that I know not.

They would pick up old bones, and cut them to pieces at the joynts, and if they were full of wormes and magots, they would scald them over the fire to make the vermine come out, and then boile them, and drink up the Liquor, and then beat the great ends of them in a Morter, and so eat them. They would eat Horses guts, and ears, and all sorts of wild Birds which they could catch: also Bear, Venison, Beaver, Tortois, Frogs, Squirrels, Dogs, Skunks, Rattle-snakes; yea, the very Bark of Trees; besides all sorts of creatures, and provision which they plundered from the *English.* I can but stand in admiration to see the wonderful power of God, in providing for such a vast number of our Enemies in the *Wilderness,* where there was nothing to be seen, but from hand to mouth. Many times in a morning, the generality of them would eat up all they had, and yet have some further supply against what they wanted. It is said, *Psal.* 81. 13, 14. *Oh, that my People had hearkened to me, and* Israel *had walked in my wayes, I should soon have subdued their Enemies, and turned my hand against their Adversaries.* But now our perverse and evil carriages in the sight of the Lord, have so offended Him, that instead of turning His hand against them, the Lord feeds and nourishes them up to be a scourge to the whole Land.

5. *Another thing that I would observe is, the strange providence of God, in turning things about when the* Indians *were at the highest, and the* English *at the lowest.* I was with the Enemy eleven weeks and five dayes, and not one Week passed without the fury of the Enemy, and some desolation by fire and sword upon one place or other. They mourned (with their black faces) for their own losses, yet triumphed and rejoyced in their inhumane, and many times devilish cruelty to the *English*. They would boast much of their Victories; saying, that in two hours time they had destroyed such a *Captain*, and his *Company* at such a place; and such a *Captain* and his *Company* in such a place; and such a *Captain* and his *Company* in such a place; and boast how many *Towns* they had destroyed, and then scoffe, and say, *They had done them a good turn, to send them to Heaven so soon.* Again, they would say, *This summer that they would knock all the Rogues in the head, or drive them into the Sea, or make them flie the Countrey:* thinking surely, *Agag*-like, *The bitterness of Death is past.* Now the Heathen begins to think all is their own, and the poor Christians hopes do fail (as to man) and now their eyes are more to God, and their hearts sigh heaven-ward: and to say in good earnest, *Help Lord, or we perish:* When the Lord had brought his people to this, that they saw no help in any thing but himself: then he takes the quarrel into his own hand: and though they had made a pit, in their own imaginations, as deep as hell for the Christians that Summer, yet the Lord hurll'd themselves into it. And the Lord had not so many wayes before to preserve them, but now he hath as many to destroy them.

But to return again to my going home, where we may see a remarkable change of Providence: At first they were all against it, except my Husband would come for me; but afterwards they assented to it, and seemed much to rejoyce in it; some askt me to send them some Bread, others some Tobacco, others shaking me by the hand, offering me a Hood and Scarfe to ride in; not one moving hand or tongue against it. Thus hath the Lord answered my poor desire, and the many earnest requests of others put up unto God for me. In my travels an *In-*

dian came to me, and told me, if I were willing, he and his *Squaw* would run away, and go home along with me: I told him *No:* I was not willing to run away, but desired to wait Gods time, that I might go home quietly, and without fear. And now God hath granted me my desire. O the wonderfull power of God that I have seen, and the experience that I have had; *I have been in the midst of those roaring Lyons, and Salvage Bears, that feared neither God, nor Man, nor the Devil, by night and day, alone and in company: sleeping all sorts together, and yet not one of them ever offered me the least abuse of unchastity to me, in word or action.* Though some are ready to say, I speak it for my own credit; *But I speak it in the presence of God, and to His glory.* Gods power is as great now, and as sufficient to save, as when he preserved *Daniel* in the Lions den; or the three *Children* in the fiery Furnace. I may well say as his *Psal.* 107. 1, 2, *Oh give thanks unto the Lord for He is good, for his mercy endureth for ever.* Let the Redeemed of the Lord say so, whom He hath redeemed from the hand of the Enemy, especially that I should come away in the midst of so many hundreds of Enemies quietly and peacably, and not a Dog moving his tongue. So I took my leave of them, and in coming along my heart melted into tears, more than all the while I was with them, and I was almost swallowed up with the thoughts that ever I should go home again.

About the Sun going down, Mr. *Hoar,* and my self, and the two *Indians* came to *Lancaster,* and a solemn sight it was to me. There had I lived many comfortable years amongst my Relations and Neighbours, and now not one *Christian* to be seen, nor one house left standing. We went on to a Farm house that was yet standing, where we lay all night: and a comfortable lodging we had, though nothing but straw to ly on. The Lord preserved us in safety that night, and raised us up again in the morning, and carried us along, that before noon, we came to *Concord.* Now was I full of joy, and yet not without sorrow: joy to see such a lovely sight, so many *Christians* together, and some of them my Neighbours: There I met with my Brother, and my Brother in Law, who asked me, if I knew where his Wife was? Poor heart! he had helped to bury her, and knew it not; she being shot down by the house was partly burnt: so that those who were at *Boston* at the desolation of the *Town,* and came back afterward, and buried the dead, did not know her. Yet I was not without sorrow, to think how many were looking and longing, and my own Children amongst the rest, to enjoy that deliverance that I had now received, and I did not know whither ever I should see them again.

Being recruited with food and raiment we went to *Boston* that day, where I met with my dear Husband, but the thoughts of our dear Children, one being dead, and the other we could not tell where, abated our comfort each to other. I was not before so much hem'd in with the merciless and cruel Heathen, but now as much with pittiful, tender-hearted and compassionate Christians. In that poor, and destressed, and beggerly condition I was received in, I was kindly entertained in severall Houses: so much love I received from several (some of whom I knew, and others I knew not) that I am not capable to declare it. But the Lord knows them all by name: *The Lord reward them seven fold into their bosoms of his spirituals, for their temporals!* The *twenty pounds* the price of my redemption was raised by some *Boston* Gentlemen, and Ms. *Usher,* whose bounty and religious charity, I would not forget to make mention of. Then Mr. *Thomas Shepard* of *Charlestown* received us into his House, where we continued eleven weeks; and a Father and Mother they were to us. And many more tender-hearted Friends we met with in that place. We were now, in the midst of love, yet not without much and frequent heaviness of heart for our poor Children, and other Relations, who were still in affliction.

The week following, after my coming in, the Governour and Council sent forth to the *Indians* again; and that not without success; for they brought in my Sister, and Good-wife Kettle: Their not knowing where our Children were, was a sore tryal to us still, and yet we were not without secret hopes that we should see them again. That which was dead lay heavier upon my spirit, than those which were alive and amongst the Heathen; thinking how it suffered with its wounds, and I was in no way able to relieve it; and how it was buried by the Heathen in the *Wilderness* from among all Christians. We were hurried up and down in our thoughts, sometimes we should hear a report that they were gone this way, and sometimes that; and that they were come in, in this place or that: We kept enquiring and listening to hear concerning them, but no certain news as yet. About this time the Council had ordered a day of publick *Thanks-giving:* though I thought I had still cause of mourning, and being unsettled in our minds, we thought we would ride toward the *Eastward,* to see if we could hear anything concerning our Children. And as we were riding along (God is the wise disposer of all things) between *Ipswich* and *Rowley* we met with Mr. *William Hubbard,* who told us that our Son *Joseph* was came in to Major *Waldrens,* and another with him, which was my Sisters Son. I asked him how he knew it? He said, the Major himself told him so.

So along we went till we came to *Newbury;* and their Minister being absent, they desired my Husband to preach the *Thanks-giving* for them; but he was not willing to stay there that night, but would go over to *Salisbury,* to hear further, and come again in the morning; which he did, and Preached there that day. At night, when he had done, one came, and told him that his Daughter was come in at *Providence:* Here was mercy on both hands: Now hath God fulfilled that precious Scripture which was such a comfort to me in my distressed condition. When my heart was ready to sink into the Earth (my Children being gone I could not tell whither) and my knees trembled under me, *And I was walking through the valley of the shadow of Death:* Then the Lord brought, and now has fulfilled that reviving word unto me: Thus saith the Lord, *Refrain thy voice from weeping, and thine eyes from tears, for thy work shall be rewarded,* saith the Lord, *and they shall came again from the Land of the Enemy.* Now we were between them, the one on the *East,* and the other on the *West.* Our Son being nearest, we went to him first, to *Portsmouth,* where we met with him, and with the Major also: who told us he had done what he could, but could not redeem him under *seven pounds,* which the good People thereabouts were pleased to pay. The Lord reward the Major, and all the rest, though unknown to me, for their labour of Love. My Sisters Son was redeemed for *four pounds,* which the Council gave order for the payment of. Having now received one of our Children, we hastened toward the other: going back through *Newbury,* my Husband Preached there on the *Sabbath-day:* for which they rewarded him many fold.

On *Munday* we came to Charlestown, where we heard that the Governour of *Road-Island* had sent over for our Daughter, to take care of her, being now within his Jurisdiction: which should not pass without our acknowledgments. But she being nearer *Rehoboth* than *Road-Island,* Mr. *Newman* went over, and took care of her, and brought her to his own House. And the goodness of God was admirable to us in our low estate, in that he raised up passionate Friends on every side to us, when we had nothing to recompance any for their love. The *Indians* were now gone that way, that it was apprehended dangerous to go to her: But the Carts which carried Provision to the *English* Army, being guarded, brought her with them to *Dorchester,* where we received her safe: blessed be the Lord for it, *For great is his Power, and he can do whatsoever seemeth him good.* Her coming in was after this manner: She was travelling one day with the *Indians,* with her basket at her back; the company of *Indians* were got before her, and gone out of sight, all except one *Squaw;* she followed the

Squaw till night, and then both of them lay down, having nothing over them but the heavens, and under them but the earth. Thus she travelled three dayes together, not knowing whither she was going: having nothing to eat or drink but water, and green *Hirtle-berries.* At last they came into *Providence,* where she was kindly entertained by several of that *Town.* The *Indians* often said, that I should never have her under *twenty pounds:* But now the Lord hath brought her in upon free-cost, and given her to me the second time. The Lord make us a blessing indeed, each to others. Now have I seen that Scripture also fulfilled, *Deut.* 30. 4, 7. *If any of thine be driven out to the outmost parts of heaven, from thence will the Lord thy God gather thee, and from thence will he fetch thee. And the Lord thy God will put all their curses upon thine enemies, and on them which hate thee, which persecuted thee.* Thus hath the Lord brought me and mine out of that horrible pit, and hath set us in the midst of tender-hearted and compassionate Christians. It is the desire of my soul, that we may walk worthy of the mercies received, and which we are receiving.

 Our family being now gathered together (those of us that were living) the South Church *in* Boston *hired an House for us: Then we removed from Mr.* Shepards, *those cordial Friends, and went to* Boston, *where we continued about three quarters of a year: Still the Lord went along with us, and provided graciously for us.* I thought it somewhat strange to set up Housekeeping with bare walls; but as *Solomon* says, *Mony answers all things;* and that we had through the benevolence of Christian-friends, some in this *Town,* and some in that, and others: And some from *England,* that in a little time we might look, and see the House furnished with love. The Lord hath been exceeding good to us in our low estate, in that when we had neither house nor home, nor other necessaries, the Lord so moved the hearts of these and those towards us, that we wanted neither food, nor raiment for our selves or ours, *Prov.* 18. 24. *There is a Friend which sticketh closer than a Brother.* And how many such Friends have we found, and now living amongst? And truly such a Friend have we found him to be unto us, in whose house we lived, *viz.* Mr. *James Whitcomb,* a Friend unto us near hand, and afar off.

 I can remember the time, when I used to sleep quietly without workings in my thoughts, whole nights together, but now it is other wayes with me. When all are fast about me, and no eye open, but his who ever waketh, my thoughts are upon things past, upon the awfull dispensation of the Lord towards us; upon his wonderfull power and might in carrying of us through so many difficulties, in returning us in safety, and suffering none to hurt us. I remember in the night season, how the other day I was in the midst of thousands of enemies, & nothing but death before me: It is then hard work to perswade myself, that ever I should be satisfied with bread again. But now we are fed *with the finest of the Wheat,* and, as I may say, *with honey out of the rock.* In stead of the Husk we have the fatted Calf: The thoughts of these things in the particulars of them, and of the love and goodness of God towards us, make it true of me, what David said of himself, *Psal.* 6. 6. *I watered my couch with my tears.* Oh! the wonderfull power of God that mine eyes have seen, affording matter enough for my thoughts to run in, that when others are sleeping mine are weeping.

I have seen the extrem vanity of this World: One hour I have been in health, and wealth, wanting nothing: But the next hour in sickness and wounds, and death, having nothing but sorrow and affliction.

Before I knew what affliction meant, I was ready sometimes to wish for it. When I lived in prosperity, having the comforts of the World about me, my relations by me, my Heart chearfull: and taking little care for any thing; and yet seeing many, whom I preferred before my self, under many tryals and afflictions, in sickness, weakness, poverty, losses, crosses, and cares of the World, I should be sometimes jealous least I should have my portion in this life, and that Scripture would come to my mind, *Heb.* 12. 6. *For whom the **Lord** loveth he chasteneth, and scourgeth every Son whom he receiveth.* But now I see the Lord had his time to scourge and chasten me. The portion of some is to have their afflictions by drops, now one drop and then another; but the dregs of the Cup, the Wine of astonishment: like a sweeping rain that leaveth no food, did the Lord prepare to be my portion. Affliction I wanted, and affliction I had, full measure (I thought) pressed down and running over; yet I see, when God calls a Person to any thing, and through never so many difficulties, yet he is fully able to carry them through and make them see, and say, they have been gainers thereby. And I hope I can say in some measure, As *David* did, *It is good for me that I have been afflicted.* The Lord hath shewed me the vanity of these outward things. That they are the *Vanity of vanities, and vexation of spirit;* that they are but a shadow, a blast, a bubble, and things of no continuance. That we must rely on God himself, and our whole dependance must be upon him. If trouble from smaller matters begin to arise in me, I have something at hand to check my self with, and say, why am I troubled? It was but the other day that if I had had the world, I would have given it for my freedom, or to have been a

14

Servant to a Christian. I have learned to look beyond present and smaller troubles, and to be quieted under them, as *Moses* said, *Exod.* 14. 13. *Stand still and see the Salvation of the Lord.*

THE SINNER

Jonathan Edwards

(1703-1758)

Colonial America's most profound theologian and philosopher, Jonathan Edwards, is chiefly remembered — if at all — for the preaching of a sermon entitled *Sinners in the Hands of an Angry God* on July 8, 1741, in Enfield, Connecticut. In the midst of the revivalist excitement known as the Great Awakening, Edwards sounded a ringing call to repentance. Two and one-half centuries later, that call still rings, but it doesn't ring quite true when taken out of context. In at least a couple of ways, that notorious sermon requires a context.

First, Edwards did not preach this sermon as some mindless, shouting, sweating pulpit-pounder interested only in the emotional frenzy of the moment. Rather, he preached it in an attempt to give to words an empirical reality. To be truly meaningful, words had to be more than noises in the air; they had to touch, relate to, or evoke human experience. And any theology worth its salt had to be more than mere speculative knowledge; it had to come from the heart. As Edwards liked to say, there is a vast difference between being told that honey is sweet and having an immediate, sensory taste of that sweetness. The first, to follow William James, was a mere knowledge by description, the second, a more direct knowledge by acquaintance. Edwards aimed at that second kind of knowledge, for, as he wrote, the person who has only a speculative knowledge of religion is never truly engaged in the business of religion. Religion without passion is religion without power.

Second, when Edwards was addressing sinners, he was addressing himself. Edwards saw himself as also unworthy, wretched, wicked — held out of the pits of hell only by the strong arm of divine love. And if that love could rescue him, it could rescue others. Edwards could and did preach sermons as powerful about a loving God as an angry God, but somehow those sermons never make the anthologies for student consumption.

Edwards did not write a full autobiography, but about two years before the *Angry God* sermon, he wrote a Personal Narrative that tells of when "God shook me over the pit of hell." He had been there. But he had also come around to the other side of God's anger to His love. One cannot read this Narrative without recognizing that Edwards is speaking not of theological doctrine but of personal experience, not of books but of life. His language is sensory; he came to have not only a conviction of God's sovereignty, but "a *delightful* conviction." To his joy and comfort he found an "inward, sweet delight in God and divine things." In his religious conversion, Edwards had tasted the sweetness of honey.

[See John E. Smith, *Jonathan Edwards: Puritan, Preacher, Philosopher* (Notre Dame: Notre Dame University Press, 1992) and the *Jonathan Edwards Sermon Reader,* edited by W. H. Kimnach, K. P. Minkema, and D. A. Sweeney (New Haven: Yale University Press, 1999).]

Personal Narrative (c. 1739)

I had a variety of concerns and exercises about my soul from my childhood; but had two more remarkable seasons of awakening, before I met with that change, by which I was brought to those new dispositions, and that new sense of things, that I have since had. The first time was when I was a boy, some years before I went to college, at a time of remarkable awakening in my father's congregation. I was then very much affected for many months, and concerned about the things of religion, and my soul's salvation; and was abundant in duties. I used to pray five times a day in secret, and to spend much time in religious talk with other boys; and used to meet with them to pray together. I experienced I know not what kind of delight in religion. My mind was much engaged in it, and had much self-righteous pleasure; and it was my delight to abound in religious duties. I, with some of my schoolmates joined together, and built a booth in a swamp, in a very secret and retired place, for a place of prayer. And besides, I had particular secret places of my own in the woods, where I used to retire by myself; and used to be from time to time much affected. My affections seemed to be lively and easily

Source: John E. Smith et al., eds., *A Jonathan Edwards Reader* (New Haven, Conn.: Yale University Press, 1995), pp. 281-96.

moved, and I seemed to be in my element, when engaged in religious duties. And I am ready to think, many are deceived with such affections, and such a kind of delight, as I then had in religion, and mistake it for grace.

But in process of time, my convictions and affections wore off; and I entirely lost all those affections and delights, and left off secret prayer, at least as to any constant performance of it; and returned like a dog to his vomit, and went on in ways of sin.

Indeed, I was at some times very uneasy, especially towards the latter part of the time of my being at college. Till it pleased God, in my last year at college, at a time when I was in the midst of many uneasy thoughts about the state of my soul, to seize me with a pleurisy; in which he brought me nigh to the grave, and shook me over the pit of hell.

But yet, it was not long after my recovery before I fell again into my old ways of sin. But God would not suffer me to go on with any quietness; but I had great and violent inward struggles: till after many conflicts with wicked inclinations, and repeated resolutions, and bonds that I laid myself under by a kind of vows to God, I was brought wholly to break off all former wicked ways and all ways of known outward sin; and to apply myself to seek my salvation, and practice the duties of religion: but without that kind of affection and delight, that I had formerly experienced. My concern now wrought more by inward struggles and conflicts, and self-reflections. I made seeking my salvation the main business of my life. But yet it seems to me, I sought after a miserable manner: which has made me sometimes since to question, whether ever it issued in that which was saving; being ready to doubt, whether such miserable seeking was ever succeeded. But yet I was brought to seek salvation, in a manner that I never was before. I felt a spirit to part with all things in the world, for an interest in Christ. My concern continued and prevailed, with many exercising things and inward struggles; but yet it never seemed to be proper to express my concern that I had, by the name of terror.

From my childhood up, my mind had been wont to be full of objections against the doctrine of God's sovereignty, in choosing whom he would to eternal life, and rejecting whom he pleased; leaving them eternally to perish, and be everlastingly tormented in hell. It used to appear like a horrible doctrine to me. But I remember the time very well, when I seemed to be convinced, and fully satisfied, as to this sovereignty of God, and his justice in thus eternally disposing of men, according to his sovereign pleasure. But never could give an account, how, or by what means, I was thus convinced; not in the least imagining, in the time of it, nor a long time after, that there was any extraordinary influence of God's Spirit in it: but only that now I saw further, and my reason apprehended the justice and reasonableness of it. However, my mind rested in it; and it put an end to all those cavils and objections, that I had till then abode with me, all the preceding part of my life. And there has been a wonderful alteration in my mind, with respect to the doctrine of God's sovereignty, from that day to this; so that I scarce ever have found so much as the rising of an objection against God's sovereignty, in the most absolute sense, in showing mercy on whom he will show mercy; and hardening and eternally damning whom he will. God's absolute sovereignty, and justice, with respect to salvation and damnation, is what my mind seems to rest assured of, as much as of anything that I see with my eyes; at least it is so at times. But I have oftentimes since that first conviction, had quite another kind of sense of God's sovereignty, than I had then. I have often since, not only had a conviction, but a *delightful* conviction. The doctrine of God's sovereignty has very often appeared, an exceeding pleasant, bright and sweet doctrine to me: and absolute sovereignty is what I love to ascribe to God. But my first conviction was not with this.

The first that I remember that ever I found anything of that sort of inward, sweet delight in God and divine things, that I have lived much in since, was on reading those words, I Tim. 1:17. "Now, unto the King eternal, immortal, invisible, the only wise God, be honor and glory forever and ever, Amen." As I read the words, there came into my soul, and was as it were diffused through it, a sense of the glory of the Divine Being; a new sense, quite different from anything I ever experienced before. Never any words of Scripture seemed to me as these words did. I thought with myself, how excellent a Being that was; and how happy I should be, if I might enjoy that God, and be wrapped up to God in heaven, and be as it were swallowed up in him. I kept saying, and as it were singing over these words of Scripture to myself; and went to prayer, to pray to God that I might enjoy him; and prayed in a manner quite different from what I used to do; with a new sort of affection. But it never came into my thought, that there was anything spiritual, or of a saving nature in this.

From about that time, I began to have a new kind of apprehensions and ideas of Christ, and the work of redemption, and the glorious way of salvation by him. I had an inward, sweet sense of these things, that at times came into my heart; and my soul was led away in pleasant views and contemplations of them. And my mind was greatly engaged, to spend my time in reading and meditating on Christ; and the beauty and excellency of his person, and the lovely way of salvation, by free grace in him. I found no books so delightful to me, as those that treated of these subjects. Those words, Cant. 2:1, used to be abundantly with me: "I am the rose of Sharon, the lily of the valleys." The words seemed to me, sweetly to represent, the loveliness and beauty of Jesus Christ. And the whole Book of Canticles used to be pleasant to me; and I used to be much in reading it, about that time. And found, from time to time, an inward sweetness, that used, as it were, to carry me away in my contemplations; in what I know not how to express otherwise, than by a calm, sweet abstraction of soul from all the concerns of this world; and a kind of vision, or fixed ideas and imaginations, of being alone in the mountains, or some solitary wilderness, far from all mankind, sweetly conversing with Christ, and wrapped and swallowed up in God. The sense I had of divine things, would often of a sudden as it were, kindle up a sweet burning in my heart; an ardor of my soul, that I know not how to express.

Not long after I first began to experience these things, I gave an account to my father, of some things that had passed in my mind. I was pretty much affected by the discourse we had together. And when the discourse was ended, I walked abroad alone, in a solitary place in my father's pasture, for contemplation. And as I was walking there, and looked up on the sky and clouds; there came into my mind, a sweet sense of the glorious majesty and grace of God, that I know not how to express. I seemed to see them both in a sweet conjunction: majesty and meekness joined together: it was a sweet and gentle, and holy majesty; and also a majestic meekness; an awful sweetness; a high, and great, and holy gentleness.

After this my sense of divine things gradually increased, and became more and more lively, and had more of that inward sweetness. The appearance of everything was altered: there seemed to be, as it were, a calm, sweet cast, or appearance of divine glory, in almost everything. God's excellency, his wisdom, his purity and love, seemed to appear in everything; in the sun, moon and stars; in the clouds, and blue sky; in the grass, flowers, trees; in the water, and all nature; which used greatly to fix my mind. I often used to sit and view the moon, for a long time; and so in the daytime, spent much time in viewing the clouds and sky, to behold the sweet glory of God in these things: in the meantime, singing forth with a low voice, my contemplations of the Creator and Redeemer. And scarce anything, among all the works of nature, was so sweet to me as thunder and lightning. Formerly, nothing had been so terrible to me. I used to be a person uncommonly terrified with thunder: and it used to strike me with terror, when I saw a thunderstorm rising. But now, on the contrary, it rejoiced me. I felt God at the first appearance of a thunderstorm. And used to take the opportunity at such times, to fix myself to view the clouds, and see the lightnings play, and hear the majestic and awful voice of God's thunder: which oftentimes was exceeding entertaining, leading me to sweet contemplations of my great and glorious God. And while I viewed, used to spend my time, as it always seemed natural to me, to sing or chant forth my meditations; to speak my thoughts in soliloquies, and speak with a singing voice.

I felt then a great satisfaction as to my good estate. But that did not content me. I had vehement longings of soul after God and Christ, and after more holiness; wherewith my heart seemed to be full, and ready to break, which often brought to my mind, the words of the Psalmist, Ps. 119:28, "My soul breaketh for the longing it hath." I often felt a mourning and lamenting in my heart, that I had not turned to God sooner, that I might have had more time to grow in grace. My mind was greatly fixed on divine things; I was almost perpetually in the contemplation of them. Spent most of my time in thinking of divine things, year after year. And used to spend abundance of my time, in walking alone in the woods, and solitary places, for meditation, soliloquy and prayer, and converse with God. And it was always my manner, at such times, to sing forth my contemplations. And was almost constantly in ejaculatory prayer, wherever I was. Prayer seemed to be natural to me; as the breath, by which the inward burnings of my heart had vent.

The delights which I now felt in things of religion, were of an exceeding different kind, from those aforementioned, that I had when I was a boy. They were totally of another kind; and what I then had no more notion or idea of, than one born blind has of pleasant and beautiful colors. Those were of a more inward, pure, soul-animating and refreshing nature. Those former delights, never reached the heart; and did not arise from any sight of the divine excellency of the things of God; or any taste of the soul-satisfying, and life-giving good, there is in them.

My sense of divine things seemed gradually to increase, till I went to preach at New York; which was about a year and a half after they began. While I was there, I felt them, very sensibly, in a much higher degree, than I had done before. My longings after God and holiness, were much increased. Pure and humble, holy and heavenly Christianity, appeared exceeding amiable to me. I felt in me a burning desire to be in everything a complete Christian; and conformed to the blessed image of Christ: and that I might live in all things, according to the pure, sweet and blessed rules of the gospel. I had an eager thirsting after progress in these things. My longings after it, put me upon pursuing and pressing after them. It was my continual strife day and night, and constant inquiry, how I should be more holy, and live more holily, and more becoming a child of God, and disciple of Christ. I sought an increase of grace and holiness, and that I might live an holy life, with vastly more earnestness, than ever I sought grace, before I had it. I used to be continually examining myself, and studying and contriving for likely ways and means, how I should live holily, with far greater diligence and earnestness, than ever I pursued anything in my life: but with too great a dependence on my own strength; which afterwards proved a great damage to me. My experience had not then taught me, as it has done since, my extreme feebleness and impotence, every manner of way; and the innumerable and bottomless depths of secret corruption and deceit, that there was in my heart. However, I went on with my eager pursuit after more holiness; and sweet conformity to Christ.

The heaven I desired was a heaven of holiness; to be with God, and to spend my eternity in divine love, and holy communion with Christ. My mind was very much taken up with contemplations on heaven, and the enjoyments of those there; and living there in perfect holiness, humility and love. And it used at that time to appear a great part of the happiness of heaven, that there the saints could express their love to Christ. It appeared to me a great clog and hindrance and burden to me, that what I felt within, I could not express to God, and give vent to, as I desired. The inward ardor of my soul, seemed to be hindered and pent up, and could not freely flame out as it would. I used often to think, how in heaven, this sweet principle should freely and fully vent and express, itself. Heaven appeared to me exceeding delightful as a world of love. It appeared to me, that all happiness consisted in living in pure, humble, heavenly, divine love.

I remember the thoughts I used then to have of holiness. I remember I then said sometimes to myself, I do certainly know that I love holiness, such as the gospel prescribes. It appeared to me, there was nothing in it but what was ravishingly lovely. It appeared to me, to be the highest beauty and amiableness, above all other beauties: that it was a *divine* beauty; far purer than anything here upon earth; and that everything else, was like mire, filth and defilement, in comparison of it.

Holiness, as I then wrote down some of my contemplations on it, appeared to me to be of a sweet, pleasant, charming, serene, calm nature. It seemed to me, it brought an inexpressible purity, brightness, peacefulness and ravishment to the soul: and that it made the soul like a field or garden of God, with all manner of pleasant flowers; that is all pleasant, delightful and undisturbed; enjoying a sweet calm, and the gently vivifying beams of the sun. The soul of a true Christian, as I then wrote my meditations, appeared like such a little white flower, as we see in the spring of the year; low and humble on the ground, opening its bosom, to receive the pleasant beams of the sun's glory; rejoicing as it were, in a calm rapture; diffusing around a sweet fragrancy; standing peacefully and lovingly, in the midst of other flowers round about; all in like manner opening their bosoms, to drink in the light of the sun.

There was no part of creature-holiness, that I then, and at other times, had so great a sense of the loveliness of, as humility, brokenness of heart and poverty of spirit: and there was nothing that I had such a spirit to long for. My heart as it were panted after this, to lie low before God, and in the dust; that I might be nothing, and that God might be all; that I might become as a little child.

While I was there at New York, I sometimes was much affected with reflections on my past life, considering how late it was, before I began to be truly religious; and how wickedly I had lived till then: and once so as to weep abundantly, and for a considerable time together.

On January 12, 1722-23,* I made a solemn dedication of myself to God, and wrote it down; giving up myself, and all that I had to God; to be for the future in no respect my own; to act as one that had no right to himself in any respect. And solemnly vowed to take God for my whole portion and felicity; looking on nothing else as any part of my happiness, nor acting as if it were: and his law for the constant rule of my obedience: engaging to fight with all my might, against the world, the flesh and the devil, to the end of my life. But have reason to be infi-

---

* The year would be 1722, Old Style (when the New Year began in March), 1723, New Style (when it began in January). (ed.)

nitely humbled, when I consider, how much I have failed of answering my obligation.

I had then abundance of sweet religious conversation in the family where I lived, with Mr. John Smith, and his pious mother. My heart was knit in affection to those, in whom were appearances of true piety; and I could bear the thoughts of no other companions, but such as were holy, and the disciples of the blessed Jesus.

I had great longings for the advancement of Christ's kingdom in the world. My secret prayer used to be in great part taken up in praying for it. If I heard the least hint of any thing that happened in any part of the world, that appeared to me, in some respect or other, to have a favorable aspect on the interest of Christ's kingdom, my soul eagerly catched at it; and it would much animate and refresh me. I used to be earnest to read public newsletters, mainly for that end; to see if I could not find some news favorable to the interest of religion in the world.

I very frequently used to retire into a solitary place, on the banks of Hudson's River, at some distance from the city, for contemplation on divine things, and secret converse with God; and had many sweet hours there. Sometimes Mr. Smith and I walked there together, to converse of the things of God; and our conversation used much to turn on the advancement of Christ's kingdom in the world, and the glorious things that God would accomplish for his church in the latter days.

I had then, and at other times, the greatest delight in the holy Scriptures, of any book whatsoever. Oftentimes in reading it, every word seemed to touch my heart. I felt an harmony between something in my heart, and those sweet and powerful words. I seemed often to see so much light, exhibited by every sentence, and such a refreshing ravishing food communicated, that I could not get along in reading. Used oftentimes to dwell long on one sentence, to see the wonders contained in it; and yet almost every sentence seemed to be full of wonders.

I came away from New York in the month of April 1723, and had a most bitter parting with Madam Smith and her son. My heart seemed to sink within me, at leaving the family and city, where I had enjoyed so many sweet and pleasant days. I went from New York to Wethersfield by water. As I sailed away, I kept sight of the city as long as I could; and when I was out of sight of it, it would affect me much to look that way, with a kind of melancholy mixed with sweetness. However, that night after this sorrowful parting, I was greatly comforted in God at Westchester, where we went ashore to lodge: and had a pleasant time of it all the voyage to Saybrook. It was sweet to me to think of meeting dear Christians in heaven, where we should never part more. At Saybrook we went ashore to lodge on Saturday, and there kept sabbath; where I had a sweet and refreshing season, walking alone in the fields.

After I came home to Windsor, remained much in a like frame of my mind, as I had been in at New York; but only sometimes felt my heart ready to sink, with the thoughts of my friends at New York. And my refuge and support was in contemplations on the heavenly state; as I find in my Diary of May 1, 1723. It was my comfort to think of that state, where there is fullness of joy; where reigns heavenly, sweet, calm and delightful love, without alloy; where there are continually the dearest expressions of this love; where is the enjoyment of the persons loved, without ever parting; where these persons that appear so lovely in this world, will really be inexpressibly more lovely, and full of love to us. And how sweetly will the mutual lovers join together to sing the praises of God and the Lamb! How full will it fill us with joy, to think, that this enjoyment, these sweet exercises will never cease or come to an end; but will last to all eternity!

Continued much in the same frame in the general, that I had been in at New York, till I went to New Haven, to live there as tutor of the College; having one special season of uncommon sweetness: particularly once at Bolton, in a journey from Boston, walking out alone in the fields. After I went to New Haven, I sunk in religion; my mind being diverted from my eager and violent pursuits after holiness, by some affairs that greatly perplexed and distracted my mind.

In September 1725, was taken ill at New Haven; and endeavoring to go home to Windsor, was so ill at the North Village, that I could go no further: where I lay sick for about a quarter of a year. And in this sickness, God was pleased to visit me again with the sweet influences of his Spirit. My mind was greatly engaged there on divine, pleasant contemplations, and longings of soul. I observed that those who watched with me, would often be looking out for the morning, and seemed to wish for it. Which brought to my mind those words of the Psalmist, which my soul with sweetness made its own language. "My soul waiteth for the Lord more than they that watch for the morning: I say, more than they that watch for the morning" [Ps. 130:6]. And when the light of the morning came, and the beams of the sun came in at the windows, it refreshed my soul from one morning to another. It seemed to me to be some image of the sweet light of God's glory.

I remember, about that time, I used greatly to long for the conversion of some that I was concerned with. It seemed to me, I could gladly honor them, and with delight be a servant to them, and lie at their feet, if they were but truly holy.

But some time after this, I was again greatly diverted in my mind, with some temporal concerns, that exceedingly took up my thoughts, greatly to the wounding of my soul: and went on through various exercises, that it would be tedious to relate, that gave me much more experience of my own heart, than ever I had before.

Since I came to [Northampton], I have often had sweet complacency in God in views of his glorious perfections, and the excellency of Jesus Christ. God has appeared to me, a glorious and lovely Being, chiefly on the account of his holiness. The holiness of God has always appeared to me the most lovely of all his attributes. The doctrines of God's absolute sovereignty, and free grace, in showing mercy to whom he would show mercy; and man's absolute dependence on the operations of God's Holy Spirit, have very often appeared to me as sweet and glorious doctrines. These doctrines have been much my delight. God's sovereignty has ever appeared to me, as great part of his glory. It has often been sweet to me to go to God, and adore him as a sovereign God, and ask sovereign mercy of him.

I have loved the doctrines of the gospel: they have been to my soul like green pastures. The gospel has seemed to me to be the richest treasure; the treasure that I have most desired, and longed that it might dwell richly in me. The way of salvation by Christ, has appeared in a general way, glorious and excellent, and most pleasant and beautiful. It has often seemed to me, that it would in a great measure spoil heaven, to receive it in any other way. That text has often been affecting and delightful to me, Is. 32:2, "A man shall be an hiding place from the wind, and a covert from the tempest; as rivers of water in a dry place, as the shadow of a great rock in a weary land."

It has often appeared sweet to me, to be united to Christ; to have him for my head, and to be a member of his body: and also to have Christ for my teacher and prophet. I very often think with sweetness and longings and pantings of soul, of being a little child, taking hold of Christ, to be led by him through the wilderness of this world. That text, Matt. 18, at the beginning, has often been sweet to me: "Except ye be converted, and become as little children, ye shall not enter into the kingdom of heaven." I love to think of coming to Christ, to receive salvation of him, poor in spirit, and quite empty of self; humbly exalting him alone; cut entirely off from my own root, and to grow into, and out of Christ: to have God in Christ to be all in all; and to live by faith on the Son of God, a life of humble, unfeigned confidence in him. That Scripture has often been sweet to me, Ps. 115:1, "Not unto us, O Lord, not unto us, but unto thy name give glory, for thy mercy, and for thy truth's sake." And those words of Christ, Luke 10:21, "In that hour Jesus rejoiced in spirit, and said, I thank thee, O Father, Lord of heaven and earth, that thou hast hid these things from the wise and prudent, and hast revealed them unto babes: even so, Father; for so it seemed good in thy sight." That sovereignty of God that Christ rejoiced in, seemed to me to be worthy to be rejoiced in; and that rejoicing of Christ, seemed to me to show the excellency of Christ, and the Spirit that he was of.

Sometimes only mentioning a single word, causes my heart to burn within me: or only seeing the name of Christ, or the name of some attribute of God. And God has appeared glorious to me, on account of the Trinity. It has made me have exalting thoughts of God, that he subsists in three persons; Father, Son, and Holy Ghost.

The sweetest joys of delights I have experienced, have not been those that have arisen from a hope of my own good estate; but in a direct view of the glorious things of the gospel. When I enjoy this sweetness, it seems to carry me above the thoughts of my own safe estate. It seems at such times a loss that I cannot bear, to take off my eye from the glorious, pleasant object I behold without me, to turn my eye in upon myself, and my own good estate.

My heart has been much on the advancement of Christ's kingdom in the world. The histories of the past advancement of Christ's kingdom, have been sweet to me. When I have read histories of past ages, the pleasantest thing in all my reading has been, to read of the kingdom of Christ being promoted. And when I have expected in my reading, to come to any such thing, I have lotted upon it all the way as I read. And my mind has been much entertained and delighted, with the Scripture promises and prophecies, of the future glorious advancement of Christ's kingdom on earth.

I have sometimes had a sense of the excellent fullness of Christ, and his meetness and suitableness as a Savior; whereby he has appeared to me, far above all, the chief of ten thousands. And his blood and atonement has appeared sweet, and his righteousness sweet; which is always accompanied with an ardency of spirit, and inward strugglings and breathings and groanings, that cannot be uttered, to be emptied of myself, and swallowed up in Christ.

Once, as I rid out into the woods for my health, anno 1737; and having lit from my horse in a retired place, as my manner commonly has been, to walk for divine contemplation and prayer; I had a view, that for me was extraordinary, of the Son of God; as mediator between God and man; and his wonderful, great, full, pure and sweet grace and love, and meek and gentle condescension. This grace, that appeared to me so calm and sweet, appeared great above the heavens. The person of Christ appeared ineffably excellent, with an excellency great enough to swallow up all thought and conception. Which continued, as near as I can judge, about an hour; which kept me, the bigger part of the time, in a flood of tears, and weeping aloud. I felt withal, an ardency of soul to be, what I know not otherwise how to express, than to be emptied and annihilated; to lie in the dust, and to be full of Christ alone; to love him with a holy and pure love; to trust in him; to live upon him; to serve and follow him, and to be totally wrapped up in the fullness of Christ; and to be perfectly sanctified and made pure, with a divine and heavenly purity. I have several other times, and views very much of the same nature, and that have had the same effects.

I have many times had a sense of the glory of the third person in the Trinity, in his office of sanctifier; in his holy operations communicating divine light and life to the soul. God in the communications of his Holy Spirit, has appeared as an infinite fountain of divine glory and sweetness; being full and sufficient to fill and satisfy the soul: pouring forth itself in sweet communications, like the sun in its glory, sweetly, and pleasantly diffusing light and Life.

I have sometimes had an affecting sense of the excellency of the Word of God, as a Word of life; as the light of life; a sweet, excellent, life-giving Word: accompanied with a thirsting after that Word, that it might dwell richly in my heart.

I have often since I lived in this town, had very affecting views of my own sinfulness and vileness; very frequently so as to hold me in a kind of loud weeping, sometimes for a considerable time together: so that I have often been forced to shut myself up. I have had a vastly greater sense of my own wickedness, and the badness of my heart, since my conversion, than ever I had before. It has often appeared to me, that if God should mark iniquity against me, I should appear the very worst of all mankind; of all that have been since the beginning of the world to this time: and that I should have by far the lowest place in hell. When others that have come to talk with me about their soul concerns, have expressed the sense they have had of their own wickedness, by saying that it seemed to them, that they were as bad as the devil himself; I thought their expressions seemed exceeding faint and feeble, to represent my wickedness. I thought I should wonder, that they should content themselves with such expressions as these, if I had any reason to imagine, that their sin bore any proportion to mine. It seemed to me, I should wonder at myself, if I should express *my* wickedness in such feeble terms as they did.

My wickedness, as I am in myself, has long appeared to me perfectly ineffable, and infinitely swallowing up all thought and imagination; like an infinite deluge, or infinite mountains over my head. I know not how to express better, what my sins appear to me to be, than by heaping infinite upon infinite, and multiplying infinite by infinite. I go about very often, for this many years, with these expressions in my mind, and in my mouth, "Infinite upon Infinite. Infinite upon Infinite!" When I look into my heart, and take a view of my wickedness, it looks like an abyss infinitely deeper than hell. And it appears to me, that were it not for free grace, exalted and raised up to the infinite height of all the fullness and glory of the great Jehovah, and the arm of his power and grace stretched forth, in all the majesty of his power, and in all the glory of his sovereignty; I should appear sunk down in my sins infinitely below hell itself, far beyond sight of everything, but the piercing eye of God's grace, that can pierce even down to such a depth, and to the bottom of such an abyss.

And yet, I ben't in the least inclined to think, that I have a greater conviction of sin than ordinary. It seems to me, my conviction of sin is exceeding small, and faint. It appears to me enough to amaze me, that I have no more sense of my sin. I know certainly, that I have very little sense of my sinfulness. That my sins appear to me so great, don't seem to me to be, because I have so much more conviction of sin than other Christians, but because I am so much worse, and have so much more wickedness to be convinced of. When I have had these turns of weeping and crying for my sins, I thought I knew in the time of it, that my repentance was nothing to my sin.

I have greatly longed of late, for a broken heart, and to lie low before God. And when I ask for humility of God, I can't bear the thoughts of being no more humble, than other Christians. It seems to me, that though their degrees of humility may be suitable for them; yet it would be a vile self-exaltation in me, not to be the lowest in humility of all mankind. Others speak of their longing to be humbled to the dust. Though that may be a proper expression for them, I always think for myself, that I ought to be humbled down below hell. 'Tis an expression that it has long been natural for me to use in prayer to God. I ought to be infinitely low before God.

It is affecting to me to think, how ignorant I was, when I was a young Christian, of the bottomless, infinite depths of wickedness, pride, hypocrisy and deceit left in my heart.

I have vastly a greater sense, of my universal, exceeding dependence on God's grace and strength, and mere good pleasure, of late, than I used formerly to have; and have experienced more of an abhorrence of my own righteousness. The thought of any comfort or joy, arising in me, on any consideration, or reflection on my own amiableness, or any of my performances or experiences, or any goodness of heart or life, is nauseous, and detestable to me. And yet I am greatly afflicted with a proud and self-righteous spirit much more sensibly, than I used to be formerly. I see that serpent rising and putting forth its head, continually, everywhere, all around me.

Though it seems to me, that in some respects I was a far better Christian, for two or three years after my first conversion, than I am now; and lived in a more constant delight and pleasure: yet of late years, I have had a more full and constant sense of the absolute sovereignty of God, and a delight in that sovereignty; and have had more of a sense of the glory of Christ, as a mediator, as revealed in the gospel. On one Saturday night in particular, had a particular discovery of the excellency of the gospel of Christ, above all other doctrines; so that I could not but say to myself; "This is my chosen light, my chosen doctrine": and of Christ, "This is my chosen prophet." It appeared to me to be sweet beyond all expression, to follow Christ, and to be taught and enlightened and instructed by him; to learn of him, and live to him.

Another Saturday night, January 1738-39, had such a sense, how sweet and blessed a thing it was, to walk in the way of duty, to do that which was right and meet to be done, and agreeable to the holy mind of God; that it caused me to break forth into a kind of a loud weeping, which held me some time; so that I was forced to shut myself up, and fasten the doors. I could not but as it were cry out, "How happy are they which do that which is right in the sight of God! They are blessed indeed, they are the happy ones!" I had at the same time, a very affecting sense, how meet and suitable it was that God should govern the world, and order all things according to his own pleasure; and I rejoiced in it, that God reigned, and that his will was done.

THE PATRIOT

Benjamin Rush

(1745-1813)

Benjamin Rush, signer of the Declaration of Independence and active patriot during the American Revolution, never held a major political office. This fact he did not regret, since he saw his good friends, John Adams and Thomas Jefferson, so harshly attacked during their presidential years. But because he did not occupy a high office, his name is not as well known as it deserves to be.

A citizen of Philadelphia, Rush sailed to Edinburgh to complete his medical education there, returning to his own city in 1769 to teach chemistry in the newly opened College of Philadelphia. But he also returned home to colonies caught in the struggle against Britain. In that struggle, Rush joined with such earnestness and zest that, for the rest of his life, he regarded the time from 1774 to 1776 as the high point of his sixty-eight years. His long friendship with Adams and Jefferson provided another emotional peak, though he suffered personally when his two dear friends became partisan enemies. Indeed, Rush more than any other individual was responsible for bringing the two ex-Presidents back together during their respective retirements. As a result, the friendship renewed between Adams and Jefferson in 1811 produced the most rewarding, engaging, and sophisticated correspondence between former presidents that the American nation has ever seen.

Rush shared his friends' interest in and dedication to religious liberty, but he pulled back from some of their more liberal heterodoxies.

Jefferson's plunge into deism or natural religion particularly struck Rush as slippery, for "all that is just in principle or conduct in a Deist is taken from his previous knowledge of the Christian Religion or the influence of Christian company." Rush, greatly influenced by his mother's Presbyterianism and by her circle of staunch evangelical friends, found the abandonment of Protestant orthodoxy — notably the divinity of Jesus — more difficult than did either Jefferson or Adams. On the other hand, he found himself greatly attracted to Universalism, the doctrine that salvation would ultimately come to all. If Christians could hold that in Adam all mankind had sinned, then why not hold that in Christ all mankind were redeemed? Such an idea seemed not only more worthy of a God of mercy, but also more worthy of a new republican, egalitarian nation.

In the excerpt below, one can follow both the development of Rush's orthodoxy as well as his modest departures therefrom. The material comes from his Autobiography as well as his Commonplace Book, the latter being a kind of journal for random reflections.

[See Donald J. D'Elia, *Benjamin Rush: Philosopher of the American Revolution* (American Philosophical Society Transactions, n.s., vol. 64, part 5, 1974).]

Having briefly stated the literary, medical and political events of my life, it remains only that I say a few words upon my religious principles.

I was baptised by the Revd. Eneas Ross, an Episcopal minister, and heard divine worship for the first time in Christ Church in Philadelphia. After the death of my father I went with my mother to the Revd. Mr. Tennent's meeting,* which was held in the building afterwards converted into a College and University in 4th Street. My mother was a constant attendant upon his Presbyterian place of worship, and educated all her children in the principles taught by him, which were highly calvinistical.

At Dr. Finley's School, I was more fully instructed in these principles by means of the Westminster Catechism. I retained them but without any affection for them 'till about the year 1780. I then read for the first time Fletcher's controversy with the Calvinists in favor of the Universality of the atonement. This prepared my mind to admit the doctrine of Universal salvation, which was then preached in our city by the

---

* Gilbert Tennent, 1703-1764, was a pro-revivalist New Side Presbyterian. (ed.)

Source: George W. Corner, ed., *The Autobiography of Benjamin Rush* (Princeton, N.J.: Princeton University Press, 1948), pp. 162-66, 334-45.

Revd. Mr. Winchester.* It embraced and reconciled my ancient calvinistical, and my newly adopted Armenian [Arminian] principles. From that time I have never doubted upon the subject of the salvation of all men. My conviction of the truth of this doctrine was derived from reading the works of Stonehouse, Seigvolk, White, Chauncey, and Winchester, and afterwards from an attentive perusal of the Scriptures. I always admitted with each of those authors future punishment, and of long, long duration.

The early part of my life was spent in dissipation, folly, and in the practice of some of the vices to which young men are prone. The weight of that folly and those vices has been felt in my mind ever since. They have often been deplored in tears and sighs before God. It was from deep and affecting sense of one of them that I was first led to seek the favor of God in his Son in the 21st year of my age. It was thus the woman of Samaria was brought to a repentance of all her sins by the Son of God reminding her of but one of them, viz. her living criminally with a man who was not her husband.

The religious impressions that were made upon my mind at this time were far from issuing in a complete union to God by his Son Jesus Christ, but they left my mind more tender to sin of every kind, and begat in me constant desire for a new heart, and a sense of God's mercy in the way of his Gospel. Religious company now became most agreeable to me and I delighted in public worship, and particularly in hearing evangelical ministers of all denominations. I made conscience of secret prayer from that time, nor do I recollect to have passed a day without it while in health to the present year 1800. But I am sorry to add my devotion was often a mere form, and carelessly and irreverently performed. I lost a great deal of spiritual sensibility while I was abroad. Travelling is unfavourable to the growth and even to the existence of Religion in the soul. Thousands I believe have lost their all by it.

The scenes of my political life were likewise unfavourable to the divine life in my soul. Often, very often, have I deplored them.

About the year 1786 I thought I felt some comfortable views of the love of God. My soul was drawn out to him in constant aspirations. I now felt a strong desire to partake of the Lord's Supper. In consequence of my having renounced the Calvinistical opinions of the Presbyterians, I did not expect to be admitted to commune with them. I

---

* Elhanan Winchester, 1751-1797, was a major force in the launching of Universalism in America. (ed.)

therefore submitted to confirmation with my dear wife in the month of February 1788, and a few days afterwards received the blessed Signs of the death of Jesus Christ in St. Peter's Church. I was deeply impressed with this solemnity. In consequence of rising a night or two before, and going out too thinly clad, I was attacked upon my return from church by a severe pleurisy which had nearly put an end to my life. I realized death. My faith, it is true, was weak; but my hopes in the mercy of God as a Redeemer were strong. It pleased God to restore me, and for some time afterwards to continue upon my mind a considerable sense of divine things. In consequence of an alteration made in the forms of Baptism and the communion service, the former admitting infant regeneration, and the latter favouring transubstantiation, I declined after a year or two communing in the church, and had my children baptized by Presbyterian ministers. I still attended public worship in the Episcopal church and occasionally in the Presbyterian churches, but alas! with coldness and formality. I was under the influence of an unholy temper, and often wounded the peace of my mind by yielding to it. During the fever of 1793 my mind was strongly impressed with a sense of divine things. I was animated by a hope in God's mercy. The psalms were made comfortable to me. I read them every day. I lament that the good impressions I then felt soon wore away. To this, the impatience I felt under the opposition and hostility of medical brethren chiefly contributed. The Gospel of Jesus Christ prescribes the wisest rules for just conduct in every situation of life. Happy they who are enabled to obey them in all situations!

Of the poor services I have rendered to any of my fellow creatures I shall say nothing. They were full of imperfections and have no merit in the sight of God. I pray to have the sin that was mixed with them, forgiven. My only hope of salvation is in the infinite transcendent love of God manifested to the world by the death of his Son upon the Cross. Nothing but his blood will wash away my sins. I rely exclusively upon it. Come Lord Jesus! Come quickly! And take home thy lost, but redeemed Creature! I will believe, and I will hope in thy salvation! Amen, and amen!

Thoughts on RELIGION

All that is just in principle or conduct in a Deist is taken from his previous knowledge of the Christian Religion or the influence of Christian company. A man not educated under such circumstances would know nothing of what is good. Mr. Jefferson proposed to civilize and moralize the Indians by putting Aesop's fables into their hands.

The affairs of men are governed alternately by and contrary to their wills, to teach us both to use our Reason and to rely upon Providence in all our Undertakings.

The greatest number of infidels and atheists are to be found among those men who see most of the wisdom of God in his works, viz. Philosophers; and the most impious men are those who experience most of His goodness, viz. sailors and soldiers. See extract from Tacitus, p. 254.

An infidel to be consistent should be an atheist, for the works of nature exhibit more mysteries and contradictions than the Word of God. All natural Religion, as it is falsely called, is the result of scattered rays of Revelation. It is the moonlight of Christianity. Infidels absurdly suppose that moonlight is reflected from the earth instead of the heavens.

There are the same grades of offenses in company as of murder — as chance, medley, homicide, malice propense.

Original or native sin is favoured by the ideas of pregnancy and parturition being diseases. Sin and suffering began together.

We count moderate evils by days, more violent by hours, the most acute by moments. "I feel, said Mirabeau when dying, in a single moment the pangs of a thousand years." What makes the review of life so short to most people is it has been spent upon the whole happily. In hell each moment will be like the duration of a thousand years.

There is no man so wicked that does not under a sudden sense of good say "Thank God" or feel gratitude to Him, nor any man so wicked that does not in sudden distress or danger cry out to God for help or deliverance. It is equally true, "No man liveth and prayeth not," as that "no man liveth and sinneth not." Even devils pray, as to our Saviour not to torment them, and "to go into the hogs."

St. Paul says we know religion but in part. The same thing may be said of all subjects and every portion or atom of matter.

August 9, 1809. We are all necessarily Religious as we are reasoning and musical animals. It is true we are disposed to false Religions; so we are to false reasoning and false music, but this shows the depth of each of those principles in the human mind.

September 19. Mr. Wilmer, who has made it a practice to visit the sick and dying for 40 years, says he has often observed the timid and diffident professors of religion to die with the most triumph and joy. Mrs. Gouge.

September 26. The Saviour of the world will have all who are saved by him to be conformed to him in some *one* or more of his sufferings. May not the reason why so many millions go out of the world by means of wounds in battle be, that they may be conformed to their Saviour in their death, who went out of the world covered with wounds?

December 21. Our researches upon liberty and necessity are like the researches after perpetual motion, and our attempts to understand the Book of Revelation are like mining — they bankrupt the head.

Change or novelty so natural to man that he rejects even truth after a while, and embraces error, only because it is new.

God reveals some truths to our senses and to our first perceptions, but many errors are conveyed into the mind through both, which are to be corrected only by reason. Thus the Sun appears to our eyes to revolve around the earth. Astronomy corrects this error. Endless punishment is obvious to first perception or apprehension in the Bible. Reason corrects this error, from comparing the whole tenor of Scripture together.

There have been many disputes about those words of our Saviour in which he says he was ignorant of the "time" of the Day of Judgement. Attempts have been made to divide his humanity and divinity and to ascribe this ignorance to the former only. But may we not suppose that when He assumed the fallen nature of man he assumed everything that belonged to that nature, that is, not only sin, poverty, shame, pain, and death, but ignorance, and many other consequences of the fall. In this way only could he "bear all our infirmities," of which ignorance is a material one. This explanation of the above words should encrease our obligations to the Saviour. He disrobed himself not only of the glory which he had with his Father, before the world was, not only of his riches and power but of a part of his Omniscience, in order to complete the great work of man's redemption.

Children suffer for the sins of their fathers when they are put to death in the sacking of towns. To reconcile their sufferings to the justice of God it has been said they sinned in another and a prior state of existence, but there is no occasion for this defence of the justice of God, if we extend our ideas as far as we should do into the unity of the human race. It has been compared to a single body. Now, we see parts suffer for each other separately and together in diseases, which parts did not contract those diseases. Thus the feet suffer in the gout for the intemperance of the tongue, and the whole body for the sin of one part of it in contracting the veneral disease. The whole body suffers, too, for the sin of the hands, which steal, when it is punished by whipping or hanging. To the Deity the whole human race probably appears as much a unit as a single human body appears to be a unit to the eye of man. It was once evidently so in Adam, and will be so again, we are told, in Jesus Christ. This doctrine is calculated to produce universal love, for vicarious sufferings do that necessarily which we are commanded to do voluntarily, that is "bear one another's burdens."

But is it just in this manner to punish the innocent for the guilty? It would not be so in a man, but "the earth is the Lord's, and the fullness thereof." Good and evil are both his. He can dispose of them as he pleases. Many things would be wrong in man that are not in his Creator. He is forbidden to revenge an injury, but this injury never passes with impunity. Vengeance is the property of God, and he never fails to inflict it at the time and in the manner, and to the degree in which it shall have the most effect. This could not be done by man. It would be in his hands out of time, done in an improper manner, and in an over proportion to the injury. It would be wrong in man to kill, because he has no property in the life of a fellow creature, but all souls, or all lives are God's. He has an exclusive property in them, and may take them away when and in what manner he pleases. When he commanded Moses and Joshua to destroy the lives of the heathen nations, including women and children, he exercised his own just power over them. The sword of Moses and Joshua was no more to him than famine or pestilence. It executed his will. Without a divine command for that act, the destruction of those nations would have been murder. In like manner God does justly transfer good and evil. They are both his, and the whole race of man is one.

There is no more injustice in transferring evil than in transferring the gout from one part of the body to the other. If this gout were brought on by intemperance the tongue only offended, but the feet, the hands, the head, and the whole body suffer for it, and the tongue less than any other part. The body is a unit; equally so is the whole of Adam's family. See Joshua and the story of Achan. All Israel threatened for his crime.

The mind of man can only be moved by love. It should be by the love of God, but sin has substituted another principle of activity, viz. love of money. The first act of idolatry of the Jews showed this to be the case. They worshipped money in the form of a golden calf. Gold or its representatives is still the idol of the world. It sets the mind of man in motion, next to the love of God. The love of fame, power, &c. have but a limited operation compared with the love of gold. Should this passion be suspended for a week in the people in the country who supply a city with provisions, what distress and famine would ensue! It would nearly destroy it.

February 5, 1810. We complain that sorrows seldom come alone. This is a proof of the goodness of God. They are best borne when they are thus inflicted, than when they come in succession. The first sorrow by dissipating excitability renders the succeeding ones less sensible. Thus Job was afflicted in mercy.

The study of mathematicks the least interested study of man. All other studies are more or less selfish.

Conversation and example the best moral and religious education, without advice or precepts (Bunyan).

It would seem that natural knowledge instead of leading men to God, like wealth (his gift) led them from him. Geology and Botany have both assailed Revelation, witness Brydone's remarks on the lava of Aetna. See Clark's Commentary on the last chapter of Genesis, also story of a large tree in Africa. The early date of the world a proof of the truth of the Mosaic account of the creation. All nations ascribe a very ancient date to their origin.

August 8, 1811. There are *intellectual* as well as *physical* miracles. Whatever occurs contrary to the usual modes of acting of the understanding is a miracle. Moses in making the history of the world and of his own nation of a recent date exhibited a miracle, for all historians delight in making the history of their nations as ancient as possible. The prophets in predicting the downfall of their religion and government exhibited miracles, for all men wish their Religions to be perpetual and universal, and patriots wish their governments or their country to last to the end of time.

August 14. Man is as necessarily a praying as he is a sociable, domestic, or religious animal. As "no man liveth and sinneth not," so no man liveth and prayeth not. Distress and terror drive even atheists to call upon God. Worldly men pray for the success of their worldly schemes. Men in deep distress even call for the prayers of their friends, witness I. P. when his wife died. Prayer is an instinct of nature in man, as much so as his love of society. He cannot, he does not live without it, except in a morbid or unnatural state of his mind.

It would seem as if one of the designs of Providence in permitting the existence of so many Sects of Christians was that each Sect might be a depository of some great truth of the Gospel, and that it might by that means be better preserved. Thus to the Catholics and Moravians he has committed the Godhead of the Saviour, hence they worship and pray to him; to the Episcopal, Presbyterian, and Baptist Church the decrees of God and partial redemption, or the salvation of the first fruits, which they ignorantly suppose to include all who shall be saved. To the Lutherans and Methodists he has committed the doctrine of universal redemption, to the Quakers the Godhead and influences of the Holy Spirit, to the Unitarians, the humanity of our Saviour, or the doctrine of "God manifested in the flesh" or the "Word made flesh" which was denied, St. John tells us, in the first ages of the Church, and which is admitted in a mystical way only by one Sect of Christians. Let the different Sects of Christians not only bear with each other, but love each other for this kind display of God's goodness whereby all the truths of their Religion are so protected that none of them can ever become feeble or be lost. When united they make a great whole, and that whole is the salvation of all men.

However strange it may appear, it is highly probable that an enlightened and inquiring Christian knows more of the whole Will of God, and of the subjects of the Gospel than any one of the historians, prophets, or Apostles, whose writings are recorded in the Old and New Testaments. Each of them saw things only in part. Specific objects, events, doctrines, and precepts were revealed to them. A modern divine by comparing and collating them all is probably in a better condition to draw general and just conclusions from them than any single writer in the Bible. Besides, the early Gospel divines were under more or less pagan and Jewish influence in all their writings. We believe without attempting to explain the Mystery of the Trinity. Why believe Three in One and not believe the derived and the independent life of our Saviour, His being raised from the grave by his Father, and being the Author of His own resurrection — the Union of liberty and necessity, and the agency of divine and human efforts in bringing about the Salvation of the soul. They all appear to be true, though opposed to each other. They are like the Trinity — mysteries intelligible only, perhaps to the Creator.

Blood forbidden to the Jews first because unwholesome, 2. because a type of the Redeemer's blood, which it was necessary to "be poured out" upon the ground to render the type complete. 3. Because the life of the animal was seated in it, and therefore it became the most suitable type of the life of the Saviour given for the sins of the world. It ceased to be sacred after the death of Christ.

Meat offerings or offerings of vegetables were accepted where persons were too poor to offer living animals. May not this typify the acceptance of the worship of pious heathen who had never heard of the necessity of the shedding of blood for the remission of sins? It is common to undervalue posthumous fame, but if acquired by doing good, it will all be added to a man's reward in a future state, so that it will become as acceptable as if he had enjoyed it in his life.

On the Sleep or Mortality of the Soul till the Resurrection from Geo. Hammon, a dissenting minister of Biddenden, Kent, printed 1660. Inferred:

1. From the death of Christ, which was of *Soul* and body. See Isaiah LIII, 10 and 12.
2. If man's Soul lives after death he has two lives and two distinct essences in him, contrary to Scripture, which says by *one* man's sin death came into the world.
3. If a separate state exists, Lazarus was much injured by being called from Heaven by his resurrection.

4. Immortality only dwelling in Christ. I. Tim. VI, 15, 16.
5. Every living substance destroyed by the flood; *living Souls* destroyed by Joshua. Josh. XI, 11.
6. The mortal part or body bears the name of Soul. Hence it is said by breathing on Adam's body, he became a living Soul.
7. If the soul die not, it is unfruitful, "for it is not quickened, except it die."
8. All the promises of future happiness are only after the Resurrection, or "that day."

Objections:
1. Kill soul and body. So in Matthew, but not in Luke XII, 4, 5, and Joshua X, 35, in which the soul was killed by man.
2. I am in a strait &c., Phil. I, 23, 24; no interval between death and resurrection in Consciousness. Contradicted by other parts of his writings.
3. Thou fool, this night shall thy soul be required of thee, means thy *life* be required, &c.
4. "This day shalt thou be with me in Paradise" was not true. For the said thief did not die 'till next day. And *this* day, the *day* of my sufferings I say thou shalt be with me &c. Again, our Saviour was in the grave that day.
5. The story of Lazarus and the rich man a parable only. Soul can't feel fire. Intended to illustrate the Rejection of the Jews.
6. Souls slain under the altar cry, &c. Rev. VI, 10, that is the blood of the Saints that had been slain.
7. Went and preached to spirits in prison, that is by his spirits preached in the days of Noah.

On the punishment of children for the iniquity of their Fathers:
1. One of the prophets prays to be forgiven the "iniquity of their fathers."
2. The Children of Israel are defeated for the iniquity of Achan, an individual. Joshua VII.
3. The Children of Israel are punished for the iniquity of David in numbering them.

Do not these facts suggest the unity of the Species, and the transferring of guilt to innocent persons, and thus show the uniformity of the divine government in punishing our Saviour for the iniquities of the world?

Does it not show, too, that we are all members of one body, and that all are punished by the misery of one?

On Universal SALVATION

General *letter* of Scripture against it, *tenor* in its favor. The same may be said of Justification, the Atonement, and the Divinity of our Saviour. — texts in which he is called the Son of Man, and but — in which he is called the Son of God.

Universality expressed by *all* the earth, *all* nations, *all* families, *all* individuals, *all* flesh. See Hartley and Pistorius.

All the faculties and propensities of the mind are intended for some use. Here we know no more of them than a foetus does of its lungs, gullet, &c. before birth. All misplaced and useful passions &c. shall be employed in their supreme good. Corinthians I, chapter 15: Death, the 2nd death only. The 1st death called *sleep*. The *last* enemy must be *Hell*, for the grave is not the last enemy.

Say not *eternal* punishment necessary to restrain Sinning. No. See men submit to 1000 privations, to war and death to avoid temporal evils, particularly slavery.

As arsenic and other poisons cure physical diseases, so may not fire and brimstone cure moral evil. Physicians and Lawyers perform humble offices to their fellow men compared with pious ministers of the Gospel. The Physicians pick the thorns from their feet which stick in them on their way, the lawyers restore to them their packs which are stolen from them on their way, but the ministers conduct them by the hand on every part of their journey to its end.

All are included in Christ's purchase. Even Kings and Lords. Hence He is said to be "King of kings" and "Lord of lords." They too are invited "to kiss the Son," "to be wise" &c.

As we have now a more summary way of curing diseases than formerly, so the doctrine of restitution of God's love, &c., would render the return of the sinner to God shorter and easier.

Everything shows the Unity of the human race, and that they are included in one Salvation. Children suffer for the iniquities of their fathers, subjects for the sins of their kings, and vice versa, and all mankind for the sin of Adam. Blessings are communicated to man by man to beget universal love. Thus the Jews conveyed the Gospel to the gentiles, and the elect will finally when they become kings and priests to

God convey the Gospel to that part of the human race which perish in this world. Moses was prevented entering into the land of Canaan on account of the sins of the Children of Israel. Nehemiah prays to be forgiven the iniquities of his father.

The reprobation and destruction of the Jews predicted and connected with the general judgement in Matthew, a type of future punishment. The former are to be restored, so will the reprobate. The former punished for unbelief, so will the latter be. Unbelief the radical sin of all sins. No condemnation but for not believing the Gospel.

The ministers complain that it is impossible to make their hearers feel the truth of eternal punishment. Why? Nothing in the nature of man accords with it. Not so with other truths, as existence of a God, &c. *All* drank of the water of the Rock in the wilderness. *All* women and children came before God on a fast day. *All* come before Him, even the stranger, to hear his word in Deuteronomy, and to enter into Covenant with him. Chapter 29, verse 12. *All* put their hands upon the sacrifice to convey to it their sins.

May not the cause of so many millions perishing in war from wounds be to diffuse more extensively the fellowship of Christ's sufferings on the Cross? As there is darkness from excessive light, so wrath appears where only excessive love was intended.

"Father, forgive them, they know not what they do" a prayer for the whole world, which must be answered.

Prayer natural to man. It is as true that no man liveth and prayeth not, as that no man liveth and sinneth not.

It is no argument in favor of the truth of endless punishment and final reprobation that the preaching of those doctrines has been attended with and followed by benefits to the Souls of men. It is because they are blended with other doctrines that are true. Thus erroneous modes of practice from the stronger efforts of Nature, or from being combined with one or two medicines proper for the disease, often cure it in spite of the ignorance of a physician. The seeds of imputed Righteousness deeply sown in our natures, discovered by our esteeming hereditary honors in men who have done nothing to deserve them, but the contrary.

Why do we demand satisfaction for injuries? And why do we honour military heroism and death so much? Are they not perverted exercises of the mind intended to recognize the Atonement and to admire it? We were made for redemption. The principles of it are inherent, natural, and born with us.

The Scriptures exclude from heaven all unregenerate persons, but they do not consign them to hell. The actively and negatively wicked only are sent there. Man has a power in his Will to avoid evil and escape hell but not to renew his nature and prepare himself for heaven.

It is said the first view or first reading of the Scriptures leads to endless misery. So the first view of the Solar system leads to a belief that the sun revolves around the earth. Reason refutes both. If time is tedious in proportion to suffering, then the pains of hell may well [be] said to be eternal, though only temporal. The Marquis of Mirabeau, who died of an acute and painful disease in his bowels, said in his last hours "he endured in a moment the pangs of a thousand years."

Hostility is most intense where there is most obligation. May not the early, uniform, and intense hatred of the Devil to the Son of God be owing to his having been redeemed by him? And may not his hostility to the whole human race be owing to their all being included in the purchase of the Saviour, and of course his property? God is undivided. His mercy must be coextensive with his justice — both infinite.

Sin is not an infinite evil. Other[wise] the infinite merits of the Saviour could not cancel it — for two infinities, like two right lines, could never overtake each other. "Few that find the way that leads to life" should be translated that "are finding" the way, and "that walk therein" should be translated "that are walking therein."

It would seem as if the doctrines of partial and Universal Salvation were guarded and preserved with equal care by divine Providence. Hence Calvin and Luther were cotemporaries, hence Wesley and Whitefield were cotemporaries likewise. This was probably wisely intended to prevent either of those doctrines predominating over each other, or the extinction of them, and thus to give support to the Doctrine of Universal Salvation. Both partial and universal redemption are true. The arguments for both are unanswerable. Of course Universal Salvation must be true. It is remarkable further that 6 Protestant Sects are divided equally between *partial* and *universal redemption,* and between *necessity* and *free agency.* The Episcopalians, Presbyterians, and Baptists hold the former, the Lutherans, Methodists, and Quakers the latter. Again, it is remarkable the commentators upon the Bible are divided in the same manner. Thus Henry, Pool, Hawse, and Scott are Calvinists, Whitby, Burket, Coke and Clark are Arminians.

The ashes of the sacrifices were holy. Lev. VI, verse 21. So the bodies of the wicked after burning or purification will still be holy to the Lord. May not burnt offerings typify the application of the Gospel after the burning of the bodies of the wicked?

THE BISHOP

Richard Allen

(1760-1831)

Nearly three generations before Lincoln's Emancipation Proclamation, some black Methodists in Philadelphia achieved an emancipation of their own. This they did under the leadership of Richard Allen. Born a slave in Pennsylvania, Allen had managed to purchase his freedom by the time he was twenty-one years of age. Even before this, he had been converted under the preaching of a Methodist itinerant, Freeborn Garrettson. By 1784, Allen had been accepted by the Methodist Conference meeting in Baltimore as a "minister of promise." In this capacity, he, too, became an itinerant, preaching the Methodist gospel throughout New York, New Jersey, and Pennsylvania.

St. George's Methodist Church in Philadelphia served as his base of operations, and as his church home. But in 1787 he and other black worshipers were rudely interrupted by one of the trustees of the church who ordered the group to leave; they did leave, Allen wrote, "and they were no more plagued with us in the church." In the excerpt below, Allen vividly recalls the incident — an occasion of repression that became an opportunity for emancipation. By 1794, Allen had founded the Bethel Methodist Church, and from this small mustard seed the African Methodist Episcopal Church would emerge in 1816, at which point Allen was chosen as the new denomination's first bishop.

Despite his treatment at St. George's, Richard Allen remained a Methodist, convinced that that religious body — itself comparatively new — had more appeal to and rapport with the African American community than any other. He also owed his own conversion to Christianity to the Methodists, and this apparently cemented the relationship. He would not turn away from those who had brought him to Christ. Amazingly enough, slaves and former slaves turned in great numbers to the religion of their masters. In so doing, however, they helped introduce into Christianity a more joyful and celebratory form of worship.

In an undated address, Bishop Richard Allen spoke to those who continued to keep slaves and continued to justify the institution. He pleaded with slave owners to rescue their "property" from a state of barbarism, and to give at least a few of their enslaved children an opportunity for education. For if they did so, they would find that blacks "were not inferior in mental endowments." While he encouraged his own brethren to be forgiving, "to have all anger and bitterness removed from our minds," he kept his strongest message for the oppressors. "If you love your children, if you love your country, if you love the God of love," Allen declared, "clear your hands of slaves; burden not your children or your country with them."

[See Carol V. R. George, *Segregated Sabbaths: Richard Allen and the Emergence of Independent Black Churches* (New York: Oxford University Press, 1973).]

number of us usually attended St. George's church in Fourth street [in Philadelphia]; and when the colored people began to get numerous in attending the church, they moved us from the seats we usually sat on, and placed us around the wall, and on Sabbath morning we went to church and the sexton stood at the door, and told us to go in the gallery. He told us to go, and we would see where to sit. We expected to take the seats over the ones we formerly occupied below, not knowing any better. We took those seats. Meeting had begun, and they were nearly done singing, and just as we got to the seats, the elder said, "Let us pray." We had not been long upon our knees before I heard considerable scuffling and low talking. I raised my head up and saw one of the trustees, H—— M——, having hold of the Rev. Absalom Jones, pulling him up off of his knees, and saying, "You must get up — you must not kneel here." Mr. Jones replied, "Wait until prayer is over." Mr. H—— M—— said "No, you must get up now, or I will call for aid and force you away." Mr. Jones said, "Wait until prayer is over, and I will get up and trouble you no more." With that he beckoned to one of the other trustees, Mr. L—— S—— to come to his assistance. He came, and went to William White to pull him up. By this time prayer was over, and

Source: *The Life Experience and Gospel Labors of the Rt. Rev. Richard Allen* [1793] (Nashville: Abingdon Press, 1983), pp. 25-35.

we all went out of the church in a body, and they were no more plagued with us in the church.

This raised a great excitement and inquiry among the citizens, in so much that I believe they were ashamed of their conduct. But my dear Lord was with us, and we were filled with fresh vigor to get a house erected to worship God in. Seeing our forlorn and distressed situation, many of the hearts of our citizens were moved to urge us forward; notwithstanding we had subscribed largely towards finishing St. George's church, in building the gallery and laying new floors, and just as the house was made comfortable, we were turned out from enjoying the comforts of worshipping therein. We then hired a store-room, and held worship by ourselves. Here we were pursued with threats of being disowned, and read publicly out of meeting if we did continue worship in the place we had hired; but we believed the Lord would be our friend. We got subscription papers out to raise money to build the house of the Lord. By this time we had waited on Dr. Rush and Mr. Robert Ralston,* and told them of our distressing situation. We considered it a blessing that the Lord had put it into our hearts to wait upon those gentlemen. They pitied our situation, and subscribed largely towards the church, and were very friendly towards us, and advised us how to go on. We appointed Mr. Ralston our treasurer. Dr. Rush did much for us in public by his influence. I hope the name of Dr. Benjamin Rush and Robert Ralston will never be forgotten among us. They were the first two gentlemen who espoused the cause of the oppressed, and aided us in building the home of the Lord for the poor Africans to worship in. Here was the beginning and rise of the first African church in America.

But the elder of the Methodist Church still pursued us. Mr. John McClaskey called upon us and told us if we did not erase our names from the subscription paper, and give up the paper, we would be publicly turned out of meeting. We asked him if we had violated any rules of discipline by so doing. He replied, "I have the charge given to me by the Conference, and unless you submit I will read you publicly out of meeting." We told him we were willing to abide by the discipline of the Methodist Church, "And if you will show us where we have violated any law of discipline of the Methodist Church, we will

---

* Robert Ralston (1761-1836), like Rush a Philadelphian and a Presbyterian, used his wealth to support many benevolent enterprises. (ed.)

submit; and if there is no rule violated in the discipline we will proceed on." He replied, "We will read you all out." We told him if he turned us out contrary to rule of discipline, we should seek further redress. We told him we were dragged off of our knees in St. George's church, and treated worse than heathens; and we were determined to seek out for ourselves, the Lord being our helper. He told us we were not Methodists, and left us. Finding we would go on in raising money to build the church, he called upon us again, and wished to see us all together. We met him. He told us that he wished us well, that he was a friend to us, and used many arguments to convince us that we were wrong in building a church. We told him we had no place of worship; and we did not mean to go to St. George's church any more, as we were so scandalously treated in the presence of all the congregation present; "and if you deny us your name, you cannot seal up the scriptures from us, and deny us a name in heaven. We believe heaven is free for all who worship in spirit and truth." And he said, "So you are determined to go on." We told him "Yes, God being our helper." He then replied, "We will disown you all from the Methodist connection." We believed if we put our trust in the Lord, he would stand by us.

This was a trial that I never had to pass through before. I was confident that the great head of the church would support us. My dear Lord was with us. We went out with our subscription paper, and met with great success. We had no reason to complain of the liberality of the citizens. The first day the Rev. Absalom Jones and myself went out we collected three hundred and sixty dollars. This was the greatest day's collection that we met with. We appointed a committee to look out for a lot — the Rev. Absalom Jones, William Gray, William Wilcher and myself. We pitched upon a lot at the corner of Lombard and Sixth streets. They authorized me to go and agree for it. I did accordingly. The lot belonged to Mr. Mark Wilcox. We entered into articles of agreement for the lot. Afterwards the committee found a lot in Fifth street, in a more commodious part of the city, which we bought; and the first lot they threw upon my hands, and wished me to give it up. I told them they had authorized me to agree for the lot, and they were all well satisfied with the agreement I had made, and I thought it was hard that they would throw it upon my hands. I told them I would sooner keep it myself than to forfeit the agreement I had made. And so I did.

We bore much persecution from many of the Methodist connection; but we have reason to be thankful to Almighty God, who was our deliverer. The day was appointed to go and dig the cellar. I arose early in the morning and addressed the throne of grace, praying that the Lord would bless our endeavors. Having by this time two or three teams of my own — as I was the first proposer of the African church, I put the first spade in the ground to dig a cellar for the same. This was the first African Church or meetinghouse that was erected in the United States of America. We intended it for the African preaching-house or church; but finding that the elder stationed in this city was such an opposer to our proceedings of erecting a place of worship, though the principal part of the directors of this church belonged to the Methodist connection, the elder stationed here would neither preach for us, nor have anything to do with us. We then held an election, to know what religious denomination we should unite with. At the election it was determined — there were two in favor of the Methodist, the Rev. Absalom Jones and myself, and a large majority in favor of the Church of England. The majority carried. Notwithstanding we had been so violently persecuted by the elder, we were in favor of being attached to the Methodist connection; for I was confident that there was no religious sect or denomination would suit the capacity of the colored people as well as the Methodist; for the plain and simple gospel suits best for any people; for the unlearned can understand, and the learned are sure to understand; and the reason that the Methodist is so successful in the awakening and conversion of the colored people, the plain doctrine and having a good discipline.

But in many cases the preachers would act to please their own fancy, without discipline, till some of them became such tyrants, and more especially to the colored people. They would turn them out of society, giving them no trial, for the smallest offense, perhaps only hearsay. They would frequently, in meeting the class, impeach some of the members of whom they had heard an ill report, and turn them out, saying, "I have heard thus and thus of you, and you are no more a member of society" — without witnesses on either side. This has been frequently done, notwithstanding in the first rise and progress in Delaware state, and elsewhere, the colored people were their greatest support; for there were but few of us free; but the slaves would toil in their little patches many a night until midnight to raise their little truck and sell to get something to support them more than what their masters gave them, but we used often to divide our little support among the white preachers of the Gospel. This was once a quarter. It was in the time of the old Revolutionary War between Great Britain and the United States. The Methodists were the first people that brought glad tidings to the colored people. I feel thankful that ever I heard a Methodist preach. We are beholden to the Methodists, under God, for the light of the Gospel we enjoy; for all other denominations preached so high-flown that we were not able to comprehend their doctrine. Sure am I that reading sermons will never prove so beneficial to the colored people as spiritual or extempore preaching. I am well convinced that the Methodist has proved beneficial to thousands and ten times thousands. It is to be awfully feared that the simplicity of the Gospel that was among them fifty years ago, and that they conform more to the world and the fashions thereof, they would fare very little better than the people of the world. The discipline is altered considerably from what it was. We would ask for the good old way, and desire to walk therein.

In 1793 a committee was appointed from the African Church to solicit me to be their minister, for there was no colored preacher in Philadelphia but myself. I told them I could not accept of their offer, as I was a Methodist. I was indebted to the Methodists, under God, for what little religion I had; being convinced that they were the people of God, I informed them that I could not be anything else but a Methodist, as I was born and awakened under them, and I could go no further with them, for I was a Methodist, and would leave you in peace and love. I would do nothing to retard them in building a church as it was an extensive building, neither would I go out with a subscription paper until they were done going out with their subscription. I bought an old frame that had been formerly occupied as a blacksmith shop, from Mr. Sims, and hauled it on the lot in Sixth near Lombard street, that had formerly been taken for the Church of England. I employed carpenters to repair the old frame, and fit it for a place of worship. In July 1794, Bishop Asbury being in town I solicited him to open the church for us which he accepted. The Rev. John Dickins sung and prayed, and Bishop Asbury preached. The house was called Bethel, agreeable to the prayer that was made. Mr. Dickins prayed that it might be a bethel to the gathering in of thousands of souls. My dear Lord was with us, so that there were many hearty "amen's" echoed through the house. This house of worship has been favored with the awakening of many souls, and I trust they are in the Kingdom, both white and colored.

Our warfare and troubles now began afresh. Mr. C. proposed that we should make over the church to the Conference. This we objected to; he asserted that we could not be Methodists unless we did; we told him he might deny us their name, but they could not deny us a seat in Heaven. Finding that he could not prevail with us so to do, he observed that we had better be incorporated, then we could get any legacies that were left for us, if not, we could not. We agreed to be incorporated. He offered to draw the incorporation himself, that it would save us the trouble of paying for to get it drawn. We cheerfully submitted to his proposed plan. He drew the incorporation, but incorporated our church under the Conference, our property was then all consigned to the Conference for the present bishops, elders, ministers, etc., that belonged to the white Conference, and our property was gone. Being ignorant of incorporations we cheerfully agreed thereto. We labored about ten years under this incorporation, until James Smith was appointed to take the charge in Philadelphia; he soon waked us up by demanding the keys and books of the church, and forbid us holding any meetings except by orders from him; these propositions we told him we could not agree to. He observed he was elder, appointed to the charge, and unless we submitted to him, he would read us all out of meeting. We told him the home was ours, we had bought it, and paid for it. He said he would let us know it was not ours, it belonged to the Conference; we took counsel on it; counsel informed us we had been taken in; according to the incorporation it belonged to the white connection. We asked him if it couldn't be altered; he told us if two-thirds of the society agreed to have it altered, it could be altered. He gave me a transcript to lay before them; I called the society together and laid it before them. My dear Lord was with us. It was unanimously agreed to, by both male and female.

We had another incorporation drawn that took the church from Conference, and got it passed, before the elder knew anything about it. This raised a considerable rumpus, for the elder contended that it would not be good unless he had signed it. The elder, with the trustees of St. George's, called us together, and said we must pay six hundred dollars a year for their services, or they could not serve us. We told them we were not able so to do. The trustees of St. George's insisted that we should or should not be supplied by their preachers. At last they made a move that they would take four hundred; we told them that our home was considerably in debt, and we were poor people, and we could not agree to pay four hundred, but we agreed to give them two hundred. It was moved by one of the trustees of St. George's that the money should be paid into their treasury; we refused paying it into their treasury, but we would pay it to the preacher that served; they made a move that the preacher should not receive the money from us. The Bethel trustees made a move that their funds should be shut and they would pay none; this caused a considerable contention. At length they withdrew their motion. The elder supplied us preaching five times in a year for two hundred dollars. Finding that they supplied us so seldom, the trustees of Bethel church passed a resolution that they would pay but one hundred dollars a year, as the elder only preached five times in a year for us; they called for the money, we paid him twenty-five dollars a quarter, but he being dissatisfied, returned the money back again, and would not have it unless we paid him fifty dollars. The trustees concluded it was enough for five sermons, and said they would pay no more; the elder of St. George's was determined to preach for us no more, unless we gave him two hundred dollars, and we were left alone for upwards of one year.

Mr. Samuel Royal being appointed to the charge of Philadelphia, declared unless we should repeal the Supplement, neither he nor any white preacher, travelling or local, should preach any more for us; so we were left to ourselves. At length the preachers and stewards belonging to the Academy, proposed serving us on the same terms that we had offered to the St. George's preachers, and they preached for us better than twelve months, and then demanded $150 per year; this not being complied with, they declined preaching for us, and we were once more left to ourselves, as an edict was passed by the elder, that if any local preacher should serve us, he should be expelled from the connection. John Emory, then elder of the Academy, published a circular letter, in which we were disowned by the Methodists. A house was also hired and fitted up for worship, not far from Bethel, and an invitation given to all who desired to be Methodists to resort thither.

But being disappointed in this plan, Robert R. Roberts, the resident elder came to Bethel, insisted on preaching to us and taking the spiritual charge of the congregation, for we were Methodists he was told he should come on some terms with the trustees; his answer was, that "He did not come to consult with Richard Allen or other trustees, but to inform the congregation, that on next Sunday afternoon, he would come and take the spiritual charge." We told him he could not preach for us under existing circumstances. However, at the appointed time he came, but having taken previous advice we had our preacher in the pulpit when he came, and the house was so fixed that he could not get but more than half way to the pulpit. Finding himself disappointed he appealed to those who came with him as witnesses, that "That man (meaning the preacher), had taken his appointment." Several respectable white citizens who knew the colored people had been ill-used, were present, and told as not to fear, for they would see us righted, and not suffer Roberts to preach in a forcible manner, after which Roberts went away.

The next elder stationed in Philadelphia was Robert Birch, who, following the example of his predecessor, came and published a meeting for himself. But the method just mentioned was adopted and he had to go away disappointed. In consequence of this, he applied to the Supreme Court for a writ of mandamus, to know why the pulpit was denied him. Being elder, this brought on a lawsuit, which ended in our favor. Thus by the Providence of God we were delivered from a long, distressing and expensive suit, which could not be resumed, being determined by the Supreme Court. For this mercy we desire to be unfeignedly thankful.

About this time, our colored friends in Baltimore were treated in a similar manner by the white preachers and trustees, and many of them driven away who were disposed to seek a place of worship, rather than go to law.

Many of the colored people in other places were in a situation nearly like those of Philadelphia and Baltimore, which induced us, in April 1816, to call a general meeting, by way of Conference. Delegates from Baltimore and other places which met those of Philadelphia, and taking into consideration their grievances, and in order to secure the privileges, promote union and harmony among themselves, it was resolved: "That the people of Philadelphia, Baltimore, etc., etc., should become one body, under the name of the African Methodist Episcopal Church." We deemed it expedient to have a form of discipline, whereby we may guide our people in the fear of God, in the unity of the Spirit, and in the bonds of peace and preserve us from that spiritual despotism which we have so recently experienced — remembering that we are not to lord it over God's heritage, as greedy dogs that can never have enough. But with long suffering and bowels of compassion, to bear each other's burdens, and so fulfill the Law of Christ, praying that our mutual striving together for the promulgation of the Gospel may be crowned with abundant success.

THE FRONTIERSMAN

Peter Cartwright

(1785-1872)

Peter Cartwright was a frontier preacher, and it is difficult to know which of those two words deserves the greater emphasis. For the frontier dominated so much of what the preacher did and was. Cartwright's autobiography is what a later century would call a "good read." He presents a vivid picture of frontier life: the frauds, the healers, the genuine pietists, the sectarian jealousies, and on occasion the sectarian cooperation. Like Richard Allen, Cartwright was converted to Methodism at a young age; and, again like Allen, he accepted ordination at the hands of the grandest itinerant of them all — Francis Asbury. Cartwright shared one other feature with Allen: a white preacher, he opposed slavery with all the vigor of the black preacher.

But Cartwright never became a bishop. He was ordained a deacon in 1806 (twenty-one years old), an elder (or presbyter) in 1808, and a presiding elder ten years later. The presiding elder assumed responsibility for younger members of the clergy, as William McKendree had been his presiding elder years before. ("He selected books for me, both literary and theological; and every quarterly visit he made, he examined into my progress, and corrected my errors, if I had fallen into any. He delighted to instruct me in English grammar.") Indeed, from his experience with McKendree, Cartwright concluded that "if presiding elders would do their duty by young men," this method of ministerial training "would be more advantageous than all the colleges and Biblical institutes in the land."

Cartwright, like so many of his peers, had no college education. Bishop Francis Asbury would not object to that, but he probably did object to what Cartwright did have: a wife. Asbury, who never married, did not think highly of the married estate, since it — in Asbury's view — tended to limit the effectiveness and mobility of the itinerant preacher. Neither Cartwright's effectiveness nor his mobility appeared to be cramped by the presence of a wife (married in 1808) or the subsequent arrival of nine children. He traveled hundreds of miles, preached thousands of sermons, baptized perhaps as many as ten thousand converts in a circuit that covered Kentucky, Ohio, Indiana, and Illinois. Somehow, he even had time to serve in the Illinois state legislature from 1824 to 1840. But when he ran for the U.S. Congress in 1846, he was defeated by a relative unknown, Abraham Lincoln.

When the Methodists split in 1844 over the slavery issue into northern and southern branches, Cartwright had no hesitation in joining with the antislavery faction of the north. Indeed, he had earlier abandoned his home state of Kentucky for Illinois because of his growing dismay over the persistence and even the spread of slavery. "It is clear to my mind," he wrote in his *Autobiography,* "if Methodist preachers, had kept clear of slavery themselves, and gone on bearing honest testimony against it, that thousands upon thousands more would have been emancipated who are now groaning under an oppression almost too intolerable to be borne."

[See Helen Hardie Grant, *Peter Cartwright: Pioneer* (New York: Abingdon Press, 1931).]

At the close of this conference year, 1806, I met the Kentucky preachers at Lexington, and headed by William Burke, about twenty of us started for conference, which was held in East Tennessee, at Ebenezer Church, Nollichuckie, September 15th. Our membership had increased to twelve thousand six hundred and seventy; our net increase was about eight hundred.

This year another presiding-elder district was added to the Western Conference, called the Mississippi District. The number of our traveling preachers increased from thirty-eight to forty-nine. Bishop Asbury attended the Conference. There were thirteen of us elected and ordained deacons. According to the printed Minutes, this was placed in 1807, but it was in the fall of 1806. Two years before there were eighteen of us admitted on trial; that number, in this short space of time, had fallen to thirteen; the other five were discontinued at their own request, or from sickness, or were reduced to suffering circumstances, and compelled to desist from traveling for want of the means of support.

I think I received about forty dollars this year; but many of our preachers did not receive half that amount. These were hard times in these Western wilds; *many,* very *many,* pious and useful preachers, were literally starved into a location. I do not mean that they were starved for

Source: *The Autobiography of Peter Cartwright* [1856] (Nashville: Abingdon Press, 1984), pp. 74-82.

want of food; for although it was rough, yet the preachers generally got enough to eat. But they did not generally receive in a whole year money enough to get them a suit of clothes; and if people, and preachers too, had not dressed in home-spun clothing, and the good sisters had not made and presented their preachers with clothing, they generally must retire from itinerant life, and go to work and clothe themselves. Money was very scarce in the country at this early day, but some of the best men God ever made, breasted the stations, endured poverty, and triumphantly planted Methodism in this Western world.

When we were ordained deacons at this Conference, Bishop Asbury presented me with a parchment certifying my ordination in the following words, namely:

> Know all by these presents, That I, Francis Asbury, *Bishop of the Methodist Episcopal Church* in America, under the protection of Almighty God, and with a single eye to his glory, by the imposition of my hands and prayer, have this day set apart Peter Cartwright for the office of a DEACON in the said Methodist Episcopal Church; a man whom I judge to be well qualified for that work; and do hereby recommend him to all whom it may concern, as a proper person to administer the ordinances of baptism, marriage, and the burial of the dead, in the absence of an elder, and to feed the flock of Christ, so long as his spirit and practice are such as become the Gospel of Christ, and he continueth to hold fast the form of sound words, according to the established doctrine of the Gospel.
>
> In testimony whereof, I have hereunto set my hand and seal this sixteenth day of September, in the year of our Lord one thousand eight hundred and six
>
> Francis Asbury.

I had traveled from Zanesville, in Ohio, to East Tennessee to conference, a distance of over five hundred miles; and when our appointments were read out, I was sent to Marietta Circuit, almost right back, but still further east. Marietta was at the mouth of the Muskingum River, where it emptied into the Ohio. This circuit extended along the north bank of the Ohio, one hundred and fifty miles, crossed over the Ohio River at the mouth of the Little Kanawha, and up that stream to Hughes River, then east to Middle Island. I suppose it was three hundred miles round. I had to cross the Ohio River four times every round.

It was a poor and hard circuit at that time. Marietta and the country round were settled at an early day by a colony of Yankees. At the time of my appointment I had never seen a Yankee, and I had heard dismal stories about them. It was said they lived almost entirely on pumpkins, molasses, fat meat, and bohea tea; moreover, that they could not bear loud and zealous sermons, and they had brought on their learned preachers with them, and they read their sermons, and were always criticizing us poor backwoods preachers. When my appointment was read out, it distressed me greatly. I went to Bishop Asbury and begged him to supply my place, and let me go home. The old father took me in his arms, and said,

"O no, my son; go in the name of the Lord. It will make a man of you."

Ah, thought I, if this is the way to make men, I do not want to be a man. I cried over it bitterly, and prayed too. But on I started, cheered by my presiding elder, Brother J. Sale. If ever I saw hard times, surely it was this year; yet many of the people were kind, and treated me friendly. I had hard work to keep soul and body together. The first Methodist house I came to, I found the brother a Universalist. I crossed over the Muskingum River to Marietta. The first Methodist family I stopped with there, the lady was a member of the Methodist Episcopal Church, but a thorough Universalist. She was a thin-faced, Roman-nosed, loquacious Yankee, glib on the tongue, and you may depend on it, I had a hard race to keep up with her, though I found it a good school, for it set me to reading my Bible. And here permit me to say, of all the isms that I ever heard of, they were here. These descendants of the Puritans were generally educated, but their ancestors were rigid predestinarians; and as they were sometimes favored with a little light on their moral powers, and could just "see men as trees walking," they jumped into Deism, Universalism, Unitarianism, etc., etc. I verily believe it was the best school I ever entered. They waked me up on all sides; Methodism was feeble, and I had to battle or run, and I resolved on the former.

There was here in Marietta a preacher by the name of A. Sargent; he had been a Universalist preacher, but finding such a motley gang, as I have above mentioned, he thought (and thought correctly too) that they were proper subjects for his imposture. Accordingly, he assumed the name of Halcyon Church, and proclaimed himself the millennial messenger. He professed to see visions, fall into trances, and to converse with angels. His followers were numerous in the town and country. The Presbyterian and Congregational ministers were afraid of him. He had men preachers and women preachers. The Methodists had no meeting-house in Marietta. We had to preach in the court-house when we could get a chance. We battled pretty severely. The Congregationalists opened their Academy for me to preach in. I prepared myself, and gave battle to the Halcyons. This made a mighty commotion. In the meantime we had a camp-meeting in the suburbs of Marietta. Brother Sale, our presiding elder, was there. Mr. Sargent came and hung around and wanted to preach, but Brother Sale never noticed him. I have said before that he professed to go into trances and have visions. He would swoon away, fall, and lay a long time; and when he would come to, he would tell what mighty things he had seen and heard.

On Sunday night, at our camp-meeting, Sargent got some powder, and lit a cigar, and then walked down to the bank of the river, one hundred yards, where stood a large stump. He put his powder on the stump, and touched it with his cigar. The flash of the powder was seen by many at the camp; at least the light. When the powder flashed, down fell Sargent; there he lay a good while. In the meantime, the people found him lying there and gathered around him. At length he came to, and said he had a message from God to us Methodists. He said God had come down to him in a flash of light, and he fell under the power of God, and thus received his vision.

Seeing so many gathered around him there, I took a light, and went down to see what was going on. As soon as I came near the stump, I smelled the sulphur of the powder; and stepping up to the stump, there was clearly the sign of powder, and hard by lay the cigar with which he had ignited it. He was now busy delivering his message. I stepped up to him, and asked him if an angel had appeared to him in that flash of light.

He said, "Yes."

Said I, "Sargent, did not that angel smell of brimstone?"

"Why," said he, "do you ask me such a foolish question?"

"Because," said I, "if an angel has spoken to you at all, he was from the lake that burneth with fire and brimstone!" and raising my voice, I said, "I smell sulphur now!" I walked up to the stump, and called on the people to come and see for themselves. The people rushed up, and soon saw through the trick, and began to abuse Sargent for a vile impostor. He soon left, and we were troubled no more with him or his brimstone angels.

I will beg leave to remark here, that while I was battling successfully against the Halcyons, I was treated with great respect by the Congregational minister and his people, and the Academy was always open for me to preach in; but as soon as I triumphed over and vanquished them, one of the elders of the Congregational Church waited on me, and informed me that it was not convenient for me to preach any more in their Academy. I begged the privilege to make one more appointment in the Academy, till I could get some other place to preach in. This favor, as it was only one more time, was granted.

I then prepared myself; and when my appointed day rolled around, the house was crowded; and I leveled my whole Arminian artillery against their Calvinism; and challenged their minister, who was present, to public debate; but he thought prudence the better part of valor, and declined. This effort secured me many friends, and some persecution; but my way was opened, and we raised a little class, and had a name among the living.

I will here mention a special case of wild fanaticism that took place with one of these Halcyon preachers while I was on this circuit. He worked himself up into the belief that he could live so holy in this life that his animal nature would became immortal and that he would never die; and he conceived that he had gained this immortality, and could live without eating. In despite of all the arguments and persuasion of his friends, he refused to eat or drink. He stood it sixteen days and nights, and then died a suicidal death. His death put a stop to this foolish delusion, and threw a damper over the whole Halcyon fanaticism.

I will here state something like the circumstances I found myself in, at the close of my labors on this hard circuit. I had been from my father's house about three years; was five hundred miles from home; my horse had gone blind; my saddle was worn out; my bridle reins had been eaten up and replaced, (after a sort) at least a dozen times; and my clothes had been patched till it was difficult to detect the original. I had concluded to try to make my way home, and get another outfit. I was in Marietta, and had just seventy-five cents in my pocket. How I would get home and pay my way I could not tell.

But it was of no use to parley about it; go I must, or do worse; so I concluded to go as far as I could, and then stop and work for more means, till I got home. I had some few friends on the way, but not many; so I cast ahead.

My first day's travel was through my circuit. At about thirty-five miles' distance there lived a brother, with whom I intended to stay all night. I started, and late in the evening, within five miles of my stopping-place, fell in with a widow lady, not a member of the Church, who lived several miles off my road. She had attended my appointments in that settlement all the year. After the usual salutations, she asked me if I was leaving the circuit.

I told her I was, and had started for my father's.

"Well," said she, "how are you off for money? I expect you have received but little on this circuit."

I told her I had but seventy-five cents in the world. She invited me home with her, and told me she would give me a little to help me on. But I told her I had my places fixed to stop every night till I got to Maysville; and if I went home with her, it would derange all my stages, and throw me among strangers. She then handed me a dollar, saying it was all she had with her, but if I would go home with her she would give me more. I declined going with her, thanked her for the dollar, bade her farewell, moved on, and reached my lodging-place.

By the time I reached the Ohio River, opposite Maysville, my money was all gone. I was in trouble about how to get over the river, for I had nothing to pay my ferriage.

I was acquainted with Brother J. Armstrong, a merchant in Maysville, and concluded to tell the ferryman that I had no money, but if he would ferry me over, I could borrow twenty-five cents from Armstrong, and would pay him. Just as I got to the bank of the river he landed, on my side, with a man and a horse; and when the man reached the bank, I saw it was Colonel M. Shelby, brother to Governor Shelby, of Kentucky. He was a lively exhorter in the Methodist Episcopal Church, and an old acquaintance and neighbor of my father's.

When he saw me he exclaimed:

"Peter! is that you?"

"Yes, Moses," said I, "what little is left of me."

"Well," said he, "from your appearance you must have seen hard times. Are you trying to get home?"

"Yes," I answered.

"How are you off for money, Peter?" said he.

"Well, Moses," said I, "I have not a cent in the world."

"Well," said he, "here are three dollars, and I will give you a bill of the road and a letter of introduction till you get down into the barrens, at Pilot Knobb."

You may be sure my spirits greatly rejoiced. So I passed on very well for several days and nights on the colonel's money and credit, but when I came to the first tavern beyond the Pilot Knobb my money was out. What to do I did not know, but I rode up and asked for quarters. I told the landlord I had no money; had been three years from home, and was trying to get back to my father's. I also told him I had a little old watch, and a few good books in my saddle-bags, and I would compensate him in some way. He bade me alight and be easy.

On inquiry I found this family had lived there from an early day, totally destitute of the Gospel and all religious privileges. There were three rooms in this habitation, below — the dining-room, and a back bedroom, and the kitchen. The kitchen was separated from the other lower rooms by a thin, plank partition, set up on an end; and the planks had shrunk and left considerable cracks between them.

When we were about to retire to bed, I asked the landlord if he had any objection to our praying before we laid down. He said, "None at all;" and stepped into the kitchen, as I supposed, to bring in the family. He quickly returned with a candle in his hand, and said, "Follow me." I followed into the back bedroom. Whereupon he set down the candle, and bade me good night, saying, "There, you can pray as much as you please."

I stood, and felt foolish. He had completely ousted me; but it immediately occurred to me that I would kneel down and pray with a full and open voice; so down I knelt, and commenced praying audibly. I soon found, from the commotion created in the kitchen, that they were taken by surprise as much as I had been. I distinctly heard the landlady say, "He is crazy, and will kill us all this night. Go, husband, and see what is the matter." But he was slow to approach; and when I ceased praying he came in, and asked me what was the cause of my acting in this strange way. I replied, "Sir, did you not give me the privilege to pray as much as I pleased?" "Yes," said he, "but I did not expect you would pray out." I told him I wanted the family to hear prayer, and as he had deprived me of that privilege, I knew of no better way to accomplish my object than to do as I had done, and I hoped he would not be offended.

I found he thought me deranged, but we fell into a free conversation on the subject of religion, and, I think, I fully satisfied him that I was not beside myself, but spoke forth the words of truth with soberness.

Next morning I rose early, intending to go fifteen miles to an acquaintance for breakfast, but as I was getting my horse out of the stable the landlord came out, and insisted that I should not leave till after breakfast. I yielded, but he would not have anything for my fare, and urged me to call on him if ever I traveled that way again. I will just say here, that in less than six months I called on this landlord, and he and his lady were happily converted, dating their conviction from the extraordinary circumstances of the memorable night I spent with them.

I found other friends on my journey till I reached Hopkinsville, Christian County, within thirty miles of my father's, and I had just six and a quarter cents left. This was a new and dreadfully wicked place. I put up at a tavern kept by an old Mr. M'. The landlord knew my father. I told him I had not money to pay my bill, but as soon as I got home I would send it to him. He said, "Very well," and made me welcome.

Shortly after I laid down I fell asleep. Suddenly I was aroused by a piercing scream, or screams, of a female. I supposed that somebody was actually committing murder. I sprang from my bed, and, after getting half dressed, ran into the room from whence issued the piercing screams, and called out, "What's the matter here?" The old gentleman replied, that his wife was subject to spasms, and often had them. I commenced a conversation with her about religion. I found she was under deep concern about her soul. I asked if I might pray for her. "O, yes," she replied, "for there is no one in this place that cares for my soul."

I knelt and prayed, and then commenced singing, and directed her to Christ as an all-sufficient Saviour, and prayed again. She suddenly sprung out of the bed and shouted, "Glory to God! he has blessed my soul." It was a happy time indeed. The old gentleman wept like a child. We sung and shouted, prayed and praised, nearly all night. Next morning the old landlord told me my bill was paid tenfold, and that all he charged me was, every time I passed that way, to call and stay with them.

Next day I reached home with the six and a quarter cents unexpended. Thus I have given you a very imperfect little sketch of the early travel of a Methodist preacher in the Western Conference. My parents received me joyfully. I tarried with them several weeks. My father gave me a fresh horse, a bridle and saddle, some new clothes, and forty dollars in cash. Thus equipped, I was ready for another three years' absence.

Our Conference, this year, was held in Chillicothe, September 14, 1807. Our increase of members was one thousand one hundred and eighty; increase of traveling preachers, six. From the Conference in Chillicothe I received my appointment for 1807-8, on Barren Circuit, in Cumberland District, James Ward presiding elder, who employed Lewis Anderson to travel with me. This brother is now a member of the Illinois Conference. It was a four weeks' circuit. We had several revivals of religion in different places. The circuit reached from Barren Creek, north of Green River, to the head of Long Creek, in Tennessee State. I received about forty dollars quarterage. We had an appointment near Glasgow, the county seat of Barren County. A very singular circumstance took place in this circuit this year; something like the following:

There were two very large Baptist Churches east of Glasgow. These Churches had each very talented and popular preachers for their pastors, by the name of W. and H. The Baptists were numerous and wealthy, and the great majority of the citizens were under Baptist influence. The Methodists had a small class of about thirteen members. There lived in the settlement a gentleman by the name of L., who was raised under the Baptist influence, though not a member of the Church. His lady was a member of one of these large Baptist Churches. Mr. L. was lingering in the last stages of consumption, but without religion. These Baptist ministers visited him often, and advised, and prayed with, and for him. Learning that I was in the neighborhood, he sent for me! I went; he seemed fast approaching his end, wasted away to a mere skeleton; he had to be lifted, like a child, in and out of the bed. I found him penitent, and prayed with him, sat up with him, and in the best way I knew I pointed him to Jesus. It pleased God to own the little effort, and speak peace to his troubled soul; he was very happy after this. He told me the next morning that he wished to be baptized, join the Church, and receive the sacrament. In the meantime, the Baptist ministers came to see him, and as I knew he was raised under Baptist denominational influences, I was at a loss to know how to act. I took the two Baptist ministers out, and said to them: "This afflicted brother has obtained religion, and he desires to be baptized, join the Church, and receive the sacrament. And," said I, "brethren, you must now take the case into your own hands, and do with it as you think best. He was raised a Baptist, and, as a matter of course, he believes in immersion. And," said I, "my opinion is, if he is immersed, he cannot survive it; and as you are strong in the faith of immersion, you must administer it."

"No, no," said they; "he is your convert, and you must do all he desires. We believe, as well as you, that he cannot be immersed."

"Now," said I, "brethren, he wants not only to be baptized, but wants to join the Church, the Baptist Church of course; and if I baptize him by sprinkling or pouring, you will not receive him into the Baptist Church; or, in other words, if I do, will you receive him into your Church?"

"Well, no," said they; "we cannot do it."

"Now," said I, "brethren, this is a very solemn affair. You will not baptize him and take him into your Church; and if I baptize him, still you will not receive him. There must be something wrong about this very solemn matter."

They then said they would have nothing to do with it; that I must manage it in my own way. I then went and consulted the wife of the sick man. I told her what her ministers had said. "Now," said I, "sister, what must I do?"

Said she, "Go and ask my husband, and do as he wishes, and I will be satisfied."

I went, and said, "Brother L., if I baptize you, it must be by sprinkling or pouring; you cannot be immersed."

Said he, "I know I can't, and I am willing to be baptized in any mode; it is not essential."

As soon as preparation was made, I baptized him by sprinkling, and then proceeded to consecrate the elements and administer the sacrament. I turned and invited both of the Baptist ministers to come and commune with the dying saint, but they refused. Then I turned to his wife, and invited her to come and commemorate the dying sorrows of her Saviour with her dying husband. She paused for a moment, and then, bursting into a flood of tears, said, "I will;" and came forward, and I administered to them both.

After this I said, "Brother L., do you wish to have your name enrolled with the members of the little class of Methodists that worship in the neighborhood?"

He said, "O, yes;" and then added, "before you get round your circuit, I shall be no more on earth, and I wish you to preach my funeral."

After consultation with his wife, I left an appointment for his funeral. In a few days he breathed his last, and went off triumphant.

When I came to the appointment, there was a vast crowd. We had a very solemn time. I stated all the circumstances above narrated, and at the close I opened the door of the Church, and Mrs. L., and six others of her relatives, all members of the Baptist Church, came forward and joined the Methodists. This circumstance gave us a standing that enabled us to lift our heads and breathe more freely afterward.

In the course of this year we carried Methodist preaching into a Baptist congregation on Bacon Creek. A great many of their members gave up Calvinism, close communion, and immersion, and joined the

Methodist Church; and we took possession of their meeting-house, and raised a large society there that flourishes to this day. Out of this revival several preachers were raised up that trained and blessed the Methodist Episcopal Church for years afterward.

THE CONVERT

Orestes Brownson

(1803-1876)

The most fascinating religious pilgrimage in the nation's history is that of Orestes Brownson. Reared in a Congregational home in Royalton, Vermont, he was converted in a Methodist or Christian revival when he was only thirteen. Two years later, in Balston Spa, New York, he found himself first attracted to Universalist literature because of its emphasis on reason. Reason led him briefly to deism, and that threatened to shove him into atheism. But this did not satisfy, for "I wanted to believe, to adore. . . . I doubted my reason, became sick of myself and in this state of mind was found by a presbyterian clergyman who made a presbyterian out of me." At the age of nineteen, he was baptized and accepted into full membership in Presbyterian church in Balston. But the pilgrimage had hardly begun.

While briefly teaching in Detroit, Michigan, he yielded again to the attractions of Universalism. "The time is past," he wrote, sounding a bit like Thomas Jefferson, "when we most close our eyes and fold our hands & receive without a murmur whatever clerical machinations and priestcraft were pleased to set before us." In 1826, back in the East, he was ordained a Universalist minister in Jaffrey, New Hampshire. But in three years, he left the Universalist ministry to become a "free thinker," interested primarily in social reform. After two or three years following this tack, however, he despaired of efforts to change society without the helping hand of religion.

Influenced by the cogent writings of Unitarian spokesman William Ellery Channing, Brownson by 1832 decided to enter the Unitarian ministry, accepting a pastoral charge in Walpole, New Hampshire. The pilgrim had at this point concluded that man was by nature religious and that religion was "the poetry of the soul." By means of this poetry, humankind can "solve by a sort of intuition all the great problems relating to God and to human destiny." In 1836 Brownson moved to Boston to direct a "Society for Christian Union and Progress." While in the Boston area, he drew closer to the Transcendentalist movement associated most closely with the name of Ralph Waldo Emerson. He found the Transcendentalist emphasis on intuition congenial, but soon concluded that intuition was not enough. One must also respect tradition. Nor was the emphasis on the individual sufficient; one must also consider the force and claims of the community.

By 1844, Brownson took one last great step: he entered into the Roman Catholic Church. He had concluded that "either the church in communion with See of Rome is the one holy catholic apostolic church, or the one holy catholic church does not exist. We have tried every possible way to escape this conclusion, but escape it we cannot." By the time that he wrote his autobiography, he had been a Catholic for thirteen years. He had also seen the large influx of Catholic immigrants into the United States, with a corresponding growth of strong anti-Catholic sentiment. Thus, his Conclusion (excerpted below) is an apologia — quite necessary at the time — both for himself and his newly embraced church.

[See Arthur M. Schlesinger, Jr., *A Pilgrim's Progress: Orestes A. Brownson* (Boston: Little, Brown and Co., 1939).]

I have now completed the sketch I proposed to give of my intellectual struggles, failures, and successes, from my earliest childhood till my reception by the Bishop of Boston into the communion of the Catholic Church. I have not written to vindicate my ante-Catholic life, or to apologize for my conversion. I have aimed to record facts, principles, and reasonings, trials and struggles, which have a value independent of the fact that they relate to my personal history. Yet even as the personal history of an earnest soul, working its way, under the grace of God, from darkness to light, from the lowest abyss of unbelief to a firm, unwavering, and not a blind faith in the old religion, so generally rejected and decried by my countrymen, I think my story not wholly worthless, or altogether uninstructive, — especially when taken in connection with the glimpses it incidentally affords of American thought and life during the greater portion of the earlier half of the present century. Whether what I have written proves me to have been intellectually weak, vacillating, constantly changing, all things by turns, and nothing long, or tolerably firm, consistent, and persevering in my search after truth; whether it shows that my seeking admission into the Church for the reasons, and in the way and manner I did, was a sudden caprice, an act of folly, perhaps of despair, or that it was an act of deliberation, wise,

Source: Orestes A. Brownson, *The Convert; Or, Leaves From My Experience* [1857] (New York: D. and J. Sadlier & Co., 1877), pp. 315-27, 330-39.

79

judicious, and for a sufficient reason, my readers are free to judge for themselves.

This much only will I add, that, whether I am believed or not, I can say truly that, during the nearly thirteen years of Catholic experience, I have found not the slightest reason to regret the step I took. I have had much to try me, and enough to shake me, if shaken I could be, but I have not had even the slightest temptation to doubt, or the slightest inclination to undo what I had done; and have every day found new and stronger reasons to thank Almighty God for his great mercy in bringing me to the knowledge of his Church, and permitting me to enter and live in her communion. I know all that can be said in disparagement of Catholics. I am well versed, perhaps no man more so, in Catholic scandals, but I have not been deceived; I have found all that was promised me, all I looked for. I have found the Church all that her ministers represented her, all my imagination painted her, and infinitely more than I had conceived it possible for her to be. My experience as a Catholic, so far as the Church, her doctrines, her morals, her discipline, her influences are concerned, has been a continued succession of agreeable surprises.

I do not pretend that I have found the Catholic population perfect, or that I have found in them or in myself no shortcomings, nothing to be censured or regretted; yet I have found that population superior to what I expected, more intellectual, more cultivated, more moral, more active, living, and energetic. Undoubtedly, our Catholic population, made up in great part of the humbler classes of the Catholic populations of the Old World, for three hundred years subjected to the bigotry, intolerance, persecutions, and oppressions of Protestant or *quasi*-Protestant governments, have traits of character, habits, and manners, which the outside non-Catholic American finds unattractive, and even repulsive. Certainly in our cities and large towns may be found, I am sorry to say, a comparatively numerous population, nominally Catholic, who are no credit to their religion, to the land of their birth, or to that of their adoption. No Catholic will deny that the children of these are to a great extent shamefully neglected, and suffered to grow up without the simplest elementary moral and religious instruction, and to become recruits to our vicious population, our rowdies, and our criminals. This is certainly to be deplored, but can easily be explained without prejudice to the Church, by adverting to the condition to which these individuals were reduced before coming here; to their disappointments and discouragements in a strange land; to their exposure to new and unlooked-for temptations; to the fact that they were by no means the best of Catholics even in their native countries; to their poverty, destitution, ignorance, insufficient culture, and a certain natural shiftlessness and recklessness, and to our great lack of schools, churches, and priests. The proportion, too, that these bear to our whole Catholic population is far less than is commonly supposed; and they are not so habitually depraved as they appear, for they seldom or never consult appearances, and have little skill in concealing their vices. As low and degraded as they are, they never are so low or so vicious as the corresponding class of Protestants in Protestant nations. A Protestant vicious class is always worse than it appears, a Catholic vicious population is less bad. In the worst there is always some gem that with proper care may be nursed into life, that may blossom and bear fruit. In our narrow lanes, blind courts, damp cellars, and unventilated garrets, where our people swarm as bees; in the midst of filth and the most squalid wretchedness, the fumes of intemperance and the shouts and imprecations of blasphemy, in what by the outside world would be regarded as the very dens of vice, and crime, and infamy, we often find individuals who, it may well be presumed, have retained their baptismal innocence, real Fleurs de Marie, who remain pure and unsullied, and who, in their humble sphere, exhibit brilliant examples of the most heroic Christian virtues.

The majority of our Catholic population is made up of the unlettered peasantry, small mechanics, servant-girls, and common laborers, from various European countries; and however worthy in themselves, or useful to the country to which they have migrated, cannot, in a worldly and social point of view at least, be taken as a fair average of the Catholic population in their native lands. The Catholic nobility, gentry, easy classes, and the better specimens of the professional men, have not migrated with them. Two or three millions of the lower, less prosperous, and less cultivated, and sometimes less virtuous class of the European Catholic populations, have in a comparatively brief period been cast upon our shores, with little or no provision made for their intellectual, moral, or religious wants. Yet, if we look at this population as it is, and is every year becoming, we cannot but be struck with its marvellous energy and progress. The mental activity of Catholics, all things considered, is far more remarkable than that of our non-Catholic countrymen, and, in proportion to their numbers and means, they contribute far more than any other class of American citizens to the purposes of education, both common and liberal; for they receive little or nothing from the public treasury, and, in addition to supporting numerous schools of their own, they contribute their quota to the support of those of the State.

I do not pretend that the Catholic population of this country are a highly literary people, or that they are in any adequate sense an intellectually cultivated people. How could they be, when the great mass of them have had to earn their very means of subsistence, and have had as much as they could do to provide for the first wants of religion, and of themselves and families? Yet there is a respectable Catholic-American literature springing up among us, and Catholics have their representatives among the first scholars and scientific men in the land. In metaphysics, in moral and intellectual philosophy, they take already the lead; in natural history and the physical sciences, they are not far behind; and let once the barrier between them and the non-Catholic public be broken down, and they will soon take the first position in general and polite literature. As yet our own literary public, owing to the causes I have mentioned, I admit is not large enough to give adequate encouragement to authors, and the general public makes it a point not to recognize our literary labors. But this will not last, for it is against the interest and the genius of liberal scholarship, and Catholic authors will soon find a public adequate to their wants. Non-Catholics do themselves great wrong in acting on the principle, No good can come out of Nazareth; for we have already in what we ourselves write, in what we reprint from our brethren in the British Empire, and in what we translate from French, German, Spanish, and Italian Catholics, a literature far richer and more important, even under a literary and scientific point of view, than they suspect.

I have known long and well the Protestant clergy of the United States, and I am by no means disposed to underrate their native abilities or their learning and science, and, although I think the present generation of ministers falls far below its predecessor, I esteem highly the contributions they have made and are making to the literature and science of our common country; but our Catholic clergy, below in many respects what for various reasons they should be, can compare more than favorably with them, except those among them whose mother tongue was foreign from ours, in the correct and classical use of the English language. They surpass them as a body in logical training, in theological science, and in the accuracy, and not unfrequently in the variety and extent of their erudition. Indeed, I have found among Catholics a higher tone of thought, morals, manners, and society, than I have ever found, with fair opportunities, among my non-Catholic countrymen; and taking the Catholic population of the country, even as it actually is, under all its disadvantages, there is nothing in it that need make the most cultivated and refined man of letters or of society blush to avow himself a Catholic.

Certainly, I have found cause to complain of Catholics at home and abroad, not indeed as falling below non-Catholic populations, but as falling below their own Catholic standard. I find among them, not indeed as universal — far from it — but as too prevalent, habits of thought and modes of action, a lack of manly courage, energy, and directness, which seem to me as unwise as they are offensive to the better class of English and American minds. In matters not of faith, there is less unanimity, and less liberality, less courtesy, and less forbearance, in regard to allowable differences of opinion, than might be expected. But I have recollected that I am not myself infallible, and may complain where I should not. Many things may seem to me wrong, only because I am not accustomed to them. Something must be set down to peculiarity of national temperament and development; and even what cannot be justified or excused on either ground, can in all cases be traced to causes unconnected with religion. The habits and peculiarities which I find it most difficult to like, are evidently due to the fact that the Catholics of this country have migrated for the most part from foreign Catholic populations, that have either been oppressed by non-Catholic governments directing their policy to crush and extinguish Catholicity, or by political despotisms which sprang up in Europe after the disastrous Protestant revolt in the sixteenth century, and which recognized in the common people no rights, and allowed them no equality with the ruling class. Under the despotic governments of some Catholic countries, and the bigotry and intolerance of Protestant states, they could hardly fail to acquire habits not in accordance with the habits of those who have never been persecuted, and have never been forced, in order to live, to study to evade tyrannical laws or the caprices of despotism. Men who are subjected to tyranny, who have to deal with tyrants, and who feel that power is against them, and that they can never carry their points by main force, naturally study diplomacy, and supply by art what they lack in strength. This art may degenerate into craft. That it occasionally does so with individuals here and elsewhere, it were useless to deny; but the cause is not in the Church or anything she teaches or approves. In fact, many things which Englishmen and Americans complain of in Catholics and the populations of Southern Europe, have been inherited from the craft and refinement of the old Graeco-Roman civilization, and transmitted from generation to generation in spite of the Church.

As yet our Catholic population, whether foreign-born or native-born, hardly dare feel themselves freemen in this land of freedom. They have so long been an oppressed people, that their freedom here seems hardly real. They have never become reconciled to the old Puritan Commonwealth of England, and they retain with their Catholicity too many reminiscences of the passions and politics of the Bourbons and the Stuarts. They are very generally attached to the republican institutions of the country, no class of our citizens more so, and would defend them at the sacrifice of their lives, but their interior life has not as yet been moulded into entire harmony with them; and they have a tendency, in seeking to follow out American democracy, to run into extreme radicalism, or, when seeking to preserve law and order, to run into extreme conservatism. They do not always hit the exact medium. But this need not surprise us, for no one can hit that medium unless his interior life and habits have been formed to it. Non-Catholic foreigners are less able than Catholic foreigners to do it, if we except the English, who have been trained under a system in many respects analogous to our own; and no small portion of our own countrymen, "to the manner born," make even more fatal mistakes than we made by any portion of our Catholic population, — chiefly, however, because they adopt a European instead of an American interpretation of our political and social order. Other things being equal, Catholic foreigners far more readily adjust themselves to our institutions than any other class of foreigners; and among Catholics, it must be observed that they succeed best who best understand and best practise their religion. They who are least truly American, and yield most to the demagogues, are those who have very little of Catholicity except the accident of being born of Catholic parents, who had them baptized in infancy. These are they who bring reproach on the whole body.

Undoubtedly there is in Catholic, as well as in non-Catholic states, much that no wise man, no good man, can defend, or fail to deplore. I have not travelled abroad, but I have listened to those who have, and I claim to know a little of the languages and literatures of Southern Europe. From the best information I can get, I do not believe that things are so bad in Spain, Portugal, and Italy, as Protestant travellers tell us; nor that the political and social condition of the people in those states is so beautiful or so happy as now and then a Catholic, who imagines that he must eulogize whatever he finds in a Catholic state, or done by men who call themselves Catholic, in his pious fervor pretends. Yet, be the political and social condition of the people in these countries as bad as it may be, it does not disturb my Catholic faith, or damp my Catholic ardor. All the modern Catholic states of Europe grew up under Catholicity, and were more Catholic than they are now at the period of their greatest prosperity and power. The decline which is alleged, and which I have no disposition to deny, in the Italian and Spanish Peninsulas, is fairly traceable to political, economical, commercial, and other causes, independent in their operation of Catholicity, or of religion of any sort. Moreover, as, a Catholic, I am under no obligation to defend the policy or the administration of so-called Catholic governments, not even the policy and administration of the temporal government of the Papal States. The Pope, as Supreme Doctor and Judge of the Deposit of faith, in teaching and defining the faith of the Church, I hold is, by the supernatural assistance of the Holy Ghost promised to his office, infallible, and I accept his definitions, *ex animo,* the moment they reach me in an authentic shape; but I am aware of no law of the Church, of no principle of Catholicity, that requires me to believe him infallible in matters of simple administration, which our Lord has left to human prudence. In these matters, so far as they are directly or indirectly ecclesiastical, I obey him as the Supreme Governor of the Church, as I obey the constitution and laws of my country, not because it is impossible for him to err, but because he is my divinely-appointed ruler. Much less am I bound to believe in the infallibility or impeccability of nominally Catholic sovereigns and states. I am as free to criticise, to blame the acts of the Catholic as I am non-Catholic governments, and as free to dispute the political doctrines of Catholics, whether monarchical, aristocratical, or democratical, as I am the political doctrines of non-Catholics. The Church prescribes and proscribes no particular form of government; she simply asserts that power, in whose hands soever lodged, or however constituted, is a trust, and to be administered for the common good on pain of forfeiture.

As a matter of fact, no doubt that much of what is objectionable or deplorable in Catholic Europe is due to the character of the governments which have existed and governed the Catholic populations since the epoch of the Protestant revolt; and the chief obstacle to the revival and progress of Catholic civilization in Catholic states, as well as the recovery to the Church of the mass of European Liberals, now bitterly hostile to Catholicity, there is just as little doubt, is to be found in the habits and manners generated by political and civil despotism. Catholicity leaves to every people its own nationality, and to every state its independence; and it ameliorates the political and social order only by infusing into the hearts of the people and their rulers the principles of justice and love, and a sense of accountability to God. The action of the Church in political and social matters is indirect, not direct, and in strict accordance with the free-will of individuals and the autonomy of states. Individuals may hold very erroneous notions on government, and sustain their rulers in a very unwise and disastrous policy, without necessarily impeaching their Catholic faith or piety. To be a good Catholic and save his soul, it is not necessary that a man should be a wise and profound statesman.

The horrors of the French Revolution; the universal breaking up of society it involved; the persecution of the Church and of her clergy and her religious it shamelessly introduced in the name of liberty; the ruthless war it waged upon religion, virtue, all that wise and good men hold sacred, not unnaturally, to say the least, tended to create in the minds of the clergy and the people who remained firm in their faith, and justly regarded religion as the first want of man and society, a deeper distrust of the practicability of liberty, and a deeper horror of all movements attempted in its name. This, again, as naturally tended to alienate the party clamoring for political and social reform still more from Catholicity; which in its turn has reacted with new force on the Catholic party, and made them still more determined in their anti-Liberal convictions and efforts. These tendencies on both sides have been aggravated by the recent European revolutions and repressions, till now almost everywhere the lines are well defined, and the so-called Liberals are, almost to a man, bitterly anti-Catholic, and the sovereigns seem to have succeeded in forcing the issue: The Church and Caesarism, or Liberty and Infidelity.

Certainly, as religion is of the highest necessity to man and society, infinitely more important than political freedom and social well-being, I am unable to conceive how the Catholic party, under the circumstances, could well have acted differently. Their error was in their want of vigilance and sagacity in the beginning, in suffering the political Caesarism to revive and consolidate itself in the state, or the sovereigns in the outset to force upon the Catholic world so false an issue, or to place them in so unnatural and so embarrassing a position. How they will extricate themselves in the Old World from that position, I am unable to foresee, for every movement on either side only makes the matter worse. Yet the internal peace and tranquillity of Catholic states cannot be restored, and the Liberals brought back to the Church in any human way that I can see, unless the Catholic party abate something of their opposition, exert themselves to change the issue the sovereigns have forced upon them, and take themselves the lead in introducing, in a legal and orderly way, such changes in the present political order as will give the body of the nation an effective voice in the management of public affairs. Rebellions, when they break out, must of course be put down; but, at the same time, every effort should be made to disconnect religion from the cause of despotism, and to remove every legitimate source of discontent. All attempts to remedy the existing evil by decrying liberty, by sneers or elaborate essays against parliamentary governments and their advocates, by permanently strengthening the hands of power, by muzzling the press, abridging the freedom of thought and speech, or by resorting to a merely repressive policy, which silences without convincing, and irritates without healing, are short-sighted and unstatesmanlike. They can at best be only momentary palliatives which leave the disease, uneradicated, to spread in the system, and to break out anew with increased virulence and force. The truth is, the Catholic party, yielding to the sovereigns, lost to some extent, for the eighteenth century, the control of the mind of the age, and failed to lead its intelligence. They must now recover their rightful leadership, and be first and foremost in every department of human thought and activity; and to be so, they must yield in matters not of faith, not essential to sound doctrine, or to the free and full operation of the Church in all her native rights, integrity, and force; but, in political and social matters subjected to human prudence, they must, I say, yield something to the changes and demands of the times.

That the struggles in Europe have an influence on Catholic thought in this country is very true, and sometimes an unfavorable influence, cannot be denied. A portion of our foreign-born Catholics, subjected at home to the restraints imposed by despotism, feel on coming here that they are loosed from all restraints, and forgetting the obedience they owe to their pastors, to the prelates whom the Holy Ghost has placed over them, become insubordinate, and live more as Protestants than as Catholics; another portion, deeply alarmed at the revolutionary spirit and the evils that it has produced in the Old World, distrust the independence and personal dignity the American always preserves in the presence of authority, and are half disposed to look upon every American as a rebel at heart, if not an unbeliever. They do not precisely understand the American disposition that bows to the law, but never to persons, and is always careful to distinguish between the man and the office; and they are disposed to look upon it as incompatible with the true principle of obedience demanded by the Gospel. But I think these and their conservative brethren in Europe mistake the real American character. There is not in Christendom a more loyal or a more law-abiding people than the genuine people of the United States. I think European Catholics of the conservative party have an unfounded suspicion of our loyalty, for I think it a higher and truer loyalty than that which they seem to inculcate. I have wholly mistaken the spirit of the Church, if an enlightened obedience, — obedience that knows wherefore it obeys, and is yielded from principle, from conviction, from free will, and from a sense of obligation, is not more grateful to her material heart than the blind, unreasoning, and cringing submission of those who are strangers to freedom. Servile fear does not rank very high with Catholic theologians; and the Church seeks to govern men as freemen, as Almighty God governs them, that is, in accordance with the nature with which he has created them, as beings endowed with reason and free-will. God adapts his government to our rational and voluntary faculties, and governs us without violence to either, and by really satisfying both. The Church does the same, and resorts to coercive measures only to repress disorders in the public body. Hence our ecclesiastical rulers are called shepherds, not lords, and shepherds of their Master's flock, not of their own, and are to feed, tend, protect the flock, and take care of its increase for him, with sole reference to his will, and his honor and glory. We must love and reverence them for his sake, for the great trust he has confided to them, not for their own sakes, as if they owned the flock, and governed it in their own name and right, for their own pleasure and profit. This idea of power whether in Church or State, as a delegated power or trust, is inseparable from the American mind; and hence the American feels always in its presence his native equality as a man, and asserts, even in the most perfect and entire submission, his own personal independence and dignity, knowing that he bows only to the law or to the will of a common Master. His submission he yields, because he knows that it is due, but without servility or pusillanimity.

But though I entertain these views of what have been for a long time the policy of so-called Catholic governments, and, so to speak, the politics of European Catholics, I find in them nothing that reflects on the truth or efficiency of the Church; for she has no responsibility in the matter, since, as I have said, she governs men, discharges her mission with a scrupulous regard to the free-will of individuals and the autonomy of states. She proffers to all every assistance necessary for the attainment of the most heroic sanctity, but she forces no man to accept that assistance. In her view, men owe all they have and are to God, but they are neither slaves nor machines.

In speaking of Catholic nations and comparing them with the Catholic standard, I find, I confess, much to regret, to deplore, and even to blame; but in comparing them with non-Catholic nations, the case is quite different, and I cannot concede that the Catholic population of any country is inferior to any Protestant population, even in those very qualities in respect to which Catholics are usually supposed to be the most deficient. In no Catholic population will you find the flunkyism which Carlyle so unmercifully ridicules in the middling classes of Great Britain; or that respect to mere wealth, that worship of the money-bag, or that base servility to the mob or to public opinion, so common and so ruinous to public and private virtue in the United States. I do not claim any very high merit for our Catholic press — it lacks, with some exceptions, dignity, grasp of thought, and breadth of view, and seems intended for an unlettered community; but it has an earnestness, a sincerity, a freedom, an independence, which will be looked for in vain in our non-Catholic press, whether religious or secular. The Catholic population of this country, too, taken as a body, have a personal freedom, an independence, a self-respect, a conscientiousness, a love of truth, and a devotion to principle, not to be found in any other class of American citizens. Their moral tone, as well as their moral standard, is higher, and they act more uniformly under a sense of deep responsibility to God and to their country. Owing to various circumstances as well as national peculiarities, a certain number of them fall easily under the influences of demagogues; but as a body, they are far less demagogical, and far less under the influence of demagogues, than are non-Catholic Americans. He who knows both classes equally well, will not pretend to the contrary. The Catholics of this country, by no means a fair average of the Catholic populations of old Catholic countries, do, as to the great majority, act from honest principle, from sincere and earnest conviction, and are prepared to die sooner than, in any grave matters, swerve from what they regard as truth and justice. They have the principle and the firmness to stand by what they believe true and just, in good report and evil report, whether the world be with them or be against them. They can, also, be convinced by arguments addressed to their reason, and moved by appeals to conscience, to the fear of God, and the love of justice. The non-Catholic has no conception of the treasure the Union possesses in these two or three millions of Catholics, humble in their outward circumstances as the majority of them are. I have never shown any disposition to palliate or disguise their faults; but, knowing them and my non-Catholic countrymen as I do, I am willing to risk the assertion that, with all their faults and shortcomings, they are the salt of the American community, and the really conservative element in the American population.

I have found valid, after thirteen years of experience, none of those objections to entering the Catholic communion which I enumerated in a previous chapter, and which made me for a time hesitate to follow the convictions of my own understanding. To err is human, and I do not pretend that I have found Catholics in matters of human prudence, in what belongs to them and not the Church, all that I could wish. I have found much I do not like, much I do not believe reasonable or prudent; but it is all easily explained without any reflection on the truth or efficiency of the Church, or the general wisdom and prudence of her prelates and clergy. Undoubtedly our Catholic population, made up in great part of emigrants from every nation of Europe, with every variety of national temper, character, taste, habit, and usage, not yet moulded, save in religion, into one homogeneous body, may present features more or less repulsive to the American wedded to his own peculiar nationality, and but recently converted to the Catholic faith; but the very readiness with which these heterogeneous elements amalgamate, and the rapidity with which the Catholic body assumes a common character, falls into the current of American life, and takes, in all not adverse to religion, the tone and features of the country, proves the force of Catholicity, and its vast importance in forming a true and noble national character, and in generating and sustaining a true, generous, and lofty patriotism. In a few years they will be the Americans of the Americans, and on them will rest the performance of the glorious work of sustaining American civilization, and realizing the hopes of the founders of our great and growing Republic.

Such are the views, feelings, convictions, and hopes of the Convert. But he would be unjust to himself and to his religion, if he did not say that, not for these reasons, or any like them, is he a Catholic. He loves his country, loves her institutions, he loves her freedom, but he is a

Catholic, because he believes the Catholic Church the Church of God, because he believes her the medium through which God dispenses his grace to man, and through which alone we can hope for heaven. He is a Catholic, because he would believe, love, possess, and obey the truth; because he would know and do God's will; because he would escape hell and gain heaven. Considerations drawn from this world are of minor importance, for man's home is not here, his bliss is not here, his reward is not here, he is made for God, for endless beatitude with him, hereafter; and, let him turn as he will, his supreme good, as well as duty, lies in seeking "the kingdom of God and his justice." That the Church serves the cause of patriotism; that, if embraced, it is sure to give us a high-toned and chivalric national character; that it enlists conscience in the support of our free institutions and the preservation of our republican freedom as the established order of the country, is a good reason why the American people should not oppose her, and why they should wish her growth and prosperity in our country; but the real reason why we should become Catholics and remain such, is, because she is the new creation, regenerated Humanity, and without communion with her, we can never see God as he is, or become united to him as our Supreme Good in the supernatural order.

THE SLAVE

Frederick Douglass

(C. 1817-1895)

Growing up as a slave on Maryland's Eastern Shore, Frederick Douglass managed when he was about twenty years of age to escape to freedom in New York, then later to Massachusetts. Within three years, he won recognition as a popular lecturer, speaking first of his own experience in slavery, then more broadly about the institution in general. By 1845, the year that he published his autobiography, his reputation had grown to the point where he was invited to the British Isles to speak against slavery and for temperance.

Possessed of a strong and deep voice, also of a commanding physical presence, Douglass quickly won the attention and then the hearts of such major abolitionists as William Lloyd Garrison and Wendell Phillips. Garrison, who provided a preface for the autobiography, heard the first speech that Douglass delivered at an antislavery convention in New Bedford, Massachusetts. Garrison describes how Douglass "came forward to the platform with a hesitancy and embarrassment, necessarily the attendants of a sensitive mind in such a novel situation." But the hesitancy soon disappeared as the fugitive moved from the story of his own experience "to many noble thoughts and thrilling reflections." When he was finished, he received unrestrained applause. And Garrison rose to assert that Patrick Henry "never made a speech more eloquent in the cause of liberty, than the one we had just listened to from the lips of that hunted fugitive."

In the first excerpt below, Douglass describes in clear narrative fashion his escape from Maryland and his exaltation in reaching New York: "a moment of the highest excitement I ever experienced." But one also reads below his quite negative appraisal of the role of religion in America with respect to slavery. Unlike Richard Allen, for example, Douglass finds no solace in the denominations, black or white, no comfort in the churches that stand next to the slaves' prisons. "The slave auctioneer's bell and the church-going bell chime in with each other, and the bitter cries of the heart-broken slave are drowned in the religious shouts of his pious master." The picture that Frederick Douglass paints of religious hypocrisy is unrelievedly gloomy. The only light that emerges comes from his assertion that "between the Christianity of this land, and the Christianity of Christ, I recognize the widest possible difference — so wide, that to receive the one as good, pure, and holy, is of necessity to reject the other as bad, corrupt, and wicked."

[See William S. McFeeley, *Frederick Douglass* (New York: W. W. Norton, 1995).]

I now come to that part of my life during which I planned, and finally succeeded in making, my escape from slavery. But before narrating any of the peculiar circumstances, I deem it proper to make known my intention not to state all the facts connected with the transaction. My reasons for pursuing this course may be understood from the following: First, were I to give a minute statement of all the facts, it is not only possible, but quite probable, that others would thereby be involved in the most embarrassing difficulties. Secondly, such a statement would most undoubtedly induce greater vigilance on the part of slaveholders than has existed heretofore among them; which would, of course be the means of guarding a door whereby some dear brother bondman might escape his galling chains. I deeply regret the necessity that impels me to suppress any thing of importance connected with my experience in slavery. It would afford me great pleasure indeed, as well as materially add to the interest of my narrative, were I at liberty to gratify a curiosity, which I know exists in the minds of many, by an accurate statement of all the facts pertaining to my most fortunate escape. But I must deprive myself of this pleasure, and the curious of the gratification which such a statement would afford. I would allow myself to suffer under the greatest imputations which evil-minded men might suggest, rather than exculpate myself, and thereby run the hazard of closing the slightest avenue by which a brother slave might clear himself of the chains and fetters of slavery.

Source: Benjamin Quarles, ed., *Narrative of the Life of Frederick Douglass: An American Slave* [1845] (Cambridge, Mass.: The Belknap Press of Harvard University Press, 1960), pp. 135-44; 155-63.

I have never approved of the very public manner in which some of our western friends have conducted what they call the *underground railroad*, but which, I think, by their open declarations, has been made most emphatically the *upperground railroad*. I honor those good men and women for their noble daring, and applaud them for willingly subjecting themselves to bloody persecution, by openly avowing their participation in the escape of slaves. I, however, can see very little good resulting from such a course, either to themselves or the slaves escaping; while, upon the other hand, I see and feel assured that those open declarations are a positive evil to the slaves remaining, who are seeking to escape. They do nothing towards enlightening the slave, whilst they do much towards enlightening the master. They stimulate him to greater watchfulness, and enhance his power to capture his slave. We owe something to the slaves south of the line as well as to those north of it; and in aiding the latter on their way to freedom, we should be careful to do nothing which would be likely to hinder the former from escaping from slavery. I would keep the merciless slaveholder profoundly ignorant of the means of flight adopted by the slave. I would leave him to imagine himself surrounded by myriads of invisible tormentors, ever ready to snatch from his infernal grasp his trembling prey. Let him be left to feel his way in the dark; let darkness commensurate with his crime hover over him; and let him feel that at every step he takes, in pursuit of the flying bondman, he is running the frightful risk of having his hot brains dashed out by an invisible agency. Let us render the tyrant no aid; let us not hold the light by which he can trace the footprints of our flying brother. But enough of this. I will now proceed to the statement of those facts, connected with my escape, for which I am alone responsible, and for which no one can be made to suffer but myself.

In the early part of the year 1838, I became quite restless. I could see no reason why I should, at the end of each week, pour the reward of my toil into the purse of my master. When I carried to him my weekly wages, he would, after counting the money, look me in the face with a robber-like fierceness, and ask, "Is this all?" He was satisfied with nothing less than the last cent. He would, however, when I made him six dollars, sometimes give me six cents, to encourage me. It had the opposite effect. I regarded it as a sort of admission of my right to the whole. The fact that he gave me any part of my wages was proof, to my mind, that he believed me entitled to the whole of them. I always felt worse for having received any thing; for I feared that the giving me a few cents would ease his conscience, and make him feel himself to be a pretty honorable sort of rob-

96

ber. My discontent grew upon me. I was ever on the look-out for means of escape; and, finding no direct means, I determined to try to hire my time, with a view of getting money with which to make my escape. In the spring of 1838, when Master Thomas came to Baltimore to purchase his spring goods, I got an opportunity, and applied to him to allow me to hire my time. He unhesitatingly refused my request, and told me this was another stratagem by which to escape. He told me I could go nowhere but that he could get me; and that, in the event of my running away, he should spare no pains in his efforts to catch me. He exhorted me to content myself, and be obedient. He told me, if I would be happy, I must lay out no plans for the future. He said, if I behaved myself properly, he would take care of me. Indeed, he advised me to complete thoughtlessness of the future, and taught me to depend solely upon him for happiness. He seemed to see fully the pressing necessity of setting aside my intellectual nature, in order to contentment in slavery. But in spite of him, and even in spite of myself, I continued to think, and to think about the injustice of my enslavement, and the means of escape.

About two months after this, I applied to Master Hugh for the privilege of hiring my time. He was not acquainted with the fact that I had applied to Master Thomas, and had been refused. He too, at first, seemed disposed to refuse; but, after some reflection, he granted me the privilege, and proposed the following term: I was to be allowed all my time, make all contracts with those for whom I worked, and find my own employment; and, in return for this liberty, I was to pay him three dollars at the end of each week; find myself in calking tools, and in board and clothing. My board was two dollars and a half per week. This, with the wear and tear of clothing and calking tools, made my regular expenses about six dollars per week. This amount I was compelled to make up, or relinquish the privilege of hiring my time. Rain or shine, work or no work, at the end of each week the money must be forthcoming, or I must give up my privilege. This arrangement, it will be perceived, was decidedly in my master's favor. It relieved him of all need of looking after me. His money was sure. He received all the benefits of slaveholding without its evils; while I endured all the evils of a slave, and suffered all the care and anxiety of a freeman. I found it a hard bargain. But, hard as it was, I thought it better than the old mode of getting along. It was a step towards freedom to be allowed to bear the responsibilities of a freeman, and I was determined to hold on upon it. I bent myself to the work of making money. I was ready to work at night as well as day, and by the most untiring perseverance and industry, I made enough to meet my expenses, and lay up a little money every week. I went on thus from May till August. Master Hugh then refused to allow me to hire my time longer. The ground for his refusal was a failure on my part, one Saturday night, to pay him for my week's time. This failure was occasioned by my attending a camp meeting about ten miles from Baltimore. During the week, I had entered into an engagement with a number of young friends to start from Baltimore to the camp ground early Saturday evening; and being detained by my employer, I was unable to get down to Master Hugh's without disappointing the company. I knew that Master Hugh was in no special need of the money that night. I therefore decided to go to camp meeting, and upon my return pay him the three dollars. I staid at the camp meeting one day longer than I intended when I left. But as soon as I returned, I called upon him to pay him what he considered his due. I found him very angry; he could scarce restrain his wrath. He said he had a great mind to give me a severe whipping. He wished to know how I dared go out of the city without asking his permission. I told him I hired my time, and while I paid him the price which he asked for it, I did not know that I was bound to ask him when and where I should go. This reply troubled him; and, after reflecting a few moments, he turned to me, and said I should hire my time no longer; that the next thing he should know of, I would be running away. Upon the same plea, he told me to bring my tools and clothing home forthwith. I did so; but instead of seeking work, as I had been accustomed to do previously to hiring my time, I spent the whole week without the performance of a single stroke of work. I did this in retaliation. Saturday night, he called upon me as usual for my week's wages. I told him I had no wages; I had done no work that week. Here we were upon the point of coming to blows. He raved, and swore his determination to get hold of me. I did not allow myself a single word; but was resolved, if he laid the weight of his hand upon me, it should be blow for blow. He did not strike me, but told me that he would find me in constant employment in future. I thought the matter over during the next day, Sunday, and finally resolved upon the third day of September, as the day upon which I would make a second attempt to secure my freedom. I now had three weeks during which to prepare for my journey. Early on Monday morning, before Master Hugh had time to make any engagement for me, I went out and got employment of Mr. Butler, at his ship-yard near the drawbridge, upon what is called the City Block, thus making it unnecessary for him to seek employment for me. At the end of the week, I brought him between eight and nine dollars. He seemed very well pleased, and asked me why I did not do the same the week before. He little knew what my plans were. My object in working steadily was to remove any suspicion he might entertain of my intent to run away; and in this I succeeded admirably. I suppose he thought I was never better satisfied with my condition than at the very time during which I was planning my escape. The second week passed, and again I carried him my full wages; and so well pleased was he, that he gave me twenty-five cents, (quite a large sum for a slaveholder to give a slave,) and bade me to make a good use of it. I told him I would.

Things went on without very smoothly indeed, but within there was trouble. It is impossible for me to describe my feelings as the time of my contemplated start drew near. I had a number of warm-hearted friends in Baltimore, — friends that I loved almost as I did my life, — and the thought of being separated from them forever was painful beyond expression. It is my opinion that thousands would escape from slavery, who now remain, but for the strong cords of affection that bind them to their friends. The thought of leaving my friends was decidedly the most painful thought with which I had to contend. The love of them was my tender point, and shook my decision more than all things else. Besides the pain of separation, the dread and apprehension of a failure exceeded what I had experienced at my first attempt. The appalling defeat I then sustained returned to torment me. I felt assured that, if I failed in this attempt, my case would be a hopeless one — it would seal my fate as a slave forever. I could not hope to get off with any thing less than the severest punishment, and being placed beyond the means of escape. It required no very vivid imagination to depict the most frightful scenes through which I should have to pass, in case I failed. The wretchedness of slavery, and the blessedness of freedom, were perpetually before me. It was life and death with me. But I remained firm, and, according to my resolution, on the third day of September, 1838, I left my chains, and succeeded in reaching New York without the slightest interruption of any kind. How I did so, — what means I adopted, — what direction I travelled, and by what mode of conveyance, — I must leave unexplained, for the reasons before mentioned.

I have been frequently asked how I felt when I found myself in a free State. I have never been able to answer the question with any satisfaction to myself. It was a moment of the highest excitement I ever experienced. I suppose I felt as one may imagine the unarmed mariner to feel when he is rescued by a friendly man-of-war from the pursuit of a pirate. In writing to a dear friend, immediately after my arrival at New York, I said I felt like one who had escaped a den of hungry lions. This state of mind, however, very soon subsided; and I was again seized with a feeling of great insecurity and loneliness. I was yet liable to be taken back, and subjected to all the tortures of slavery. This in itself was enough to damp the ardor of my enthusiasm. But the loneliness overcame me. There I was in the midst of thousands, and yet a perfect stranger; without home and without friends, in the midst of thousands of my own brethren — children of a common Father, and yet I dared not to unfold to any one of them my sad condition. I was afraid to speak to any one for fear of speaking to the wrong one, and thereby falling into the hands of money-loving kidnappers, whose business it was to lie in wait for the panting fugitive, as the ferocious beasts of the forest lie in wait for their prey. The motto which I adopted when I started from slavery was this — "Trust no man!" I saw in every white man an enemy, and in almost every colored man cause for distrust. It was a most painful situation; and, to understand it, one must needs experience it, or imagine himself in similar circumstances. Let him be a fugitive slave in a strange land — a land given up to be the hunting-ground for slaveholders — whose inhabitants are legalized kidnappers — where he is every moment subjected to the terrible liability of being seized upon by his fellowmen, as the hideous crocodile seizes upon his prey! — I say, let him place himself in my situation — without home or friends — without money or credit — wanting shelter, and no one to give it — wanting bread, and no money to buy it, — and at the same time let him feel that he is pursued by merciless men-hunters, and in total darkness as to what to do, where to go, or where to stay, — perfectly helpless both as to the means of defense and means of escape, — in the midst of plenty, yet suffering the terrible gnawings of hunger, — in the midst of houses, yet having no home, — among fellow-men, yet feeling as if in the midst of wild beasts, whose greediness to swallow up the trembling and half-famished fugitive is only equalled by that with which the monsters of the deep swallow up the helpless fish upon which they subsist, — I say, let him be placed in this most trying situation, — the situation in which I was placed, — then, and not till then, will he fully appreciate the hardships of, and know how to sympathize with, the toil-worn and whip-scarred fugitive slave.

~

I find, since reading over the foregoing Narrative that I have, in several instances, spoken in such a tone and manner, respecting religion, as may possibly lead those unacquainted with my religious views to suppose me an opponent of all religion. To remove the liability of such misapprehension, I deem it proper to append the following brief explanation. What I have said respecting and against religion, I mean strictly to apply to the *slaveholding religion* of this land, and with no possible reference to Christianity proper; for, between the Christianity of this land, and the Christianity of Christ, I recognize the widest possible difference — so wide, that to receive the one as good, pure, and holy, is of necessity to reject the other as bad, corrupt, and wicked. To be the friend of the one, is of necessity to be the enemy of the other. I love the pure, peaceable, and impartial Christianity of Christ: I therefore hate the corrupt, slaveholding, women-whipping, cradle-plundering, partial and hypocritical Christianity of this land. Indeed, I can see no reason, but the most deceitful one, for calling the religion of this land Christianity. I look upon it as the climax of all misnomers, the boldest of all frauds, and the grossest of all libels. Never was there a clearer case of "stealing the livery of the court of heaven to serve the devil in." I am filled with unutterable loathing when I contemplate the religious pomp and show, together with the horrible inconsistencies, which every where surround me. We have men-stealers for ministers, women-whippers for missionaries, and cradle-plunderers for church members. The man who wields the blood-clotted cowskin during the week fills the pulpit on Sunday, and claims to be a minister of the meek and lowly Jesus. The man who robs me of my earnings at the end of each week meets me as a class-leader on Sunday morning, to show me the way of life, and the path of salvation. He who sells my sister, for purposes of prostitution, stands forth as the pious advocate of purity. He who proclaims it a religious duty to read the Bible denies me the right of learning to read the name of the God who made me. He who is the religious advocate of marriage robs whole millions of its sacred influence, and leaves them to the ravages of wholesale pollution. The warm defender of the sacredness of the family relation is the same that scatters whole families, — sundering husbands and wives, parents and children, sisters and brothers, — leaving the hut vacant, and the hearth desolate. We see the thief preaching against theft, and the adulterer against adultery. We have men sold to build churches, women sold to support the gospel, and babes sold to purchase Bibles for the *poor heathen! all for the glory of God and the good of souls!* The slave auctioneer's bell and the church-going bell chime in with each other, and the bitter cries of the heart-broken slave are drowned in the religious shouts of his pious master. Revivals of religion and revivals in the slave-trade go hand in hand together. The slave prison and the church stand near each other. The clanking of fetters and the rattling of chains in the prison, and the pious psalm and solemn prayer in the church, may be heard at the same time. The dealers in the bodies and souls of men erect their stand in the presence of the pulpit, and they mutually help each other. The dealer gives his blood-stained gold to support the pulpit, and the pulpit, in return, covers his infernal business with the garb of Christianity. Here we have religion and robbery the allies of each other — devils dressed in angels' robes, and hell presenting the semblance of paradise.

"Just God! and these are they,
    Who minister at thine altar, God of right!
Men who their hands, with prayer and blessing, lay
    On Israel's ark of light.

"What! preach, and kidnap men?
    Give thanks, and rob thy own afflicted poor?
Talk of thy glorious liberty, and then
    Bolt hard the captive's door?

"What! servants of thy own
    Merciful Son, who came to seek and save
The homeless and the outcast, fettering down
    The tasked and plundered slave!

"Pilate and Herod friends!
    Chief priests and rulers, as of old, combine!
Just God and holy! is that church which lends
    Strength to the spoiler thine?"

The Christianity of America is a Christianity, of whose votaries it may be as truly said, as it was of the ancient scribes and Pharisees, "They bind heavy burdens, and grievous to be borne, and lay them on men's shoulders, but they themselves will not move them with one of their fingers. All their works they do for to be seen of men. — They love the uppermost rooms at feasts, and the chief seats in the synagogues, ... and to be called of men, Rabbi, Rabbi. — But woe unto you scribes and Pharisees, hypocrites! for ye shut up the kingdom of heaven against men; for ye neither go in yourselves, neither suffer ye them that are entering to go in. Ye devour widows' houses, and for a pretense make long prayers; therefore ye shall receive the greater damnation. Ye compass sea and land to make one proselyte, and when he is made, ye make him two-fold more the child of hell than yourselves. — Woe unto you, scribes and Pharisees, hypocrites! for ye pay tithe of mint, and anise, and cumin, and have omitted the weightier matters of the law, judgment, mercy, and faith; these ought ye to have done, and not to leave the other undone. Ye blind guides! which strain at a gnat, and swallow a camel. Woe unto you, scribes and Pharisees, hypocrites! for ye make clean the outside of the cup and of the platter; but within, they are full of extortion and excess. — Woe unto you, scribes and Pharisees, hypocrites! for ye are like unto whited sepulchres, which indeed appear beautiful outward, but are within full of dead men's bones, and of all uncleanness. Even so ye also outwardly appear righteous unto men, but within ye are full of hypocrisy and iniquity."

Dark and terrible as is this picture, I hold it to be strictly true of the overwhelming mass of professed Christians in America. They strain at a gnat, and swallow a camel. Could any thing be more true of our churches? They would be shocked at the proposition of fellowshipping a *sheep*-stealer; and at the same time they hug to their communion a *man*-stealer, and brand me with being an infidel, if I find fault with them for it. They attend with Pharisaical strictness to the outward forms of religion, and at the same time neglect the weightier matters of the law, judgment, mercy, and faith. They are always ready to sacrifice, but seldom to show mercy. They are they who are represented as professing to love God whom they have not seen, whilst they hate their brother whom they have seen. They love the heathen on the other side of the globe. They can pray for him, pay money to have the Bible put into his hand, and missionaries to instruct him; while they despise and totally neglect the heathen at their own doors.

Such is, very briefly, my view of the religion of this land; and to avoid any misunderstanding, growing out of the use of general terms, I mean, by the religion of this land, that which is revealed in the words, deeds, and actions, of those bodies, north and south, calling themselves Christian churches, and yet in union with slaveholders. It is against religion, as presented by these bodies, that I have felt it my duty to testify.

I conclude these remarks by copying the following portrait of the religion of the south, (which is, by communion and fellowship, the religion of the north,) which I soberly affirm is "true to the life," and without caricature or the slightest exaggeration. It is said to have been drawn, several years before the present anti-slavery agitation began, by a northern Methodist preacher, who, while residing at the south, had an opportunity to see slaveholding morals, manners, and piety, with his own eyes. "Shall I not visit for these things? saith the Lord. Shall not my soul be avenged on such a nation as this?"

"A PARODY.

"Come, saints and sinners, hear me tell
How pious priests whip Jack and Nell,
And women buy and children sell,
And preach all sinners down to hell,
    And sing of heavenly union.

"They'll bleat and baa, [go on] like goats,
Gorge down black sheep, and strain at motes,
Array their backs in fine black coats,
Then seize their negroes by their throats,
    And choke, for heavenly union.

"They'll church you if you sip a dram,
And damn you if you steal a lamb;
Yet rob old Tony, Doll, and Sam,
Of human rights, and bread and ham;
    Kidnapper's heavenly union.

"They'll loudly talk of Christ's reward,
And bind his image with a cord,
And scold, and swing the lash abhorred,
And sell their brother in the Lord
    To handcuffed heavenly union.

"They'll read and sing a sacred song,
And make a prayer both loud and long,
And teach the right and do the wrong,
Hailing the brother, sister throng,
    With words of heavenly union.

"We wonder how such saints can sing,
Or praise the Lord upon the wing,
Who roar, and scold, and whip, and sting,
And to their slaves and mammon cling,
    In guilty conscience union.

"They'll raise tobacco, corn, and rye,
And drive, and thieve, and cheat, and lie,
And lay up treasures in the sky,
By making switch and cowskin fly,
    In hope of heavenly union.

"They'll crack old Tony on the skull,
And preach and roar like Bashan bull,
Or braying ass, of mischief full,
Then seize old Jacob by the wool,
    And pull for heavenly union.

"A roaring, ranting, sleek man-thief,
Who lived on mutton, veal, and beef,
Yet never would afford relief
To needy, sable sons of grief,
    Was big with heavenly union.

"'Love not the world,' the preacher said,
And winked his eye, and shook his head;
He seized on Tom, and Dick, and Ned,
Cut short their meat, and clothes, and bread,
    Yet still loved heavenly union.

"Another preacher whining spoke
Of One whose heart for sinners broke:
He tied old Nanny to an oak,
And drew the blood at every stroke,
    And prayed for heavenly union.

"Two others oped their iron jaws,
And waved their children-stealing paws;
There sat their children in gewgaws;
By stinting negroes' backs and maws,
    They kept up heavenly union.

"All good from Jack another takes,
And entertains their flirts and rakes,
Who dress as sleek as glossy snakes,
And cram their mouths with sweetened cakes;
    And this goes down for union."

Sincerely and earnestly hoping that this little book may do something toward throwing light on the American slave system, and hastening the glad day of deliverance to the millions of my brethren in bonds — faithfully relying upon the power of truth, love, and justice, for success in my humble efforts — and solemnly pledging myself anew to the sacred cause, — I subscribe myself,

Frederick Douglass

THE AMERICANIZER

Isaac Mayer Wise

(1819-1900)

Arriving in America in 1846, Rabbi Wise liked what he saw. Even more, he liked what he viewed as the exciting possibilities for Judaism in this new land. He saw no reason to import all of Europe's problems and all of Europe's religious divisions into the United States. Rather, Jews — freed from ghettoes and pogroms — should discard the insularity that had been imposed on them, and join wholeheartedly in America's freedom of religion and the modern world's many new possibilities. Like Orestes Brownson, Wise believed in and was charmed by the allure of "progress."

Wise and his family settled first in Charleston, South Carolina, but soon after in Albany, New York, where he became rabbi of Congregation Beth-El. There he began introducing the reforms with which his name soon became identified: men and women sitting together in the pews, use of choirs in the synagogue, and impatient dismissal of the dietary regulations and laws. Judaism, he believed, resided not in the kitchen or the ritual slaughtering of animals, but in the fear of the Lord and the love of justice. But he moved too far too fast for many of his Albany congregation to willingly or happily follow. The division among his people grew so vigorous that on at least one occasion the sheriff had to be called in to restore order. By 1850, Wise found it expedient to withdraw from Beth-El and form a separate congregation.

In 1854, however, he was called to Cincinnati, Ohio, to lead Congregation B'nai. But he felt called to lead much else besides. Here in the West, he found the freedom that to him represented what America was all about — and represented what Judaism could become. A new kind of Judaism, ultimately to take the name of Reform Judaism, properly looks to Isaac Mayer Wise as its founding father. In 1873 he directed the creation of the Union of American Hebrew Congregations (with emphasis on the American). Two years later he led in the founding of Hebrew Union College in Cincinnati; he became the institution's first president, and remained in that post until his death a quarter-century later. By 1889, when the Central Conference of American Rabbis was formed, one could readily predict that Reform Judaism would be the dominant form of religious expression among America's Jews. But the flood of Jewish immigrants early in the twentieth century from eastern Europe — most of them of strongly orthodox persuasion — changed all that.

In his *Reminiscences,* excerpted below, Rabbi Wise explains — no, exclaims — that the European Jew must become an American Jew, setting aside "the century-long oppression [that] has demoralized the German and Polish Jew, and robbed him of his self-respect." He added: "The Jew must become an American, in order to gain the proud self-consciousness of the free-born man. From that hour I began to Americanize with all my might . . ."

[See Sefton Temkin, *Isaac Mayer Wise, Shaping American Judaism* (New York: Oxford University Press, 1992).]

Upon assuming office in the *B'ne Yeshurun* congregation and the *Talmid Yelodim* Institute at the end of April, 1854, I found myself not one whit different from what I had been eight years before. I was the same incorrigible idealist and optimist, enthusiast and world-improver, full of great world-revolutionizing and world-redeeming plans, without any executive ability, and without sufficient insight or discretion. In my imagination I accomplished everything quickly, surely, and finely. Because I was able to write and speak in two languages, and because I had been called to Cincinnati on the strength of my literary reputation, I persuaded myself that I would be able to accomplish any and every thing, and that all that was necessary was to nod my head *a la* Zeus. There were two things particularly that had become fixed ideas in my mind; viz., that I had talent for all things, and that I was a child of destiny. Naturally, when I acted upon my theories, I had ample opportunities to discover that I had often reckoned without my host.

Although I was very fiery, thoughtless, and rash, as a general thing, yet I was very moderate, considerate, and argumentative (as far as externalities were concerned) in the pulpit, and chiefly for the following reasons: I was the only Jewish preacher in Cincinnati, or, rather, in the

Source: Isaac M. Wise, *Reminiscences* (Cincinnati: Leo Wise and Co., 1901), pp. 257-61, 324-32.

entire West. Therefore I had to address every Saturday a very large but very mixed audience. My hearers comprised, not only members of the three other congregations of Cincinnati, but also the inhabitants of near and distant towns, because business brought many merchants of the West and South to Cincinnati at that time. I was therefore compelled to speak tactfully and carefully if I wished to succeed, and I was determined to succeed. I was fortunate in finding a splendid element in the congregation — men who, without any great exertion on my part, desired, favored, and actively supported every forward and progressive movement. I met with no obstacles in the congregation itself; everything was peaceful and harmonious. The congregation consisted for the most part of natives of Bavaria, Wurtemberg, and Baden, who had been favorable to reform even before they had left their old homes. As early as the second Sabbath of my incumbency, the president, Marcus Fechheimer, without calling a meeting for the purpose, made the following announcement in the synagogue: Since English and German sermons are preached alternately during the morning service, the *piutim** have become superfluous; they are therefore abolished till further notice. This settled the fate of the *piutim:* they were never again made the subject of discussion. Soon thereafter the sale of the *mitzvoth*** was abolished. I recognized that all things would turn out right if I would be content to make haste slowly.

The introduction of a choir was not accomplished so readily. Upon my approaching the *parnass†* on this subject, he was free to confess that he did not consider it feasible, because a number of attempts had already been made in vain, and the congregation had spent several hundred dollars without being able to establish a choir. I was assured, however, that the necessary funds for the purpose would be forthcoming if I would pledge myself to bring the project to a successful issue. Thereupon I went to work actively. I called together a number of young people, among others, A. J. Friedlander, Frederick Eichberg, L. Loeb, David Wise, Ludwig Brandeis, Gideon, and others, who organized a society, induced a number of young girls to join them, engaged Junkerman at once as singing-teacher, and Cincinnati began to sing. The voices were quite good; the young people were exceedingly enthusiastic; the *chazan,‡* Marx Moses, had not only a good voice, but was possessed of

*liturgical poems
**certain religious functions sold to the highest bidder
†president
‡cantor

the necessary musical training, so that it required but a few weeks for the young people to study the evening service composed by Sulzer. The choir now appeared in the synagogue without further ado.

That was a great Friday evening for Cincinnati. Members of all the congregations flocked to the synagogue, and filled it. The harmonious strains of Sulzer's music resounded for the first time in a synagogue in the western part of America, to glorify the dawn of a new era. The venture proved completely successful. Cincinnati listened, and all hearts glowed with enthusiasm. "That is what we wish," was said on all sides. Marcus Fechheimer celebrated a veritable triumph, and the members of the choir were transported by their great feats. They continued to study, and before the autumn had denuded the trees of their leaves, they had learned and introduced the morning service.

It is scarcely conceivable now what a victory for culture and progress the introduction of a synagogal choir was at that time. No reform of the Jewish service was possible until the Jewish ear had again become accustomed to harmony and beauty. The service would have disappeared gradually altogether if it had not been reinstated in its old dignity and uplifting solemnity by song. Many who longed unconsciously for, or who even opposed the introduction of the choir into the synagogue, surely recognize now how the harmonious strains affect and edify the worshiper, and exert an uplifting effect even upon the whole of life. The first choral songs in the *B'ne Yeshurun* synagogue in Cincinnati were a new pathfinder of culture for the Israelites of the West.

Although the external reforms were introduced slowly, I was much less timorous in regard to enlightenment in the school and in the pulpit. I took the instruction of the young in charge, and carried out my own ideas and convictions on the subject. The enlightenment of the people has always seemed to me the most important reform. Of all things, the prime essential has ever appeared to me to awaken the spirit, to force it to activity, and to give it fresh and healthy nourishment. I thought that the external forms would fit themselves of their own accord to the newly-awakened spirit. I preached, therefore, in the same rationalistic style that I had employed in writing history. I never failed to prove whatever theories I advanced. To my thinking, proof was of prime importance. I did not wish either my word or my faith to decide. Therefore my opponents called me the "jurist of the pulpit." I pursued the same course in my school. Before long I had made rationalists of all connected with the *Talmid Yelodim* Institute — teachers, pupils, and officers.

111

Generally speaking, but little attention was paid in Cincinnati to what was spoken or written elsewhere. There was peace at home. In the fall of 1855, Zion College was opened with fourteen students, two of whom were Christians, and five professors. The three paid teachers were: Rothenheim, instructor in Hebrew and German; Cohn, a young attorney from Charleston, S. C., instructor in English; Junkerman, a teacher of the *Talmid Yelodim* Institute, instructor in mathematics. Lilienthal, who was to teach Latin and French, and Wise, who was to impart instruction in history, geography, and archaeology, tendered their services gratis. The beginning was full of encouragement. The class was composed of intelligent youths, and the teachers were experts, from whose teachings good results were to be expected.

True, there was no enthusiasm among the people at large; but, on the other hand, the few who were deeply interested in education and culture, of whom the majority are still living, were all the more active. They have grown older, but not colder. This noble band was always to the fore when there was work to be done in the cause of progress, the rebirth of Judaism, the weal of humanity. Some of these noble friends have been called to their eternal reward; but those that are still alive work on as undauntedly as at that time.

The opening of Zion College was celebrated by a banquet given in Masonic Hall. The elite of Cincinnati was present. The governor of the State, the late Chief-Justice Salmon P. Chase, Judge Carter, and others, were among the speakers. About eight hundred dollars were subscribed for the college that evening. Everything looked encouraging, and the friends of the movement indulged the fondest hopes.

If American Jewry had been ripe for such an undertaking at that time, as some few men in Cincinnati and Louisville were, what could not a school such as that college have accomplished within the space of twenty years? There would have been no necessity to look to-day with a Diogenes' lantern for educated preachers and teachers fully acquainted with the English language and conversant with the customs and habits of the country. But American Jewry was not ripe for such an undertaking at that time. Zion College had been open but a few weeks when a protest appeared in the *Asmonean*, of New York, in which the Zion Collegiate Association of that city declared itself dissolved. Most bitter and venomous attacks emanated one after the other from the East. If we had been horse-thieves, gamblers, sharks, and tramps, we could not have been more shamefully treated; and yet, up to this moment, no one has been able to discover what our offense really was. Lilienthal and I taught gratis. We were never reproached with being ignoramuses or incapable of teaching. The faithful band of energetic men who stood at the helm of the movement and paid all outlays were certainly not deserving of reproach, and yet we were reviled as though we were veritable street gamins. I will not deny that I often gnashed my teeth; for I was carried out of myself with indignation at the thought that there were people to whom nothing, absolutely nothing, is sacred; but I forced myself to swallow my wrath and to keep silent, because a public scandal was distasteful to me. True, several Eastern papers were at my disposal. I was even requested by a prominent Eastern editor to use the columns of his paper for this purpose; but I remained silent rather than give the scandal wider publicity. Domestic family polemics were revolting to me, and I therefore held my peace. It may be readily imagined that all this did not conduce greatly to my health, my energy, my enthusiasm, or my desire for work. At times I succumbed to despair, and it seemed to me that Judaism in America was nigh to dissolution. I knew well that orthodoxy had been conquered; but these bitter recriminations in place of struggle for principle's sake in the camp of reformed Judaism seemed to me the beginning of the end. True, I had forgotten to take into account the chief factor, Providence. I overlooked the fact also that the general public would learn little or nothing of these polemics, since they were written in the German language.

My opponents put forth every effort to displace the *Israelite* and the *Deborah* wherever they had any influence. In this they succeeded frequently. A further circumstance which reduced the number of subscribers to both papers was the many Rabbinic-Talmudical expositions and discussions which, though very learned, have little interest for the general reader. At the same time I came into conflict with an atheistical weekly published at that time in Cincinnati, and was attacked by all the aesthetes who, to be in the fashion, affected atheism. There was no lack of these worthies in Cincinnati at that time. Their campaign cry was, "Priest! priest!" This was to intimidate me, who had fought for progress with all the powers at my command.

Their efforts were fruitless as far as I personally was concerned; but some wounded apostles of the atheistical stripe who had some influence in certain houses where they served as book-keepers, clerks, and the like, contributed not a little towards the downfall of Zion College. Their sympathy with the opponents in the East was truly touching.

These people drove me out of the Republican party, which was just forming at that time, although I sat at the round table at which that party was born and baptized. I would have nothing to do with these people even politically. True, Salmon P. Chase called my attention several times to the fact that it would be much better to attach myself to the young progressive party at whose head my best friends stood, than to work for a religious idea in a narrow circle; but I did not listen, I would not listen. I submitted to all the public affronts, even though the future of American Judaism seemed to me dark indeed.

The worst feature of the whole matter was, that I was unable to confide in any one. I wrote in my diary, and kept silent. People were surprised at my worn and sickly appearance; my poor wife wept often enough. But I had to keep silent in order not to aggravate the evil. It was my peculiar good fortune that I was treated with especial regard and love by my congregation and my family, that I had so many, many friends in Cincinnati round about me, or else my opponents in all likelihood would have defeated or killed me.

Quite a heavy European mail lay on my table on March 14, 1856. A letter, postmarked Paris, attracted my attention first of all. Upon opening it I read: "Heine is dead! He died on the eighteenth (of February). To-morrow (the twentieth) he will be buried in Montmartre.

'Keine Messe wird man lesen,
Keinen Kaddish wird man sagen.'*

I shall not go to the funeral, although Alexander Weill and the others have already taken their gala clothes out of pawn for the purpose, for I will have the toothache. The teeth of the many dogs that have bit Heine will hurt me for many a day. If you impart this information to the Americans, do not forget to add that Heine had the double misfortune of being a German and a Jew. Every German soldier felt justified in whipping him publicly, because he was a German poet and author, and because he was a Jew. Every Jew considered it his duty to procure for him *cheleq l'olam habba; i.e.,* to let him starve temporarily, in order to erect a monument to him fifty years hence. We Jews are very proud of our great men after they are dead, and we Germans are so honest that we tear one another to pieces bravely, etc., etc."

*no mass will they celebrate,
 no Kaddish will they say.

I had read quite enough for that day. The letters and newspapers remained untouched upon my table. I called a carriage, and drove to the lunatic asylum in order to pass the reminder of the day among the mentally sick. I succeeded admirably in not hearing a sensible word the whole day long, although the physicians took great pains to explain to me the secrets of mental diseases. After arriving home in the evening I had my wife read to me from Davis's "Discoveries in the Spirit Realm." Thereupon I went with her to drink a glass of beer, all, all in order to keep from thinking. I wanted to force myself not to think and reason, for being also a German and a Jew I wanted to escape the clubbing of the German soldiers and the sympathetic "Nebbich" of the Jews at any time. My wife thought me very stupid and ill-humored. I would not grant the latter, and in proof thereof I wrote some silly poetry for her amusement.

My object was gained. I felt convinced that I had gotten rid of troublesome Madame Reason, and could return home with easy conscience. However, the insistent lady reappeared early in the morning, I was compelled to return to my work, and again go to thinking. I was vexed and struggled against it; but all to no avail. I had to begin again to think.

The fact that the Germans tear one another to pieces, and that no German writer escapes brutal attacks and bloody contests, seemed to me to be the outcome of the political disruption of Germany. The Bavarian had to hate, or at least mock and revile, the Hessian; both of them the Saxon, each of these the Prussian, and all combined the Austrian. This explained to me sufficiently the mutual ill-will and the incapacity of the German Jewish congregations to unite and work together. They were Germans who had learned the lessons of disunion and hatred thoroughly under the tutelage of thirty-six rulers. I attributed the coarseness and rudeness of their public mouthpieces, as given expression to in their published polemics, to their village life, for seventy per cent of all Germans, be they Jews or Christians, spend their life among peasants and boors, and have therefore no conception of higher culture and refinement, elegance of behavior or manners. Even in the cities they remain peasants for a long time. It was very plain to me that the Jew had brought all these characteristics from Germany to this country; for the Germany of that time was not the Germany of to-day.

But why have Jews so little regard for one another, that they revile and traduce each other? How is it that a highly-honored public applauds loudly whenever literary rowdies squabble like street gamins, and throw mud at decent people? Whence comes this wretched imitation of Christian customs, good and bad, by Jews; this clinging to every Christian fashion; this eager association with, this humble attitude towards every Christian, even though he be a knave, for no other reason than that he is not a Jew? Whence this disgusting phenomenon? I could find but one answer to these questions: The century-long oppression has demoralized the German and Polish Jew, and robbed him of his self-respect. He has no self-respect, no pride left. The hep! hep! times still weigh him down; he bows and scrapes, he crawls and cringes. The Jew respects not the fellow-man in another Jew, because he lacks the consciousness of manhood in himself. He parodies and imitates, because he has lost himself. After diagnosing the evil, I set myself to seeking a remedy.

The Jew must be Americanized, I said to myself, for every German book, every German word reminds him of the old disgrace. If he continues under German influences as they are now in this country, he must become either a bigot or an atheist, a satellite or a tyrant. He will never be aroused to self-consciousness or to independent thought. The Jew must become an American, in order to gain the proud self-consciousness of the free-born man. From that hour I began to Americanize with all my might, and was as enthusiastic for this as I was for reform. Since then, as a matter of course, the German element here, as well as in Germany, has completely changed, although Judeophobia and uncouthness have survived in many; but at that time it appeared to me that there was but one remedy that would prove effective for my co-religionists, and that was to Americanize them thoroughly. We must be not only American citizens, but become Americans through and through outside of the synagogue. This was my cry then and many years thereafter. This, too, increased the hatred of my opponents considerably.

"But, if I succeed in Americanizing my co-religionists, will not Judaism disappear in Americanism," I asked myself, "even as the native Jewish element has approached the different sects so closely in various localities? This must be counteracted by a better knowledge of Jewish history and Jewish sources." My conviction was that a Jewish patriotism, a pride in being a Jew, must be aroused; for this it was that the Jew had lost in the ages of oppression.

The all-important question now forced itself — how? The means to Americanize were easy to find and apply; the means to Judaize were, however, not so apparent. I could not preach my ideas to the whole world, nor could I create an Americanizing-Judaizing literature single-handed. After lengthy reflection I arrived at the following conclusions:

1. To emphasize strongly the historical mission of Israel in all my speeches and writings, in order to arouse a consecrated self-consciousness.

2. To bring before the public the bright side of the Jewish character, and to leave it to the enemy to exploit our faults; thus to arouse a feeling of self-respect.

3. To popularize by spoken and written words as much Jewish learning as I might possess, in order to inculcate in others respect for Jewish literature.

4. To familiarize the reading public with the brilliant periods of Jewish history in fictional form, in order to appeal by this means to the growing youth so as to awaken in them Jewish patriotism, for there could be no doubt that they would Americanize themselves.

THE HOLY MAN

Black Elk

(1863-1950)

In the United States, the majority culture's treatment of the Native Americans has few, if any, bright spots. As Commissioner on Indian Affairs John Collier noted, beginning around 1870 (when Black Elk was only a child), "a leading aim of the United States was to destroy the Plains Indians societies through destroying their religions; and it may be that the world has never witnessed a religious persecution so implacable and so variously implemented." The slaughter at Wounded Knee, South Dakota, in 1890 was only one of the more dramatic expressions of national policy. In the twentieth century, some reversal of policy took place, as Indians were granted citizenship in 1924 and as they received a specific guarantee of their religious freedom in 1978 — a freedom all other Americans had enjoyed since 1791.

Black Elk, a Holy Man of the Ogalala Sioux, was twenty-seven years of age when the Wounded Knee horror occurred. He rode onto the scene while some shooting still went on, but many dead and wounded already lay in full view. The winter day had been sunny and bright, but with nightfall came snow and bitter winds, adding to the misery that afflicted those who survived. The snow drifted into a deep gulch, Black Elk reported, "and it was one long grave of butchered women and children and babies, who had never done any harm and were only trying to run away." But the Holy Man concluded that something else had died at Wounded Knee: "A people's dream died there. It was a beautiful dream. . . . There is no center any longer, and the sacred tree is dead."

Before that fateful day, Black Elk had shared the dream that in the 1880s spread widely among many different tribes: from Paiute to Shoshone to Cheyenne, Arapaho, and Sioux. The Ghost Dance religion represented an effort to resist the white man's ever enlarging political and military superiority. Conventional warfare would no longer work: supernatural forces must come to the aid of the Native American. Through dancing, singing, praying, and purifying, all Indians now living and even ancestors long deceased could bring about that new and wondrous dawning when the now-mighty enemy would be brought low and the now-despised natives would be exalted. In his own vision, Black Elk "saw again how beautiful the day was — the sky all blue and full of yellow light above the greening earth. And I saw that all the people were beautiful and young. There were no old ones there, nor children either — just people of about one age, and beautiful."

[For a book that places greater emphasis on the Holy Man's tribal context, see Julian Rice, *Black Elk's Story: Distinguishing Its Lakota Purpose* (Albuquerque: University of New Mexico Press, 1991).]

The Messiah

There was hunger among my people before I went away across the big water, because the Wasichus* did not give us all the food they promised in the Black Hills treaty. They made that treaty themselves; our people did not want it and did not make it. Yet the Wasichus who made it had given us less than half as much as they promised. So the people were hungry before I went away.

But it was worse when I came back. My people looked pitiful. There was a big drouth, and the rivers and creeks seemed to be dying. Nothing would grow that the people had planted, and the Wasichus had been sending less cattle and other food than ever before. The Wasichus had slaughtered all the bison and shut us up in pens. It looked as though we might all starve to death. We could not eat lies, and there was nothing we could do.

And now the Wasichus had made another treaty to take away from us about half the land we had left. Our people did not want this treaty either, but Three Stars came and made the treaty just the same, because the Wasichus wanted our land between the Smoky Earth and the Good River. So the flood of Wasichus, dirty with bad deeds, gnawed away half of the island that was left to us. When Three Stars came to kill us on the Rosebud, Crazy Horse whipped him and drove him back. But when he came this time without any soldiers, he whipped us and drove us back. We were penned up and could do nothing.

* The white people. (ed.)

Source: *Black Elk Speaks*... as told through John G. Neihardt (Lincoln: University of Nebraska Press, 1995), pp. 230-47.

All the time I was away from home across the big water, my power was gone, and I was like a dead man moving around most of the time. I could hardly remember my vision, and when I did remember, it seemed like a dim dream.

Just after I came back, some people asked me to cure a sick person, and I was afraid the power would not come back to me; but it did. So I went on helping the sick, and there were many, for the measles had come among the people who were already weak because of hunger. There were more sick people that winter when the whooping cough came and killed little children who did not have enough to eat.

So it was. Our people were pitiful and in despair.

But early that summer when I came back from across the big water (1889) strange news had come from the west, and the people had been talking and talking about it. They were talking about it when I came home, and that was the first I had heard of it. This news came to the Ogalalas first of all, and I heard that it came to us from the Shoshones and Blue Clouds (Arapahoes). Some believed it and some did not believe. It was hard to believe; and when I first heard of it, I thought it was only foolish talk that somebody had started somewhere. This news said that out yonder in the west at a place near where the great mountains (The Sierras) stand before you come to the big water, there was a sacred man among the Paiūtes who had talked to the Great Spirit in a vision, and the Great Spirit had told him how to save the Indian peoples and make the Wasichus disappear and bring back all the bison and the people who were dead and how there would be a new earth. Before I came back, the people had got together to talk about this and they had sent three men, Good Thunder, Brave Bear and Yellow Breast, to see this sacred man with their own eyes and learn if the story about him was true. So these three men had made the long journey west, and in the fall after I came home, they returned to the Ogalalas with wonderful things to tell.

There was a big meeting at the head of White Clay Creek, not far from Pine Ridge, when they came back, but I did not go over there to hear, because I did not yet believe. I thought maybe it was only the despair that made people believe, just as a man who is starving may dream of plenty of everything good to eat.

I did not go over to the meeting, but I heard all they had to tell. These three men all said the same thing, and they were good men. They said that they traveled far until they came to a great flat valley* near the last great mountains before the big water, and there they saw the

---

* Mason Valley, Nevada (J. G. Neihardt).

Wanekia, who was the son of the Great Spirit, and they talked to him. Wasichus called him Jack Wilson, but his name was Wovoka. He told them that there was another world coming, just like a cloud. It would come in a whirlwind out of the west and would crush out everything on this world, which was old and dying. In that other world there was plenty of meat, just like old times; and in that world all the dead Indians were alive, and all the bison that had ever been killed were roaming around again.

This sacred man gave some sacred red paint and two eagle feathers to Good Thunder. The people must put this paint on their faces and they must dance a ghost dance that the sacred man taught to Good Thunder, Yellow Breast, and Brave Bear. If they did this they could get on this other world when it came, and the Wasichus would not be able to get on, and so they would disappear. When he gave the two eagle feathers to Good Thunder, the sacred man said: "Receive these eagle feathers and behold them, for my father will cause these to bring your people back to him."

This was all that was heard the whole winter.

When I heard this about the red paint and the eagle feathers and about bringing the people back to the Great Spirit, it made me think hard. I had had a great vision that was to bring the people back into the nation's hoop, and maybe this sacred man had had the same vision and it was going to come true, so that the people would get back on the red road. Maybe I was not meant to do this myself, but if I helped with the power that was given me, the tree might bloom again and the people prosper. This was in my mind all that winter, but I did not know what vision the sacred man out there had seen, and I wished I could talk to him and find out. This was sitting deeper in my mind every day, and it was a very bad winter, with much hunger and sickness.

My father died in the first part of the winter from the bad sickness that many people had. This made me very sad. Everything good seemed to be going away. My younger brother and sister had died before I came home, and now I was fatherless in this world. But I still had my mother. I was working in a store for the Wasichus so that I could get something for her to eat, and I just kept on working there and thinking about what Good Thunder, Yellow Breast, and Brave Bear had told; but I did not feel sure yet.

During that winter the people wanted to hear some more about this sacred man and the new world coming, so they sent more men out there to learn what they could. Good Thunder and Yellow Breast, with two others, went from Pine Ridge. Some went with them from other agencies, and two of these were Kicking Bear and Short Bull. News came back from these men as they traveled west, and it seemed that everywhere people believed all that we had heard, and more. Letters came back telling us this. I kept on working in the store and helping sick people with my power.

Then it was spring (1890), and I heard that these men had all come back from the west and that they said it was all true. I did not go to this meeting either, but I heard the gossip that was everywhere now, and people said it was really the son of the Great Spirit who was out there; that when he came to the Wasichus a long time ago, they had killed him; but he was coming to the Indians this time, and there would not be any Wasichus in the new world that would come like a cloud in a whirlwind and crush out the old earth that was dying. This they said would happen after one more winter, when the grasses were appearing (1891).

I heard many wonderful things about the Wanekia that these men had seen and heard, and they were good men. He could make animals talk, and once while they were with him he made a spirit vision, and they all saw it. They saw a big water, and beyond it was a beautiful green land where all the Indians that had ever lived and the bison and the other animals were all coming home together. Then the Wanekia, they said, made the vision go out, because it was not yet time for this to happen. After another winter it would happen, when the grasses were appearing.

And once, they said, the Wanekia held out his hat for them to look into; and when they did this, all but one saw there the whole world and all that was wonderful. But that one could see only the inside of the hat, they said.

Good Thunder himself told me that, with the power of the Wanekia, he had gone to a bison skin tepee; and there his son, who had been dead a long time, was living with his wife, and they had a long talk together.

This was not like my great vision, and I just went on working in the store. I was puzzled and did not know what to think.

Afterwhile I heard that north of Pine Ridge at the head of Cheyenne Creek, Kicking Bear had held the first ghost dance, and that people who danced had seen their dead relatives and talked to them. The next thing I heard was that they were dancing on Wounded Knee Creek just below Manderson.

I did not believe yet, but I wanted to find out things, because all this was sitting more and more strongly in my heart since my father died. Something seemed to tell me to go and see. For awhile I kept from going, but at last I could not any more. So I got on my horse and went to this ghost dance on Wounded Knee Creek below Manderson.

I was surprised, and could hardly believe what I saw; because so much of my vision seemed to be in it. The dancers, both women and men, were holding hands in a big circle, and in the center of the circle they had a tree painted red with most of its branches cut off and some dead leaves on it. This was exactly like the part of my vision where the holy tree was dying, and the circle of the men and women holding hands was like the sacred hoop that should have power to make the tree to bloom again. I saw too that the sacred articles the people had offered were scarlet, as in my vision, and all their faces were painted red. Also, they used the pipe and the eagle feathers. I sat there looking on and feeling sad. It all seemed to be from my great vision somehow and I had done nothing yet to make the tree to bloom.

Then all at once great happiness overcame me, and it all took hold of me right there. This was to remind me to get to work at once and help to bring my people back into the sacred hoop, that they might again walk the red road in a sacred manner pleasing to the Powers of the Universe that are One Power. I remembered how the spirits had taken me to the center of the earth and shown me the good things, and how my people should prosper. I remembered how the Six Grandfathers had told me that through their power I should make my people live and the holy tree should bloom. I believed my vision was coming true at last, and happiness overcame me.

When I went to the dance, I went only to see and to learn what the people believed; but now I was going to stay and use the power that had been given me. The dance was over for that day, but they would dance again next day, and I would dance with them.

Visions of the Other World

So I dressed myself in a sacred manner, and before the dance began next morning I went among the people who were standing around the withered tree. Good Thunder, who was a relative of my father and later married my mother, put his arms around me and took me to the sacred tree that had not bloomed, and there he offered up a prayer for me. He said: "Father, Great Spirit, behold this boy! Your ways he shall see!" Then he began to cry.

I thought of my father and my brother and sister who had left us, and I could not keep the tears from running out of my eyes. I raised my face up to keep them back, but they came out just the same. I cried with my whole heart, and while I cried I thought of my people in despair. I thought of my vision, and how it was promised me that my people should have a place in this earth where they could be happy every day. I thought of them on the wrong road now, but maybe they could be brought back into the hoop again and to the good road.

Under the tree that never bloomed I stood and cried because it had withered away. With tears on my face I asked the Great Spirit to give it life and leaves and singing birds, as in my vision.

Then there came a strong shivering all over my body, and I knew that the power was in me.

Good Thunder now took one of my arms, Kicking Bear the other, and we began to dance. The song we sang was like this:

"Who do you think he is that comes?
It is one who seeks his mother!"

It was what the dead would sing when entering the other world and looking for their relatives who had gone there before them.

As I danced, with Good Thunder and Kicking Bear holding my arms between them, I had the queer feeling that I knew and I seemed to be lifted clear off the ground. I did not have a vision all that first day. That night I thought about the other world and that the Wanekia himself was with my people there and maybe the holy tree of my vision was really blooming yonder right then, and that it was there my vision had already come true. From the center of the earth I had been shown all good and beautiful things in a great circle of peace, and maybe this land of my vision was where all my people were going, and there they would live and prosper where no Wasichus were or could ever be.

Before we started dancing next day, Kicking Bear offered a prayer, saying: "Father, Great Spirit, behold these people! They shall go forth to-day to see their relatives, and yonder they shall be happy, day after day, and their happiness will not end."

Then we began dancing, and most of the people wailed and cried as they danced, holding hands in a circle; but some of them laughed with happiness. Now and then some one would fall down like dead, and others would go staggering around and panting before they would fall. While they were lying there like dead they were having visions, and we kept on dancing and singing, and many were crying for the old way of living and that the old religion might be with them again.

After awhile I began to feel very queer. First, my legs seemed to be full of ants. I was dancing with my eyes closed, as the others did. Suddenly it seemed that I was swinging off the ground and not touching it any longer. The queer feeling came up from my legs and was in my heart now. It seemed I would glide forward like a swing, and then glide back again in longer and longer swoops. There was no fear with this, just a growing happiness.

I must have fallen down, but I felt as though I had fallen off a swing when it was going forward, and I was floating head first through the air. My arms were stretched out, and all I saw at first was a single eagle feather right in front of me. Then the feather was a spotted eagle dancing on ahead of me with his wings fluttering, and he was making the shrill whistle that is his. My body did not move at all, but I looked ahead and floated fast toward where I looked.

There was a ridge right in front of me, and I thought I was going to run into it, but I went right over it. On the other side of the ridge I could see a beautiful land where many, many people were camping in a great circle. I could see that they were happy and had plenty. Everywhere there were drying racks full of meat. The air was clear and beautiful with a living light that was everywhere. All around the circle, feeding on the green, green grass, were fat and happy horses; and animals of all kinds were scattered all over the green hills, and singing hunters were returning with their meat.

I floated over the tepees and began to come down feet first at the center of the hoop where I could see a beautiful tree all green and full of flowers. When I touched the ground, two men were coming toward me, and they wore holy shirts made and painted in a certain way. They came to me and said: "It is not yet time to see your father, who is happy. You have work to do. We will give you something that you shall carry back to your people, and with it they shall come to see their loved ones."

I knew it was the way their holy shirts were made that they wanted me to take back. They told me to return at once, and then I was out in the air again, floating fast as before. When I came right over the dancing place, the people were still dancing, but it seemed they were not making any sound. I had hoped to see the withered tree in bloom, but it was dead.

Then I fell back into my body, and as I did this I heard voices all around and above me, and I was sitting on the ground. Many were crowding around, asking me what vision I had seen. I told them just what I had seen, and what I brought back was the memory of the holy shirts the two men wore.

That evening some of us got together at Big Road's tepee and decided to use the ghost shirts I had seen. So the next day I made ghost shirts all day long and painted them in the sacred manner of my vision. As I made these shirts, I thought how in my vision everything was like old times and the tree was flowering, but when I came back the tree was dead. And I thought that if this world would do as the vision teaches, the tree could bloom here too.

I made the first shirt for Afraid-of-Hawk and the second for the son of Big Road.

In the evening I made a sacred stick like that I had seen in my first vision and painted it red with the sacred paint of the Wanekia. On the top of it I tied one eagle feather, and this I carried in the dance after that, wearing the holy shirt as I had seen it.

Because of my vision and the power they knew I had, I was asked to lead the dance next morning. We all stood in a straight line, facing the west, and I prayed: "Father, Great Spirit, behold me! The nation that I have is in despair. The new earth you promised you have shown me. Let my nation also behold it."

After the prayer we stood with our right hands raised to the west, and we all began to weep, and right there, as they wept, some of them fainted before the dance began.

As we were dancing I had the same queer feeling I had before, as though my feet were off the earth and swinging. Kicking Bear and Good Thunder were holding my arms. Afterwhile it seemed they let go of me, and once more I floated head first, face down, with arms extended, and the spotted eagle was dancing there ahead of me again, and I could hear his shrill whistle and his scream.

I saw the ridge again, and as I neared it there was a deep, rumbling sound, and out of it there leaped a flame. But I glided right over it. There were six villages ahead of me in the beautiful land that was all clear and green in living light. Over these in turn I glided, coming down on the south side of the sixth village. And as I touched the ground, twelve men were coming towards me, and they said: "Our Father, the two-legged chief, you shall see!"

Then they led me to the center of the circle where once more I saw the holy tree all full of leaves and blooming.

But that was not all I saw. Against the tree there was a man standing with arms held wide in front of him. I looked hard at him, and I could not tell what people he came from. He was not a Wasichu and he was not an Indian. His hair was long and hanging loose, and on the left side of his head he wore an eagle feather. His body was strong and good to see, and it was painted red. I tried to recognize him, but I could not make him out. He was a very fine-looking man. While I was staring hard at him, his body began to change and became very beautiful with all colors of light, and around him there was light. He spoke like singing: "My life is such that all earthly beings and growing things belong to me. Your father, the Great Spirit, has said this. You too must say this."

Then he went out like a light in a wind.

The twelve men who were there spoke: "Behold them! Your nation's life shall be such!"

I saw again how beautiful the day was — the sky all blue and full of yellow light above the greening earth. And I saw that all the people were beautiful and young. There were no old ones there, nor children either — just people of about one age, and beautiful.

Then there were twelve women who stood in front of me and spoke: "Behold them! Their way of life you shall take back to earth." When they had spoken, I heard singing in the west, and I learned the song I heard.

Then one of the twelve men took two sticks, one painted white and one red, and, thrusting them in the ground, he said: "Take these! You shall depend upon them. Make haste!"

I started to walk, and it seemed as though a strong wind went under me and picked me up. I was in the air, with outstretched arms, and floating fast. There was a fearful dark river that I had to go over, and I was afraid. It rushed and roared and was full of angry foam. Then I looked down and saw many men and women who were trying to cross the dark and fearful river, but they could not. Weeping, they looked up to me and cried: "Help us!" But I could not stop gliding, for it was as though a great wind were under me.

Then I saw my earthly people again at the dancing place, and fell back into my body lying there. And I was sitting up, and people were crowding around me to ask what vision I had seen.

I told my vision through songs, and the older men explained them to the others. I sang a song, the words of which were those the Wanekia spoke under the flowering tree, and the air of it was that which I heard in the West after the twelve women had spoken. I sang it four times, and the fourth time all the people began to weep together because the Wasichus had taken the beautiful world away from us.

I thought and thought about this vision. The six villages seemed to represent the Six Grandfathers that I had seen long ago in the Flaming Rainbow Tepee, and I had gone to the sixth village, which was for the Sixth Grandfather, the Spirit of the Earth, because I was to stand for him in the world. I wondered if the Wanekia might be the red man of my great vision, who turned into a bison, and then into the four-rayed herb, the daybreak-star herb of understanding. I thought the twelve men and twelve women were for the moons of the year.

THE POLEMICIST

Harry Emerson Fosdick

(1878-1969)

In the 1920s the Protestant community was noisily divided into two camps: fundamentalists on the one hand, and modernists on the other. The former emphasized what were not necessarily traditional doctrines, but had become in the twentieth century testing points of orthodoxy: the virgin birth of Jesus, the inerrancy of the Bible, the imminent Second Coming of Christ, and a tendency to withdraw from the modern world. The latter, on the other hand, embraced current cultural developments, including the theory of evolution with its implicit support for the idea of progress. Modernists saw God as operative more within history than above or outside it, and the Bible as more of a progressive revelation than a static book of scientific and historical fact.

While the two sides shouted at each other across a wide valley, the majority of the nation's Protestants dwelled in that valley — unaware of or largely indifferent to the strident voices. Harry Emerson Fosdick, fully caught up in the theological and ecclesiastical strife, tried in many of his books to mediate or at least to explain to the larger Protestant audience just what was going on. In his *Modern Use of the Bible* (1924), for example, he labored to describe just what was going on with the much-maligned "higher criticism" of the Bible. He accepted such scholarship, but endeavored to show how it made the Bible more meaningful, more relevant — not less so. And though clearly, even notoriously, a liberal, Fosdick also demonstrated in book after book the depth of his own Christian commitment.

Fosdick bore battle wounds himself. Serving as pastor of the First Presbyterian Church in New York City, he drew down upon his head the wrath of the fundamentalists who demanded that he be expelled from the Presbyterian church. Though this did not happen, he voluntarily left the denomination in 1924 to become pastor of the Park Avenue Baptist Church in the same city. With John D. Rockefeller as patron and counselor, Fosdick moved in a few years into the magnificent new Riverside Church, remaining as its chief minister until 1946. His was a powerful pulpit and, as already indicated, he wielded a powerful pen.

At the beginning of the twenty-first century, theological quarrels — at least among the cultural elite — seem somewhat passé. But not in the lifetime of Harry Emerson Fosdick. In 1956 he wrote his autobiography, skillfully introducing us to an earlier, stormier time.

[See Robert Moats Miller, *Harry Emerson Fosdick: Preacher, Pastor, Prophet* (New York: Oxford University Press, 1985).]

The Fundamentalist Controversy

The conflict between liberal and reactionary Christianity had long been moving toward a climax. There were faults, on both sides. The modernists were tempted to make a supine surrender to prevalent cultural ideas, accepting them wholesale, and using them as the authoritarian standard by which to judge the truth or falsity of classical Christian affirmations. The reactionaries, sensing the peril in this shift of authority, were tempted to retreat into hidebound obscurantism, denying the discoveries of science, and insisting on the literal acceptance of every biblical idea, which even Christians of the ancient church had avoided by means of allegorical interpretation. As Reinhold Niebuhr neatly sums it up: "That part of the church which maintained an effective contact with modern culture stood in danger of capitulating to all the characteristic prejudices of a 'scientific' and 'progressive' age; and that part of the church which was concerned with the evangelical heritage chose to protect it in the armor of a rigorous biblicism."

When the storm did break, chance placed me near the center, and I tell the story of the controversy, as I experienced it, not because my

Source: Harry E. Fosdick, *The Living of These Days: An Autobiography* (New York: Harper & Brothers, 1956), pp. 144-53, 157-65.

share in it was more important than many others', but because I did have an interesting opportunity to see it from the inside.

My sermon, "Shall the Fundamentalists Win?" was a plea for tolerance, for a church inclusive enough to take in both liberals and conservatives without either trying to drive the other out. I stated the honest differences of conviction dividing these two groups on such matters as the virgin birth of Jesus, the inerrancy of the Scriptures and the second coming of Christ, and then made my plea that the desirable solution was not a split that would tear the evangelical churches asunder, but a spirit of conciliation that would work out the problem within an inclusive fellowship.

Since the liberals had no idea of driving the fundamentalists out of the church, while the fundamentalists were certainly trying to drive the liberals out, the impact of this appeal fell on the reactionary group. "Just now," I said, "the fundamentalists are giving us one of the worst exhibitions of bitter intolerance that the churches of this country have ever seen. As one watches them and listens to them, one remembers the remark of General Armstrong of Hampton Institute: 'Cantankerousness is worse than heterodoxy.' There are many opinions in the field of modern controversy concerning which I am not sure whether they are right or wrong, but there is one thing I am sure of: courtesy and kindliness and tolerance and humility and fairness are right. Opinions may be mistaken, love never is."

If ever a sermon failed to achieve its object, mine did. It was a plea for good will, but what became of it was an explosion of ill will, for over two years making headline news of a controversy that went the limit of truculence. The trouble was, of course, that in stating the liberal and fundamentalist positions, I had stood in a Presbyterian pulpit and said frankly what the modernist position on some points was — the virgin birth no longer accepted as historic fact, the literal inerrancy of the Scriptures incredible, the second coming of Christ from the skies an outmoded phrasing of hope.

There might have been no unusual result had it not been for Ivy Lee. Head of one of the nation's foremost publicity organizations, he was a liberal Presbyterian, and the sermon, printed in pamphlet form by the church, caught his attention. He asked the privilege of distributing it to his nation-wide clientele, and I consented. Mr. Lee cut out a few innocuous sentences of the homiletical introduction and conclusion, provided a fresh title, "The New Knowledge and the Christian Faith," broke up the sermon into sections with attractive subcaptions, and distributed it with a commendatory message calling attention to its importance. None of us foresaw the stormy consequence. Mr. Lee and I subsequently became warm friends, and I know that he always took pride in the way he put that sermon over.

The attack that followed was launched by Clarence Edward Macartney, then minister of a Presbyterian church in Philadelphia. He was very decent and dignified in his attitude. While his theological position was in my judgment incredible, he was personally fair-minded and courteous. Indeed, when the storm was just breaking, he wrote me directly, in order to be sure that he was not misquoting me. After that we had some frank and not unfriendly correspondence, in which he presented his own unbending orthodoxy, shocked at my doctrinal looseness; and I, still hoping that tolerance might win, tried in a conciliatory way to make him see that while I differed from him in my intellectual formulations, I was endeavoring to maintain, just as much as he was, the timeless values and truths of the gospel. It was, however, a vain attempt.

I returned to my preaching after a summer's vacation in 1922 to face a tense situation. The congregation at the church was solidly behind me, but around the horizon storm clouds were gathering. Fundamentalism, especially among Presbyterians and Baptists, was fighting mad, and I was an easily accessible object of attack. One immediate result was that the congregations at the church, which always had filled the auditorium, now overflowed all available auxiliary spaces and took up every foot of standing room. This went on until even the chancel steps were crowded, and when I went into the pulpit someone sat down in the seat I vacated until the sermon was finished.

Among fundamentalist Presbyterians the attack naturally took the form of a determined endeavor to get me out of that pulpit. It was bad enough, they thought, to have heresy preached in a Presbyterian church, but to have a Baptist do it was intolerable. The General Assembly of the Presbyterian Church which met in 1923 had before it overtures from ten presbyteries wanting something done to stop my heretical preaching. William Jennings Bryan, then at the top of his form as a defender of the faith against evolution, was one of the leading figures of the Assembly, and his oratory helped to achieve a fundamentalist victory. Anyone who ever heard Bryan speak can understand that. I had the privilege twice, once at Westfield in 1896 when a crowd of us, carrying goldenrod, heard him plead for free silver, and once at Harvard where, before an audience which jammed Sanders Theater, Bryan attacked evolution. It was an extraordinary performance. What he said was nonsense, but the way he said it — his voice, his inflection, his sincerity — was fascinating. At any rate, he dominated the General Assembly in 1923.

The Committee on Bills and Overtures brought in a majority report, referring my case to the judgment of the New York Presbytery; but, by a vote of 439 to 359, a minority report was adopted, expressing "profound sorrow that doctrines contrary to the standards of the Presbyterian Church" were being proclaimed in the Old First pulpit, and directing the Presbytery of New York to take such action "as will require the preaching and teaching in the First Presbyterian Church of New York City to conform to the system of doctrines taught in the Confession of Faith." Moreover, the minority report specified five doctrines, in particular, which they had in mind: the inerrant Bible; the virgin birth; the substitutionary atonement, Jesus' death "a sacrifice to satisfy divine justice"; the physical resurrection of Christ "with the same body in which he suffered"; and Christ's supernatural miracles.

Both as a gentleman and as a Christian I found myself in a difficult position. I was a guest in a denomination to which I did not belong and was causing trouble in the household of my host; and I was a lover of peace and harmony, wanting a church more united, not more divided, who instead was occasioning vehement discord. Upon hearing of the General Assembly's decision, therefore, I presented my resignation to the session of the church. The fact remained, however, that I was being attacked as a representative of liberal Christianity — "modernism's Moses" one humorous fundamentalist dubbed me — and I had an obligation not to leave my fellow liberals in the lurch with a defeat on their hands when patience and persistence might yet win a victory. When, therefore, the session unanimously declined to present my resignation to the congregation, I let them have their way, to see if the conflict, whose first battle we had lost, might turn out to be a war whose ultimate victory might be ours.

That next church season, 1923-24, was one of the most strenuous I ever spent. The part of it which I recall with greatest distaste was the political maneuvering, the drafting and redrafting of statements, and all the questionable compromises involved in trying so to present the matter to the next Presbyterian Assembly that our arrangement at Old First could somehow continue. I found myself caught in a long process of ecclesiastical intrigue which I thoroughly disliked.

I had seriously and, I think, rightly committed myself to a tolerant policy, believing that the belated doctrinal issues then crowding into the center of attention were really marginal and would so turn out to be, and that, therefore, the church ought not to split because of them but hold together and ride out the storm. My mind and conscience were thus on the side of conciliation, but in the end it involved more than I had bargained for.

The committee of the New York Presbytery, under the chairmanship of Edgar Whitaker Work, at once started to prepare for the General Assembly in 1924 a report that would mollify the opposition. Appeasement was their policy, and I presume inevitably so. They were my stanch friends; they wanted my ministry at Old First to go on; they saw that it could not go on unless they won over a majority of the next Assembly; and so they began painting my portrait in as orthodox outlines as possible and portraying the background situation at Old First to make it seem innocuous.

Dr. Work's committee wanted a statement from me to include in its report. I sent a tentative draft. They were very complimentary about it, calling it "a straightforward, manly and magnificent statement," but that exaggerated praise was only setting for their discontent. They were troubled by the "absence of any even remote hint or suggestion of admission or concession" in it. They wanted me, so they wrote, to "express some doubt as to your own judgment in preaching the Sermon, 'Shall the Fundamentalists Win?'" They very much wanted me to rephrase my affirmation of faith, using words with a more orthodox aroma than the ones I had employed, and in general they wanted me to assume that the aggrieved party in the dispute was not myself but the General Assembly, and so to approach the Assembly with concession and even apology. Of course I could not do it. I recall yet my struggle over that letter for Dr. Work, torn as I was between the desire to help my friends and my entire unwillingness to say what they wanted me to say.

The covering letter which I sent along with my formal statement reflects my difficulty. I regretted the necessity of disappointing Dr. Work's expectations. I protested that while he pictured my statement being read by conservative Presbyterians, I pictured it being read by young men and women who had looked to me in some measure for spiritual leadership and who would be wondering whether I had "stood by my colors" or had "trimmed, hedged, and compromised." I was glad to calm down a few phrases "needlessly aggressive and perhaps strident," but "putting a positively apologetic and concessive note" into the letter, I could not do. So far as the troublesome sermon was concerned, I said that "far from having searching of conscience because I preached the sermon, I should have had desperate and intolerable searching of conscience if I had not preached it or something like it"; and I added: "I have thought and rethought the problem in the hope of finding some way of making a statement for your purposes, but every time I tried, I framed a statement even less concessive than the one I thought of at first." The best I could do was to omit all reference to the sermon. I was willing to substitute "deity" for "divinity" in affirming my faith about Christ, "because they mean the same thing," but I could not make the other verbal changes he asked for. And I ended by saying:

> Even if I could write the letter which you have suggested, I am positively certain that it would do no good whatever, and for the simple reason that I must not take in this letter a tone which I don't take anywhere else. No one who knows me personally, hears me preach, lecture, or reads my books, can for a moment suppose that I take an apologetic and deprecatory attitude toward the gospel which I preach. Upon the contrary, I am proud of it; I believe in it, I stand by it. With all the inevitable limitations and mistakes, I am sure that it has in it the seeds of hope for the future generation. I do not apologize for it, I proclaim it and everybody knows it. It would therefore convince nobody (even if it were honest) for me to take in this letter to you under these special circumstances a tone of voice which I never take anywhere else. The letter which I am now sending you seems to me to be a natural and straightforward expression of the thing that I say in my private conversation, in my sermons, lectures, and books. Whether you can use it or not I do not know. If you find it impossible to use it I shall of course understand thoroughly.

And all this fuss was about a statement in which if I erred at all, I erred on the side of conservatism.

Meanwhile, as the months passed the controversial uproar grew ever louder and more obstreperous across the country. The headlines screamed and even the Episcopalians entered the fray, so that in 1924 Bishop William T. Manning of the New York Diocese begged his clergy to observe a truce during the Christmas season. My own situation became correspondingly warm, with three groups throwing fagots on the flame.

First, the fundamentalists themselves grew increasingly vehement. In pulpits, magazines, pamphlets and mass meetings they assailed the liberals and called on them to leave the evangelical churches. Their slogan was concisely stated in a mass meeting of Presbyterian fundamentalists in New York: "We have a right to demand that those who serve as pastors of our churches shall 'hew to the line' in matters of faith." When my ministry came within their range of fire another factor added ammunition. "Dr. Fosdick," cried an outraged Presbyterian at another New York mass meeting, "is a foreigner within our gates, without standing or credentials that have been considered; one who is considered a usurper and whom the Supreme Court of our Church has told very plainly he was not welcome."

If the Presbyterian fundamentalists disliked me, their Baptist brethren went them, if anything, one better. They held a series of mass meetings of their own, at the opening session of which John Roach Straton, pastor of the Calvary Baptist Church in New York, tore loose. "We are driven," he said, "to the conclusion that Dr. Fosdick is not only a Baptist bootlegger, but that he is also a Presbyterian outlaw; without the slightest personal ill will and with no desire to injure him personally, I nevertheless declare, in the light of Bible teaching, and in the name of eternal truth, that Dr. Harry Emerson Fosdick is a religious outlaw — he is the Jesse James of the theological world."

The second party in the conflict was made up of my friends. They did not all agree with me doctrinally, but they were in general on the liberal side, and in particular were deeply concerned about maintaining personal freedom in the church. The outcome that would follow a fundamentalist victory was clear. As one typical Presbyterian reactionary put it: "How can men who are honest stay in the Presbyterian Church when they no longer believe in her doctrines? There is only one honest way for these brethren to act. Let them get out!" This meant, however, that the church's doctrines were finally to be frozen in terms which the fundamentalists chose and that both all liberty of interpretation and all possibility of progress were to be denied. This raised an issue much larger than any individual; I was only by chance thrust into a representative position, standing for a kind of Christian liberty that all liberals had to stand for if they were not to be driven from the evangelical churches.

My friends, therefore, were contending not so much for me — although personal loyalty often warmed their efforts — as for the essential liberties of the Christian ministry. To have the General Assembly try to enforce five such definitions of indispensable belief as it was requiring the New York Presbytery to impose on me was more than they could stand. They rose in revolt and fought for their freedom.

On the first Sunday after the 1923 Assembly John Kelman, a Scottish Presbyterian, then minister of the Fifth Avenue Presbyterian Church, New York, made a typical statement:

> When I came here in 1919 I had never heard of that declaration of the Assembly. In the questions which were addressed to me no reference was made to any such declaration. If there had been any such reference and if it had been necessary for me to profess my agreement with it, I could not have accepted a call to any church in America.
>
> The impression that ministers of this church are bound to consider these forms of statement as essential is one which would have the most serious consequences upon the minds of thinking men and women around us, and especially upon the mind of the rising generation. For their sake, as well as for my own, I therefore feel it my duty to associate myself with those who entered their protest against the action of the General Assembly.*

Many of the most impressive voices in the Presbyterian church, such as Henry Sloane Coffin and William P. Merrill, spoke in similar fashion. Henry van Dyke, then a professor at Princeton, came back for a Sunday in his former pulpit at the Brick Presbyterian Church, New York, to say roundly: "These famous 'Five Points' of the Assembly . . . are

---

*New York Times, May 28, 1923.

not valid as a definition of the fundamentals of Christian faith. They have no binding force. You do not need to trouble about them." And Presbyterian editors such as Nolan R. Best and James E. Clarke risked serious damage to their publications and the loss of their own positions to take their stand for freedom in the church.

Altogether it was a hot situation for me, caught as I was between the attacks of my foes and the defenses of my friends, and compelled Sunday after Sunday to face overflowing congregations expectantly awaiting some message worthy of the occasion. I had been reared in a church which has no authoritative written creeds and which gives to each congregation autonomous control over its own affairs. As I watched the operation of the Presbyterian system, making individual congregations subservient to the Presbytery and the Presbytery subservient to the General Assembly, with a written Confession of Faith that modern minds can subscribe to only with mental reservations, I was ill at ease.

Nevertheless, fundamentalism was no peculiarly Presbyterian problem; it was an urgent peril in all the evangelical churches; and by the selection of the reactionaries I had been made for the time being a symbol of liberalism. It would have been easy to insist on my resignation from Old First, but had I done so my liberal friends would have called me a quitter. It clearly looked as though I could best serve the cause by staying on and fighting it out.

Meanwhile, I never knew before that I had so many friends. A letter signed by several hundred professors and students of Cornell University strongly backed me up, writing, they said, "in solemn protest against these misinformed and unchristian attacks and in pledging our unqualified loyalty to you as the leading American interpreter of the Christian religion for men and women of scientific training." Letters of similar import came from institutions as far apart as Mount Holyoke College in Massachusetts and the Southern Methodist University in Texas, and one that I especially valued was sent by five hundred and sixty professors and students at Columbia.

President John Grier Hibben of Princeton, himself a Presbyterian minister, came to my defense in a baccalaureate sermon, saying that "a part of the Christian church has recently been stampeded through fear of a great teacher and prophet of righteousness in New York City, because the group which would call him to account does not speak his language or understand his thought." President W. H. P. Faunce of Brown gave me his spirited support: "Nearly all Christian ministers with whom I am personally acquainted and all the college teachers that I know believe substantially what Dr. Fosdick has been preaching with such lucidity and power as to win the approval of two continents. If any particular denomination does not wish to hear his message, that denomination is the loser and not Dr. Fosdick."

As for the secular press, I never can be sufficiently grateful for the loyal backing of men like John Finley, of the *New York Times*. The outrageous escapade of the Scopes trial in Tennessee, backed by William Jennings Bryan, was to come in 1925, but its foreshadowings were apparent and many citizens who would ordinarily have given a religious controversy only amused or disgusted attention were awakened to the public menace involved in rampant fundamentalism, so that the secular press commonly reflected sympathy with the liberal cause.

I marvel yet at editorials such as one that John Finley wrote for the *New York Times* when it became apparent that my days at Old First were numbered:

It is plain that the whole loss will fall not upon Dr. Fosdick, but upon the Presbyterian Church. It will have convicted itself in the eyes of the lay public not only of a certain denominational narrowness, but of the folly of giving up the services of a preacher whose good report has filled the whole city, become known throughout the entire country and reached the knowledge of the churches in England. Such a voice as that of Dr. Fosdick's is in no danger of being silenced by any technical ecclesiastical veto. He has but to speak, anywhere, and people will flock to hear him. Without artifice in the pulpit, or the slightest trick of ministerial sensationalism, he has moved thousands by the quality of his thought and the depth and sincerity of his religious emotions. When a church, no matter of what denomination, has at its disposal such a preacher of spiritual power in a time of dominant materialism, it is so stupid as to be almost wicked to let him go. It seems very close to a violation of the Scriptural injunction to quench not the spirit. But Dr. Fosdick need not think of abandoning his great following or his high mission. If not in one pulpit, then eventually in another, his exceptional vocation for the ministry will, no doubt, be exemplified so long as strength and life do not fail him.*

New York Times, October 7, 1924.

With a good deal of hesitancy I include these tributes, not only because they are part of the record, but because I wish to remove any possibility of supposing that in this bitter controversy I was in any sense a martyr. Some of my too enthusiastic friends were tempted to add that halo to me, but there was no occasion for it. I thoroughly disliked the whole contentious and embittered episode; at times I seriously wondered what the ultimate effect upon my opportunities as a Christian minister would be; but I was all the time supported by powerful backing from those by whom one would most choose to be backed, so that there was never any occasion for developing a martyr complex.

Especially at the Old First Church I was unanimously sustained by a friendliness for which I can never be sufficiently thankful. My colleagues in the ministry there, Dr. Alexander and Mr. Speers, bore a heavy load on my behalf, and their loyalty never failed. Dr. Alexander was a great personality, more conservative than I in his theological opinions, but devoted to large-spirited, inclusive Christianity. Under his leadership the whole congregation rallied around my ministry, and amid the tumult on the outside, the parish within was not only harmonious but vigorously active in its work, as though the best answer to attack was not recrimination but a practical illustration of what a church like ours could mean in a modern metropolis.

It was not alone the fundamentalists and liberals, however, who heated the fires of controversy; a third group, smaller in number but vociferous in expression, added to its vehemence. This group was made up of left-wing religious radicals. Many of them had been ministers or members of evangelical churches, and finding the constraints intolerable had left them. They took the same position the fundamentalists did on one point: that the liberals should leave the evangelical denominations. Common honesty, they thought, demanded that the liberals get out. No criticism of my attitude from the fundamentalists was more harsh than some that came from this left-wing group. They insisted that my only decent course was to do as they had done — shake the dust of the evangelical denominations from my feet.

The difference in point of view between the evangelical liberals and this left-wing group was important. The radicals, motivated by disgust with the evangelical churches, wanted them left to their own hidebound, obscurantist devices. We, on the other hand, were determined not to surrender to the fundamentalists the control of the great historic denominations. We saw in them priceless values; we treasured the Christian heritage of which, with all their faults, they were the most influential conservers; we felt ourselves one with them in the abiding, substantial truths they stood for, despite our disagreement with their outgrown theological formulas. For all the liberals to desert them, leaving their long-accumulated prestige, their powerful influence and their multitudes of devoted Christian people in the hands of fundamentalist leadership, seemed to us an unthinkable surrender and an intolerable tragedy to the Christian cause.

Moreover, the left-wing group, so we thought, lost their perspective in exaggerating the importance of the controversy. They commonly saw it as the crack of doom for the old denominations, the beginning of a final split that would line up the evangelical churches under reactionary control, on one side, and all honest, outspoken modernists on the other. I recall a conversation with one of these radicals. He could with difficulty repress his contempt for my attitude. He thought the controversy was one of the most momentous events in the church's history, a kind of new Reformation that would force the withdrawal of all intelligent, sincere modern minds from the old-line institutions. He thought this, in part, because he wanted it; and the popular tumult of the controversy encouraged him to see his hopes in process of fulfillment. As for evangelical liberals in general and for me in particular, we seemed to him to be trimming. Why did we not see that the great split had now come, that the time for toleration and conciliation had passed, and that the only honest thing for all of us to do was to quit the old denominations?

We, on the other hand, thought that the controversy, despite the noise it made, was an ephemeral affair, with the matters in dispute, such as the five points the General Assembly raised, insufficient in importance to disrupt the historic churches. I often confided to my friends my sense of shame that I was unwittingly made the front and center of a controversy over such belated issues. The questions in dispute were not the great matters that confronted modern Christianity; they were trivial in comparison with the real issues of the day; and the whole uproar was not the noise of the main battle but the flare-up of a rear-guard action. The idea of splitting the great churches over such obscurantism as William Jennings Bryan stood for seemed to us absurd; the slow but inevitable processes of education were bound in time to put an end to such outdated thinking; and meanwhile our place was inside the evangelical churches, patiently standing our ground, claiming our liberty, and biding our time. The outcome, I am sure, has validated our stand.

THE EDITOR

John LaFarge, S.J.

(1880-1963)

Born in Newport, Rhode Island, and educated at Harvard, John LaFarge stood out as an aristocratic intellectual, distinct from much clerical leadership that provoked Catholic historian John Tracy Ellis to bemoan the "anti-intellectualism" of American Catholicism. LaFarge was anything but anti-intellectual, even if he did have some blind spots, such as his unwavering support for Franco throughout Spain's civil war. In 1905, at the age of twenty-five, he entered the Society of Jesus, or Jesuit order, an institution steadily devoted to elevating the life of the mind.

Father LaFarge flourished in the period before Vatican II, when institutional rigidity was more the rule than the exception. And as a Jesuit, he manifested strict loyalty both to his order and his church. It is a bit surprising, then, that in the 1930s he challenged his church to be more progressive, more daring, with respect to matters of race. He helped create the Catholic Interracial Council of New York in 1934, published *Interracial Justice* in 1937, *The Race Question and the Negro* in 1943, and *No Postponement: U.S. Moral Leadership and the Problem of Racial Minorities* in 1950. To try to win more friends for his cause among Catholic authorities, he emphasized how the Catholic Church's efforts in this area would thwart the appeal of the Communists to African Americans; he also pointed to the fact that his own church lagged behind the Protestants in bringing blacks into their ranks.

From the perspective of the later civil rights movements, LaFarge's labors seem a bit tame — though, to be sure, some fellow Catholics condemned him as a visionary radical. And LaFarge himself admitted that the meetings of the Interracial Council struck some visitors as too quietly intellectual. A French journalist, LaFarge reports, expected the meetings to "protest not only against prejudice, but against the economically corrupt situation of the modern, industrialized word." But, LaFarge explained, that was not their mode of operation. We "met for an hour or so, exchanged views and wishes, and then parted to [our] several ways resolving simply to behave like decent citizens in [our] contacts with various ethnic groups." No power structures collapsed.

But John LaFarge had his greatest influence as editor of *America,* a Roman Catholic weekly of considerable influence. Though associated with the magazine in one capacity or another from 1926 on, he was asked to become its editor-in-chief in 1944, "an usually difficult time, the climax of World War II." In the excerpt below, he takes us into that time period, into the contest between fascism, communism, and democracy. He also illuminates the challenges that a religious periodical faced in a postwar, post-atomic age.

[See Robert A. Hecht, *Unordinary Man: A Life of Father John LaFarge, S.J.* (Lanham, Md.: Scarecrow Press, 1996).]

On July 12, 1942, Father Francis X. Talbot, editor-in-chief of *America,* asked me to take the job of executive editor. He wished to devote himself to promotion work for the magazine and believed that its direction would be helped by a division of editorial work.

America was unique among religious periodicals of its type. The magazine first saw the light in 1909 at 32 Washington Square West, and its first editor was Father John J. Wynne, S.J., renowned organizer and editor of the *Catholic Encyclopedia.* Jesuit students and priests were canvassed for a name for the new periodical and suggested the usual quota of Reviews, Journals, Proceedings, etc. Then a former Provincial, the Rev. Thomas Gannon, S.J., proposed the name *America.* It was immediately adopted.

The press which issued the magazine was exceptional in possessing a constitution, or *Ordinatio,* provided for it by the General of the Society, Very Rev. Father F. X. Wernz. The *Ordinatio* provided that the ultimate responsibility for the magazine should be vested in a Board of Governors consisting of the heads of the several Jesuit Provinces in the United States. These were five in 1909; there are eight at the present day. The staff was to be drawn as far as possible from each of the American Provinces, as well as from the English-speaking Province of Canada.

The Constitution provided that once a year the Governor should assemble to consider the problems of the America Press: a deliberation

Source: John LaFarge, S.J., *The Manner Is Ordinary* (New York: Harcourt, Brace & Co., 1954), pp. 254-61.

which later was expanded to other works of the Society in the United States. The editor at the same time was summoned to appear before this plenary session in order to render an account of his year's stewardship, receive advice, and ask for what he needed in the way of additional help, materials, and whatnot. Two of the meetings I attended as executive editor; the other four as editor-in-chief (except that at one of the four, being prevented by illness, I was represented by our treasurer, Father Joseph Carroll of the California Province).

Before each of these appearances I felt much the same sinking of heart as that experienced by a pastor when he receives notice to come down to the Bishop's office and explain what is happening in his parish and why. Anything can happen in a magazine, and if one dignitary can make you feel uncomfortable, how about eight at once? However, the anticipation always proved far worse than the reality. Since I wrote to the Fathers Provincial once a month during the year, I found they were pretty well posted and were ready to support the work and sustain it against objections and criticism. Moreover, I was urged to speak out and state my views, needs, and objections. The treasurer took care of the bad news, if any, in the financial report.

In October of 1944 Father Talbot called me into his office on the ground floor and notified me, in his own inimitably gracious, encouraging manner, that I was appointed editor-in-chief.

I was therefore called on to direct a national religious weekly magazine at an unusually difficult time, the climax of World War II. The problems of any war are appalling, but none were ever as vexatious as at that catastrophic time. For the first time in history, our country was engaged in war against an armed ideology quite as much as against a nation in arms. In fighting for our country the situation was enormously complicated by the fact that we were allied with a great and powerful nation whose ideas, aims, and ultimate policies we were obliged in conscience to combat to the very end. Communism was not simply an excess, or a distortion of the truth, it was, in the words of Pope Pius XI, intrinsically wrong. It was wrong beyond the possibility of any conciliation, as Father Gaston Fessard had so clearly demonstrated in his discussions with the Parisian Communist leaders. As he said, the first condition of discussion is that the Communist be ready to grant that there is a *possibility* of other opinions besides his own in the matter of religion. But no orthodox Marxist could grant any possibility of an error in dogma on his part. And this dogmatic intransigence in the field of anti-religious propaganda applied to the whole field of social and political action.

The Nazi ideology was inflamed with hatred of Christ the God-Man and His Church, as I had seen on my visit to Germany in 1938. Yet in the United States some religious people were deceived and confused by the fact that Hitler was professedly an enemy of Stalin. The fact that Hitler was warring on the Mystical Body of Christ itself was ignored or was even attributed to Jewish or British propaganda. Yet the war between Hitler and Stalin was ideologically unreal, as was shown by the Nazi-Soviet pact. On November 5, 1938, I had already written that Nazism might salvage for its own purposes the irreligious tyranny of Communism — "in short, that Brown and Red Bolshevism may come to terms more easily and more readily than we dared suspect." A similar opinion was expressed a month later in the *Saturday Evening Post* by Demaree Bess. Denunciations of Bolshevism in Nazi Germany had given place very largely to attacks on democracy and the "democratic powers." The most basic sign of all, as I observed, was the evident fact that Nazism did not oppose Bolshevism on religious grounds. I looked to the "ultimate union of the two greatest anti-Christian forces of the world."

I was convinced that a Catholic weekly needed to tackle the ideological question more thoroughly than was the case with the usual organs of current news. Communism was not just an instance of ordinary political ambition or greed. A vast difference separated the ideas of the thoroughgoing Marxist from the simple power-philosophy of the anarchistic free-booter, such as a Calles, or a Carranza, who had initiated revolution in Mexico and paved the way for the spread of Communist influence.

Such a philosophical approach was somewhat unpopular and open to considerable misunderstanding. Typical was a banquet in one of our New England cities when some one thousand Catholic laymen were told by the reverend director of a retreat, as reported: "Don't worry about the spirit of the modern age; don't worry about Communism. Communism can never touch the United States; Communism can never take over its government or desecrate its homes or its churches, as long as there are men filled with the spirit of Jesus Christ." A prominent citizen of the aforesaid city quoted the report with the remark, "How sensible!"

Men, including pious men, naturally follow the line of least resistance, and considerable mental effort and spiritual energy is needed to follow up the devious windings of Communist propaganda through daily study and effective action, particularly when such following up is frowned on by local Catholic politicians.

It has taken a long time for our American thought to disengage itself from the notion that the problem of Communism is wholly a matter of economics. This was the type of thinking that was bedazzled by the Soviet industrial development and by its vast agricultural co-operative and state farms, the type of thinking that made Senator Borah in 1933 urge recognition of Russia, and made Senator Brookhart exclaim, "Never was there such industrial development and so little indebtedness" as in Soviet Russia. It was against that mentality that Joseph Motta, the President of Switzerland, argued when he opposed vainly the admission of Soviet Russia to the League of Nations. "We cannot believe in the peaceful evolution of the Bolshevist regime, which we hope for as you do. We cannot sacrifice, even to the principle of universality, the idea of a necessary minimum of moral and political conformity between states." Until bitter experience drove them home to unwilling minds, those were hard words to express to a reluctant world. They were truths that had to be expressed on grounds that could be accepted by those to whom they were addressed. An editor could not rely too much on the authoritarian language of dogma.

American liberals regarded anyone who spoke against the Communists or Stalin or compared his conduct to that of Hitler as betraying the Resistance, as in league with Nazism and Vichy. I willingly recognized the honesty of those liberals who finally expressed their disillusionment with the Communists and Communism. They had been taken in by a naive idealism, and they have shown great courage in finally acknowledging the truth. Yet it is hard for one like myself, who has suffered a painfully clear vision of the perversity of organized political atheism ever since the very beginning of its operations at the close of the First World War, to avoid a certain touch of bitterness. If I were of the brooding type — which, thank God, I am not — I would be tempted to brood over the quiet assumptions of my stupidity expressed by intelligent, cultivated people when I was disturbed and shocked at flagrant violations of basic human rights and ordinary justice by the anarchist elements.

It is still a mystery to me how the great top-flight intellectual and literary leaders in this country and abroad could have been blind to the savagery of the Leftist Spanish revolution, to such scenes of savagery as occurred when Barcelona was seized on Red Sunday, July 9, 1936, when the Anarcho-Syndicalists were then in power. Those were the days when the American friends of Spanish "Loyalists" demonstrated in Madison Square Garden. It took a long time for them to learn what George Orwell, who had fought courageously for those same Anarcho-Syndicalists, finally discovered — "about this being a 'war for Democracy,' it was plain eyewash" (*Homage to Catalonia*, p. 180).

Yet the very difficulty of adopting a philosophical approach to these problems was itself a challenge. The function of the magazine, which I believed to be in line with *America's* tradition, was, first to rectify consciences as to the matter of the defense of our country. I rejected pacifist doctrine. "No Christian," I held, "can maintain consistently that all war, all use of military force, is invariably and necessarily wrong." As Cardinal della Costa, Archbishop of Florence, said after that city had been liberated by the Allies in October 1944, if the Allies had not constructed their great armaments, "we don't know what would have happened to Christian civilization, human civilization."

On the other hand, our task was to make every effort to point out the foundations of a just and durable peace, looking to the postwar world. Our philosophy was summed up in the famous statement, the seven-point *Pattern for Peace*. Originated in 1943 by Father Edward A. Conway, S.J., who became an associate editor of *America* in 1948, the *Pattern* was issued separately but in identical form by outstanding representative organizations of the three major faiths, namely, the National Catholic Welfare Conference, the Synagogue Council of America, and the Federal Council of the Churches of Christ in America. The points, in summary, were as follows: (1) the moral law must govern world society; (2) the rights of the individual must be asserted; (3) the rights of the oppressed, weak, or colonial peoples must be protected; (4) the rights of minorities must be secured; (5) international institutions to maintain peace with justice must be organized; (6) international economic cooperation must be developed; (7) a just social order within each state must be developed. These conclusions represented the indispensable minimum of moral law, as Pope Pius XII had urged in his appeals to the Christian conscience in his various Christmas discourses.

Moreover, we felt that a religious periodical was obligated to devote attention to specific postwar problems of human welfare, of refugees, of migration, of religious persecution, of the treatment of war criminals, and so on, as well as discuss the complete disruption of the social order.

It was clear to me that any defense of human freedom against totalitarianism as a total assault on man — on the human race — was doomed to failure unless it defended the totality of man. Issues back in 1928, in my first years with the Review, were fewer and in general simpler and easier to handle than those of 1942 and after. And yet those later issues were somehow blended into one great issue, which shaped up with startling clarity. In the words of President Truman to Pope

Pius XII, it was "the preservation and support of the principles of freedom and justice"; the issue of the Christian concept of liberty as opposed to totalitarianism. We see now that what looked to us in those earlier years as trifling or transitory was pregnant with the horrors of the future.

Such a defense of the totality of man implied on the one hand the defense of his religious and moral being and dignity, and on the other hand regard for the concrete conditions, earthly and temporal, under which he worked out his destiny. The mere proclaiming of generalities without ever reducing them to deeds brought the doctrine itself into contempt and was apt to gain more enemies than disciples for the truth. Both of these ideas I had seen stressed by Pope Pius XI and his successor Pius XII. Father Ledóchowski, with whom I had conversed in Rome in 1938, expressly encouraged in the United States the formation of the Institute of Social Order among the American Jesuits for the purpose of coming to grips with the concrete problems of the social order in view of our time, our country, and our Faith.

One of the strongest statements to this effect that I know was made in *America* by the former Secretary General of the Communist organization of Spain, Don Enrique Matorras, in an article describing his disillusionment with Communism:

> We cannot escape the truth; we Catholics must face it and may not evade the issues. We who know and have the remedy must also fight in order to master the situation. We who are fortunately acquainted with the full teachings of Christ have the moral obligation even at the risk of our position, prejudice, and persecution to raise our voices in protest against social injustice and to command once more reverence for the dignity of the workingman.

Convinced as I was on this point I regretted that I was not equipped with the specialized study to enable me to handle it adequately. I had spent many years in practical pastoral work when theoretically I should have been working for degrees in sociology, social ethics, or political science. When stationed at Leonardtown I did borrow a case of books on some of these topics from the Congressional Library in Washington, through the kindness of its librarian Mr. Herbert Putnam, and did a little exploring in spare moments. But without guidance, one could not get very far. However, I had the advantage of having already probed into a number of problems of our time.

154

All this made me desire to keep the line entirely clear on two cardinal points: First, the complete integrity of personal responsibility before God; for we cannot fob off on society or circumstances what in the last analysis is an affair of our own personal conscience. Second, the scope of that claim on our integrity; for the burden on our conscience is not confined to purely personal matters.

Man's social nature affects controversial questions like those of sexual morality, such as birth control, or the indissolubility of matrimony. The Catholic Church stubbornly refuses to look upon the exercise of the sexual function and conduct in the marriage relation as matters to be guided by one's own personal choices alone, but insists that these functions carry a wide social implication. No matter how secretly and privately they may be exercised, they invariably affect the entire structure of society. It is as guardian of the principles of decency, justice, and order on which our society rests that the Church preaches certain standards of sexual and family morality.

With equally controversial insistence, the Church preaches the morality of the marketplace. The pursuit of gain cannot be the affair of the individual alone, but is always subject to the responsibilities which rest upon him as a consequence of his place in society. This frequently leads the editor of a Church organ into highly unpopular positions, first with one group, then with another. Yet his position is fundamentally reasonable, and it is his task to see that it should be expounded as far as possible in a manner acceptable to the general public.

If anyone asked me what were the issues that most threatened the poise of my editorial chair during the years I was in charge of the Review I would be at a loss to choose, since every issue dealing with concrete affairs starts a controversy, even if you merely discuss the weather. However, the following items particularly stand out. They reflect the positions *America* took as a journal of opinion in line with its long tradition, and still holds to, as far as I know. They may be summed up as follows: (1) our duties toward the international community and its organization; (2) our obligation of charity toward the war-stricken peoples of the world; (3) the issue of morality in the marketplace and the consequent reform of certain economic institutions; and (4) the question of civil rights of minority groups — whether religious, as in the case of Catholics and the public school question, or racial minorities, as in the case of the Negroes, the Jews, and others in our community. All of these issues were explosive; each touched some neuralgic point in one reader or another.

THE IMMIGRANT

Mary Antin

(1881-1949)

Raised as a young girl in the Jewish ghetto of Polotzk, Russia, Mary Antin emigrated with her mother, brother, and two sisters to the United States in 1894. (Her father had gone on before in 1891 to find work and prepare for his family's arrival.) As an early editor, Ellery Sedgwick, commented, "Mary Antin was twelve years old when she stepped out of the Old Testament into the new world." And as Mary herself wrote regarding that Old Testament world back in Russia, despite persecution and brutal oppression, "I yet arose and held my head high, sure that I should find my kingdom in the end, although I had lost my way in exile." She added: "for He who had brought my ancestors safe through a thousand perils was guiding my feet as well. God needed me, and I needed Him, for we two together had a work to do, according to an ancient covenant between Him and my forefathers."

Her feet were guided to Boston where she would, of course, find freedom of religion. But the more immediate promise held out to her and her siblings was free public education. This was the gate to the whole world of modern wonder, a gate firmly shut against her in the ghetto. With pride and eager anticipation, her father escorted his children to the public school. "He would not have delegated that mission to the President of the United States," Mary wrote. "The boasted freedom of the New World," she noted, "meant to him far more than the right to reside, travel, and work wherever he pleased; it meant the freedom to speak his thoughts, to throw off the shackles of superstition, to test his own fate, unhindered by political or religious tyranny."

Yet, the public school in the 1890s still revealed a Christian if not an identifiably Protestant flavor. When the teacher led the class in the Lord's Prayer, Mary Antin — still working on her use of English — followed along as best she could. But "my mind could not go beyond the word 'hallowed,' for which I had not found the meaning." Then, a Jewish boy in the class nudged her foot, and whispered that she should not be trying to say or understand the prayer at all because it was a Christian prayer. On the other hand, the young immigrant from Russia reasoned that the name of Christ appeared nowhere in the prayer, "and I was bound to do everything that the class did. If I had any Jewish scruples, they were lagging way behind my interest in school affairs."

Indeed, that interest was so keen, so zealous that the young student soon mastered the English language, doing so with a gusto that enabled her before long to write poetry in her adopted language and to get it published in the Boston papers. "How long would you say, wise reader, it takes to make an American?" Antin asked. In her case, it took less than two years for her proudly to claim the United States as "my country." Polotzk, she explains, was never her country — only her exile.

[See Oscar Handlin's biographical sketch in Edward T. James et al., *Notable American Women, 1607-1950: A Biographical Dictionary,* 3 vols. (Cambridge, Mass.: Harvard University Press, 1971).]

"My Country"

The public school has done its best for us foreigners, and for the country, when it has made us into good Americans. I am glad it is mine to tell how the miracle was wrought in one case. You should be glad to hear of it, you born Americans; for it is the story of the growth of your country; of the flocking of your brothers and sisters from the far ends of the earth to the flag you love; of the recruiting of your armies of workers, thinkers, and leaders. And you will be glad to hear of it, my comrades in adoption; for it is a rehearsal of your own experience, the thrill and wonder of which your own hearts have felt.

How long would you say, wise reader, it takes to make an American? By the middle of my second year in school I had reached the sixth grade. When, after the Christmas holidays, we began to study the life of Washington, running through a summary of the Revolution, and the early days of the Republic, it seemed to me that all my reading and study had been idle until then. The reader, the arithmetic, the song book, that had so fascinated me until now, became suddenly sober exercise books, tools wherewith to hew a way to the source of inspiration.

Source: Mary Antin, *The Promised Land* (Boston: Houghton Mifflin, 1912), pp. 222-30.

When the teacher read to us out of a big book with many bookmarks in it, I sat rigid with attention in my little chair, my hands tightly clasped on the edge of my desk; and I painfully held my breath, to prevent sighs of disappointment escaping, as I saw the teacher skip the parts between bookmarks. When the class read, and it came my turn, my voice shook and the book trembled in my hands. I could not pronounce the name of George Washington without a pause. Never had I prayed, never had I chanted the songs of David, never had I called upon the Most Holy, in such utter reverence and worship as I repeated the simple sentences of my child's story of the patriot. I gazed with adoration at the portraits of George and Martha Washington, till I could see them with my eyes shut. And whereas formerly my self-consciousness had bordered on conceit, and I thought myself an uncommon person, parading my schoolbooks through the streets, and swelling with pride when a teacher detained me in conversation, now I grew humble all at once, seeing how insignificant I was beside the Great.

As I read about the noble boy who would not tell a lie to save himself from punishment, I was for the first time truly repentant of my sins. Formerly I had fasted and prayed and made sacrifice on the Day of Atonement, but it was more than half play, in mimicry of my elders. I had no real horror of sin, and I knew so many ways of escaping punishment. I am sure my family, my neighbors, my teachers in Polotzk — all my world, in fact — strove together, by example and precept, to teach me goodness. Saintliness had a new incarnation in about every third person I knew. I did respect the saints, but I could not help seeing that most of them were a little bit stupid, and that mischief was much more fun than piety. Goodness, as I had known it, was respectable, but not necessarily admirable. The people I really admired, like my Uncle Solomon, and Cousin Rachel, were these who preached the least and laughed the most. My sister Frieda was perfectly good, but she did not think the less of me because I played tricks. What I loved in my friends was not inimitable. One could be downright good if one really wanted to. One could be learned if one had books and teachers. One could sing funny songs and tell anecdotes if one travelled about and picked up such things, like one's uncles and cousins. But a human being strictly good, perfectly wise, and unfailingly valiant, all at the same time, I had never heard or dreamed of. This wonderful George Washington was as inimitable as he was irreproachable. Even if I had never, never told a lie, I could not compare myself to George Washington; for I was not brave

— I was afraid to go out when snowballs whizzed — and I could never be the First President of the United States.

So I was forced to revise my own estimate of myself. But the twin of my new-born humility, paradoxical as it may seem, was a sense of dignity I had never known before. For if I found that I was a person of small consequence, I discovered at the same time that I was more nobly related than I had ever supposed. I had relatives and friends who were notable people by the old standards, — I had never been ashamed of my family, — but this George Washington, who died long before I was born, was like a king in greatness, and he and I were Fellow Citizens. There was a great deal about Fellow Citizens in the patriotic literature we read at this time; and I knew from my father how he was a Citizen, through the process of naturalization, and how I also was a citizen, by virtue of my relation to him. Undoubtedly I was a Fellow Citizen, and George Washington was another. It thrilled me to realize what sudden greatness had fallen on me; and at the same time it sobered me, as with a sense of responsibility. I strove to conduct myself as befitted a Fellow Citizen.

Before books came into my life, I was given to stargazing and daydreaming. When books were given me, I fell upon them as a glutton pounces on big meat after a period of enforced starvation. I lived with my nose in a book, and took no notice of the alternations of the sun and stars. But now, after the advent of George Washington and the American Revolution, I began to dream again. I strayed on the common after school instead of hurrying home to read. I hung on fence rails, my pet book forgotten under my arm, and gazed off to the yellow-streaked February sunset, and beyond, and beyond. I was no longer the central figure of my dreams; the dry weeds in the lane crackled beneath the tread of Heroes.

What more could America give a child? Ah, much more! As I read how the patriots planned the Revolution, and the women gave their sons to die in battle, and the heroes led to victory, and the rejoicing people set up the Republic, it dawned on me gradually what was meant by *my country*. The people all desiring noble things, and striving for them together, defying their oppressors, giving their lives for each other — all this it was that made *my country*. It was not a thing that I *understood*; I could not go home and tell Frieda about it, as I told her other things I learned at school. But I knew one could say "my country" and *feel* it, as one felt "God" or "myself." My teacher, my schoolmates, Miss

Dillingham, George Washington himself could not mean more than I when they said "my country," after I had once felt it. For the Country was for all the Citizens, and *I was a Citizen*. And when we stood up to sing "America," I shouted the words with all my might. I was in very earnest proclaiming to the world my love for my new-found country.

> "I love thy rocks and rills,
> Thy woods and templed hills."

Boston Harbor, Crescent Beach, Chelsea Square — all was hallowed ground to me. As the day approached when the school was to hold exercises in honor of Washington's Birthday, the halls resounded at all hours with the strains of patriotic songs; and I, who was a model of the attentive pupil, more than once lost my place in the lesson as I strained to hear, through closed doors, some neighboring class rehearsing "The Star-Spangled Banner." If the doors happened to open, and the chorus broke out unveiled —

> "O! say, does that Star-Spangled Banner yet wave
> O'er the land of the free, and the home of the brave?" —

delicious tremors ran up and down my spine, and I was faint with suppressed enthusiasm.

Where had been my country until now? What flag had I loved? What heroes had I worshipped? The very names of these things had been unknown to me. Well I knew that Polotzk was not my country. It was *goluth* — exile. On many occasions in the year we prayed to God to lead us out of exile. The beautiful Passover service closed with the words, "Next year, may we be in Jerusalem." On childish lips, indeed, those words were no conscious aspiration; we repeated the Hebrew syllables after our elders, but without their hope and longing. Still not a child among us was too young to feel in his own flesh the lash of the oppressor. We knew what it was to be Jews in exile, from the spiteful treatment we suffered at the hands of the smallest urchin who crossed himself; and thence we knew that Israel had good reason to pray for deliverance. But the story of the Exodus was not history to me in the sense that the story of the American Revolution was. It was more like a glorious myth, a belief in which had the effect of cutting me off from the actual world, by linking me with a world of phantoms. Those moments of exaltation which the contemplation of the Biblical past afforded us, allowing us to call ourselves the children of princes, served but to tinge with a more poignant sense of disinheritance the long humdrum stretches of our life. In very truth we were a people without a country. Surrounded by mocking foes and detractors, it was difficult for me to realize the persons of my people's heroes or the events in which they moved. Except in moments of abstraction from the world around me, I scarcely understood that Jerusalem was an actual spot on the earth, where once the Kings of the Bible, real people, like my neighbors in Polotzk, ruled in puissant majesty. For the conditions of our civil life did not permit us to cultivate a spirit of nationalism. The freedom of worship that was grudgingly granted within the narrow limits of the Pale by no means included the right to set up openly any ideal of a Hebrew State, any hero other than the Czar. What we children picked up of our ancient political history was confused with the miraculous story of the Creation, with the supernatural legends and hazy associations of Bible lore. As to our future, we Jews in Polotzk had no national expectations; only a life-worn dreamer here and there hoped to die in Palestine. If Fetchke and I sang, with my father, first making sure of our audience, "Zion, Zion, Holy Zion, not forever is it lost," we did not really picture to ourselves Judea restored.

So it came to pass that we did not know what *my country* could mean to a man. And as we had no country, so we had no flag to love. It was by no far-fetched symbolism that the banner of the House of Romanoff became the emblem of our latter-day bondage in our eyes. Even a child would know how to hate the flag that we were forced, on pain of severe penalties, to hoist above our housetops, in celebration of the advent of one of our oppressors. And as it was with country and flag, so it was with heroes of war. We hated the uniform of the soldier, to the last brass button. On the person of a Gentile, it was the symbol of tyranny; on the person of a Jew, it was the emblem of shame.

So a little Jewish girl in Polotzk was apt to grow up hungry-minded and empty-hearted; and if, still in her outreaching youth, she was set down in a land of outspoken patriotism, she was likely to love her new country with a great love, and to embrace its heroes in a great worship. Naturalization, with us Russian Jews, may mean more than the adoption of the immigrant by America. It may mean the adoption of America by the immigrant.

On the day of the Washington celebration I recited a poem that I had composed in my enthusiasm. But "composed" is not the word. The process of putting on paper the sentiments that seethed in my soul was really very discomposing. I dug the words out of my heart, squeezed the rhymes out of my brain, forced the missing syllables out of their hiding-places in the dictionary. May I never again know such travail of the spirit as I endured during the fevered days when I was engaged on the poem. It was not as if I wanted to say that snow was white or grass was green. I could do that without a dictionary. It was a question now of the loftiest sentiments, of the most abstract truths, the names of which were very new in my vocabulary. It was necessary to use polysyllables, and plenty of them; and where to find rhymes for such words as "tyranny," "freedom," and "justice," when you had less than two years' acquaintance with English! The name I wished to celebrate was the most difficult of all. Nothing but "Washington" rhymed with "Washington." It was a most ambitious undertaking, but my heart could find no rest till it had proclaimed itself to the world; so I wrestled with my difficulties, and spared not ink, till inspiration perched on my penpoint, and my soul gave up its best.

When I had done, I was myself impressed with the length, gravity, and nobility of my poem. My father was overcome with emotion as he read it. His hands trembled as he held the paper to the light and the mist gathered in his eyes. My teacher, Miss Dwight, was plainly astonished at my performance, and said many kind things, and asked many questions; all of which I took very solemnly, like one who had been in the clouds and returned to earth with a sign upon him. When Miss Dwight asked me to read my poem to the class on the day of celebration, I readily consented. It was not in me to refuse a chance to tell my schoolmates what I thought of George Washington.

I was not a heroic figure when I stood up in front of the class to pronounce the praises of the Father of his Country. Thin, pale, and hollow, with a shadow of short black curls on my brow, and the staring look of prominent eyes, I must have looked more frightened than imposing. My dress added no grace to my appearance. "Plaids" were in fashion, and my frock was of a red-and-green "plaid" that had a ghastly effect on my complexion. I hated it when I thought of it, but on the great day I did not know I had any dress on. Heels clapped together, and hand glued to my sides, I lifted up my voice in praise of George Washington. It was not much of a voice; like my hollow cheeks, it suggested consumption. My pronunciation was faulty, my declamation flat. But I had the courage of my convictions. I was face to face with twoscore Fellow Citizens, in clean blouses and extra frills. I must tell them what George Washington had done for their country — for *our* country — for me.

Reinhold Niebuhr

(1892-1971)

For at least a generation, say from around 1940 to 1970, the word "theologian" brought to the minds of many Americans the name of Reinhold Niebuhr. He gave lectures from coast to coast, as well as abroad; he wrote weekly columns along with a flood of books; he was quoted endlessly on questions ranging from politics and war to the nature of man and the necessity of faith. In 1948 he even achieved the equivalent of an American canonization: his picture on the cover of *Time Magazine*. But long before reaching these dizzying heights of public attention and acclaim, Niebuhr served as pastor of the Bethel Evangelical Church in Detroit, Michigan, from 1915 to 1928.

A graduate of Elmhurst College in Illinois and Eden Seminary in Missouri, both institutions affiliated with the Evangelical Synod of North America, Niebuhr went on to Yale for further graduate work in 1914 and 1915. He then assumed the pastorate of his denomination's small church in Detroit. During this long apprenticeship, if it might be so termed, both Niebuhr and the city of Detroit grew rapidly. Henry Ford was making his mark, for both good and ill, upon the American economy and upon the theological development of Reinhold Niebuhr. Protestantism could all too easily allow itself to become the comfortable ally of capitalism; it could all too easily settle for pious platitudes and moral complacency. Rather, what was needed was a moral rigor, a moral courage, a prophetic voice that addressed itself to the challenges and crises of the day: World War I, the Ku Klux Klan, the organization of labor, the secularization of religious values, and the "criminal indifference on the part of the strong to the fate of the weak." In the years from 1915 to 1928, Niebuhr found his prophetic voice.

Soon after he left the Bethel pastorate for Union Theological Seminary in New York City in 1928, he published his autobiographical reflections: *Leaves From the Notebook of a Tamed Cynic*. In this work, excerpted below, one sees how the external pressures of an industrial world forced Niebuhr's creative, probing mind to search for the hard answers rather than settle for the easy ones. In the words of Richard Fox, this small book is a "relentless record of a unique man's attempt to become a prophet without succumbing to the obvious threat of pride and self-satisfaction."

[See Richard Fox, *Reinhold Niebuhr: A Biography* (New York: Harper & Row, 1985).]

Now that I have preached about a dozen sermons I find I am repeating myself. A different text simply means a different pretext for saying the same thing over again. The few ideas that I had worked into sermons at the seminary have all been used, and now what? I suppose that as the years go by life and experience will prompt some new ideas and I will find some in the Bible that I have missed so far. They say a young preacher must catch his second wind before he can really preach. I'd better catch it pretty soon or the weekly sermon will become a terrible chore.

You are supposed to stand before a congregation, brimming over with a great message. Here I am trying to find a new little message each Sunday. If I really had great convictions I suppose they would struggle for birth each week. As the matter stands, I struggle to find an idea worth presenting and I almost dread the approach of a new sabbath. I don't know whether I can ever accustom myself to the task of bringing light and inspiration in regular weekly installments.

How in the world can you reconcile the inevitability of Sunday and its task with the moods and caprices of the soul? The prophet speaks only when he is inspired. The parish preacher must speak

Source: Reinhold Niebuhr, *Leaves From the Notebook of a Tamed Cynic* [1929] (Louisville, Ky.: Westminster/John Knox Press, 1990), pp. 12, 31-32, 45, 65-66, 76-77, 86-87, 118-19, 137-38.

whether he is inspired or not. I wonder whether it is possible to live on a high enough plane to do that without sinning against the Holy Spirit.

$$\backsim$$

I spoke to the —— club today and was introduced by the chairman as a pastor who had recently built a new church at "the impressive cost of $170,000." While the figure was not quite correct it gave me somewhat of a start to find how much emphasis was placed upon what was regarded as a great business achievement. Here was a group of business men, and the chairman knew of no way to recommend me to them but by suggesting that I was myself a business man of no mean ability. That would have given the good men of my church council a laugh. Knowing how little I had to do with the raising of the money for the new church and how I have always failed to put on the kind of "pressure" they desired when we were raising money, they would certainly have smiled wryly at this eulogy.

But it is all natural enough. America worships success and so does the world in general. And the only kind of success the average man can understand is obvious success. There must be

"Things done that took the eye, that had the price;
O'er which from level stand,
The low world laid its hand,
Found straightway to its mind, could value in a trice."

After all the real work of a minister is not easily gauged and the world may not be entirely wrong in using external progress as an outward sign of an inward grace. Even those who value the real work of the ministry sometimes express their appreciation in rather superficial phrases. I remember when dear old —— celebrated his twenty-fifth anniversary the good toastmaster pathetically described his pastor's successful ministry by explaining that under his leadership the congregation had "doubled its membership, installed a new organ, built a parsonage, decorated the church and wiped out its debt." Not a word about the words of comfort the good pastor had spoken or the inspiration he had given to thirsting souls.

Perhaps it is foolish to be too sensitive about these inevitable secularizations of religious values. Let us be thankful that there is no quarterly meeting in our denomination and no need of giving a district superintendent a bunch of statistics to prove that our ministry is successful.

~

A revival meeting seems never to get under my skin. Perhaps I am too fish-blooded to enjoy them. But I object not so much to the emotionalism as to the lack of intellectual honesty of the average revival preacher. I do not mean to imply that the evangelists are necessarily consciously dishonest. They just don't know enough about life and history to present the problem of the Christian life in its full meaning. They are always assuming that nothing but an emotional commitment to Christ is needed to save the soul from its sin and chaos. They seem never to realize how many of the miseries of mankind are due not to malice but to misdirected zeal and unbalanced virtue. They never help the people who corrupt family love by making the family a selfish unit in society or those who brutalize industry by excessive devotion to the prudential virtues.

Of course that is all inevitable enough. If you don't simplify issues you can't arouse emotional crises. It's the melodrama that captivates the crowd. Sober history is seldom melodramatic. God and the devil may be in conflict on the scene of life and history, but a victory follows every defeat and some kind of defeat every victory. The representatives of God are seldom divine and the minions of Satan are never quite diabolical.

I wonder whether there is any way of being potent oratorically without over-simplifying truth. Or must power always be bought at the expense of truth? Perhaps some simplification of life is justified. Every artist does, after all, obscure some details in order to present others in bolder relief. The religious rhetorician has a right to count himself among, and take his standards from, the artists rather than the scientists. The trouble is that he is usually no better than a cartoonist.

~

We went through one of the big automobile factories today. So artificial is life that these factories are like a strange world to me though I have lived close to them for many years. The foundry interested me particularly. The heat was terrific. The men seemed weary. Here manual labor is a drudgery and toil is slavery. The men cannot possibly find any satisfaction in their work. They simply work to make a living. Their sweat and their dull pain are part of the price paid for the fine cars we all run. And most of us run the cars without knowing what price is being paid for them.

Looking at these men the words of Markham's "The Man with the Hoe" came to me. A man with a hoe is a happy creature beside these suffering souls.

"The emptiness of ages in his face"
. . . .
"Who made him dead to rapture and despair,
A thing that grieves not and that never hopes,
Stolid and stunned, a brother to the ox?"

We are all responsible. We all want the things which the factory produces and none of us is sensitive enough to care how much in human values the efficiency of the modern factory costs. Beside the brutal facts of modern industrial life, how futile are all our homiletical spoutings! The church is undoubtedly cultivating graces and preserving spiritual amenities in the more protected areas of society. But it isn't changing the essential facts of modern industrial civilization by a hair's breadth. It isn't even thinking about them.

The morality of the church is anachronistic. Will it ever develop a moral insight and courage sufficient to cope with the real problems of modern society? If it does it will require generations of effort and not a few martyrdoms. We ministers maintain our pride and self-respect and our sense of importance only through a vast and inclusive ignorance. If we knew the world in which we live a little better we would perish in shame or be overcome by a sense of futility.

～

Cynics sometimes insinuate that you can love people only if you don't know them too well; that a too intimate contact with the foibles and idiosyncrasies of men will tempt one to be a misanthrope. I have not found it so. I save myself from cynicism by knowing individuals, and knowing them intimately. If I viewed humanity only from some distant and high perspective I could not save myself from misanthropy. I think the reason is simply that people are not as decent in their larger relationship as in their more intimate contacts.

Look at the industrial enterprise anywhere and you find criminal indifference on the part of the strong to the fate of the weak. The lust for power and the greed for gain are the dominant note in business. An industrial overlord will not share his power with his workers until he is forced to do so by tremendous pressure. The middle classes, with the exception of a small minority of intelligentsia, do not aid the worker in exerting this pressure. He must fight alone.

The middle classes are in fact quite incapable of any high degree of social imagination. Their experience is too limited to give them a clear picture of the real issues in modern industrial life. Nonunion mines may organize in West Virginia and reduce miners to a starvation wage without challenging the conscience of a great middle class nation. If the children of strikers are starving it is more difficult to find support for them than to win contributors for the missions of the church. America may arouse the resentment of the world by its greed and all the good people of the American prairie will feel nothing but injured innocence from these European and Asiatic reactions to our greed.

Men are clearly not very lovely in the mass. One can maintain confidence in them only by viewing them at close range. Then one may see the moral nobility of unselfish parenthood, the pathetic eagerness of father and mother to give their children more of life than they enjoyed, the faithfulness of wives to their erring husbands; the grateful respect of mature children for their old parents, the effort of this and that courageous soul to maintain personal integrity in a world which continually tempts to dishonesty, and the noble aspirations of hearts that must seem quite unheroic to the unheeding world.

The same middle classes which seem so blind to the larger moral problems of society have, after all, the most wholesome family life of any group in society.

Spoke tonight to the Churchmen's Club of ———. The good Bishop who introduced me was careful to disavow all my opinions before I uttered them. He assured the brethren, however, that I would make them think. I am getting tired of these introductions which are intended to impress the speaker with the Christian virtue of the audience and its willingness to listen to other than conventional opinions. The chairman declares in effect, "Here is a harebrained fellow who talks nonsense. But we are Christian gentlemen who can listen with patience and sympathy to even the most impossible opinions." It is just a device to destroy the force of a message and to protect the sensitive souls who might be rudely shocked by a religious message which came in conflict with their interests and prejudices.

There is something pathetic about the timidity of the religious leader who is always afraid of what an honest message on controversial issues might do to his organization. I often wonder when I read the eleventh chapter of Hebrews in which faith and courage are practically identified whether it is psychologically correct to assume that the one flows from the other. Courage is a rare human achievement. If it seems to me that preachers are more cowardly than other groups, that may be because I know myself. But I must confess that I haven't discovered much courage in the ministry. The average parson is characterized by suavity and circumspection rather than by any robust fortitude. I do not intend to be mean in my criticism because I am a coward myself and find it tremendously difficult to run counter to general opinion. Yet religion has always produced some martyrs and heroes.

I suppose religion in its most vital form does make men indifferent to popular approval. The apostle Paul averred that it was a small thing to be judged of men because he was seeking the approval of God. In a genuinely religious soul faith does seem to operate in that way. Issues are regarded *sub specie aeternitatis* and the judgment of contemporaries becomes insignificant. But the average man fashions his standards in the light of prevailing customs and opinions. It could hardly be expected that every religious leader would be filled with prophetic ardor and heedless courage. Many good men are naturally cautious. But it does seem that the unique resource of religion ought to give at least a touch of daring to the religious community and the religious leader.

~

I wonder if it is really possible to have an honest Thanksgiving celebration in an industrial civilization. Harvest festivals were natural enough in peasant communities. The agrarian feels himself dependent upon nature's beneficence and anxious about nature's caprices. When the autumnal harvest is finally safe in the barns there arise, with the sigh of relief, natural emotions of gratitude that must express themselves religiously, since the bounty is actually created by the mysterious forces of nature which man may guide but never quite control.

All that is different in an industrial civilization in which so much wealth is piled up by the ingenuity of the machine, and, at least seemingly, by the diligence of man. Thanksgiving becomes increasingly the business of congratulating the Almighty upon his most excellent co-workers, ourselves. I have had that feeling about the Thanksgiving proclamations of our Presidents for some years. An individual living in an industrial community might still celebrate a Thanksgiving day uncorrupted by pride, because he does benefit from processes and forces which he does not create or even guide. But a national Thanksgiving, particularly if it is meant to express gratitude for material bounty, becomes increasingly a pharisaic rite.

The union Thanksgiving service we attended this morning was full of the kind of self-righteous bunk which made it quite impossible for me to worship. There was indeed a faint odor of contrition in one of the prayers and in an aside of the sermon, but it did not spring from the heart. The Lord who was worshiped was not the Lord of Hosts, but the spirit of Uncle Sam, given a cosmic eminence for the moment which the dear old gentleman does not deserve.

It is a bad thing when religion is used as a vehicle of pride. It would be better to strut unashamedly down the boardwalk of nations than to go through the business of bowing humbly before God while we say, "We thank thee Lord that we are not as other men."

175

A very sophisticated young man assured me in our discussion today (student discussion at a middle western university) that no intelligent person would enter the ministry today. He was sure that the ministry was impossible as a vocation not only because too many irrationalities were still enmeshed with religion but also because there was no real opportunity for usefulness in the church. I tried to enlighten this sophomoric wise man.

Granted all the weaknesses of the church and the limitations of the ministry as a profession, where can one invest one's life where it can be made more effective in as many directions?

You can deal with children and young people and help them to set their life goals and organize their personalities around just and reasonable values.

You can help the imperiled family shape the standards and the values by which the institution of family life may be saved and adjusted to the new conditions of an industrial civilization.

You can awaken a complacent civilization to the injustices which modern industrialism is developing. While ministers fail most at this point there is nothing to prevent a courageous man from making a real contribution to his society in this field.

You can soften the asperities of racial conflict and aid the various groups of a polyglot city to understand one another and themselves.

You can direct the thoughts and the hopes of men to those facts and those truths which mitigate the cruelty of the natural world and give man the opportunity to assert the dignity of human life in the face of the contempt of nature.

You can help them to shape and to direct their hopes and aspirations until their lives are determined and molded by the ideal objects of their devotion. While it is true that magic and superstition are still entwined, seemingly inextricably intertwined, with the highest hopes and assurances of mankind, you may find real joy as a skillful craftsman in separating hopes from illusions so that the one need not perish with the other.

Here is a task which requires the knowledge of a social scientist and the insight and imagination of a poet, the executive talents of a business man and the mental discipline of a philosopher. Of course none of us meets all the demands made upon us. It is not easy to be all things to all men. Perhaps that is why people are so critical of us. Our task is not specific enough to make a high degree of skill possible or to result in tangible and easily measured results. People can find fault with us easily enough and we have no statistics to overawe them and to negate their criticisms.

THE YOGI

Paramahansa Yogananda

(1893-1952)

Hinduism, by and large, is not as readily transportable as such more demonstrably mobile religions as Buddhism, Christianity, and Islam. Hinduism is so closely tied to India — its geography, its social patterns, its history — that it has never "conquered" another country in the way that the three religions named above have done. Certainly, it has never invaded the United States in force. And yet, from the English translations of such Hindu classics as the Upanishads, the Bhagavad Gita, and the Laws of Manu late in the eighteenth century, Hinduism as an intellectual force has been present in America. During the heyday of Transcendentalism in the 1840s, that force was more widely felt among many of New England's elite.

The general public saw Hinduism favorably presented in the World's Parliament of Religions gathered in Chicago in 1893. There Swami Vivekananda made a persuasive case for a kind of Hinduism that was transportable — not necessarily tied to India. His Vedanta Society, founded in New York in 1894, paved the way for other centers across the country. Vedanta attracted such highly visible converts as Christopher Isherwood and Aldous Huxley, with the former's writings being a major influence in intellectual circles. But since the movement remained more philosophical than popular, it never won a wide following.

Yogananda, through the Self-Realization Fellowship founded in 1920, won greater attention by way of his widely read *Autobiography*, first published in 1946 and reprinted countless times thereafter. Coming to the United States in 1920 to address the International Congress of Religious Liberals in Boston, Yogananda remained in this country to become a full-time Hindu missionary. Establishing his headquarters ultimately in Los Angeles, Yogananda — like Vivekananda — found many admirers among recognized leaders. He even dedicated his *Autobiography* to Luther Burbank, "an American saint."

The Self-Realization Fellowship relies on the teaching of a sacred instructor, a guru, who in this case is Yogananda. It also employs a Hindu discipline, in this instance *kriya yoga,* as a way of achieving spiritual liberation. One's true spiritual nature, otherwise dormant, is by this means awakened so that all illusions drop away. In reading the excerpt below, one also sees that for Yogananda all religions are valid. The challenge is to rise above ethnic and national limitations in order to discover the essential unity underlying all. This approach has the virtue of not alienating those of other faiths that one may wish to convert; it also has the virtue of asserting that Hinduism, or at least some major elements of it, can be appropriated without having to take on all of India as well.

[See John Y. Fenton, *Transplanting Religious Traditions: Asian Indians in America* (New York: Praeger, 1988).]

The Years 1940-1951

"We have indeed learned the value of meditation, and know that nothing can disturb our inner peace. In the last few weeks during the meetings we have heard air-raid warnings and listened to the explosion of delayed-action bombs, but our students still gather and thoroughly enjoy our beautiful service."

This brave message, written by the leader of the London Self-Realization Fellowship Center, was one of many letters sent to me from war-ravaged England and Europe during the years that preceded America's entry into World War II.

Dr. L. Cranmer-Byng of London, noted editor of *The Wisdom of the East Series*, wrote me in 1942 as follows:

"When I read *East-West* I realized how far apart we seemed to be, apparently living in two different worlds. Beauty, order, calm, and peace come to me from Los Angeles, sailing into port as a vessel laden with the blessings and comfort of the Holy Grail to a beleaguered city.

Source: Paramahansa Yogananda, *Autobiography of a Yogi* [1946] (Self-Realization Fellowship, 1993), pp. 549-69.

"I see as in a dream your palm-tree grove, and the temple in Encinitas with its ocean stretches and mountain views; and above all its fellowship of spiritually minded men and women — a community comprehended in unity, absorbed in creative work, and replenished in contemplation. . . . Greetings to all the Fellowship from a common soldier, written on the watchtower waiting for the dawn."

A Church of All Religions in Hollywood, California, was built by Self-Realization Fellowship workers and dedicated in 1942. A year later another temple was founded in San Diego, California; and, in 1947, one in Long Beach, California.

One of the most beautiful estates in the world, a floral wonderland in the Pacific Palisades section of Los Angeles, was donated in 1949 to Self-Realization Fellowship. The ten-acre site is a natural amphitheater, surrounded by verdant hills. A large natural lake, a blue jewel in a mountain diadem, has given the estate its name of Lake Shrine. A quaint Dutch-windmill house on the grounds contains a peaceful chapel. Near a sunken garden a large waterwheel splashes a leisurely music. Two marble statues from China adorn the site — a statue of Lord Buddha and one of Kwan Yin (the Chinese personification of the Divine Mother). A life-size statue of Christ, its serene face and flowing robes strikingly illuminated at night, stands on a hill above a waterfall.

A Mahatma Gandhi World Peace Memorial at the Lake Shrine was dedicated in 1950, the year that marked the thirtieth anniversary of Self-Realization Fellowship in America. A portion of the Mahatma's ashes, sent from India, was enshrined in a thousand-year-old stone sarcophagus.

A Self-Realization Fellowship "India Center" in Hollywood was founded in 1951. Mr. Goodwin J. Knight, Lieutenant Governor of California, and Mr. M. R. Ahuja, Consul General of India, joined me in the dedicatory services. On the site is India Hall, an auditorium seating 250 persons.

Newcomers to the various centers often want further light on yoga. A question I sometimes hear is this: "Is it true, as certain organizations state, that yoga may not be successfully studied in printed form but should be pursued only with the guidance of a nearby teacher?"

In the Atomic Age, yoga should be taught by a method of instruction such as the *Self-Realization Fellowship Lessons,* or the liberating science will again be restricted to a chosen few. It would indeed be a price-less boon if each student could keep by his side a guru perfected in divine wisdom; but the world is composed of many "sinners" and few saints. How then may the multitudes be helped by yoga, if not through study in their homes of instructions written by true yogis?

The only alternative is that the "average man" be ignored and left without yoga knowledge. Such is not God's plan for the new age. Babaji has promised to guard and guide all sincere *Kriya Yogis* in their path toward the Goal. Hundreds of thousands, not dozens merely, of *Kriya Yogis* are needed to bring into manifestation the world of peace and plenty that awaits men when they have made the proper effort to reestablish their status as sons of the Divine Father.

The founding in the West of a Self-Realization Fellowship organization, a "hive for the spiritual honey," was a duty enjoined on me by Sri Yukteswar and Mahavatar Babaji. The fulfillment of the sacred trust has not been devoid of difficulties.

"Tell me, truly, Paramahansaji, has it been worth it?" This laconic question was put to me one evening by Dr. Lloyd Kennell, a leader of the temple in San Diego. I understood him to mean: "Have you been happy in America? What about the falsehoods circulated by misguided people who are anxious to prevent the spread of yoga? What about the disillusionments, the heartaches, the center leaders who could not lead, the students who could not be taught?"

"Blessed is the man whom the Lord doth test!" I answered. "He has remembered, now and then, to put a burden on me." I thought, then, of all the faithful ones, of the love and devotion and understanding that illumines the heart of America. With slow emphasis I went on: "But my answer is yes, a thousand times yes! It *has* been worthwhile, more than ever I dreamed, to see East and West brought closer in the only lasting bond, the spiritual."

The great masters of India who have shown keen interest in the West have well understood modern conditions. They know that, until there is better assimilation in all nations of the distinctive Eastern and Western virtues, world affairs cannot improve. Each hemisphere needs the best offerings of the other.

In the course of world travel I have sadly observed much suffering: in the Orient, suffering chiefly on the material plane; in the Occident, misery chiefly on the mental or spiritual plane. All nations feel the painful effects of unbalanced civilizations. India and many other Eastern lands can greatly benefit from emulation of the practical grasp of affairs, the material efficiency, of Western nations like America. The Occidental peoples, on the other hand, require a deeper understanding of the spiritual basis of life, and particularly of scientific techniques that India anciently developed for man's conscious communion with God.

The ideal of a well-rounded civilization is not a chimerical one. For millenniums India was a land of both spiritual light and widespread material prosperity. The poverty of the last 200 years is, in India's long history, only a passing karmic phase. A byword in the world, century after century, was "the riches of the Indies." Abundance, material as well as spiritual, is a structural expression of *rita*, cosmic law or natural righteousness. There is no parsimony in the Divine nor in Its goddess of phenomena, exuberant Nature.

The Hindu scriptures teach that man is attracted to this particular earth to learn more completely in each successive life, the infinite ways in which the Spirit may be expressed through and dominant over, material conditions. East and West are learning this great truth in different ways, and should gladly share with each other their discoveries. Beyond all doubt it is pleasing to the Lord when His earth-children struggle to attain a world civilization free from poverty, disease, and soul ignorance. Man's forgetfulness of his divine resources (the result of his misuse of free will) is the root cause of all other forms of suffering.

The ills attributed to an anthropomorphic abstraction called "society" may be laid more realistically at the door of Everyman. Utopia must spring in the private bosom before it can flower in civic virtue, inner reforms leading naturally to outer ones. A man who has reformed himself will reform thousands.

The time-tested scriptures of the world are one in essence, inspiring man on his upward journey. One of the happiest periods of my life was spent in dictating, for *Self-Realization Magazine,* my interpretation of part of the New Testament. Fervently I implored Christ to guide me in divining the true meaning of his words, many of which have been grievously misunderstood for twenty centuries.

One night while I was engaged in silent prayer, my sitting room in the Encinitas hermitage became filled with an opal-blue light. I beheld the radiant form of the blessed Lord Jesus. A young man, he seemed, of about twenty-five, with a sparse beard and moustache; his long black hair, parted in the middle, was haloed by shimmering gold.

His eyes were eternally wondrous; as I gazed, they were infinitely changing. With each divine transition in their expression, I intuitively understood the wisdom conveyed. In his glorious gaze I felt the power that upholds the myriad worlds. A Holy Grail appeared at his mouth; it came down to my lips and then returned to Jesus. After a few moments he uttered beautiful words, so personal in their nature that I keep them in my heart.

I spent much time in 1950 and 1951 at a tranquil retreat near the Mojave Desert in California. There I translated the Bhagavad Gita and wrote a detailed commentary that presents the various paths of yoga.

Twice referring explicitly to a yogic technique (the only one mentioned in the Bhagavad Gita and the same one that Babaji named, simply, *Kriya Yoga*), India's greatest scripture has thus offered a practical as well as moral teaching. In the ocean of our dream-world, the breath is the specific storm of delusion that produces the consciousness of individual waves — the forms of men and of all other material objects. Knowing that mere philosophical and ethical knowledge is insufficient to rouse man from his painful dream of separate existence, Lord Krishna pointed out the holy science by which the yogi may master his body and convert it, at will, into pure energy. The possibility of this yogic feat is not beyond the theoretical comprehension of modern scientists, pioneers in an Atomic Age. All matter has been proved to be reducible to energy.

The Hindu scriptures extol the yogic science because it is employable by mankind in general. The mystery of breath, it is true, has occasionally been solved without the use of formal yoga techniques, as in the cases of non-Hindu mystics who possessed transcendent powers of devotion to the Lord. Such Christian, Moslem, and other saints have indeed been observed in the breathless motionless trance *(sabikalpa samadhi)*, without which no man has entered the first stages of God-perception. (After a saint has reached *nirbikalpa* or the highest *samadhi*, however, he is irrevocably established in the Lord — whether he be breathless or breathing, motionless or active.)

Brother Lawrence, the 17th-century Christian mystic, tells us his first glimpse of God-realization came about by viewing a tree. Nearly all human beings have seen a tree; few, alas, have thereby seen the tree's Creator. Most men are utterly incapable of summoning those irresistible powers of devotion that are effortlessly possessed only by a few *ekantins,* "singlehearted" saints found in all religious paths, whether of East or West. Yet the ordinary man is not therefore shut out from the possibility of divine communion. He needs, for soul recollection, no more than the *Kriya Yoga* technique, a daily observance of the moral precepts, and an ability to cry sincerely: "Lord I yearn to know Thee!"

The universal appeal of yoga is thus its approach to God through a daily usable scientific method, rather than through a devotional fervor that, for the average man, is beyond his emotional scope.

Various great Jain teachers of India have been called *tirthakaras,* "ford-makers," because they reveal the passage by which bewildered humanity may cross over and beyond the stormy seas of *samsara* (the karmic wheel, the recurrence of lives and deaths). *Samsara* (literally, "a flowing with" the phenomenal flux) induces man to take the line of least resistance. "Whosoever therefore will be a friend of the world is the enemy of God." To become the friend of God, man must overcome the devils or evils of his own karma or actions that ever urge him to spineless acquiescence in the mayic delusions of the world. A knowledge of the iron law of karma encourages the earnest seeker to find the way of final escape from its bonds. Because the karmic slavery of human beings is rooted in the desires of *maya*-darkened minds, it is with mind-control that the yogi concerns himself. The various cloaks of karmic ignorance are laid away, and man views himself in his native essence.

The mystery of life and death, whose solution is the only purpose of man's sojourn on earth, is intimately interwoven with breath. Breathlessness is deathlessness. Realizing this truth, the ancient rishis of India seized on the sole clue of the breath and developed a precise and rational science of breathlessness.

Had India no other gift for the world, *Kriya Yoga* alone would suffice as a kingly offering.

The Bible contains passages which reveal that the Hebrew prophets were well aware that God has made the breath to serve as the subtle link between body and soul. Genesis states: "The Lord God formed man of the dust of the ground, and breathed into his nostrils the breath of life; and man became a living soul." The human body is composed of chemical and metallic substances that are also found in the "dust of the ground." The flesh of man could never carry on activity nor manifest energy and motion were it not for the life currents transmitted by soul to body through the instrumentality, in unenlightened men, of the breath (gaseous energy). The life currents, operating in the human body as the fivefold *prana* or subtle life energies, are an expression of the *Aum* vibration of the omnipresent soul.

The reflection, the verisimilitude, of life that shines in the fleshly cells from the soul source is the only cause of man's attachment to his body; obviously he would not pay solicitous homage to a clod of clay. A human being falsely identifies himself with his physical form because the life currents from the soul are breath-conveyed into the flesh with such intense power that man mistakes the effect for a cause, and idolatrously imagines the body to have life of its own.

Man's conscious state is an awareness of body and breath. His subconscious state, active in sleep, is associated with his mental, and temporary, separation from body and breath. His superconscious state is a freedom from the delusion that "existence" depends on body and breath. God lives without breath; the soul made in his image becomes conscious of itself, for the first time, only during the breathless state.

When the breath-link between soul and body is severed by evolutionary karma, the abrupt transition called "death" ensues; the physical cells revert to their natural powerlessness. For the *Kriya Yogi*, however, the breath link is severed at will by scientific wisdom, not by the rude intrusion of karmic necessity. Through actual experience, the yogi is already aware of his essential incorporeity, and does not require the somewhat pointed hint given by Death that man is badly advised to place his reliance on a physical body.

Life by life, each man progresses (at his own pace, be it ever so erratic) toward the goal of his own apotheosis. Death, no interruption in this onward sweep, simply offers man the more congenial environment of an astral world in which to purify his dross. "Let not your heart be troubled. . . . In my Father's house are many mansions." It is indeed unlikely that God has exhausted His ingenuity in organizing this world, or that, in the next world, He will offer nothing more challenging to our interest than the strumming of harps.

Death is not a blotting-out of existence, a final escape from life; nor is death the door to immortality. He who has fled his Self in earthly joys will not recapture It amidst the gossamer charms of an astral world. There he merely accumulates finer perceptions and more sensitive responses to the beautiful and the good, which are one. It is on the anvil of this gross earth that struggling man must hammer out the imperishable gold of spiritual identity. Bearing in his hand the hard-won golden treasure, as the sole acceptable gift to greedy Death, a human being wins final freedom from the rounds of physical reincarnation.

For several years I conducted classes in Encinitas and Los Angeles on the *Yoga Sutras* of Patanjali and other profound works of Hindu philosophy.

"Why did God ever join soul and body?" a class student asked one evening. "What was His purpose in setting into initial motion this evolutionary drama of creation?" Countless other men have posed such questions; philosophers have sought, in vain, fully to answer them.

"Leave a few mysteries to explore in Eternity," Sri Yukteswar used to say with a smile. "How could man's limited reasoning powers comprehend the inconceivable motives of the Uncreated Absolute? The rational faculty in man, tethered by the cause-effect principle of the phenomenal world, is baffled before the enigma of God, the Beginningless, the Uncaused. Nevertheless, though man's reason cannot fathom the riddles of creation, every mystery will ultimately be solved for the devotee by God Himself."

He who sincerely yearns for wisdom is content to start his search by humbly mastering a few simple ABC's of the divine schema, not demanding prematurely a precise mathematical graph of life's "Einstein Theory."

"*No man hath seen God at any time* (no mortal under 'time,' the relativities of *maya,* can realize the Infinite); *the only begotten Son, which is in the bosom of the Father* (the reflected Christ Consciousness or outwardly projected Perfect Intelligence that, guiding all structural phenomena through *Aum* vibration, has issued forth from the 'bosom' or deeps of the Uncreated Divine in order to express the variety of Unity), *he hath declared* (subjected to form, or manifested) *him.*"

"Verily, verily, I say unto you," Jesus explained, "the Son can do nothing of himself, but what he seeth the Father do: for what things soever he doeth, these also doeth the Son likewise."

The threefold nature of God as He demonstrates Himself in the phenomenal worlds is symbolized in Hindu scriptures as Brahma the Creator, Vishnu the Preserver, and Shiva the Destroyer-Renovator. Their triune activities are ceaselessly displayed throughout vibratory creation. As the Absolute is beyond the conceptual powers of man, the devout Hindu worships It in the august embodiments of the Trinity.

The universal creative-preservative-destructive aspect of God, however, is not His ultimate or even His essential nature (for cosmic creation is only His *lila,* creative sport). His intrinsicality cannot be grasped even by grasping all the mysteries of the Trinity, because His outer nature, as manifested in the lawful atomic flux, merely expresses Him without revealing Him. The final nature of the Lord is known only when "the Son ascends to the Father." The liberated man overpasses the vibratory realms and enters the Vibrationless Original.

All great prophets have remained silent when requested to unveil the ultimate secrets. When Pilate asked: "What is truth?" Christ made no reply. The large ostentatious questions of intellectualists like Pilate seldom proceed from a burning spirit of inquiry. Such men speak rather with the empty arrogance that considers a lack of conviction about spiritual values to be a sign of "open-mindedness."

"To this end was I born, and for this cause came I into the world , that I should bear witness unto the truth. Everyone that is of the truth heareth my voice." In these few words Christ spoke volumes. A child of God "bears witness" *by his life.* He embodies truth; if he expounds it also, that is generous redundancy.

Truth is no theory, no speculative system of philosophy, no intellectual insight. Truth is exact correspondence with reality. For man, truth is unshakable knowledge of his real nature, his Self as soul. Jesus, by every act and word of his life, proved that he knew *the truth* of his being — his source in God. Wholly identified with the omnipresent Christ Consciousness, he could say with simple finality: "Everyone that is of the truth heareth my voice."

Buddha, too, refused to shed light on the metaphysical ultimates, dryly pointing out that man's few moments on earth are best employed in perfecting the moral nature. The Chinese mystic Lao-tzu rightly taught: "He who knows, tells it not; he who tells, knows it not." The final mysteries of God are not "open to discussion." The decipherment of His secret code is an art that man cannot communicate to man; here the Lord alone is the Teacher.

"Be still, and know that I am God." Never flaunting His omnipresence, the Lord is heard only in the immaculate silences. Reverberating throughout the universe as the creative *Aum* vibration, the Primal

Sound instantly translates Itself into intelligible words for the devotee in attunement.

The divine purpose of creation, so far as man's reason can grasp it, is expounded in the Vedas. The rishis taught that each human being has been created by God as a soul that will uniquely manifest some special attribute of the Infinite before resuming its Absolute Identity. All men, endowed thus with a facet of Divine Individuality, are equally dear to God.

The wisdom garnered by India, the eldest brother among the nations, is a heritage of all mankind. Vedic truth, as all truth, belongs to the Lord and not to India. The rishis, whose minds were pure receptacles to receive the divine profundities of the Vedas, were members of the human race, born on this earth, rather than on some other, to serve humanity as a whole. Distinctions by race or nation are meaningless in the realm of truth, where the only qualification is spiritual fitness to receive.

God is Love; His plan for creation can be rooted only in love. Does not that simple thought, rather than erudite reasonings, offer solace to the human heart? Every saint who has penetrated to the core of Reality has testified that a divine universal plan exists and that it is beautiful and full of joy.

To the prophet Isaiah, God revealed His intentions in these words:

> So shall my word [creative *Aum*] be that goeth forth out of my mouth: it shall not return unto me void, but it shall accomplish that which I please, and it shall prosper in the thing whereto I sent it. For ye shall go out with joy, and be led forth with peace: the mountains and the hills shall break forth before you into singing, and all the trees of the field shall clap their hands. (Isaiah 55:11-12)

"Ye shall go out with joy and be led forth with peace." The men of a hard-pressed twentieth century hear longingly that wondrous promise. The full truth within it is realizable by every devotee of God who strives manfully to repossess his divine heritage.

The blessed role of *Kriya Yoga* in East and West has hardly more than just begun. May all men come to know that there exists a definite, scientific technique of Self-realization for the overcoming of all human misery!

In sending loving thought vibrations to the thousands of *Kriya Yogis* scattered like shining jewels over the earth, I often think gratefully: "Lord, Thou hast given this monk a large family!"

THE EDUCATOR

Benjamin E. Mays

(1895-1984)

Born near the end of the nineteenth century, Benjamin Mays through his long life saw civil rights for black Americans take some great strides — not soon enough, not fast enough, and not far enough. But when he died, he left behind a world that his parents and grandparents never knew. And it was a world that he had done much to create.

Forsaking the rural poverty of his South Carolina birthplace, Mays worked his way through college in Maine (Bates, a Baptist school), then through graduate school at the University of Chicago where he received a master's degree in 1925 and his doctorate ten years later. From 1921 to 1934 he held a variety of teaching posts, as well as the pastorate of Shiloh Baptist Church in Atlanta. His professional visibility rose sharply when he became dean of the School of Religion at Howard University in 1934, a position that he filled for the next six years. Then in 1940, he assumed the presidency of Morehouse College in Atlanta; there for over a quarter of a century, he served as mentor and model for generations of African American students. Martin Luther King Jr. spoke of him as his spiritual guide.

In the midst of all these heavy duties, Mays took on ever larger responsibilities nationally and internationally. He served on the national boards of the Ford Foundation, the YMCA, the World Council of Churches, and the Baptist World Alliance. When the Progressive National Baptist Convention was organized in 1961, Mays, King, and others led in giving black Baptists a clearer voice on behalf of the civil rights movements. For, as Mays notes in his Preface to the autobiography excerpted here, "The segregated system was so cruel, so inhuman, and so destructive to the development of manhood and character that white America can never really know the damage it did to the mind and spirit of millions of Negroes who lived and died under that system." He made a similar point when he was asked to deliver the eulogy at the funeral of Martin Luther King Jr. — his former student at Morehouse College. "A century after Emancipation, and after the enactment of the 13th, 14th, and 15th Amendments, it should not have been necessary," Mays declared, "for Martin Luther King, Jr., to stage marches in Montgomery, Birmingham, and Selma, and to go to jail thirty times trying to achieve for his people those rights which people of lighter hue get by virtue of their being born white."

And it should not have been necessary for Benjamin Mays to grow up with a lynch mob as his earliest memory, nor to endure much abuse and scorn throughout a great deal of his later life. In an appreciative introduction to Mays's autobiography, Samuel DuBois Cook of the Ford Foundation wrote of Mays's many remarkable qualities: his "strength of character, gifts of mind, vision, ability to grow and courage to change, creative restlessness and zest for life, stubborn moral courage, prophetic imagination, deep commitment to social justice, boundless energy and eagerness to tackle new tasks, devotion to academic excellence, capacity for independence and critical judgment, single-minded commitment to the most precious and enduring values of the human enterprise, and lifelong romance with the world of higher possibilities." Many of these qualities can be discerned below, in portions of his chapter entitled "The Church and Race."

[See Stephen B. Oates, *Let the Trumpet Sound: The Life of Martin Luther King, Jr.* (New York: New American Library, 1982).]

The Church and Race

I believe that throughout my lifetime, the local white church has been society's most conservative and hypocritical institution in the area of White-Negro relations. Nor has the local black church a record of which to be proud. The states, schools, business enterprises, industries, theaters, recreation centers, hotels, restaurants, hospitals, trains, boats, waiting rooms, and filling stations, have all played their ignominious roles in the tragedy of segregating the black man and discriminating against him, but at least none of these enterprises claims to have a divine mission on earth. The church boasts of its unique origin, maintaining that God, not man, is the source of its existence. The church alone calls itself the House of God, sharing this honor with no other American institution. The church is indeed sui generis.

The local white churches, the vast majority of them, have not lived up to their professed Christianity, because Christian fellowship across racial barriers is so inherent in the very nature of the church that to deny fellowship in God's House, on the basis of race or color, is a profanation of all that the church stands for. Secular organizations make no commitments, nor do they prate about brotherhood among men and a gospel of redemption and salvation. When the church maintains a segregated house, and simultaneously preaches the fatherhood of God and the brotherhood of man, then surely "hypocrisy" is the mildest term we can apply. "Whited sepulchre" comes to mind.

Source: Benjamin E. Mays, *Born to Rebel* (New York: Charles Scribner's Sons, 1971), pp. 241-45; 251-56; 259-60.

Although the local black church has never denied white people the privilege of entrance for worship in their churches, and has often inflated the white man's already bloated ego by giving him preferential seating, Negro church members would hardly welcome large numbers of white people to membership in their congregations. I believe this attitude is not based so much on race, as it is on the desire of Negroes to maintain control of their churches. Then too, Negroes would hardly want to run the risk of being hurt or humiliated by whites who so often exhibit a superior air in their association with Negroes. The basic difference between the black and white churches is that the black church has never had a policy of racial exclusiveness. The white church has.

Leadership in the church is supposedly different from that in secular life. In earlier years, and even today, the minister was said to be specially "called of God" to do His work, to preach His truth. Early in my life I became aware of the dichotomy in the preaching and the practice of the church leadership. Now and then the Reverend James F. Marshall, my pastor, would invite white ministers to preach at Mount Zion, especially the Methodist minister, the Reverend Pierce Kinard. My father, though illiterate, was never impressed with the Reverend Kinard's message. He once remarked about the Reverend Kinard's emphasis on living right in order to be assured of God's blessings and of eternal salvation, while at the same time Negroes were being cheated, beaten, and lynched throughout South Carolina. As young as I was, I got the message. The few Negroes who attended the Reverend Kinard's tent meetings were thoroughly segregated. Members of my family never attended because they were Methodist meetings for whites, and, frankly, we were actually afraid to attend a white church.

The gospel in Negro and white churches alike was definitely otherworld-oriented and never even hinted at bringing whites and blacks of the county closer together for the improvement of social and economic conditions. After all, if the "righteous" were to be rewarded in heaven, where there would be no more night, no sickness, no death, where the angels had wings and the streets were paved with gold, it mattered little that black people were exploited and mistreated here on earth! The Negro's song, "Take All the World and Give Me Jesus," was never considered seriously by the white man, even though he may have believed in heaven. He had as much of Jesus as the Negro — and the world besides!

My early unhappy racial experiences explain my cynicism about the sincerity of many white ministers. I have never cared to listen to any minister who would deny fellowship on a racial basis. More than once I have turned off the radio or the television rather than listen to the preaching of a man known to advocate a segregated church. I tuned out Billy Graham as long as he held revivals under segregated conditions. When he came to Atlanta early in his career, the Council of Presidents of the Atlanta University Center was asked to provide a segregated meeting for the students and faculties of the Center. Needless, to say, we refused, and we felt it was an insult to us to be asked to do this. I listen to Billy Graham now with appreciation of what he says and the hope that he is a sincere convert of his own teaching. Segregation in the House of God has been a great strain on my religion.

In the process of writing this book, I read widely the most reputable newspapers of the South published between 1880 and 1910. I was anxious to find out what they had to say about lynching, the most vicious evil of my early years, and what their attitude was toward the Negro. I do not recall ever having seen a single article by a minister, a group of ministers, or by anyone speaking in the name of the church and Christianity that condemned the horrible crime of lynching. During this time, the church was truly both in the world and of the world. Earlier in this book, I have related in detail examples of the horrifying lynchings which took place in Phoenix, South Carolina, in the county of my birth. The Phoenix Riot, with its accompanying lynchings, is one of the most hideous records in the history of this country. One would think that somewhere, in at least one of the South Carolina newspapers, the voice of the church would have been heard speaking out for justice and stamping its disapproval upon such savagery. I found no record of a church voice raised in protest. The church was so much a part of the system that lynching was accepted as part of the Southern way of life just as casually as was segregation. Ironically enough, when the Southern people did begin to cry out against lynching, it was not the voice of organized southern and northern ministers but of southern white women under the leadership of the Commission on Interracial Cooperation. The Southern Association of Women for the Prevention of Lynching was organized in Atlanta in 1930, under the leadership of Jessie Daniel Ames, and did much to denigrate lynching in the South. Time has not done much to change the silence of the local church in the midst of racial ills.

The local white church has always been conservative when it comes to taking a stand on social issues, especially so if the issue involves black people. Local black churches have been far more prophetic than the local white churches. So-called radical movements, such as the National Association for the Advancement of Colored People, have always had access to black churches. The Southern Christian Leadership Conference, under the leadership of Martin Luther King, Jr., and, since 1968, under Ralph David Abernathy, and the National Conference of Black Churchmen have involved the local Negro churches in programs designed to bring about social and economic justice for black people. But North and South, Negro and white churches remain highly segregated. A thoroughly desegregated church, embracing a representative number of blacks and whites, is a *rara avis* in the United States.

In the area of race, local churches have followed, not led. When segregation in the public schools was declared unconstitutional on May 17, 1954, one would have expected the local churches to urge compliance on moral and religious grounds. But for too long a time the local white ministers in Atlanta and in other Southern cities were silent, and when they did speak it was as a group. For the most part, the individual pastor was afraid to urge compliance, afraid to stand alone. He wanted protection from the group as well as the benefit of the impact that the group might make if he were to speak out.

The local Atlanta white ministers certainly did not lead in a program to abolish segregation in the public schools. Indeed, it can hardly be said that they even followed. It was three and a half years after the May 17, 1954, decision of the Supreme Court before some eighty white ministers in Atlanta broke their silence on the Court's decision. It is disgraceful that it took the Atlanta white ministers forty-two months to come out with a statement on segregation in the public schools, and it is even more shameful that when they did speak it was only as individuals, for they did not dare speak for their congregations. They felt that they had to say they were opposed to intermarriage and against the amalgamation of the races. They expressed belief in "preserving the integrity of both races through the free choice of both." It is utterly fantastic for white ministers to speak for white men against the amalgamation of the races. The white man's activities in this area of behavior are a matter of history the world around. The black race in America has been amalgamated for centuries. I suppose these men of the cloth felt compelled to say such things to please the white public.

Speaking three and a half years after the 1954 decision outlawing segregation in the public schools, the white ministers of Atlanta issued a statement both weak and inconclusive. They said, in part:

As Americans and as Christians we have an obligation to obey the law. This does not mean that all loyal citizens need approve the 1954 decision of the Supreme Court with reference to segregation in the public schools. Those who feel that this decision was in error have every right to work for an alteration in the decree, either through a further change in the Supreme Court's interpretation of the law, or through an amendment to the Constitution of the United States. It does mean that we have no right to defy the constituted authority in the government of our nation. Assuredly also it means that resorts to violence and to economic reprisals as a means to avoid the granting of legal rights to other citizens are never justified.

If I had been a segregationist, I could have freely signed this document.

A year later 312 Atlanta ministers spoke somewhat more pointedly to the issue at hand. This group was speaking in the interest of preserving the public schools. These ministers were also cautious. They were against massive integration and sincerely opposed to the amalgamation of the races. They pleaded for time where desegregation of schools was most difficult and expressed the hope that state and local authorities would be allowed to do the job when good faith in compliance had been shown. This group, too, urged law and order, and said that those who were dissatisfied with the decision should seek legal ways to change it. They insisted, however, that closing the public schools would be a tragedy.

All in all, their November, 1958, manifesto was a plea for gradualism. It called for intelligent discussion of the issues of integration, asked that creative thought be given to preserving the public schools, and advocated a citizens' committee to preserve harmony within the community. It was clearly not a manifesto for integration but rather one for law and Christian duty. And its sponsors did what "Christian" and "religious" people usually do when they lack the will to act: They called on God. They said, "Man cannot will himself to do this. The Christian, or Jew, can do this only with the help of God." They called for prayer and the strength to do it. It is indeed strange that when man does evil, he has the will, but when he faces a moral crisis and needs to do what is right, he calls on God to give him the strength to do it.

Although my career has been in education for thirty-four years and in research and social work for six years, I have been fortunate in having extensive contact — local, national, and worldwide — with the church and the Young Men's Christian Association. National and world gatherings have been more Christian in character than have local ones, in that fellowship has never been denied. Even when national bodies have been all too cautious, in an effort to placate those coming from segregated sections of the country or the world, and those who are dyed-in-the-wool segregationists, fellowship across racial barriers in assembly and worship has always obtained. This has been true in the score or more national and world gatherings in which I have been a participant. However, it must be remembered that national and world gatherings are not empowered to pass resolutions which are binding on local bodies, and so are not subject to the same pressures. Nor do I mean to imply that race has not been a problem in national and world church bodies.

For the race problem is ubiquitous; and I have never been able to escape it. It came up in every national and world Christian conference I ever attended. It is ever present. One often hears that Negroes never forget the race problem, that they talk about it all the time. This is equally true of white people. In church and state alike, the black man has been continually in the white man's mind. One need only read anti-Negro newspapers reaching back a hundred years, and anti-Negro books written over the decades, or study the laws the various states and the federal government have enacted against the Negro to find that the black man has dominated the white man's thinking since the first Africans landed here in 1619. The Negro, I am convinced, is the white man's obsession.

The black-white relationship has been so crucial that black and white alike are inclined to attach great significance to any slight breakthrough a black man may make in this relationship. Thus it was national news when the Federal Council of Churches of Christ in America elected me its vice-president in Pittsburgh, Pennsylvania, in 1944. It was national news because it was the first time that the Federal Council, organized in 1912, had chosen a black man to serve in the second spot of the Council. The president of the Federal Council at that time was Bishop G. Bromley Oxnam of the Methodist Church. The Negro and the white press headlined my election, and *Time* magazine called me a "religious liberal," citing as proof that though I was a Baptist I had never tried to convert my Methodist wife to the Baptist faith!

I became widely known in church circles, and was invited to speak to white and black groups all over the nation, in state and city federations of churches — even in church councils in the South, especially in Virginia and North Carolina, and in the Baptist Convention of Florida. I was not invited to the local white churches, for few such churches in the South, in the mid-1940's, would have dared invite a black man to preach to them. I doubt that a single one would have had the temerity. Even to this day, excluding Glenn Memorial on Emory University's campus, only two white churches in Atlanta and vicinity have ever invited me to speak to their congregations — Trinity Presbyterian Church in Atlanta and Saint Paul United Methodist Church in Marietta. And Atlanta has been my home for thirty years.

Two experiences which happened during my two years as vice-president of the Federal Council are worth relating here.

First, the Council held a special meeting in Columbus, Ohio, March 5-7, 1946. President Truman was a guest speaker. Winston Churchill was traveling on the presidential train with Truman. Mr. Churchill chose to remain on the train while the President spoke to the delegates of the Federal Council. The officers of the Council thought it would be a good gesture if we went down to the train to greet Winston Churchill, and we did. He showed no particular enthusiasm for our visit, and I thought he received us rather coldly. Consequently, I felt no particular enthusiasm for nor was I impressed by this great man.

Though vice-president of the Council, I evidently posed a problem to some of the Council leadership. Where was I to sit — on the platform with the President of the United States or in a special seat up front in the audience? I have always wondered whether there would have been any debate if the vice-president of the Council had been white. As the second officer in the Council, I should have helped decide who would sit on the rostrum. The decision was made for me to sit in the front row, in the audience. Several rows in front were being left for dignitaries and secret service men. I was advised to take my seat in the front row before the presidential party came in and before other guests had taken the reserved seats.

Several persons came to request me to move, saying that the place where I was sitting was reserved for special people. I didn't move. Finally Earl F. Adams, secretary of the Protestant Council of New York, came to me and said, "Why are you sitting here? As vice-president of the Council, you belong on the rostrum with the President of the United States." He said, "Wait, I'll fix it." Another chair was placed on the rostrum and, when the President came in, I was escorted to the rostrum. Evidently I had presented a problem which Earl Adams solved. People in the audience had wondered why I didn't move as requested. When I went to the rostrum, the mystery seemed solved. They thought it was planned from the beginning that I would sit on the rostrum. Not so.

Secondly, at the same Conference, the Federal Council took a giant step. It issued an official document stating in forceful language that it was opposed to segregation in any form and that the Council from that moment on would work to eliminate it. This was, I believe, the first time the Federal Council had made such a declaration, and so was assuming national leadership among church bodies. It was significant, too, that Will W. Alexander, who had been head of the Commission on Interracial Cooperation until the new organization, the Southern Regional Council, was organized, was chairman of the seminar on race. The Commission on Interracial Cooperation never did declare itself against the segregated system. The seminar on race of the Federal Council, chaired by Alexander, raised its voice in opposition to segregation in every area of life. I think it important to quote one paragraph of a document from the seminar on church and race of which I was a member:

> The Federal Council of the Churches of Christ in America hereby renounces the pattern of segregation in race relations as unnecessary and undesirable and a violation of the gospel of love and human brotherhood. Having taken this action, the Federal Council requests its constituent communion to do likewise. As proof of their sincerity in this renunciation, they will work for a non-segregated church and a non-segregated society.

I was glad to see Will Alexander move to this position. He fought for this statement vigorously, and I am mighty glad that I was a member of the seminar that assisted in its formulation. The Federal Council, and now the National Council, never retreated from this position. The National Council has gone beyond mere pronouncements to participation in the arena where the action is. It has taken a leading role in such action projects as: The Delta Ministry; The Ghetto Investment Program; the Crisis in the Nation Program; and The Mississippi Summer Project on Voter Registration. It has also been active in the field of legislation, has participated in Project Equality, and given encouragement to the National Urban Coalition.

Two years after my term as vice-president of the Federal Council of Churches of Christ in America expired, I was a participant in the organization of the World Council of Churches in Amsterdam, Holland, in 1948. Unfortunately, the Second World War had made it necessary to delay the establishment of this great body. The seed of ecumenism, however, had been germinating for a long time. The historic moment came the second day of the Assembly, August 23, 1948, when delegates from 750 communions and 43 countries voted unanimously to organize the World Council of Churches. It was a great moment, and the delegates and visitors cheered long and lustily.

The United States was so heavily segregated in 1948 that I was always glad to get a breath of fresh air somewhere in Europe. Since the people in the Assembly came from the ends of the earth, there could not possibly be any segregation or discrimination. All hotels, restaurants, streetcars, churches, and government organizations were opened to everybody, a thing unheard of in most sections of the United States. One would have to be in an Assembly of the World Church really to know what Christian fellowship is. Segregated and discriminated against all my life, I believe that I can sense any form of discrimination instinctively. I found none in Amsterdam. At a communion service, I noted a Methodist sitting next to a Baptist, an Anglican sitting next to a Presbyterian, a Chinese communing beside a Japanese, an American white man seated with an American Negro, and an African communing with a Dutchman. As I sat there in the World Church, my mind reverted sadly to the United States, where local churches were the most segregated bodies in our country.

The same catholicity obtained in social affairs. The reception given by Her Majesty's government and the one given by the burgomaster and the aldermen of the City of Amsterdam were lovely, representing all shades and colors, ranging from the pure black to the lightest of the light. One of the persons to introduce the attendants to the burgomaster was an African delegate.

Despite the fact that this delegation of 450 people was mainly ecumenical, designed to bring about the unity of the non-Catholic churches, the race problem is so universal that it has to be considered whenever people meet. Thus in several sections, race prejudice and discrimination were condemned. Section I of the Assembly's "The Universal Church in God's Design" said: "Even where there are no differences of theology, language, or liturgy, there exist churches segregated by race and color, a scandal within the Body of Christ." From Section III, dealing with "Disorder of

Society," came these words: "if the church can overcome the national and social barriers which now divide it, it can help society to overcome those barriers. This is especially clear in the case of racial barriers. It is here that the church has failed most lamentably — it knows that it must call society away from racial prejudice and from the practice of discrimination and segregation based on color and race as denials of justice and human dignity, but it cannot say a convincing word to society unless it takes steps to eliminate these from the Christian community because they contradict all that it believes about God's love for all his children."

When participating in a World Church gathering, black people often need to see to it that the church takes a strong position on race, and also that Negroes are not left out when offices and positions are being voted on. In world gatherings, as elsewhere, the Negro is likely to be the forgotten man. Several times in plenary sessions at Amsterdam, I or some other black man had to see to it that a section dealing with race was strengthened. On this point, the Pittsburgh *Courier* reported my own stand as follows:

> Dr. Benjamin E. Mays, president of Morehouse College and *Courier* columnist, electrified the World Council of Churches here last week when he vigorously proposed amending a resolution involving the Universal Church to include a specific attitude on the racial situation within the Church proper. His amendment was passed. Noting that the report on *The Universal Church in God's Design* covered the racial aspect throughout the world in just ten words, Dr. Mays took the floor of the assembly and proposed the following amendment:

> > In addition to differences in theology which divide the Universal Church, it is further divided into racial churches based entirely on race and color. It is to be regretted that this division is so deeply established that even where there is unity in theology, creed, ritual, liturgy and language, we find the body of Christ divided on grounds of race and color. This condition must be strongly condemned by the World Council of Churches and it should urge the churches to eliminate this condition within its fellowship.

There were six of us as delegates representing the National Baptist Convention, Incorporated. On discovering that a central committee of ninety persons was to be the official voice of the World Council between Assemblies (a five-year interval), we knew that the National Baptist Convention, Incorporated, despite its four million members, would not be represented unless we pushed for membership.

So I called our delegation together and we worked out a strategy. Fortunately, the chairman of the nominating group saw the reasonableness of our attitude and I and another American Negro were chosen. From 1948 to 1954, when the Second Assembly of the World Council of Churches met in Evanston at Northwestern University, I represented the Central Committee in Rolle, Switzerland; Chichester, England; Toronto, Canada; and Lucknow, India.

~

The Central Committee meetings in Rolle, Switzerland, in 1951, and in Lucknow, India, in 1952 and 1953, moved along about like other world gatherings. There was no segregation and no discrimination based on racial and ethnic origins. My great experience in Lucknow came when reporters from all over India questioned me for ninety minutes, not quite believing me when I gave evidence that Negro-white relations were better at that time in the United States than they had been when I was in India in 1937.

Back home again we had to answer the question: Where in the United States could we meet and be certain that Negroes and other dark people would not be humiliated and embarrassed in hotels, motels, and restaurants? We wanted to meet on some campus where facilities were adequate and space ample. Bishop G. Bromley Oxnam, one of the six vice-presidents of the World Council, and a leader of note in the movement, was anxious to have the assembly on a Methodist university campus. We examined the situation at Duke University in Durham, North Carolina. The university was satisfactory, but as no guarantee could be given that there would be no discrimination in Durham, Duke was out. Some Eastern campuses were ruled out for lack of space for all the activities of the Second Assembly. Bishop Oxnam was threatening to use his power to take the Assembly back to Europe. Some of us protested. Finally Northwestern University, in Evanston, Illinois, was chosen as the place for the Second Assembly of the World Council of Churches, August 14-31, 1954.

THE PACIFIST

Dorothy Day

(1897-1980)

Dorothy Day was a most remarkable social reformer: remarkable in her fervor, in her steady devotion to the causes she deemed significant, and in her unwillingness to compromise or retreat. She did not preach sermons on poverty: she fed the poor. She did not appoint a committee to explore the problems of the homeless; she built hospitality houses to care for them, and died herself in one of her homes for the homeless. She did not issue pronouncements on race; she created and lived in the midst of a caring interracial community. She did not merely condemn war, but went to jail countless times for refusing to support the war effort in any form, even civil defense. Her legacy was her life.

Born in Brooklyn, she moved with her family to San Francisco, then Chicago, and — on her own — back to New York. At the age of thirty, she converted to Roman Catholicism and, like many a new convert, took her Catholicism with a seriousness that confounded or even angered those whose religious commitment was somewhat more relaxed. Under the influence of Peter Maurin, a French-born Catholic philosopher, she moved toward ways of melding her religious faith and her political-moral vision into a "Reconstruction of the Social Order," to use the title of a 1931 papal encyclical that Day found congenial and supportive. In 1933 she and Maurin launched a penny newspaper, *The Catholic Worker,* in imitation of and in response to the Marxist *Daily Worker.* Appearing in the midst of America's deep depression, her paper found a ready audience and its circulation leaped from a few thousand to 150,000 in just three years. Readers — jobless, homeless, hopeless — eagerly searched for whatever solution or solace Christian love might have to offer.

Some readers, of course, were shocked. *The Catholic Worker* must be Communist, or Communist-inspired. The Houses of Hospitality were radical communes, reveling in their poverty rather than curing it. The interracial character of Day's movement offended some, and her pacifism — especially during World War II — offended even more. Americans knew of pacifists, but they were mainly visible in small Protestant sects such as the Mennonites and the Church of the Brethren. But the huge Roman Catholic Church a pacifist institution? Of course, it was not, and many bishops took pains to separate themselves openly and, if necessary, repeatedly from Dorothy Day and her movement.

She was not being realistic, they said. She was a mere sentimentalist, they added. Pacifism had no place in the epic struggle for human decency and moral values. But on that point, Day had her opponents just where she wanted them. When it came to moral crusades, the bishops proved to be the real pacifists. She had been fighting for human decency and moral values for ten years, or more, and what had she been faced with? Pacifism. Indifference. Cold neglect. Too many Roman Catholics seemed content to leave the fate of the hungry, the homeless, and the destitute to the Communists and the Salvation Army. Dorothy Day was not. She believed in revolution, but a revolution of love, not hate.

[See William D. Miller, *Dorothy Day: A Biography* (New York: Harper & Row, 1982); and June E. O'Connor, *The Moral Vision of Dorothy Day* (New York: Crossroad, 1991).]

"War Is the Health of the State"

One Christmas at the close of World War II, we received a card from the Rochester group saying that they had liked *The Catholic Worker* much better before the pacifists got hold of it. Another letter came from Boston, from an elderly worker who had been responsible for the first house of hospitality in Boston. She too reproached me for the extremism of our revolutionary pacifist position. She was a good trade unionist and was thinking in terms of the immediate steps to be taken, while we tried to keep the vision of a new social order, brought about by peaceful means.

It struck me then how strange a thing it was; here we had been writing about pacifism for fifteen years and members of two of our groups were just beginning to realize what it meant.

We had been pacifist in class war, race war, in the Ethiopian war, in the Spanish Civil War, all through World War II, as we are now during the Korean war. We had spoken in terms of the Sermon on the Mount and all of our traders were familiar enough with that. We had lost subscriptions and bundle orders, but these cancellations came

---

Source: Dorothy Day, *The Long Loneliness* (New York: Harper & Row, 1952), pp. 263-73.

from those who frankly disagreed with us and the matter was settled at once.

But there were a very great many who had seemed to agree with us who did not realize for years that *The Catholic Worker* position implicated them; if they believed the things we wrote, they would be bound, sooner or later, to make decisions personally and to act upon them.

Union workers in steel plants, auto and airplane factories — many in industry and business would have to find other jobs, jobs not tied up with the war effort. And where could they get them? If they worked in the garment factories, they would have to fill government orders for uniforms. Mills turned out blankets, parachutes. Raising food, building houses, baking bread — whatever you did you kept the wheels of industrial capitalism moving, and industrial capitalism kept the wheels moving on war orders. You could not live without compromise. Teachers sold war stamps and bonds. Children were asked to bring aluminum pots and scrap metal to school. The Pope asked that war be kept out of the schools, but there it was.

We wrote as much as we could on the subject, and Father John J. Hugo wrote articles and pamphlets — "The Immorality of Conscription." "Catholics Can Be Conscientious Objectors," "The Weapons of the Spirit," "The Gospel of Peace." The last two were printed as *Catholic Worker* pamphlets under the imprimatur of the Archdiocese of New York.

In Europe, Father Stratman, a Belgian Dominican, wrote *The Church and War* and *Peace and the Clergy,* and Father Ude of Austria wrote a monumental book, *"Thou Shalt Not Kill."* Only the first two appeared in English. All of these set forth our stand.

In addition to the theological articles in our own paper, many young men wrote of war and peace. The most lively articles we published were those of Ammon Hennacy, Christian anarchist, a modern Thoreau in his monthly account of his life on the land. He began with a series on his term, largely spent in solitary confinement, in Atlanta Penitentiary during World War I, where he met Alexander Berkman and studied American history and anarchism with him. Ammon had been a Socialist before he was won by the personalist approach of Berkman. Forced to rely on himself, he recognized the importance of beginning with oneself, starting here and now, and not waiting for someone else to start the revolution. He became a pacifist even in the class war and he came to see the dangers of the modern state, and the inefficiency and waste of bureaucracy.

Reading the Bible while he was in solitary confinement, he was completely won by the Sermon on the Mount and all the teachings of Jesus. Upon reading Tolstoi he recognized himself as a Christian anarchist and from then on, Tolstoi, Gandhi and Jesus became his teachers. Organized religion, as he calls it, he rejects.

"He has seen so great a light, it has blinded him," the rector of a seminary said to me after reading his articles.

(Ammon is not the only non-Catholic contributor to *The Catholic Worker*. Fritz Eichenberg, a Quaker artist, contributes many illustrations, great in their understanding and compassion.)

Ammon's articles were always personal, since he wrote of what he knew, himself and his own experience. His life in jail, his work on dairy farms in Colorado and New Mexico, and on truck farms in Arizona have constituted a moving series about "Life at Hard Labor" and show how a man can live without compromise, and yet earn a living. For years he has paid no income tax. He worked by the day at the "stoop labor" the Mexicans usually performed, at irrigating, at ditchdigging, wood chopping, cotton picking.

He has supported himself and his two daughters, sending both through Northwestern University and in addition to his back-breaking work and his writing, he has found time to sell *The Catholic Worker* at churches and public meetings every week.

He has fasted and prayed for peace; he has picketed the tax collector's office twice a year. For the last few years on the anniversary of the dropping of the atomic bomb he has fasted as penance for six days, picketing the Internal Revenue office at Phoenix while he fasted, and distributing literature. Ammon considers himself a propagandist, an agitator, a one-man revolution. I doubt that he has ever considered himself a sociologist or an anthropologist, yet he could be classed in these categories too. His articles on the Indians of the Southwest, especially the Hopi, who are anarchist and pacifist, are of vital interest.

Ammon is fifty-eight, a tall lank Ohioan of tremendous physical strength and endurance. For all of us at the Catholic Worker headquarters, he epitomizes the positive pacifist. He is trying to change conditions that bring about wars, and as he does not accept from Caesar, he does not render to Caesar. With all his absolutism and certitude, he is friendly and lovable, truly looking upon all as his brothers, overcoming opposition by understanding and affection.

On the other hand, Bob Ludlow, one of the editors of the paper, a convert to the Catholic Church, has been the theorist of our pacifism for the past five years. Son of a Scranton coal miner, educated by the

Christian Brothers, he was converted by reading Newman. All his life he has been a student and teacher, and knows little of manual labor. When we have gotten him to work a few hours in our asparagus patch or to mend a leaky faucet, he has felt triumphant for weeks. He has cared for the babies of one of our Catholic Worker families, however, sitting helplessly in the middle of the kitchen while they circled like wild savages around him, and he has walked for miles on picket lines.

During the war, he served as a conscientious objector in the Rosewood Training School at Owings Mills, Maryland, working twelve hours a day, seven days a week, among human monstrosities and idiots as well as "children" with varying degrees of feeble-mindedness. Once every month he had an accumulated four days off which he spent with us in New York, helping us to catch up on correspondence and filing. This went on for three years.

Since the end of the war he has written a monthly article which has aroused our readers to the consciousness that they also are involved in the duty of making moral judgments, that they must begin to think, not only of the pacifism of the Sermon on the Mount, but of the natural law.

Robert is doctrinaire and dogmatic, sometimes belligerent in tone so that we find ourselves in hot water and are forced to reconsider and re-present our position. And yet he is the mildest of mortals, meek and disciplined in his personal life, ready to withdraw or subside, to hold his position alone, if need be, accepting without question the authority of the Church, yet determined to call attention to, and take advantage of, the freedom in the Church to discuss, question, and clarify the stand various theologians have taken on finance capitalism, the state, and on war and the morality of the means used in war.

His writings have aroused the conscience, have spotlighted attention on the grave questions of freedom and authority.

In the last generation, Chesterton, Belloc, Eric Gill and Father Vincent McNabb were the great distributists who opposed the servile state, the "providential state" as Pius XII recently called it. Of the four only Eric Gill was a pacifist and anarchist. The others would have feared the word, "anarchist," and understood it only in its popular connotation. I myself would prefer the word "libertarian," as less apt to offend. But I do not like to censor the writings of the editors. Peter used to say, "It makes to think." Peter himself liked to shock people, and one article of his entitled "Feed the Poor, Starve the Bankers" did lose us a very good friend. He called himself an anarchist, but privately however. He liked the term Christian Communist, but when that too was misunderstood, he called himself a communitarian.

Bob's anarchism, however, has provoked much thought and has forced many a student to realize that there were other positions on the left besides that of the Marxist.

When correspondents ask him how we can do without government, he says,

Both among Catholics and anarchists in general a great deal of misunderstanding comes about by a confusion of the terms State, government and society. Father Luigi Sturzo's book *Inner Laws of Society* is the best Catholic treatment of the subject I have read. He brings out the point that the State is only *one* form of government. When you analyze what anarchists advocate (particularly the anarcho-syndicalists) it really boils down to the advocacy of decentralized self-governing bodies. It *is* a form of government.

The confusion results because some anarchist writers use the term government as synonymous with the term State and will make the categorical statement that they do not believe in government, meaning by that the State.

The State is government by *representation* (when it is a democracy) but there is no reason why a Catholic must believe that people must be governed by representatives — the Catholic is free to believe one way or the other as is evident from St. Thomas' treatment of law in the Summa Theologica. In Question 90, Art. 3, St. Thomas states: A law, properly speaking, regards first and foremost the order to the common good. Now to order anything to the common good belongs *either* to the whole people, or to someone who is the viceregent of the whole people. Hence, the making of law belongs either to the whole people or to a public personage who has care of the whole people; for in all other matters the directing of anything to the end concerns him to whom the end belongs.

Anarchists believe that the *whole* people composing a community should take care of what governing is to be done rather than have a distant and centralized State do it. You can see from the quotation from St. Thomas there is nothing heretical about such a belief. It certainly is possible for a Christian to be an anarchist. As to government proceeding from sin, St. Augustine distinguishes between coercive government and directive government. The former he says is the result of sin. The latter is not, as man is a social being. It could be said that anarchists advocate directive government (mutual aid) but reject coercive government (the State).

Our Lord taught us to pray "Thy kingdom come on earth as it is in heaven" — in other words the nearer earthly government approximates what things are in heaven the more Christian it is. I do believe — whether it can be realized or not — that the anarchist society approaches nearer to this ideal than do other forms of government. As the Christian lives in hope so may we set this as the idea, towards which we work even if it seems as impractical as Calvary.

Bob is one of the most disciplined members of the Catholic Worker family. He needs no rules, no laws — he imposes a very rigid regime on himself. Like Peter Maurin, he follows a rule and it seldom varies. He attends seven o'clock Mass, which means rising a little after six, walks a mile to the post office for the mail and a mile back. His breakfast is a bowl of cereal. From nine until five he is at his desk, aside from half an hour after lunch when he goes to his room to say the Little Office of the Blessed Mother. In the evening he reads from six to ten-thirty, goes out for coffee and a short walk, and is in bed at eleven. You can set your clock by him. Over his desk hangs a picture of the Blessed Virgin and a newsprint photograph of Gandhi.

In stating the Catholic Worker pacifist position, Bob puts it this way:

The question of pacifism may be treated from the natural or supernatural viewpoint. From the natural viewpoint it derives its validity from reason, and natural morality, which is derived from the nature of man, is susceptible of development in that we understand more its implications as we understand more the nature of man. From an ethical and psychological standpoint it seems evident that pacifism, as exemplified in non-violent procedure, is more reasonable than is violent procedure, and therefore is more in accord with man's nature which differs from sub-human nature precisely in that man is capable of rationality.

As the Catholic religion is not in opposition to nature but rather completes and confirms nature it would seem then that there could be no opposition between a pacifism basing its validity on man's reason and the official teaching of the Church.

The supernatural viewpoint takes into consideration the revelation of Christ. Here we find that, in the early Church, there was division of opinion. Some of the early saints and Fathers were definitely pacifist. All were critical of the army. The general rule of the early Church was that one who was baptized should not join the army. Those who were already in the army when baptized were admonished to shed no blood even in a war. So there has been a tradition of pacifism in the Church, though this has fallen into obscurity and awaits doctrinal development to become explicit. Some of this tradition survives in canon law wherein the clergy are forbidden to shed blood. The increasing horror and immorality of modern war which, because of the means used, necessitate the slaying of the innocent, should serve to recall this latent pacifist tradition so that the Sermon on the Mount will be seen to confirm and sanction non-violent procedure which is already sanctioned by reason.

If it is remarked that pacifism places too much of a burden on the ordinary Catholic it can then be replied in truth that it places not so much a burden as does Catholic sexual morality with its day to day difficulties and the heroism it requires of many in these days. And yet the Church will not compromise in this regard. It would seem that the day must come when we refuse to compromise on this matter of war — otherwise we will sink to sub-human bestiality and will most certainly stray far from the spirit of Christ.

What would you do if an armed maniac were to attack you, your child, your mother? How many times have we heard this. Restrain him, of course, but not kill him. Confine him if necessary. But perfect love casts out fear and love overcomes hatred. All this sounds trite but experience is not trite.

On one occasion an armed maniac did try to kill Arthur Sheehan, one of our editors during the war. A victim of World War I, who had already assaulted several other men in the house and almost broken my wrist one day when I tried to turn off the radio in the kitchen, took a large breadknife and a crucifix and announced he was going to kill Arthur. Another woman and I seized him, forcing him to drop the knife. We could not hold him, however, and after he had hurled a gallon can of vegetables at Arthur and smashed a hole in the wall, we restrained him long enough to allow Arthur to escape. We called the police, and asked that Harry be confined to Bellevue for observation, but since we would not bring charges against him, the hospital released him the next day. Later we persuaded them to keep him for a month in the psychiatric ward. He was returned to the hospital, but at the end of thirty days he was out again, and continued to eat on our breadline during the war. Some time later we heard that he had shipped out on an oil tanker.

There were many other incidents that would have resulted in violence if moral force had not been substituted for coercion, which would have resulted in greater trouble.

David Mason was another pacifist member of our group. David came from Philadelphia, where he had been one of the leaders of the house of hospitality there, to work during the war in our New York house. A large stout man, forty-five at that time, with white hair and a peculiar short-stepping gait as though his legs were not properly matched to his big body, he was a paternal figure around the place when most of the young men were called. He served as one of the editors of the paper, took care of the mail, wrote articles, cooked meals. In fact, he was cooking the evening the FBI came to pick him up for failure to report.

I was away on a speaking trip at the time but I can imagine the picture. Two men drove up to the house at Mott Street and stalked in looking very official.

"Where is David Mason?"

"Upstairs in the kitchen. Shall we get him?"

"No, we will get him," and the two agents went through the long hall, the courtyard, up the stairs, and found David, an apron around his large middle, making gelatine for the evening dessert.

"And that night we had gelatine at the Federal House of Detention," he said ruefully, "and it was like leather, not as good as mine."

They kept him only a few weeks, much to his regret. He was obviously not the physical material our infantry needs. "I wanted to write a book," he said as they released him. He came back to the soup kitchen and editorial office instead. Arthur Sheehan, who was exempt as a former tuberculosis patient, is now working for CARE and David for a new Catholic daily.

Younger men, such as Tom Sullivan from our Chicago house, who went to war and served in the Pacific, and Jack English, formerly of our Cleveland house, another veteran, will not call themselves pacifist, though Tom is an editor of our pacifist paper. Tom was brought up on the West Side of Chicago and his heart is always with the underdog. He would scoff at the idea of being called a mystic, but I can only explain his attitude toward war on mystical grounds. He agrees with the condemnation of the means used in modern war. He probably would never lift a hand to injure another man, but his attitude is that if other men have to suffer in the war, he will suffer with them.

He poses the question — how explain the two thousand years of Christianity during which time Crusades were preached, wars were fought with the blessing of the Church, and warriors were canonized?

"I do not consider myself strong enough to court martyrdom," he says, "and that is what it means if atheistic communism wins out. Since nobody seems to be using the spiritual weapons you are always talking about, we may have to use the material ones."

He says nothing about means and ends. He is leaving that to the theologians. And his is the general opinion of the rank and file in the church today.

It is a matter of grief to me that most of those who are Catholic Workers are not pacifists, but I can see too how good it is that we always have this attitude represented among us. We are not living in an ivory tower.

Jack English suffered more in the war than the others. A gunner on a bomber, he was shot down and spent a year in a Rumanian prison camp. He was rescued by the Russians, only to go through the blitz in London. Jack has theologian friends whose opinions keep him away from the extreme pacifist position.

Tony Aratari, also from a prison camp, Charlie McCormick, Joe Monroe, members of the Catholic Worker group, and younger men in their early twenties just with us to help as long as the draft board permits, talk the issue over constantly. Can there be a just war? Can the conditions laid down by St. Thomas ever be fulfilled? What about the morality of the use of the atom bomb? What does God want me to do? And what am I capable of doing? Can I stand out against state and Church? Is it pride, presumption, to think I have the spiritual capacity to use spiritual weapons in the face of the most gigantic tyranny the world has ever seen? Am I capable of enduring suffering, facing martyrdom? And alone?

Again the long loneliness to be faced.

THE SCHOOLGIRL

Mary McCarthy

(1912-1987)

Some memoirs are unforgettable because of the experiences they relate, others because of the superior quality of the writing. Mary McCarthy's "memories" happily fall in the second category. With rich humor and a lively style, McCarthy invites us into her parochial school and into her youthful crisis concerning the eternal salvation — or more likely the eternal damnation — of her Protestant grandfather whom she deeply loved.

But before that, in a long Note to the Reader, the author tells of the reactions to her autobiographical reflections (they were first published serially in a magazine, before appearing in book form). The Catholic laity, she reported, detested her memories, regarding them as cheap, bigoted, and poisonous. "I have sometimes thought," McCarthy writes, "that Catholicism is a religion not suited to the laity, or not suited, at any rate, to the American laity, in whom it seems to bring out some of the worst traits in human nature and to lend them a sort of sanctification." On the other hand, the priests and nuns who wrote to her found her work sincere, probing, brilliant. "None of these correspondents," she notes, "feels obliged to try to convert me; they seem to leave that to God to worry about."

Though in her maturity a "lapsed Catholic," Mary McCarthy professed her continuing gratitude for a Catholic education that taught her Latin, introduced her to the treasures of western civilization, and even gave her some understanding of theology. She rather pitied those lacking this background. "Having to learn a little theology as an adult is like being taught the Bible as Great Literature in a college humanities course; it does not stick to the ribs. Yet most students in America have no other recourse than to take these vitamin injections to make good the cultural deficiency."

Born in the West (Seattle, Washington), Mary McCarthy lived much of her life in the East and abroad, in France. A caustic reviewer and a sparkling writer, she wrote several novels, among them being the hilariously satirical *Groves of Academe* (1952) and *The Group* (1953), loosely based on her own undergraduate education at Vassar (A.B., 1933). She also contributed to the *New Yorker, Harper's, Encounter,* and other publications. Her work in its totality, *Newsweek* concluded, entitled her "to be called our only real woman of letters." That judgment may well be challenged, but few would question her liveliness — either in her writing or in her life. Orphaned at the age of six, she was reared by a rather severe great-aunt and uncle. Her parochial school experience, deliciously described below, comes from this period of her life.

[See Irvin Stock, *Mary McCarthy* (Minneapolis: University of Minnesota Press, 1968).]

The Blackguard

Were he living today, my Protestant grandfather would be displeased to hear that the fate of his soul had once been the occasion of intense theological anxiety with the Ladies of the Sacred Heart. While his mortal part, all unaware, went about its eighteen holes of golf, its rubber of bridge before dinner at the club, his immortal part lay in jeopardy with us, the nuns and pupils of a strict convent school set on a wooded hill quite near a piece of worthless real estate he had bought under the impression that Seattle was expanding in a northerly direction. A sermon delivered at the convent by an enthusiastic Jesuit had disclosed to us his danger. Up to this point, the disparity in religion between my grandfather and myself had given me no serious concern. The death of my parents, while it had drawn us together in many senses, including the legal one (for I became his ward), had at the same time left the gulf of a generation between us, and my grandfather's Protestantism presented itself as a natural part of the grand, granite scenery on the other side. But the Jesuit's sermon destroyed this ordered view in a single thunderclap of doctrine.

As the priest would have it, this honest and upright man, a great favorite with the Mother Superior, was condemned to eternal torment by the accident of having been baptized. Had he been a Mohammedan, a Jew, a pagan, or the child of civilized unbelievers, a place in Limbo would have been assured him; Cicero and Aristotle and Cyrus the Per-

---

Source: Mary McCarthy, *Memories of a Catholic Girlhood* (New York: Harcourt, Brace & World, 1957), pp. 83-91.

sian might have been his companions, and the harmless souls of unbaptized children might have frolicked about his feet. But if the Jesuit were right, all baptized Protestants went straight to Hell. A good life did not count in their favor. The baptismal rite, by conferring on them God's grace, made them also liable to His organizational displeasure. That is, baptism turned them Catholic, whether they liked it or not, and their persistence in the Protestant ritual was a kind of asseverated apostasy. Thus my poor grandfather, sixty years behind in his Easter duty, actually reduced his prospects of salvation every time he sat down in the Presbyterian church.

The Mother Superior's sweet frown acknowledged me, an hour after the sermon, as I curtsied, all agitation, in her office doorway. Plainly, she had been expecting me. Madame MacIllvra, an able administrator, must have been resignedly ticking off the names of the Protestant pupils and parents all during the concluding parts of the morning's service. She had a faint worried air, when the conversation began, of depreciating the sermon: doctrinally, perhaps, correct, it had been wanting in delicacy; the fiery Jesuit, a missionary celebrity, had lived too long among the Eskimos. This disengaged attitude encouraged me to hope. Surely this lady, the highest authority I knew, could find a way out for my grandfather. She could see that he was a special case, outside the brutal rule of thumb laid down by the Jesuit. It was she, after all, in the convent, from whom all exemptions flowed, who created arbitrary holidays (called *congés* by the order's French tradition); it was she who permitted us to get forbidden books from the librarian and occasionally to receive letters unread by the convent censor. (As a rule, all slang expressions, violations of syntax, errors of spelling, as well as improper sentiments, were blacked out of our friends' communications, so unless we moved in a circle of young Addisons or Burkes, the letters we longed for came to us as fragments from which the original text could only be conjectured.) To my twelve-year-old mind, it appeared probable that Madame MacIllvra, our Mother Superior, had the power to give my grandfather *congé*, and I threw myself on her sympathies.

How could it be that my grandfather, the most virtuous person I knew, whose name was a byword among his friends and colleagues for a kind of rigid and fantastic probity — how could it be that this man should be lost, while I, the object of his admonition, the despair of his example — I, who yielded to every impulse, lied, boasted, betrayed — should, by virtue of regular attendance at the sacraments and the habit of easy penitence, be saved?

Madame MacIllvra's full white brow wrinkled, her childlike blue eyes clouded. Like many headmistresses, she loved a good cry, and she clasped me to her plump, quivering, middle-aged bosom. She understood; she was crying for my grandfather and the injustice of it too. She and my grandfather had, as a matter of fact, established a very amiable relation, in which both took pleasure. The masculine line and firmness of his character made an aesthetic appeal to her, and the billowy softness and depth of the Mother Superior struck him favorably, but, above all, it was their difference in religion that suited their conversations. Each of them enjoyed, whenever they met in her straight, black-and-white little office, a sense of broadness, of enlightenment, of transcendent superiority to petty prejudice. My grandfather would remember that he wrote a check every Christmas for two Sisters of Charity who visited his office; Madame MacIllvra would perhaps recall her graduate studies and Hume. They had long, liberal talks which had the tone of *performances;* virtuoso feats of magnanimity were achieved on both sides. Afterward, they spoke of each other in nearly identical terms: "A very fine woman," "A very fine man."

All this (and possibly the suspicion that her verdict might be repeated at home) made Madame MacIllvra's answer slow. "Perhaps God," she murmured at last, "in His infinite mercy . . ." Yet this formulation satisfied neither of us. God's infinite mercy we believed in, but its manifestations were problematical. Sacred history showed us that it was more likely to fall on the Good Thief or the Woman Taken in Adultery than on persons of daily virtue and regular habits, like my grandfather. Our Catholic thoughts journeyed and met in a glance of alarmed recognition. Madame MacIllvra pondered. There were, of course, she said finally, other loopholes. If he had been improperly baptized . . . a careless clergyman . . . I considered this suggestion and shook my head. My grandfather was not the kind of man who, even as an infant, would have been guilty of a slovenly baptism.

It was a measure of Madame MacIllvra's intelligence, or of her knowledge of the world, that she did not, even then, when my grandfather's soul hung, as it were, pleadingly between us, suggest the obvious, the orthodox solution. It would have been ridiculous for me to try to convert my grandfather. Indeed, as it turned out later, I might have dropped him into the pit with my innocent traps (the religious books left open beside his cigar cutter, or "Grandpa, won't you take me to Mass this Sunday? I am so tired of going alone"). "Pray for him, my dear," said Madame MacIllvra, sighing, "and I will speak to Madame Barclay. The point may be open to interpretation. She may remember something in the Fathers of the Church. . . ."

A few days later, Madame MacIllvra summoned me to her office. Not only Madame Barclay, the learned prefect of studies, but the librarian and even the convent chaplain had been called in. The Benedictine view, it seemed, differed sharply from the Dominican but a key passage in Saint Athanasius seemed to point to my grandfather's safety. The unbeliever, according to this generous authority, was not to be damned unless he rejected the true Church with sufficient knowledge and full consent of the will. Madame MacIllvra handed me the book and I read the passage over. Clearly, he was saved. Sufficient knowledge he had not. The Church was foreign to him; he knew it only distantly, only by repute, like the heathen Hiawatha, who had heard strange stories of missionaries, white men in black robes who bore a Cross. Flinging my arms about Madame MacIllvra, I blessed for the first time the insularity of my grandfather's character, the long-jawed, shut face it turned toward ideas and customs not its own. I resolved to dismantle at once the little altar in my bedroom at home, to leave off grace before meals, elaborate fasting, and all ostentatious practices of devotion, lest the light of my example shine upon him too powerfully and burn him with sufficient knowledge to a crisp.

Since I was a five-day boarder, this project had no time to grow stale, and the next Sunday, at home, my grandfather remarked on the change in me, which my feeling for the dramatic had made far from unobtrusive. "I hope," he said in a rather stern and ironical voice, "that you aren't using the *irreligious* atmosphere of this house as an excuse for backsliding. There will be time enough when you are older to change your beliefs if you want to." The unfairness of this rebuke delighted me. It put me solidly in the tradition of the saints and martyrs; Our Lord had known something like it, and so had Elsie Dinsmore at the piano. Nevertheless, I felt quite angry and slammed the door of my room behind me as I went in to sulk. I almost wished that my grandfather would die at once, so that God could furnish him with the explanation of my behavior — certainly he would have to wait till the next life to get it; in this one he would only have seen in it an invasion of his personal liberties.

As though to reward me for my silence, the following Wednesday brought me the happiest moment of my life. In order to understand my happiness, which might otherwise seem perverse, the reader must yield himself to the spiritual atmosphere of the convent. If he imagines that the life we led behind those walls was bare, thin, cold, austere, sectarian, he will have to revise his views; our days were a tumult of emotion. In the first place, we ate, studied, and slept in that atmosphere of intrigue, rivalry, scandal, favoritism, tyranny, and revolt that is common to all girls' boarding schools and that makes "real" life afterward seem a long and improbable armistice, a cessation of the true anguish of activity. But above the tinkling of this girlish operetta, with its clink-clink of changing friendships, its plot of smuggled letters, notes passed from desk to desk, secrets, there sounded in the Sacred Heart convent heavier, more solemn strains, notes of a great religious drama, which was also all passion and caprice, in which salvation was the issue and God's rather sultan-like and elusive favor was besought, scorned, despaired of, connived for, importuned. It was the paradoxical element in Catholic doctrine that lent this drama its suspense. The Divine Despot we courted could not be bought, like a piece of merchandise, by long hours at the *prie-dieu,* faithful attendance at the sacraments, obedience, reverence toward one's superiors. These solicitations helped, but it might well turn out that the worst girl in the school, whose pretty, haughty face wore rouge and a calm, closed look that advertised even to us younger ones some secret knowledge of men, was in the dark of her heart another Mary of Egypt, the strumpet saint in our midst. Such notions furnished a strange counterpoint to discipline; surely the Mother Superior never could have expelled a girl without recalling, with a shade of perplexity, the profligate youth of Saint Augustine and of Saint Ignatius of Loyola.

This dark-horse doctrine of salvation, with all its worldly wisdom and riddling charm, was deep in the idiom of the convent. The merest lay sister could have sustained with spiritual poise her end of a conversation on the purification through sin with Mr. Auden, Herr Kafka, or *Gospodin* Dostoevski; and Madame MacIllvra, while she would have held it bad taste to bow down, like Father Zossima, before the murder in Dmitri Karamazov's heart, would certainly have had him in for a series of long, interesting talks in her office.

Like all truly intellectual women, these were in spirit romantic desperadoes. They despised organizational heretics of the stamp of Luther and Calvin, but the great atheists and sinners were the heroes of the costume pictures they taught as a subject called history. Marlowe, Baudelaire — above all, Byron — glowed like terrible stars above their literature courses. Little girls of ten were reciting "The Prisoner of Chillon" and hearing stories of Claire Clairmont, Caroline Lamb, the Segatti, and the swim across the Hellespont. Even M. Voltaire enjoyed a left-handed popularity. The nuns spoke of him with horror and admiration mingled: "A great mind, an unconquerable spirit — and what fearful use they were put to." In Rousseau, an unbuttoned, middle-class figure, they had no interest whatever.

These infatuations, shared by the pupils, were brought into line with official Catholic opinion by a variety of stratagems. The more highly educated nuns were able to accept the damnation of these great Luciferian spirits. A simple young nun, on the other hand, who played baseball and taught arithmetic to the sixth and seventh grades, used to tell her pupils that she personally was convinced that Lord Byron in his last hours must have made an act of contrition.

It was not, therefore, unusual that a line from the works of this dissipated author should have been waiting for us on the blackboard of the eighth-grade rhetoric classroom when we filed in that Wednesday morning which remains still memorable to me. *"Zoe mou, sas agapo"*: the words of Byron's last assurance to the Maid of Athens stood there in Madame Barclay's French-looking script, speaking to us of the transiency of the passions. To me, as it happened, it spoke a twice-told tale. I had read the poem before, alone in my grandfather's library; indeed, I knew it by heart, and I rather resented the infringement on my private rights in it, the democratization of the poem which was about to take place. Soon, Madame Barclay's pointer was rapping from word to word: "My . . . life . . . I . . . love . . . you," she sharply translated. When the pointer started back for its second trip, I retreated into hauteur and began drawing a picture of the girl who sat next to me. Suddenly the pointer cracked across my writing tablet.

"You're just like Lord Byron, brilliant but unsound."

I heard the pointer being set down and the drawing being torn crisply twice across, but I could not look up. I had never felt so flattered in my life. Throughout the rest of the class, I sat motionless, simulating meekness, while my classmates shot me glances of wonder, awe, and congratulation, as though I had suddenly been struck by a remarkable disease, or been canonized, or transfigured. Madame Barclay's pronouncement, which I kept repeating to myself under my breath, had for us girls a kind of final and majestic certainty. She was the severest and most taciturn of our teachers. Her dark brows met in the middle; her skin was a pure olive; her upper lip had a faint mustache; she was the iron and authority of the convent. She tolerated no infractions, overlooked nothing, was utterly and obdurately fair, had no favorites; but her rather pointed face had the marks of suffering, as though her famous discipline had scored it as harshly as one of our papers. She had a bitter and sarcastic wit, and had studied, it was said, at the Sorbonne. Before this day, I had once or twice dared to say to myself that Madame Barclay liked me. Her dark, quite handsome eyes would sometimes move in my direction as her lips prepared an aphorism or a satiric gibe. Yet hardly had I estimated the look, weighed and measured it to store it away in my memory book of re-quited affections when a stinging penalty would recall me from my dream and I could no longer be sure. Now, however, there was no doubt left. The reproof was a declaration of love as plain as the sentence on the blackboard, which shimmered slightly before my eyes. My happiness was a confused exaltation in which the fact that I was Lord Byron and the fact that I was loved by Madame Barclay, the most puzzling nun in the convent, blended in a Don Juanesque triumph.

In the refectory that noon, publicity was not wanting to enrich this moment. Insatiable, I could hardly wait for the week end, to take Madame Barclay's words home as though they had been a prize. With the generosity of affluence I spoke to myself of sharing this happiness, this honor, with my grandfather. Surely, *this* would make up to him for any worry or difficulty I had caused him. At the same time, it would have the practical effect of explaining me a little to him. Phrases about my prototype rang in my head: "that unfortunate genius," "that turbu-lent soul," "that gifted and erratic nature."

My grandfather turned dark red when he heard the news. His fore-head grew knotty with veins; he swore; he looked strange and young; it was the first time I had ever seen him angry. Argument and explanation were useless. For my grandfather, history had interposed no distance be-tween Lord Byron and himself. Though the incestuous poet had died forty years before my grandfather was born, the romantic perspective was lacking. That insularity of my grandfather's that kept him intimate with morals and denied the reality of the exotic made him judge the poet as he judged himself or one of his neighbors — that is, on the merit of his ac-tions. He was on the telephone at once, asking the Mother Superior in a thundering, courtroom voice what right one of her sisters had to associ-ate his innocent granddaughter with that degenerate blackguard, Byron. On Monday, Madame Barclay, with tight-drawn lips, told her class that she had a correction to make: Mary McCarthy did not resemble Lord By-ron in any particular; she was neither brilliant, loose-living, nor unsound.

The interviews between my grandfather and Madame MacIllvra came to an end. To that remarkable marriage of mind the impediment had at last been discovered. But from this time on, Madame Barclay's marks of favor to me grew steadily more distinct, while the look of suffering tightened on her face, till some said she had cancer (a theory supported by the yellowness of her skin) and some said she was being poisoned by an antipathy to the Mother Superior.

THE WESTERNER

Virginia Sorensen

(1912-1991)

A native of Utah and a graduate of Brigham Young University, Virginia Sorensen understood Mormonism in the best way possible: as the all-surrounding, all-sustaining atmosphere of her life. As a great grand-daughter of the original Mormon settlers in Utah, the Church of Jesus Christ of Latter-day Saints was even in her blood. This easy familiarity enables her to write of her childhood memories with warmth and affection, but also with the distance that the passing of many years provides. And, like Mary McCarthy, Sorensen does know how to write: eight novels, almost as many children's books, and a good many short stories. The reader has reason to be grateful for such literary skill.

Mormonism is built into the American experience, and yet seems to stand apart from it. In the earliest years, this apart-ness was deliberate, both on the part of the faithful and on the part of the "Gentiles" who feared, denounced, ridiculed, and persecuted them. The migration of the tiny church (organized in 1830) from Palmyra, New York, to Kirtland Hills, Ohio, to Independence, Missouri, then to Nauvoo, Illinois, and finally to Salt Lake City in Utah is a story filled with such drama and sacrifice as to be the stuff of myth. But it is history, and no group has preserved and protected that history more zealously than the Mormons. When Sorensen was born in 1912, Mormon membership had reached about one-quarter million — a large number by Illinois or Missouri standards. But the period of great growth was just beginning: by mid-century well over a million Mormons, and by the end of the century over ten times that number, both in the United States and abroad.

One of the reasons for this sharp growth was the large immigration of converts from Great Britain and western Europe. Sorensen is especially concerned with the immigrants from Denmark, and even wrote a novel on the Mormon missionaries to that country: *Kingdom Come* (1960). The protagonist in the story given below is Danish; the Mormon bishop is Danish; and Virginia Sorensen even received a Guggenheim fellowship that took her to Denmark. Her story was first published in the *New Yorker,* and while it is a story, her book carries the subtitle of "Memories of a Mormon Childhood." Those memories probably come from the years around 1920 — before and after. They tell us not only of Mormonism, but also of the American West in the days when settlers fought for survival — and for water.

[See L. L. Lee and Sylvia B. Lee, *Virginia Sorensen,* Western Writers Series, No. 31 (Boise, Idaho: Boise State University, 1978).]

"Where Nothing Is Long Ago"

"You'll probably remember Brother Tolsen and that awful thing that happened when you were a little girl," my mother wrote me recently. Her fat script traveled the whole way around the photograph and obituary she had clipped from our Mormon newspaper. "The killing wasn't even mentioned at his funeral. All the speakers just said what a good man he always was."

Remember Brother Tolsen? I looked at his square jaw and his steady eyes, and it was as if I had seen him yesterday. Well, I thought, another one is gone; soon there won't be a real Danish accent left in that whole valley. Mormon converts from Denmark came to Utah by the thousands during the second half of the nineteenth century. Now there were only a few survivors. Not long before, it had been old Bishop Petersen himself who had died.

I was with Bishop Petersen, in his garden, the morning the Tolsen trouble happened. My mother thought I had a morbid interest in the affair, and I guess I had. It was the summer I was nine, and I was morbid about almost everything. I was absolutely certain for years afterward

Source: Virginia Sorensen, *Where Nothing Is Long Ago* (New York: Harcourt, Brace & World, 1963), pp. 3-14.

that two piles of bloody rabbits' ears I saw on the courthouse lawn at the time of Brother Tolsen's trial had something to do with the killing he was being tried for. They hadn't. They were merely tokens of the fact that the annual county rabbit hunt had gone off according to schedule.

Mother, who loves accuracy, often complains about the peculiar quality of my memories, and likely she's right. The Tolsen case, for instance, tends to get mixed in my mind with other water-thief murders I've heard of. My mother sent me a clipping about one in Utah Valley, near Provo, just last year. This man was killed with a gun, however, instead of a shovel — as Brother Tolsen killed *his* thief — and then the killer turned the gun on himself. Mother wrote on that latest clipping, "Dad and I don't see why he had to shoot himself, too. Do you?"

That's a very Western query. A poem written by Thomas Hornsby Ferril begins: "Here in America nothing is long ago . . . " and that's very Western, too. People out West remember when important things were settled violently, and they remember the wide, dry wastes before the mountain water was captured and put to use. Even now, the dry spaces, where the jack rabbits hop through the brush as thick as mites on a hen, are always there, waiting to take over; dryness hugs the green fields, pushing in, only the irrigation ditches keeping it at bay.

July was when the Tolsen trouble happened. In Utah, that's when the dry heat is most intense. Our whole valley floor is like a spot on a piece of paper when you focus the sun on it through a glass; you feel as if, any second, it is going to brown and then smoke and then burst into flame. Around it there are the quiet mountains, cool and blue, but long, dusty roads and scrubby hills lie between them and the simmering town. The river is the single link, flowing down between dusty-leaved cottonwoods from the mountains to the people in the valley.

Not that I minded heat in those days. There was no need to be hot when, on either side of the wide streets, there was cold water, brought from the river by the town's main ditch and diverted into smaller channels that ran along the sidewalks. It rushed constantly there, between banks lined with mint and grass. Wearing huge black bloomers and white pantywaists with the garters off, I spent most of my summer days in the ditches. Main Ditch was deep and lined with stones; when I skated along it in wintertime, I could hardly see over its banks. The ditches leading from it along the streets were shallow, having perhaps a foot of water in them at the peak of the spring supply.

Each household in town had its own dam — often nothing more than a couple of broad boards with a short handle nailed to them — and its own water turn when the dam was put to use. Set across the streams in the streetside ditches, and packed in with wet turf, these dams were sufficient to turn the water onto lawns and gardens, and nothing short of a calamity could prevent a householder from putting in his dam at the proper time. Every spring, the Water Master — an official of great importance in a Utah town — provided each family with a list of Water Turns, carefully worked out. We always kept our list tacked inside the door of the kitchen cupboard.

We children followed the water like pioneers, finding what dams were in and wading in the ditches where the water was highest. We kept ourselves rosy and crisp with it. Sometimes my grandmother would go with us and put her feet into the water to cool off. I recall her saying many times that Brigham Young must have been a true prophet, because he had said that Utah was The Place right in the middle of July, when nobody would think, to look at it without water, that it would ever grow a respectable bean. It was on the twenty-fourth of July that Brigham Young made his historic pronouncement, and as far as I know not a drop of rain has ever fallen to spoil the parades, the fireworks, and the pageants that take place every year on that day.

The Tolsen trouble must have been on the twenty-fifth of July, because I remember Mother's saying I couldn't wade in the grass, which was about to be flooded, unless I first collected every burned-out sparkler that had been left on the ground the night before. So, early that morning, I was busily searching the grass for wires when I saw Bishop Petersen, whose dam was in, working with the water in his garden next door. The full stream was running into it, as it would presently run into ours, for our turn followed his. His garden, like every other one in Utah, had a series of shallow furrows between the rows of vegetables, and he was damming them with chunks of turf and opening one or two at a time, so that each, in turn, received the stream. It was beautiful to see the tall green vegetables in precise lines and the moving water twinkling between them.

In half a minute, I was paddling alongside Bishop Petersen. The water in the furrows was warmer than that in the ditches, and it was glorious to feel the soft mud between my toes. And I loved to hear Bishop Petersen tell about Denmark, from which he had come as a young man. I asked him all sorts of questions to keep him talking, for his odd accent and his laughter pleased me. I recall how the robins sang and hopped down into the furrows as water darkened them and lured out long, fat worms.

Bishop Petersen said that to leave the lovely land of Denmark one had to be very certain it was to God's Kingdom he was coming. He himself had been sure of it when he heard about the mountain water, so pure, so shining, so cold, so free. Whenever his turn came to speak at Testimony Meeting, which followed Sunday school on the first Sunday of every month, he spoke about the water. It was to him, next to the Gospel itself, the unmistakable sign of the Kingdom.

That twenty-fifth of July, he talked as usual, his white beard wobbling like an elf's, and now and then I had to turn my back to prevent him from seeing that I was smiling. He thought that, as one descended from Danes myself, I ought to know that the crisp peas I was picking and eating were *uahmindelig god* (usually good). He wanted me to repeat the phrase, but I couldn't. The very sound of most Danish words made me giggle until I was weak. The language bristled with "g's" and "k's" exactly the way Bishop Petersen bristled with white whiskers. Yet goodness and kindness and excellent husbandry went along with all the things about him that made me laugh. I loved him dearly, as my parents did, and to most of us to be Danish — as to be Mormon — meant to be virtuous, kind, and of good report.

Mother came out to call me for breakfast, and she stood awhile, leaning on the fence, to talk. What she said and what Bishop Petersen replied is lost to me now, but while they talked, I saw Brother Tolsen coming. He ran into the yard with so urgent and desperate a look on his usually cheerful face that even I knew at once that he was in bad trouble. "Come in now," Mother said sharply to me. "The eggs will be cold already."

By suppertime, it was known all over town that Brother Tolsen had killed a man.

"But why did he hit him like that?" Mother asked my father. "It's not like Brother Tolsen to strike anybody. Such a gentle man!"

"Twice he had turned Brother Tolsen's water off his fields in the night. *Twice!*" My father spoke with the patience of a man obliged to explain violence to a woman. "Brother Tolsen says he had no notion of hitting so hard, but he hit him with a shovel, after all. From what I hear, it struck on the edge and went over the forehead, and one eye came — "

"Finish your supper and go out to play," Mother said to me severely, and to my father, "Is it necessary to go into those terrible details in front of the children? It's enough to curdle their souls, the way you men tell it — as if you enjoyed it!"

It may seem an odd thing to remember, but I do remember that I was eating cottage cheese that night. It was made by my mother on the back of the stove and served in great bowls. Cream was poured over it, and there was a great, lovely red blob of jelly in the middle of it, from which one took a little chip of a jewel with every bite, eating one curd of the cheese at a time. It was a common summer supper. I also had a bowl of fresh lettuce, with cream and sugar, and I ate that slowly, too, leaf by leaf.

My parents said no more about Brother Tolsen until I had finished and gone outside, but I lingered on the porch in the shadows of the Virginia creepers. I heard my father say how big my ears were — ". . . as big as soup ladles. She never misses a thing" — but he laughed when he said it. It was a family joke about me and my big ears, and how I was as deaf as a post when it suited me. Presently, they were talking about the killing again — how the victim's head had been bashed in and he had been found in a pool of blood near Brother Tolsen's dam.

I remember sitting there on the porch and holding my hands up against the setting sun. Sunset was huge and red and terribly intense in July, over the western hills. Against it, I could see my own blood shining red through my skin. Heads were brimful of blood, too — I knew that from nosebleed and from teeth coming out, and from the time I hit a stump and went over the handlebars of my bicycle square onto my skull. The man Brother Tolsen had killed was not very well known to me, probably because, as Grandmother remarked, he had "fallen away from the faith" and didn't often come to church. Now, losing the faith, I knew, was one of the greatest of sins, but murder was worse; it was the greatest sin of them all. And Brother Tolsen I knew very well indeed. He was important in our Ward of the Church, and I had often heard his testimony at meeting, just as I had heard Bishop Petersen's, and in the same delightful accent. In fact, he was so good a speaker that I had heard him more than once making sermons at funerals.

I liked funerals very much then, and I find them rather stimulating now. The philosophy I learned as a child made death more fascinating than terrible. The first corpse I ever saw was the mother of one of my grade-school friends. She had died in childbirth. I had received fresh cookies from her hands a day or so before, but now she lay exactly like

Snow White, like one dreaming in a lovely bed, with an infinitely small and doll-like child in the crook of her arm. I stood and gazed at her with awe and admiration.

After that, I went to every funeral remotely connected with anybody I knew. They were never forbidden to me. The corpses of men and women alike were always dressed in pure white, with bright-green aprons cheerfully embroidered to look like the fig leaves of the Garden of Eden. It was perfectly reasonable to me to believe that, as I was assured, they had just stepped "through the veil between earth and heaven." It seemed to me that they were always much handsomer than they had ever been in life, in their common house aprons or in their overalls stained with manure. I pictured them, in their clean new clothes, walking slowly westward with the sun and vanishing in a tremendous scarlet smile of sunset. I had even seen something like that in the movies, so I suspected that the miracle happened not only in Utah but also in California.

When Mother told me I could not go to the funeral of the man Brother Tolsen had killed, I was devastated, especially because there were rumors that Brother Tolsen himself would attend. He had been in jail a few hours and then had been released to attend to his work until the trial. He had a big family and a farm, and goodness only knew, people said, what would happen to them if he had to spend the rest of the summer in the jail.

"But Mother — " I cried, over and over.

"No! Absolutely not!" she said each time. She knew full well, of course, that I had a morbid interest in seeing a corpse with its head bashed in, and also that I wanted to enjoy the spectacle of a man going to the funeral of someone he had knocked headlong "through the veil" with a shovel.

In the end, I was not only forbidden to go, I was even given a neighbor's baby to tend, and in agony of spirit I saw Mother and Dad and Grandmother and just about everybody else in town go marching off to the dead man's house. No sooner were they gone, however, than I bundled the baby into his buggy and pushed him rapidly to that street. There I could at least see all the people standing around in the yard silent and serious, and I thought I might catch a glimpse of Brother Tolsen coming or going. Back and forth I walked, back and forth, pushing the buggy in the heat, envying the people as they filed slowly into the house and slowly out again after viewing the remains.

And then I really did see Brother Tolsen. Walking with his wife and oldest son, he passed so close to me on the sidewalk that he would have brushed against me if I had not drawn the buggy quickly off onto the grass. He nodded to me but did not smile, and I thought he appeared much as he always did when he went to church. People looked down at their shoes as he entered the dead man's gate, but when he moved along the walk toward the house, many stepped forward and greeted him. Between the gate and the porch, he must have stopped to shake hands twenty times. The front door opened and he went inside, and I found myself standing with my stomach pressed against the fence to watch. I could hear a breeze of comment among the people nearest me.

"It won't be easy for him to see Lena today."

"She knows it was an accident."

"But how can she believe her own husband would steal water?"

Presently, Brother Tolsen and his wife and son came out of the house. This time, he did not pause to shake the hand of anyone, but walked quickly from the yard. Then the door of the house remained closed for a while, and most of the people started toward the church, a few blocks away. When Mother and Dad and Grandmother came out of the yard, I began to push the buggy toward home, but I turned back as soon as they were out of sight. The hearse and a leading car, filled with flowers, were waiting in front of the house, and nobody was going to deny me a sight of the coffin.

I heard someone say "Poor Lena!" and the door opened again. Lena is still, to me, a vision of total sorrow. She leaned forward as she walked after the coffin, doubled over like a person with a violent stomach-ache. She was dressed in heavy black, with a black veil, and I think now how hot she must have been on that blistering day. After she had been carried off in a car that followed the hearse, the people who were left went away, and the whole house and yard looked empty and bedraggled. I walked back and forth, staring in. On the path, just inside the gate, lay one red rose, but I only looked at it. I wouldn't any more have touched it than I would have stirred my finger in a pool of blood.

Poor Lena! I knew that since her husband had fallen away from the faith she could never get much glory in the next world. Even if he had not been a water-thief, he wouldn't have done her much good in heaven. In the Mormon Church, every man can aspire to some sort of ordination — every small boy of any virtue whatever is a Deacon and can go on to be a Priest and an Elder and a Teacher and a High Priest and all sorts of important-sounding things. But a woman has no Priesthood and must depend on her husband to take her to The Highest Degree. I visualized dazzling marble steps stretching up and up to the throne of God Himself, with winged people arranged thereon according to their just deserts.

Not once, as I recall, did I think Poor Brother Tolsen! The two figures are clear in my mind. Brother Tolsen had looked sad but very straight and dignified as he walked into the house where the corpse lay, shaking hands with his Brethren as he went. Sister Lena, stooping and wild, had hidden her face in her handkerchief as she was led away. Later, I heard some talk of "poor Lena," who was "young yet, after all" and "should marry a real believer," but after the funeral I never laid eyes on her again, though I often rode my bicycle past her house, and looked and looked.

The next thing I remember about the Tolsen case is walking after school with my best friend, Carol. We went past the courthouse, where we knew the jury was being selected, and there were those great piles of bloody rabbits' ears on the courthouse lawn, being counted. The hunters were always divided into two teams, and the losers had to give the winners what was called a Rabbit Supper. I learned later, with relief, that they did not eat the ears or even the jack rabbits, but had chicken pies at the church, cooked by the women of the Relief Society. Nevertheless, those piles of ears I see to this day.

That night, there was talk at our supper table, and on the porch afterward, about how difficult it had been to find jurors "without prejudice." The trial itself lasted only three short afternoons. At home, it was discussed freely, and the talk consisted mostly of repeating what character witnesses had said. There had been no witness to the killing itself, and Brother Tolsen had given up at once to the authorities: first to his Bishop, which was entirely proper in all eyes, and then — in company with Bishop Petersen — to the sheriff. As for Lena, she did not come to the trial at all, but was said to have disappeared into that vast place where there were yellow streetcars, blue-coated policemen, a shining capitol building, and a merry-go-round in Liberty Park — Great Salt Lake City.

Almost all that was left to be done after the character witnesses were through was to hear the simple story told by Brother Tolsen himself and repeated in the town with nods of understanding and respect. His friends and neighbors considered him innocent of any real wrongdoing, and in this the jury soon concurred. I remember Dad repeating the words of somebody who had been very important at the trial — probably Brother Tolsen's lawyer. "If a thief enters a man's own house in the night and means to rob him of all he has, all his clothing and all his food, thereby meaning to take the very lives of his wife and his little children — then what shall that householder do? Would his actions be judged as malice aforethought? Is it not true that he who steals water is stealing life itself?"

It was a joyful thing for Brother Tolsen's friends to see him at home again, and they have all been safer because of him. There has been no water-stealing that I have heard of in that valley since.

One other memory remains. I recall an evening, months after the trial was over, when my parents and I were driving along the road where his fields lay and saw Brother Tolsen working with the little streams that were running among his young corn. Dad and Mother waved and called to him. He lifted an arm to answer, and I saw that he held a shovel in the other hand. "I wonder if he bought a new shovel," I said suddenly.

For a minute, the air seemed to have gone dead about us, in the peculiar way it sometimes can, which is so puzzling to a child. Then Mother turned to me angrily. "Don't you ever let me hear you say a thing like that again!" she said. "Brother Tolsen is a good, kind man!"

So until this very hour I never have.

THE MONK

Thomas Merton

(1915-1968)

Americans, overwhelmingly Protestant for centuries, approach monasticism with caution if they approach it at all. In the passions of nineteenth-century nativism, the sentiments or fears of a great many Protestants found expression in an ugly book, *The Awful Disclosures of Maria Monk* (1836). That none of it was true was quite beside the point; to many, it symbolized everything wrong with monastic life and the Roman Catholicism of which it was an integral part.

Thomas Merton changed all that, and it is perhaps not too strong a claim to say that he changed all that permanently. Not only was Merton a sophisticated, socially sensitive, and incredibly productive monk, he was a monk of the most rigid sort: a member of the Cistercians of the Strictest Observance, after the eighteenth century generally called Trappists. In addition to the traditional monastic vows of poverty, chastity, and obedience, Trappists took a further vow of silence. Their exacting ritual life included the singing of the night office at 2:00 A.M., the execution on their rural land of a farmer's labors without anything like the farmer's typical diet. Somehow, in the midst of all this, Merton managed to write some forty volumes of poetry and prose, together with countless letters to an amazing array of correspondents — including Dorothy Day.

He also somehow managed to keep a sense of humor, even when resisted and censored by his own abbot, even when charged with producing pacifist tracts that must have been influenced by the Commu-

241

nists. And in 1948 he wrote what no American monk before him had ever managed to bring forth: a best-seller. *The Seven Storey Mountain* sold some 400,000 copies in its first year, transforming Merton — to his dismay and distaste — from a withdrawn hermit to a popular celebrity, a cult figure. It became chic to cite Merton nearly everywhere, from Protestant pulpits and Buddhist temples to talk shows and night clubs. Remarkably, he survived his following.

Losing his mother when still a child, Merton then lost his father at the age of fifteen. Passed around among French and British boarding schools (he was born in France) and among a variety of relatives, Merton in his late twenties made his way to America and to Columbia University where he fell under the spell of Carl Van Doren. At the time he was receiving his Columbia degrees (B.A. and M.A.), he converted from a nominal Anglicanism to Roman Catholicism. In 1941, after a young life of hedonistic indulgence, he entered the Trappist monastery in Gethsemani, Kentucky. The excerpt below describes some of the agonies of soul that led him to this decision.

Like Martin Luther, Thomas Merton entered the monastery primarily to save his own soul. Like Martin Luther, he soon shook the world.

[See Monica Furlong, *Merton: A Biography* (San Francisco: Harper & Row, 1980); and Lawrence S. Cunningham, *Thomas Merton and the Monastic Vision* (Grand Rapids: William B. Eerdmans, 1999).]

There were still about three weeks left until Easter. Thinking more and more about the Trappist monastery where I was going to spend Holy Week, I went to the library one day and took down the *Catholic Encyclopaedia* to read about the Trappists. I found out that the Trappists were Cistercians, and then, in looking up Cistercians, I also came across the Carthusians, and a great big picture of the hermitages of the Camaldolese.

What I saw on those pages pierced me to the heart like a knife.

What wonderful happiness there was, then, in the world! There were still men on this miserable, noisy, cruel earth, who tasted the marvelous joy of silence and solitude, who dwelt in forgotten mountain cells, in secluded monasteries, where the news and desires and appetites and conflicts of the world no longer reached them.

They were free from the burden of the flesh's tyranny, and their clear vision, clean of the world's smoke and of its bitter sting, was raised to heaven and penetrated into the deeps of heaven's infinite and healing light.

They were poor, they had nothing, and therefore they were free and possessed everything, and everything they touched struck off something of the fire of divinity. And they worked with their hands, silently

---

Source: Thomas Merton, *The Seven Storey Mountain* (New York: Harcourt, Brace & World, 1948), pp. 382-88; 396-405.

ploughing and harrowing the earth, and sowing seed in obscurity, and reaping their small harvests to feed themselves and the other poor. They built their own houses and made, with their own hands, their own furniture and their own coarse clothing, and everything around them was simple and primitive and poor, because they were the least and the last of men, they had made themselves outcasts, seeking, outside the walls of the world, Christ poor and rejected of men.

Above all, they had found Christ, and they knew the power and the sweetness and the depth and the infinity of His love, living and working in them. In Him, hidden in Him, they had become the "Poor Brothers of God." And for His love, they had thrown away everything, and concealed themselves in the Secret of His Face. Yet because they had nothing, they were the richest men in the world, possessing everything: because in proportion as grace emptied their heart of created desire, the Spirit of God entered in and filled the place that had been made for God. And the Poor Brothers of God, in their cells, they tasted within them the secret glory, the hidden manna, the infinite nourishment and strength of the presence of God. They tasted the sweet exultancy of the fear of God, which is the first intimate touch of the reality of God, known and experienced on earth, the beginning of heaven. The fear of the Lord is the beginning of heaven. And all day long, God spoke to them: the clean voice of God, in His tremendous peacefulness, spending truth within them as simply and directly as water wells up in a spring. And grace was in them, suddenly, always in more and more abundance, they knew not from where, and the coming of this grace to them occupied them altogether, and filled them with love, and with freedom.

And grace, overflowing in all their acts and movements, made everything they did an act of love, glorifying God not by drama, not by gesture, not by outward show, but by the very simplicity and economy of utter perfection, so utter that it escapes notice entirely.

Outside in the world were holy men who were holy in the sense that they went about with portraits of all the possible situations in which they could show their love of God displayed about them: and they were always conscious of all these possibilities. But these other hidden men had come so close to God in their hiddenness that they no longer saw anyone but Him. They themselves were lost in the picture: there was no comparison between them receiving and God giving, because the distance by which such comparison could be measured had dwindled to nothing. They were in Him. They had dwindled down to nothing and had been transformed into Him by the pure and absolute humility of their hearts.

And the love of Christ overflowing in those clean hearts made them children and made them eternal. Old men with limbs like the roots of trees had the eyes of children and lived, under their grey woolen cowls, eternal. And all of them, the young and the old, were ageless, the little brothers of God, the little children for whom was made the Kingdom of Heaven.

Day after day the round of the canonical hours brought them together and the love that was in them became songs as austere as granite and as sweet as wine. And they stood and they bowed in their long, solemn psalmody. Their prayer flexed its strong sinews and relaxed again into silence and suddenly flared up again in a hymn, the color of flame, and died into silence: and you could barely hear the weak, ancient voice saying the final prayer. The whisper of the *amens* ran around the stones like sighs and the monks broke up their ranks and half emptied the choir, some remaining to pray.

And in the night they also rose, and filled the darkness with the strong, patient anguish of their supplication to God: and the strength of their prayer (the Spirit of Christ concealing His strength in the words their voices uttered) amazingly held back the arm of God from striking and breaking at last the foul world full of greed and avarice and murder and lust and all sin.

The thought of those monasteries, those remote choirs, those cells, those hermitages, those cloisters, those men in their cowls, the poor monks, the men who had become nothing, shattered my heart.

In an instant the desire of those solitudes was wide open within me like a wound.

I had to slam the book shut on the picture of Camaldoli and the bearded hermits standing in the stone street of cells, and I went out of the library, trying to stamp out the embers that had broken into flame, there, for an instant, within me.

No, it was useless: I did not have a vocation, and I was not for the cloister, for the priesthood. Had I not been told that definitely enough? Did I have to have that beaten into my head all over again before I could believe it?

Yet I stood in the sun outside the dining hall, waiting for the noon Angelus, and one of the Friars was talking to me. I could not contain the one thing that filled my heart:

"I am going to a Trappist monastery to make a retreat for Holy

Week," I said. The things that jumped in the Friar's eyes gave him the sort of expression you would expect if I had said: "I am going to go and buy a submarine and live on the bottom of the sea."

"Don't let them change you!" he said, with a sort of a lame smile. That meant "Don't go reminding the rest of us that all that penance might be right, by getting a vocation to the Trappists."

I said: "It would be a good thing if they did change me."

It was a safe, oblique way of admitting what was in my heart — the desire to go to that monastery and stay for good.

On the morning of the Saturday before Palm Sunday I got up before five, and heard part of a Mass in the dark chapel and then had to make a run for the train. The rain fell on the empty station straight and continuous as a tower.

All the way down the line, in the pale, growing day, the hills were black, and rain drenched the valley and flooded the sleeping valley towns. Somewhere past Jamestown I took out my Breviary and said the Little Hours, and when we got into Ohio the rain stopped.

We changed stations at Galion, and on the fast train down to Columbus I got something to eat, and in southern Ohio the air was drier still, and almost clearing. Finally, in the evening, in the long rolling hills that led the way in to Cincinnati, you could see the clouds tearing open all along the western horizon to admit long streaks of sun.

It was an American landscape, big, vast, generous, fertile, and leading beyond itself into limitless expanses, open spaces, the whole West. My heart was full!

So when we entered Cincinnati, in the evening, with the lights coming on among all the houses and the electric signs shining on the hills, and the huge freight yards swinging open on either side of the track and the high buildings in the distance, I felt as if I owned the world. And yet that was not because of all these things, but because of Gethsemani, where I was going. It was the fact that I was passing through all this, and did not desire it, and wanted no part in it, and did not seek to grasp or hold any of it, that I could exult in it, and it all cried out to me: God! God!

I went to Mass and Communion the next morning in Cincinnati, and then took the train for Louisville, and waited in Louisville all the rest of the day because I did not have the sense to take a bus to one of the towns near Gethsemani and buy a ride from there to the monastery.

It was not until after night fell that there was a train out to Gethsemani, on the line to Atlanta.

It was a slow train. The coach was dimly lighted, and full of people whose accents I could hardly understand, and you knew you were in the South because all the Negroes were huddled in a separate car. The train got out of the city into country that was abysmally dark, even under the moon. You wondered if there were any houses out there. Pressing my face to the window, and shading it with my hands, I saw the outline of a bare, stony landscape with sparse trees. The little towns we came to looked poor and forlorn and somewhat fierce in the darkness.

And the train went its slow way through the spring night, branching off at Bardstown junction. And I knew my station was coming.

I stepped down out of the car into the empty night. The station was dark. There was a car standing there, but no man in sight. There was a road, and the shadow of a sort of a factory a little distance away, and a few houses under some trees. In one of them was a light. The train had hardly stopped to let me off, and immediately gathered its ponderous momentum once again and was gone around the bend with the flash of a red tail light, leaving me in the middle of the silence and solitude of the Kentucky hills.

I put my bag down in the gravel, wondering what to do next. Had they forgotten to make arrangements for me to get to the monastery? Presently the door of one of the houses opened, and a man came out, in no hurry.

We got in the car together, and started up the road, and in a minute we were in the midst of moonlit fields.

"Are the monks in bed?" I asked the driver. It was only few minutes past eight.

"Oh, yes, they go to bed at seven o'clock."

"Is the monastery far?"

"Mile and a half."

I looked at the rolling country and at the pale ribbon of road in front of us, stretching out as grey as lead to the light of the moon. Then suddenly I saw a steeple that shone like silver in the moonlight, growing into sight from behind a rounded knoll. The tires sang on the empty road, and, breathless, I looked at the monastery that was revealed before me as we came over the rise. At the end of an avenue of trees was a big rectangular block of buildings, all dark, with a church crowned by a tower and a steeple and a cross: and the steeple was as bright as platinum and the whole place was as quiet as midnight and lost in the all-absorbing silence and solitude of the fields. Behind the monastery was a dark curtain of woods, and over to the west was a wooded valley, and beyond that a rampart of wooded hills, a barrier and a defense against the world.

And over all the valley smiled the mild, gentle Easter moon, the full moon in her kindness, loving this silent place.

At the end of the avenue, in the shadows under the trees, I could make out the lowering arch of the gate, and the words: *"Pax Intrantibus."*

The driver of the car did not go to the bell rope by the heavy wooden door. Instead he went over and scratched on one of the windows and called, in a low voice:

"Brother! Brother!"

I could hear someone stirring inside.

Presently the key turned in the door. I passed inside. The door closed quietly behind me. I was out of the world.

There were no longer any pure hermits or anchorites in the world: but the Carthusians were the ones who had gone the furthest, climbed the highest on the mountain of isolation that lifted them above the world and concealed them in God.

We could see the Cistercians here going out to work in a long line with shovels tucked under their arms with a most quaint formality. But the Carthusian worked alone, in his cell, in his garden or workshop, isolated. These monks slept in a common dormitory, the Carthusian slept in a hidden cell. These men ate together while someone read aloud to them in their refectory. The Carthusian ate alone, sitting in the window-alcove of his cell, with no one to speak to him but God. All day long and all night long the Cistercian was with his brothers. All day long and all night long, except for the offices in choir and other intervals, the Carthusian was with God alone. *O beata solitudo!* . . .

The words were written on the walls of this Trappist guest house, too. *O beata solitudo, O sola beatitudo!*

There was one thing the Cistercians had in their favor. The Carthusians had a kind of recreation in which they went out for walks together and conversed with one another, to prevent the possibilities of strain that might go with too uncompromising a solitude, too much of that *sola beatitudo*. Could there be too much of it, I wondered? But the Trappist with his unbroken silence — at least as far as conversations were concerned — had one advantage!

And yet what did it matter which one was the most perfect Order? Neither one of them was for me! Had I not been told definitely enough a year ago that I had no vocation to any religious Order? All these comparisons were nothing but fuel for the fire of that interior anguish, that hopeless desire for what I could not have, for what was out of reach.

The only question was not which Order attracted me more, but which one tortured me the more with a solitude and silence and contemplation that could never be mine.

Far from wondering whether I had a vocation to either one, or from instituting a comparison between them, I was not even allowed the luxury of speculation on such a subject. It was all out of the question.

However, since the Carthusians were, after all, far way, it was what I had before my eyes that tortured me the most. The Carthusians were more perfect, perhaps, and therefore more to be desired: but they were doubly out of reach because of the war and because of what I thought was my lack of a vocation.

If I had had any supernatural common sense I would have realized that a retreat like this would be the best time to take that problem by the horns and overcome it, not by my own efforts and meditations but by prayer and by the advice of an experienced priest. And where would I find anyone more experienced in such matters than in a monastery of contemplatives?

But what was the matter with me? I suppose I had taken such a beating from the misunderstandings and misapprehensions that had arisen in my mind by the time that Capuchin got through with me, in his confessional, the year before, that I literally feared to reopen the subject at all. There was something in my bones that told me that I ought to find out whether my intense desire to lead this kind of a life in some monastery were an illusion: but the old scars were not yet healed, and my whole being shrank from another scourging.

That was my Holy Week, that mute, hopeless, interior struggle. It was my share in the Passion of Christ which began, that year, in the middle of the night with the first strangled cry of the Vigils of Holy Thursday.

It was a tremendous thing to hear the terrible cries of Jeremias resounding along the walls of that dark church buried in the country. "... Attend and see if there be any sorrow like unto my sorrow ... From above He hath sent fire into my bones, and hath chastised me: He hath spread a net for my feet, He hath turned me back, He hath made me desolate, wasted with sorrow all the day long."

It was not hard to realize Whose words these were, not difficult to detect the voice of Christ, in the liturgy of His Church, crying out in the sorrows of His Passion, which was now beginning to be relived, as it is relived each year, in the churches of Christendom.

At the end of the office, one of the monks came solemnly out and extinguished the sanctuary light, and the sudden impression froze all hearts with darkness and foreboding. The day went on solemnly, the Little Hours being chanted in a strange, mighty, and tremendously sorrowful tone, plain as its three monotonously recurring notes could possibly make it be, a lament that was as rough and clean as stone. After the *Gloria in Excelsis,* of the Conventual Mass, the organ was at last altogether silent: and the silence only served to bring out the simplicity and strength of the music chanted by the choir. After the general Communion, distributed to the long slow line of all the priests and monks and brothers and guests, and the procession of the Blessed Sacrament to the altar of repose — slow and sad, with lights and the *Pange Lingua* — came the Maundy, the *Mandatum,* when, in the cloister, the monks washed the feet of some seventy or eighty poor men, and kissed their feet and pressed money into their hands.

And through all this, especially in the *Mandatum,* when I saw them at close range, I was amazed at the way these monks, who were evidently just plain young Americans from the factories and colleges and farms and high-schools of the various states, were nevertheless absorbed and transformed in the liturgy. The thing that was most impressive was their absolute simplicity. They were concerned with one thing only: doing the things they had to do, singing what they had to sing, bowing and kneeling and so on when it was prescribed, and doing it as well as they could, without fuss or flourish or display. It was all utterly simple and unvarnished and straightforward, and I don't think I had ever seen anything, anywhere, so unaffected, so un-self-conscious as these monks. There was not a shadow of anything that could be called parade or display. They did not seem to realize that they were being watched — and, as a matter of fact, I can say from experience that they did not know it at all. In choir, it is very rare that you even realize that there are any, or many, or few seculars in the house: and if you do realize it, it makes no difference. The presence of other people becomes something that has absolutely no significance to the monk when he is at prayer. It is something null, neutral, like the air, like the atmosphere, like the weather. All these external things recede into the distance. Remotely, you are aware of it all, but you do not advert to it, you are not conscious of it, any more than the eye registers, with awareness, the things on which it is not focused, although they may be within its range of vision.

Certainly one thing the monk does not, or cannot, realize is the effect which these liturgical functions, performed by a group as such, have upon those who see them. The lessons, the truths, the incidents and values portrayed are simply overwhelming.

For this effect to be achieved, it is necessary that each monk as an individual performer be absolutely lost, ignored, overlooked.

And yet, what a strange admission! To say that men were admirable, worthy of honor, perfect, in proportion as they disappeared into a crowd and made themselves unnoticed, by even ceasing to be aware of their own existence and their own acts. Excellence, here, was in proportion to obscurity: the one who was best was the one who was least observed, least distinguished. Only faults and mistakes drew attention to the individual.

The logic of the Cistercian life was, then, the complete opposite to the logic of the world, in which men put themselves forward, so that the most excellent is the one who stands out, the one who is eminent above the rest, who attracts attention.

But what was the answer to this paradox? Simply that the monk in hiding himself from the world becomes not less himself, not less of a person, but more of a person, more truly and perfectly himself: for his personality and individuality are perfected in their true order, the spiritual, interior order, of union with God, the principle of all perfection. *Omnis gloria ejus filiae regis ab intus.*

The logic of worldly success rests on a fallacy: the strange error that our perfection depends on the thoughts and opinions and applause of other men! A weird life it is, indeed, to be living always in somebody else's imagination, as if that were the only place in which one could at last become real!

With all these things before me, day and night, for two days, I finally came to the afternoon of Good Friday.

After a tremendous morning of ten hours of practically uninterrupted chanting and psalmody, the monks, exhausted, had disappeared from the scene of their gutted church, with its stripped altars and its empty Tabernacle wide open to the four winds. The monastery was silent, inert. I could not pray, I could not read any more.

251

I got Brother Matthew to let me out the front gate on the pretext that I wanted to take a picture of the monastery, and then I went for a walk along the enclosure wall, down the road past the mill, and around the back of the buildings, across a creek and down a narrow valley, with a barn and some woods on one side, and the monastery on a bluff on the other.

The sun was warm, the air quiet. Somewhere a bird sang. In a sense, it was a relief to be out of the atmosphere of intense prayer that had pervaded those buildings for the last two days. The pressure was too heavy for me. My mind was too full.

Now my feet took me slowly along a rocky road, under the stunted cedar trees, with violets growing up everywhere between the cracks in the rock.

Out here I could think; and yet I could not get to any conclusions. But there was one thought running around and around in my mind: "To be a monk . . . to be a monk . . ."

I gazed at the brick building which I took to be the novitiate. It stood on top of a high rampart of a retaining wall that made it look like a prison or a citadel. I saw the enclosure wall, the locked gates. I thought of the hundreds of pounds of spiritual pressure compressed and concentrated within those buildings and weighing down on the heads of the monks, and I thought, "It would kill me."

I turned my eyes to the trees, to the woods. I looked up the valley, back in the direction from which I had come, at the high wooded hill that closed off the prospect. I thought: "I am a Franciscan. That is my kind of spirituality, to be out in the woods, under the trees . . ."

I walked back across the trestle over the sunny, narrow creek, embracing my fine new error. After all I had seen of the Franciscans, where did I get the idea that they spent their time under the trees? They often lived in schools in towns and in cities: and these monks, on the contrary, did go out every day and work in the very fields and woods that I was looking at.

Human nature has a way of making very specious arguments to suit its own cowardice and lack of generosity. And so now I was trying to persuade myself that the contemplative, cloistered life was not for me, because there was not enough fresh air. . . .

Nevertheless, back in the monastery I read St. Bernard's *De Diligendo Deo* and I read the life of a Trappist monk who had died in a monastery in France, ironically enough in my own part of France, near Toulouse: Father Joseph Cassant.

The Retreat Master, in one of his conferences, told us a long story of a man who had once come to Gethsemani, and who had not been able to make up his mind to become a monk, and had fought and prayed about it for days. Finally, went the story, he had made the Stations of the Cross, and at the final station had prayed fervently to be allowed the grace of dying in the Order.

"You know," said the Retreat Master, "they say that no petition you ask at the fourteenth station is ever refused."

In any case, this man finished his prayer, and went back to his room and in an hour or so he collapsed, and they just had time to receive his request for admission to the Order when he died.

He lies buried in the monks' cemetery, in the oblate's habit.

And so, about the last thing I did before leaving Gethsemani was to do the Stations of the Cross, and to ask, with my heart in my throat, at the fourteenth station, for the grace of a vocation to the Trappists, if it were pleasing to God.

Back in the world, I felt like a man that had come down from the rare atmosphere of a very high mountain. When I got to Louisville, I had already been up for four hours or so, and my day was getting on towards its noon, so to speak, but I found that everybody else was just getting up and having breakfast and going to work. And how strange it was to see people walking around as if they had something important to do, running after busses, reading the newspapers, lighting cigarettes.

How futile all their haste and anxiety seemed.

My heart sank within me, I thought: "What am I getting into? Is this the sort of a thing I myself have been living in all these years?"

At a street corner, I happened to look up and caught sight of an electric sign, on top of a two-storey building. It read: "Clown Cigarettes."

I turned and fled from the alien and lunatic street and found my way into the nearby cathedral, and knelt, and prayed, and did the Stations of the Cross.

Afraid of the spiritual pressure in that monastery? Was that what I had said the other day? How I longed to be back there now: everything here, in the world outside, was insipid and slightly insane. There was only one place I knew of where there was any true order.

Yet, how could I go back? Did I not know that I really had no vocation? . . . It was the same old story again.

I got on the train for Cincinnati, and for New York.

Back at St. Bonaventure's, where the spring I had already met in Kentucky finally caught up with me again, several weeks later, I walked in the woods, in the sun, under the pale blossoms of the wild cherry trees.

The fight went on in my mind.

By now, the problem had resolved itself into one practical issue: why don't I consult somebody about the whole question? Why don't I write to the abbot of Gethsemani and tell him all about my case, and ask him his opinion?

More practical still, here at St. Bonaventure's there was one priest whom I had come to know well during this last year, a wise and good philosopher, Father Philotheus. We had been going over some texts of St. Bonaventure and Duns Scotus together, and I knew I could trust him with the most involved spiritual problem. Why did I not ask him?

There was one absurd, crazy thing that held me up: it was a kind of a blind impulse, confused, obscure, irrational. I can hardly identify it as it actually was, because its true nature escaped me: it was so blind, so elemental. But it amounted to a vague subconscious fear that I would once and for all be told that I definitely had no vocation. It was the fear of an ultimate refusal. Perhaps what I wanted was to maintain myself in an equivocal, indefinite position in which I would be free to dream about entering the monastery, without having the actual responsibility of doing so, and of embracing the real hardships of Cistercian life. If I asked advice, and was told I had no vocation, then the dream would be over; and if I was told I had a vocation, then I would have to walk right in to the reality.

And all this was complicated by that other dream: that of the Carthusians. If there had been a Carthusian monastery in America, things would have been much simpler. But there is still no such place in the whole hemisphere. And there was no chance of crossing the Atlantic. France was full of Germans and the Charterhouse in Sussex had been bombed flat to the ground, And so I walked under the trees, full of indecision, praying for light.

In the midst of this conflict, I suddenly got a notion which shows that I was not very far advanced in the spiritual life. I thought of praying God to let me know what I was going to do, or what I should do, or what the solution would be, by showing it to me in the Scriptures. It was the old business of opening the book and putting your finger down blindly on the page and taking the words thus designated as answer to your question. Sometimes the saints have done this, and much more often a lot of superstitious old women have done it. I am not a saint, and I do not doubt that there may have been an element of superstition in my action. But anyway, I made my prayer, and opened the book, and put my finger down definitely on the page and said to myself: "Whatever it is, this is it."

I looked, and the answer practically floored me. The words were: *"Ecce eris tacens."* "Behold, thou shalt be silent."

It was the twentieth verse of the first chapter of St. Luke where the angel was talking to John the Baptist's father, Zachary.

Tacens: there could not have been a closer word to "Trappist" in the whole Bible, as far as I was concerned, for to me, as well as to most other people, the word "Trappist" stood for "silence."

However, I immediately found myself in difficulties which show how silly it is to make an oracle out of books. As soon as I looked at the context, I observed that Zachary was being reproved for asking too many questions. Did the whole context apply to me, too, and was I also therefore reproved? And therefore was the news to be taken as ominous and bad? I thought about it a little, and soon found that I was getting completely mixed up. Besides, when I reflected, I realized that I had not put the question in any clear terms, so that, as a matter of fact I had forgotten just what I had asked. I did not know whether I had asked God to tell me His will, or merely to announce to me what would happen in the future in point of fact. By the time I had got myself completely tied up in these perplexities, the information I had asked for was more of a nuisance, and a greater cause of uncertainty than my ignorance.

In fact I was almost as ignorant as I was before, except for one thing.

Deep down, underneath all the perplexity, I had a kind of a conviction that this was a genuine answer, and that the problem was indeed some day going to end up that way: I was going to be a Trappist.

DEATH
THE NEXT DEVELOPMENT IN MAN (Mentor)
THE UNCONSCIOUS BEFORE FREUD (Basic Books)
L. von Bertalanffy THE PROBLEM OF LIFE (Torchbooks)
NEW PATHWAYS IN PIANO TECHNIQUE (Philos. Library)
Perls, Hefferline & Goodman. GESTALT THERAPY (Julian Press)
A. F. Bentley INQUIRY INTO INQUIRIES (Beacon)
Dewey & Bentley
Paperback
φυσις
natura
Firm
Yielding
Rigid

Alan Watts

(1915-1973)

Alan Watts may not have been the most authentic representative of Zen Buddhism in the West, but he was in the 1960s the most widely read and heard. The counterculture generation adopted him as their very own, and he, like a Pied Piper, led them away from establishment norms and traditional Christian or Judaic allegiances.

Watts had a pilgrimage not quite as convoluted as that of Orestes Brownson, but one that held much fascination. Born in a small town in England, he migrated to London and through reading of Zen master D. T. Suzuki found himself at an early age attracted to Buddhism. By the time he was nineteen, he wrote his first book on Zen. In 1938 he contracted the first of his three marriages, and soon he and his wife moved to New York. After graduation from Seabury-Western Theological Seminary in 1948, he accepted ordination as an Episcopal priest and served as the Episcopal chaplain at Northwestern University from 1945 to 1950. Following that position, he moved to California as professor of Asian Studies at the University of the Pacific in Stockton. All this time his interest in the East continued, and his popularity as lecturer and writer grew. By 1957 he was able to give himself full time to these latter activities.

Long before this, he had concluded that he must resign from his priestly status in the Episcopal Church. In a letter of resignation, he explained that he had seen his ministry in the Episcopal Church as a kind of refuge "from the confusion of our times." We live, Watts added, "in a world where all the traditions in which men have found security are crumbling." That being so, the natural tendency is to return to an older, familiar faith. The mind "envies the inner calm and certitude of an earlier age, where men could put absolute and childlike trust in the authority of the Church, and in the ordered beauty of an ancient doctrine." But this no longer served for him, as he exchanged the familiar Christian tradition for the "rich and venerable tradition of Mahayana Buddhism, touched by the nature-wisdom of Taoism." In contrast to the exclusivist tendencies of Christianity, this Eastern path "has seemed one of the most civilizing and humanizing and generally amiable movements in all history."

The pilgrimage was more than intellectual. By 1972 Watts had made four trips to Kyoto, Japan, and "will snatch any opportunity to go there again." He went to the city "which had been soaked in Buddhism for so many centuries . . . to gape like a yokel and simply absorb its atmosphere." Watts wrote and lectured extensively on Zen, but Zen master Suzuki regarded Thomas Merton as the most astute interpreter of Zen Buddhism to the West.

[See Monica Furlong, *Zen Effects: The Life of Alan Watts* (Boston: Houghton Mifflin, 1986); and, Thomas A. Tweed and Stephen Prothero, eds., *Asian Religions in America: A Documentary History* (New York: Oxford University Press, 1999.]

The Sound of Rain

Although I have always been following the sun to the West, I have at last come to love the rain as well, especially in these dry California hills where the burnished grass so easily takes fire. Better still, though, are the spring and autumn rains of Japan. Despite the fascination which I have had with the Far East since reading about Dr. Fu Manchu at the age of eleven, and Lafcadio Hearn's *Gleanings in Buddha-Fields* at the age of fourteen, I didn't reach Japan until I was forty-six. From all I had heard about its frantic industrialization I was prepared to be completely disillusioned. But I went, and have returned three more times.

One would suppose that in view of my lifelong interest in Zen Buddhism I would have gone there years before — like Ruth Sasaki, Gary Snyder, and many others — to undertake the monastic discipline of living Zen, sit at the feet of a master, attain enlightenment, and come back with a certificate to prove it. I have nothing against that at all, especially if one may judge by what it has done for Gary. But that

---

Source: Alan Watts, *In My Own Way: An Autobiography, 1915-1965* (New York: Pantheon Books, 1972), pp. 359-61; 362-64; 376-79; 387-88.

isn't my way. And when at last I did get to Japan I didn't rush off to a Zen school to gobble up all the wisdom I could. I went to look and to listen, and to see things in a way that insiders often miss; and I found what I wanted — albeit with the help of two Zen masters. It was the sound of rain.

Zen Buddhism fascinates Westerners because its way of teaching is quite unlike that of any other religion, if religion it is. It has no dogma, requires no particular belief, and neither deals in abstractions nor harps on morality. Then what, of religion or philosophy, is left? All and nothing, for Zen deals with reality — the universe — as it is, and not as it is thought about and described. The heart of Zen is not an idea but an experience, and when that experience happens (and "happens" is just the right word) you are set free from ideas altogether. Certainly, you can still use them, but you no longer take them seriously. Picture yourself, then, as a person very earnestly concerned with making sense of life, of a world involving intense pleasure and appalling pain, and trying to understand how and why there is this weird sensation called "myself" in the middle of it all. You have heard that there is a great master, a sage, who can give you the answer; not in terms of some fancy theory, but the thing itself, so that you will never feel the same again and that sensation called "myself" will have been turned upside down and inside out. You approach the master and, perhaps with some difficulty, get an interview. You have thought out your questions most carefully, but just as you are about to open your mouth he yells "Ho!" at the top of his voice. You are nonplussed, and he asks what's puzzling you. You begin, "Well I came to ask . . . ," but he interrupts, "And I have answered you." "But I don't . . . ," and again "Ho!" — shouted from the depths of his belly. End of interview.

The greater part of Zen literature consists of such tales, often adding, however, that the questioner was completely satisfied. He cannot think of any more questions about life to ask, other than such simple matters as, "What time does the plane leave for San Francisco?" For this reason intelligent and adventurous Westerners have, in considerable numbers, been heading for the ancient capital of Kyoto, which has long been the main center for training in Zen.

But it was not only for Zen that I went immediately to Kyoto when I first arrived in Japan. I wanted to feel the everyday life of a city which had been soaked in Buddhism for so many centuries, not analyze it like a psychologist, categorize it like an anthropologist, or study its splendid monuments like an antiquarian. I went to gape like a yokel and simply absorb its atmosphere. We went to the district called Higashi-yama, or Eastern Hills, where buildings on narrow, winding streets overlook the rest of the city, which — unusually for Japan — are laid out in the flat grid pattern of an American city in a geographical setting which slightly resembles Los Angeles. Hills, even mountains, lie to the east, north, and west, while the south is open to Osaka, Kobe, and the sea. As in Los Angeles, the best land is in the foothills, where spring-water flows into garden pools through bamboo pipes, and though there are here many quiet and sumptuous private homes, much of the area has been occupied by temples and monasteries. Originally it belonged to feudal brigands, who were scared of the Zen priests because the priests weren't scared of them, became pious Buddhists, and made generous offerings of land.

∼

With sense of time gone awry from travel by jet, I wake at four in the morning to hear what is, for me, the most magical single sound that man has made. It comes from a bronze bell some eight feet high and five feet in diameter, struck by a horizontal swinging tree-trunk, and hung close to the ground; actually more of a gong than a bell. It doesn't clang out through the sky like a church bell but booms along the ground with a note at once deep and sweet and vaguely sad, as if very very old. It sounds once and, when the hum has died way, again . . . and several times more. From the direction, I realize that this is the bell of the Nanzenji Zen monastery, signifying that, so long before sunrise, some twenty young men, skin-headed and black-robed, have gone to sit perfectly still in a quiet dark hall. When the bell finishes they will begin to intone, on a single note, the *Shingyo*, or *Heart Sutra*, which sums up everything that Buddhism has to say: *Shiki soku ze ku, ku soku ze shiki* — "What is form that is emptiness, what is emptiness that is form." Actually the language is the Japanese way of pronouncing medieval Chinese, which hardly anyone understands, and the words are chanted for their sound rather than their meaning. We shall see why.

With one side of my brain I know that these are rather bored and sleepy young men, mostly sons of priests, attending the Japanese equivalent of an ecclesiastical boys' boarding school or a Jesuit seminary. They think they ought to be there, but would really rather be chasing girls or learning to fly planes. The fine aloeswood incense, the faint candles, the sonorous gongs, and the pulsing chant are for them merely *kurai*: gloomy, musty, dank, decrepit, and old. A graveyard long gone to waste, with an old lady muttering over a stone. Only the sternest discipline will keep these boys at it. For the most part they are not, like Western seekers, *interested* in Buddhism, and they, in their turn, seldom realize that much of this seemingly esoteric discipline is simply routine drill for reluctant boys. Having been through that once, in school at Canterbury Cathedral, I have not been inclined to try it again.

But with the other side of my brain I want to be in their company, silently and unseen, with no wretched novice-master pushing me around and trying to teach me how to sit in meditation. For the antiquity and mystery of those gongs and the chant is not so much from a backward direction in time as from a vast depth inside the present, from a level of my own here-and-now being, as ancient as life itself. I wonder — what is this glamour of the mysterious and venerable East? Is it all a phony projection of my own romantic fantasies, and if so, why such fantasies? Why do Buddhist rituals and symbols evoke in me a sensation of the mysterious and the marvelous far more enthralling than any Christian equivalent, more even than astronomical revelations about the scope of distant galaxies? There is, of course, a wise-guy debunkery school of cultural anthropologists who want to insist that, seen from the familiar inside, all exotic culture-forms are just humdrum "old hat," as if Japanese and Tibetans could not feel for their traditions what we feel for Shakespeare and Beethoven. There are, indeed, orchestra men bored to death with the Ninth Symphony and schoolchildren who find *Hamlet* a drag, so why should I share these Japanese novices' lack of enthusiasm for Zen? I am sure that the paternalistic discipline with which it is forced down their throats connects it with the same emotions of guilt that I felt in the presence of God the Father and Jesus Christ. It would follow, then, that my enchantment with Zen and Buddhism is that their forms are, for me, free from this kind of static, and thus that through them I can approach the mysteries of the universe without having to feel like a small boy being bawled out because it is good for me.

~

Thus "to realize Buddha in this body" is to realize that you yourself are in fact the universe. You are not, as parents and teachers are wont to imply, a mere stranger on probation in the scheme of things; you are rather a sort of nerve-ending through which the universe is taking a peek at itself, which is why, deep down inside, almost everyone has a vague sense of eternity. Few dare admit this because it would amount to believing that you are God, and God in our culture is the cosmic Boss, so that anyone imagining himself to be God is deemed either blasphemous or insane. But for Buddhism this is no problem because they do not have this particular idea of God, and so are not troubled by the notion of sin and everlasting damnation. Their picture of the universe is not political, not a kingdom ruled by a monarch, but rather an organism in which every part is a "doing" of the whole, so that everything that happens to you is understood as your own *karma,* or "doing." Thus when things go wrong you have no one but yourself to blame. You are not a sinner but a fool, so try another way.

Now I have always found this a highly civilized and humane point of view. For Westerners, the only real alternative to the boss-God religion has been the so-called "scientific" view of the universe as a system of essentially stupid objects. This comes from looking at things in a coldly withdrawn way as in studying the behavior of machinery, while in physiology and psychology we turn this attitude inwardly upon ourselves — only to become objectionable objects to our own gaze. If this mechanical view of life gets rid of horrors about sin and guilt, it also gets rid of any real reason for sympathy or kindness. From the standpoint of mechanical efficiency all feelings and emotions are just obstructive static, and when we are through with poisoning the air there will be every reason for replacing ourselves with steady state electronic mechanisms that require no atmosphere and do nothing but solve mathematical problems. The objective attitude to oneself is finally suicidal, and it is not, therefore, surprising that the grandest flower of our technology is the hydrogen bomb.

But when Buddhists look very deeply into themselves they ask, "But who is looking?" They come up with an answer which has been hard to understand, essentially because of a language problem. For the Japanese word *ku* (translating the Sanskrit *sunya*) has the sense of sky, space, or emptiness, but when it is used for the root of one's own consciousness it means also the finally mysterious and inconceivable. Not so much emptiness or darkness as the way the head looks to its own eyes. This is the meaning of the flaming crystal ball atop the pagoda mast, which in Zen is said to be "like an eye that sees, but does not see itself." *Ku* is therefore "clarity" as of vision or hearing, and nothing is so mysterious as clarity even though we speak of clearing up mysteries. For exactly *what* is clarity itself? Could it be well-defined form? Crystal-clear form? Then, as the *Heart Sutra* says, *ku* is *shiki* — transparency is form.

Unburdened by a Christian upbringing, Gary Snyder has the humorous attitude to religion so characteristic of Zen. We found him in a Japanese-style cottage, close to the Daitokuji monastery in Kyoto, where he was making a twelve-year study of the Zen way of life. He is like a wiry Chinese sage with high cheekbones, twinkling eyes, and a thin beard, and the recipe for his character requires a mixture of Oregon woodsman, seaman, Amerindian shaman, Oriental scholar, San Francisco hippie, and swinging monk, who takes tough discipline with a light heart. He seems to be gently keen about almost everything, and needs no affectation to make himself interesting. He has taken to wife Masa, a beautiful but gutsy Japanese girl from the southern islands, who looks you straight in the eye, does not simper and giggle, gives no mock humility, yet has a quiet naturalness. Their living room is adorned with two large and colorful scrolls bearing those Shingon diagrams of multitudinous Buddha-figures, and so abounds with Buddhist ceremonial tools that Gary called it "the safest place in the galaxy."

After we have taken a communal bath in a huge cauldron over a wood fire, much saké is downed, and apropos of *ku,* the clear void, Gary suggests that we incorporate the "Null and Void Guaranty and Trust Company" with the slogan, "Register your absence with us; you *can* take it with you!" Later, I had some business cards printed for him to this effect, naming him as the company's nonrepresentative. I wonder, why is it that we can't stop laughing at the notion that none of us really exists, and that the walloping concreteness of all the hard facts to be faced is an energetic performance of nothingness?

The joke derives from the fact that, although Westerners speak of "conquering space," they have a radical prejudice and a positive blind spot with respect to the importance of nothingness. They balk at it as people used to balk at thinking of the world as round. To them, nothingness is the awful-awful, the end, the demise which, we most fervently hope, is not to be the ultimate destiny of man and the universe. Yet this is due to a freaky lapse in our logic which affects our theology, our science, our philosophy, and our most vivid emotions. No one seems to have realized that you can't have something without nothing. How can you know "is" without understanding "isn't"? Try to imagine a solid without any space through and around it. Try to imagine space without any solid, including yourself, within it. For if something implies nothing, then nothing — in turn — implies something. To be or not to be is *not* the question, for reality, like electricity, is a pulsation of positive and negative energy. The big bang with which this universe is supposed to have started was, as they say in Zen, "the Void gnashing its teeth." Put in more scientific jargon: Every approach to the limit of absolute inertia condenses by inversion into a departure from the limit of absolute energy. Flip — total void equals big bang.

Stated in bare words this looks too simple. Yet I regard it as my most important philosophical discovery, and if we could understand it thoroughly, we would no longer have the horrors about death, darkness, night, silence, and the unknown. But the remaining question is how to get one's feelings, those easy victims of habit, to recognize that it takes nothing to start something.

~

Long after this I was talking to Ali Akbar Khan, the sarod player, who is generally regarded as the greatest living master of Indian music. I have a particular personal admiration for him, for he is at once holy and sensuous, a complete man. Wine and woman go with his song; a song of unsurpassed technique which he also uses as a type of yoga-meditation in which — if one can use temporal language about things eternal — he is very advanced. Discussing this, he dropped the remark, "All music is in the understanding of one note."

Now this really ought not to be explained. But if you just listen, relating yourself to the world entirely through the sense of hearing, you will find yourself in a universe where reality — pure sound — comes immediately out of silence and emptiness, echoing away as memory in the labyrinths of the brain. In this universe everything flows backward from the present and vanishes, like the wake of a ship; the present comes out of nothing, and you cannot hear any self that is listening. This can be done with all the senses, but most easily with the ears. Simply listen, then, to the rain. Listen to what Buddhists call its "suchness" — its *tathata* or da-da-da. Like all classical music, it means nothing except itself, for only inferior music mimics other sounds or is *about* anything other than music. There is no "message" in a Bach fugue. So, too, when an ancient Zen master was asked about the meaning of Buddhism he replied, "If there is any meaning in it, I myself am not liberated." For when you have really heard the sound of rain you can hear, and see and feel everything else in the same way — as needing no translation, as being just that which it is, though it may be impossible to say what. I have tried for years as a philosopher, but in words it comes out all wrong: in black and white with no color. It comes out that life is a perfectly and absolutely meaningless happening — nothing but a display of endlessly variegated vibrations, neither good nor evil, right nor wrong — a display which, though marvelously woven together, is like a Rorschach blot upon which we are projecting the fantasies of personality, purpose, history, religion, law, science, evolution, and even the basic instinct to survive. And this projection is, in turn, part of the happening. Thus when you try to pin it down you get the banality of formal nihilism, wherein the universe is seen as "a tale told by an idiot, full of sound and fury, signifying nothing."

But this sense of "turning to ashes in one's mouth" is the result of trying to grasp something which can only come to you of itself. Trying to catch the meaning of the universe in terms of some religious, philosophical, or moral system is really like asking Bach or Ali Akbar to explain their music in words. They can explain it only by continuing to play, and you must listen until you understand, get with it, and go with it — and the same is true of the music of the vibrations. The vibrations can go so high on the scale of pain that we have to go into zero, and the way can be made richly horrible by thinking to ourselves, "This ought not to happen" — "It was all that bastard's fault" — "I am being punished for my sins" — "How could God let this happen to me?" When you say the music is abominable, listen to the sound of your own complaint. Above all, simply listen, and I (for the time being) will be silent.

THE REVIVALIST

Billy Graham
(1918-   )

The most readily recognizable name in American religion in the second half of the twentieth century was that of Billy Graham. This resulted not only from his preaching crusades that reached millions, both in the United States and abroad, but also from his high visibility in the media and in the presidential circles in Washington. Graham seemed to be everywhere, and his voice — thanks to radio and television — seemed to be heard everywhere. He had opposition, of course, but he sailed serenely above and far beyond the reach of the denigrators.

Televangelism, a booming phenomenon of the 1960s and beyond, produced a host of would-be imitators of Graham and his resounding success. But many of the electronic revivalists fell as dramatically as they had risen. Graham did not. He avoided the two great traps that had caught so many others: sex and money. He evaded the first by maintaining a happy and monogamous marriage of more than one-half a century to Ruth Bell, daughter of L. Nelson Bell, a Presbyterian medical missionary to China. He avoided the second by setting for himself a salary to be paid by the Billy Graham Evangelistic Association. Money raised at the crusades or on the airwaves went either to the Association or to a local arrangements committee — not directly to Graham. Neither greed nor lust was allowed to rear its ugly head.

Born in North Carolina, Graham's educational wanderings took him to South Carolina (Bob Jones University), Florida (Florida Bible Institute), Illinois (Wheaton College), and — as president — to Northwestern Bible College in Minneapolis, Minnesota (1947-52). Even before taking the position at Northwestern Bible College, Graham had become a full-time evangelist in the Youth for Christ movement. The Los Angeles campaign in 1949, described in the excerpt below, Graham rightly calls the "Watershed." "Overnight we had gone from being a little evangelistic team . . . to what appeared to many to be the hope for national and international revival." By the 1950s, Graham had become a household word.

In response to the flood of invitations to preach all across the country and in many cities abroad, Graham took two responsible steps: first, he would invite all Protestant denominations to join together as sponsors; second, he would countenance no segregated seating at his services. Both decisions brought criticism, and some abandonment by those who thought of themselves as his first and firmest friends. But both decisions enlarged his audience and his impact. His coziness with occupants of the White House also brought criticism, and sorrow to Graham when he learned that sin is no respecter of persons. But even with scandal and sordidness all around, Graham maintained his dignity — and his faith.

[See William Martin, *A Prophet With Honor: The Billy Graham Story* (New York: William Morrow, 1992).]

Watershed: Los Angeles 1949

If the amount of advance press coverage was any indication, the Los Angeles Campaign was going to be a failure. Not that the local organizing committee hadn't tried. They had employed Lloyd Doctor, public relations director for the local Salvation Army, to drum up interest. One day shortly before the meetings opened, he persuaded a handful of reporters to attend the first press conference I had ever conducted. Next day we eagerly scanned the newspapers to see the stories those reporters had written.

Nothing.

As far as the media were concerned, the Los Angeles Campaign — by far our most ambitious evangelistic effort to date — was going to be a nonevent.

Later Lloyd got me a brief appointment with the mayor of Los Angeles, and the *Los Angeles Times* carried a small back-page picture and story of that meeting. Except for the ads that the committee ran in the church section, that was virtually the only press exposure we got for the first couple of weeks.

The invitation to hold meetings in Los Angeles originally came

Source: Billy Graham, *Just As I Am* (New York: HarperCollins, 1997), pp. 167-85.

from a group of businessmen who called themselves "Christ for Greater Los Angeles," representing about two hundred churches. They had already sponsored several such Campaigns with other evangelists, all of which were reasonably successful. Now they wanted me to preach and to bring Cliff Barrows and George Beverly Shea. I agreed but insisted on several stringent conditions.

First, they were to try to broaden church support to include as many churches and denominations as possible. Second, they were to raise their budget from $7,000 to $25,000, in order to invest more in advertising and promotion. Third, they were to erect a much larger tent than they had planned; our limited experience in citywide Campaigns had already taught us that the crowds seemed to grow as the days went on.

The men from Los Angeles initially agreed to every point except raising the budget. They were convinced it would be impossible to come up with such a large amount.

They had a point. In those days, Campaigns were modest efforts. Even at the biggest meetings, it was unusual to hear of more than 50 people responding to the Invitation to receive Christ. Any evangelist preaching before more than 2,000 people was considered highly successful. The Christ for Greater Los Angeles committee undoubtedly felt that their commitment to raise $7,000 was an ambitious step in the right direction.

To many of those seasoned, older Christians, I came across as brash. But I found myself drafting a Los Angeles scenario bigger and bolder than anything I had imagined before. Besides insisting on the budget increase, I set yet another seemingly impossible condition: the committee had to put the public leadership and the platform duties of the Campaign entirely in the hands of local clergy. The committee, I felt, represented too limited an evangelical constituency to make an impact.

I consulted with Cliff, and he agreed. I wrote back to our hosts and told them we would be forced to cancel if they could not see their way clear to step out in faith and take that financial risk.

"I stand upon the brink of absolute fear and trembling when I think we might come to Los Angeles with only a small handful of churches," I wrote in February 1949. "The city of Los Angeles will not be touched unless the majority of the churches are actively back of this campaign."

My limited experience had already shown me that without the cooperation of the local churches and their pastors, not only would attendance suffer but so would the follow-up of new Christians.

One of my objectives was to build the church in the community. I did not simply want the audience to come from the churches. I wanted to leave something behind in the very churches themselves.

Even as I imposed these conditions on the long-suffering committee, I doubted that they could comply. Yet I burned with a sense of urgency to move forward: "I'm convinced . . . that if a revival could break out in the city of Los Angeles," I wrote to Mr. Claude Jenkins, secretary of the committee, "it would have repercussions around the world. Let's not stop at anything to make this the meeting that God could use as a spark to send a flame of revival through the nation. Your responsibilities are tremendous. Let's go forward by prayer."

Initial reports from Los Angeles indicated that I was stirring up a hornet's nest. Some opponents circulated distorted and false stories about my being a self-promoting money-grabber. The kind of conditions I was insisting on certainly might have fueled that fire. And getting the committee's agreement would take a miracle. I was soon humbled when I found out what truly big men they were in the depth of their devotion to evangelism: they agreed to do what we had asked. The Campaign was set to begin in the last week of September and run for three weeks.

Just before the Campaign began, Henrietta Mears invited me to her home in Beverly Hills to speak to the Hollywood Christian Group. That occasion gave me an opportunity for lengthy discussions with well-known actors and actresses.

One man at the meeting, Stuart Hamblen, impressed me tremendously. He was rough, strong, loud, and earthy. Every inch of his six-foot-two frame was genuine cowboy, and his 220 pounds seemed all bone and muscle. His name was legendary up and down the West Coast for his popular radio show, heard every afternoon for two hours. He said he would invite me on as a guest. I took an instant liking to him and coveted him for Christ. Only half-jokingly, he said he could fill the tent if he gave his endorsement.

In the months ahead, I would meet other Hollywood celebrities of the time, especially in visits to Miss Mears's "out of this world" home, as Ruth described it — people such as Tim Spencer (who wrote a number-one song on the hit parade, "Room Full of Roses"), Mickey Finn, Jon Hall, Connie Haines, and Jane Russell. Edwin Orr led these meetings, so they were both intellectually stimulating and spiritually stirring. Many of these stars were so earnest about learning the Word of

God and translating it into daily living that Ruth felt they put to shame our Thursday afternoon prayer meetings back home in the Bible Belt.

I was inspired especially by the testimony of actress Colleen Townsend, who had a contract with Twentieth Century–Fox and whose picture had just been on the cover of *Life* magazine. She was one of the most dedicated Christians I had met, and yet she was working in the film industry — an industry that was anathema to many of the supporters of the Crusade. She became engaged to Louis Evans, Jr., whose father was pastor of Hollywood's First Presbyterian Church. They would actively participate in the tent meetings. It was she who thoughtfully wrote a note to Ruth after meeting me at Forest Home. "Billy mentioned how much he'd like to have you here," she said, "so I thought I'd just drop you a note of added encouragement."

Ruth did come, a month earlier than she intended. She wanted to be with me for my birthday on November 7 but got mixed up on the date and arrived on October 7 instead! "I tell you, I have a brain tumor," she wrote back to North Carolina. "I've never felt so foolish in my life, and got ribbed good and properly." Gigi had been left in the care of Grandmother Bell in Montreat, and Anne was staying with her Aunt Rosa and Uncle Don Montgomery in Los Alamos, New Mexico. (Bunny hadn't yet been born, of course.)

I was overjoyed to have Ruth with me so soon. Having gotten to California well ahead of the September 25 starting date to allow time for getting acquainted with the leaders and the special challenges of the area, I had been missing her terribly.

The attendance at our early Los Angeles meetings averaged about 3,000 each night and 4,000 on Sunday afternoons, so the tent was never filled to capacity.

I sensed that interest was building, though, and the crowds were getting larger. However, I found that I was preaching mainly to Christians. As Ruth observed in a letter home to her folks in October, "It isn't easy to get unconverted to a tent."

Nevertheless, I was preaching with a new confidence and fervor. I had always been loud and enthusiastic (and some said authoritative). But since my pivotal experience in the mountain woods at Forest Home, I was no longer struggling internally. There was no gap between what I said and what I knew I believed deep in my soul. It was no coincidence that the centerpiece of the 150-foot platform in the tent, right in front of the pulpit, was a replica of an open Bible — twenty feet high and twenty feet wide.

Stuart Hamblen did indeed invite me to be a guest on his radio show. I hesitated at first. Would the Campaign committee want me on that kind of program, sponsored by a tobacco company, even if Hamblen was the number one radio personality on the West Coast?

The more I thought about it, the more intriguing the idea seemed. Hadn't Christ Himself spent time with sinners? Hadn't He been criticized by the religious leaders of His day for that very thing? Why should I not take the risk? I said yes.

On his show, he surprised me by telling all his listeners, in his own rough-and-ready manner, to "go on down to Billy Graham's tent and hear the preaching." Even more surprising, to his listeners as well as to me, was his next remark: "I'll be there too!"

The first night Stuart attended, we would find out later, he became deeply convicted of his own sins and the need for Christ to save him. Not understanding what was going on in his soul, he became angry and stalked out. For two or three nights he stayed away. Then he came back. Each time he showed up, he had the same reaction, getting so mad once that he actually shook his fist at me as he walked out of the tent.

We were approaching the scheduled closing-night meeting — Sunday, October 16 — of our three-week Campaign. During the week before that final meeting, since there was evident blessing, some committee members advocated extending the Campaign a short time. Others thought it should stop as planned; the choir, the counselors, and other workers were tired, and we might risk an anticlimax. The budget had been met, and now the organizers just took love offerings for Cliff and me. Everybody was confident the tent would be filled on the closing Sunday to give us a grand finale to an excellent series of meetings.

Should the Campaign be extended? It was not simply for the committee to decide. We needed a clear sense of direction from the Lord. Grady, Cliff, Bev, and I prayed together over and over again as the last week wore on. At last we decided to follow the example of Gideon in the Old Testament and put out a fleece, asking God to give us a decisive sign of His purpose.

It came at four-thirty the next morning.

I was awakened in my room at the Langham Hotel by the jangling of the telephone. In a voice broken by tears, a man begged to see me right away. It was Stuart Hamblen. I woke up Grady and Wilma Wilson, and they went with Ruth into another room to pray.

By the time I was up and dressed, Stuart and his praying, godly wife, Suzy, were at my door. We talked together and prayed, and the rugged cowboy gave his life to Christ in a childlike act of faith. He came forward in the next service. The first thing he did after he received Christ was to call his father, who was an old-fashioned Methodist preacher in west Texas. I could hear his father shout with joy over the phone!

It would not be long before Stuart put his vibrant experience into a song that was inspired by a conversation he'd had with John Wayne: "It Is No Secret [What God Can Do]." That still remains one of the favorites people like to hear Bev Shea sing. Shortly after, he wrote another testimony song, "This Ole House," which I think was number one for several weeks on the national radio show *Your Hit Parade*.

Years later, when we were back in Los Angeles for a Crusade at the Coliseum, Cliff, Grady, Bev, and I went to Stuart's home for breakfast. "Billy," Stuart said at one point, "it's terrible that these planes come over the stadium while you're trying to preach. I'm a member of the President's Club of Western Airlines, and I think I'll call the president. If he won't do anything about it, I think I'll get my old longhorn rifle out and see if I can't stop those planes from here!"

That very night I was telling the crowd how Stuart was willing to get his longhorn rifle out to bag a few of the low-flying airplanes . . . when there was a terribly loud bang at the other end of the stadium.

"Stuart, is that you?" I called out.

The crowd roared.

That night back in 1949, Cliff and I knew that we had our answer about continuing the Campaign. Clearly, the Lord had unfinished business to do in the lives of people who were just beginning to hear about the meetings and think about the Gospel. We told the committee that the Campaign had to go on, and they agreed.

But for how long? During the next week — the first week of our extension — we were thrilled to hear Stuart Hamblen give his testimony over his radio program, telling listeners how Christ had changed his life. People were talking about it all along the West Coast. Did this justify *another* extension of the Campaign?

Cliff and I had not experienced such mounting interest and enthusiasm during our previous Campaigns. In our uncertainty about what to do, we agreed that the best thing was to put out the fleece again, as Gideon had done, and ask the Lord for another sign. We were relatively inexperienced young men with a lot to learn. (Cliff was four and a half years younger than I.) Our wives were coping with our unpredictable lifestyles, but we wanted to be considerate of their feelings too. Would God give us another clear indication what to do?

When I arrived at the tent for the next meeting, the scene startled me. For the first time, the place was crawling with reporters and photographers. They had taken almost no notice of the meetings up until now, and very little had appeared in the papers. I asked one of the journalists what was happening.

"You've just been kissed by William Randolph Hearst," he responded.

I had no idea what the reporter was talking about, although I knew the name. Hearst, of course, was the great newspaper owner. I had never met the man, but like most Americans I had read his papers. The next morning's headline story about the Campaign in the *Los Angeles Examiner,* followed by an evening story in the *Los Angeles Herald Express* — both owned by Hearst — stunned me. The story was picked up by the Hearst papers in New York, Chicago, Detroit, and San Francisco, and then by all their competitors. Until then, I doubt if any newspaper editor outside the area had heard of our Los Angeles Campaign.

Puzzled as I was, my curiosity was never satisfied. Hearst and I did not meet, talk by phone, or correspond as long as he lived. Supposedly, he had sent a message to his editors, "Puff Graham," but there were so many stories about how we might have come to his notice and about why he might have been interested in promoting us that I did not know which, if any, was true. One of the more intriguing ones was that Hearst and his controversial partner, Marion Davies, disguised themselves and attended a tent meeting in person. I doubted it.

Time magazine pulled out all the rhetorical stops in its November 14, 1949, issue: "Blond, trumpet-lunged North Carolinian William Franklin Graham Jr., a Southern Baptist minister who is also president of the Northwestern Schools in Minneapolis, dominates his huge audience from the moment he strides onstage to the strains of *Send the Great Revival in My Soul.* His lapel microphone, which gives added volume to his deep, cavernous voice, allows him to pace the platform as he talks, rising to his toes to drive home a point, clenching his fists, stabbing his finger at the sky and straining to get his words to the furthermost corners of the tent."

The newspaper coverage was just the beginning of a phenomenon. As more and more extraordinary conversion stories caught the public's attention, the meetings continued night after night, drawing overflow crowds. Something was happening that all the media coverage in the world could not explain. And neither could I. God may have used Mr. Hearst to promote the meetings, as Ruth said, but the credit belonged solely to God. All I knew was that before it was over, we were on a journey from which there would be no looking back.

A veteran police officer in Medford, Oregon, who had attended a Los Angeles meeting at the start of the third week, wrote to me shortly after he got home: "I am glad you have continued on. . . . and I pray God will continue to bless you and your good work there." He added a postscript explaining the gift he had enclosed: "A small token to help you — and keep spreading that tent out."

That was exactly what we had to do. As November began with a further extension of the Campaign, headlines as far away as Indiana screamed, "OLD-TIME RELIGION SWEEPS LOS ANGELES." Reporters were comparing me with Billy Sunday; church leaders were quoted as saying that the Campaign was "the greatest religious revival in the history of Southern California."

One evening when the Invitation was given, I noticed a giant of a man, tears rolling down his cheeks, coming up with his wife to receive Christ. I did not know who he was, but I asked Cliff to have the audience sing one more verse of the final song to give them time to reach the front. Reporters recognized him, and the next day's newspaper made a big thing of it. "EVANGELIST CONVERTS VAUS, SOUND ENGINEER IN VICE PROBE." Jim Vaus was the electronics wizard who had allegedly served as reputed mobster Mickey Cohen's personal wiretapper.

A few days after his conversion, Jim came to visit me.

"Billy, I told Mickey Cohen what happened to me. Instead of his getting angry, he said, 'Jim, I'm glad you did it. I hope you stick to it.'"

There was a contract out on Jim's life, but apparently it was not from Cohen.

"Billy, would you be willing to talk to Mickey if I could arrange it?" he asked.

"I'll go anywhere to talk to anybody about Christ," I shot back without thinking.

By arrangement, then, we slipped out of the tent by a back exit after the meeting one night, in order to avoid the press, and got away undetected in Jim's car. As he drove toward Mickey Cohen's home, I had mixed feelings — a little uncertainty and hesitation, to be sure, yet a deep-down boldness as well, because I knew I was going to witness to a well-known mobster in the name of Jesus Christ.

As we drove up to an unimpressive house in the exclusive Brentwood section of Los Angeles, I noticed a car parked across the street with a man sitting in it.

When we got out of our car in the driveway, Cohen opened the front door to greet us. I was surprised to see how short he was. He reminded me of Zacchaeus in the New Testament, the undersized tax collector who shinnied up a tree in order to see Jesus over the heads of the crowd (*see* Luke 19:1-10). Looking straight at me with curiosity in his big brown eyes, he invited us in.

"What'll you have to drink?" Cohen asked.

"I'll have a Coca-Cola," I replied.

"That's fine," he said. "I think I'll have one, too."

He went to get the drinks himself. Apparently, there was no one else in the house.

Jim told Mickey again how he had accepted Christ and planned to change his entire life; he described the peace and joy he now had.

Then I explained to Mickey, as simply and forthrightly as I could, the Gospel from A to Z. As we talked, I prayed inwardly (as I did when preaching to thousands in the tent) that God would help me to find the right words.

Mickey responded with some items about his own life, especially mentioning the charitable organizations he had supported and the good works he had done. Although he was of a different religious belief than I, he told me he respected me and certainly respected what Jim Vaus had done. Before we left, we had a prayer.

"WIRETAPPER IN CONFESSION AS EVANGELIST TRIES TO SAVE COHEN."

That was one paper's headline the next day. Without my knowledge or approval, the story of that visit had been leaked to the press — perhaps by the man I had seen in the car parked across the street, perhaps by a reporter who had been tipped off by someone in the Campaign organization, perhaps even by Cohen himself (who had a reputation for promoting his own notoriety).

Cohen denied the story. "I think the whole thing is a publicity stunt," one newspaper reported him as saying, "and that's what I'm tryin' to avoid — publicity. . . . I don't want to meet the guy. I haven't got time."

Lies of that magnitude were startlingly new to me but I could not be discouraged about them. Ruth's mother wrote to us about a prayer Gigi had offered on Cohen's behalf. "Dear Jesus, thank You for the meetings and dear Jesus, thank You for Mickey Cohen. Make him good and make him let Jesus put His blood in his heart."

As the Campaign went into its fifth week, we rearranged the seating to accommodate 3,000 more chairs. When that wasn't enough, crowds overflowed into the street. We added an extension, doubling the size of the 480-foot-long tent. Reporters were on hand to cover every meeting, and press accounts were positive.

The Associated Press put it on their priority "A" wire that went throughout the world. Both *Life* and *Time* magazines carried major stories. And the *Los Angeles Times* (the main competitor to the Hearst-owned papers) picked up the Campaign in a big way, of course.

People came to the meetings for all sorts of reasons, not just religious ones. No doubt some were simply curious to see what was going on. Others were skeptical and dropped by just to confirm their prejudices. Many were desperate over some crisis in their lives and hoped they might get a last chance to set things right. A few, we learned, were even sentenced by a Los Angeles County judge, a woman who strongly supported the ministry and thought a night in the tent might do convicted offenders more good than a night in jail.

A minister from Yucca Valley took a leave of absence from his church so that he could be night watchman at the tent after each meeting ended. "Johnny" was the name he wanted us to call him by. He slept under the platform to keep an eye on the place. One night he heard something rattling the chain at the entrance.

"Who goes there?" he called out.

"Just me," came the reply.

"What do you want?"

"I just want to find Jesus."

Johnny led him to Christ right then and there.

As for Northwestern, I sent reports regularly to my secretary, Luverne Gustavson, in Minneapolis. Sometimes forgetful of the two-hour time difference between California and Minnesota, I phoned George Wilson at his home at two in the morning, his time, to tell him what had happened at that night's meeting.

Back in Los Angeles, we asked the Lord for yet another signal. Should we extend the meetings to a sixth week? Attendance was still growing, but I did not want numerical success to become our standard for discerning the will of God. We did not dare go forward without His direction.

A fierce storm was heading toward Los Angeles from the Pacific. If it hit the coast, it would wreak havoc on our huge tent and the thousands of folding chairs. We prayed that if God wanted us to continue, the storm would not reach Los Angeles. The next morning the newspapers reported that the storm had dissipated at sea, much to the surprise of the meteorologists. We entered the sixth week with high hopes and grateful hearts, but with sagging shoulders. I had never preached so much or so hard in all my life. I had run out of sermons in stockpile and was having to prepare a new one every day. That took up to six or eight hours. Increasingly, I forgot about illustrations and applications, though I knew they were supposed to be necessary to good sermon construction. In some of these later messages, I used mostly Scripture references. I had two or three old Bibles from which I clipped out passages to paste onto my outline. Then, from the platform, I read these as part of my sermon without having had to write them out longhand.

A movie star who was not a Christian offered me this word of spiritual wisdom: "Billy, you can't compete with us in entertainment. We know all the ropes. If you get up there and preach what's in the Bible, I'll be on hand every night." I tried to follow that advice.

On one or two nights at the height of the Campaign, we had new believers give their testimonies of what Christ had done for them. Their words made such an impression that afterward I sensed the Holy Spirit was already speaking to many, so I simply gave a brief explanation of the Gospel and an Invitation to receive Christ, and people came forward.

One night a man took a taxi from a tavern to the tent, and ran down the aisle while I was preaching. I asked Grady to take him into the auxiliary prayer tent and then invited anyone who wanted to join them to come forward. Scores did, even though the sermon wasn't finished. The man put his faith in Christ and began a new life by the grace of God.

Long after the crowds left, people drifted in singly or in pairs. Some were simply wanderers in the night; others, too troubled to sleep, were seeking something in that odd sanctuary. Johnny, the pastor-watchman, seated them in a row at the front and read Scripture to them, gave them the Gospel, and prayed for them.

Occasionally, I invited others to preach for me. T.W.* came two or three times from Minneapolis. One night Bob Pierce, founder of World Vision and Samaritan's Purse, spoke for me. I introduced them, and then I would come back to the pulpit and give the Invitation.

Besides the sermon preparation, I desperately needed time for prayer to unload my burdens to the Lord and to seek His direction for

---

*Thomas Walter Wilson, brother of Grady Wilson. (ed.)

the preaching and for other ministry opportunities. Some mornings as early as five o'clock, I would go to Grady's room to ask him to pray with me. Some time after the third week, he had to leave for a previous Campaign commitment back in the Midwest, but Cliff and Bev stayed with me to encourage me and do all they could to ease the load.

Under the leadership of a Lutheran spiritual leader, Armin Gesswein, organized prayer meetings were going on all over Southern California as well as in other parts of the country. Students were praying in Christian colleges, businesspeople were praying in offices, families were praying in their homes, and congregations were gathering for special prayer meetings. "The mightiest force in the world," as Frank Laubach called prayer, undergirded me and brought the blessing of God from Heaven to Los Angeles. (Laubach was a great advocate of teaching people how to read and write in areas of the world where education could not be taken for granted.)

Faithfully, day after day, 40 to 50 women prayed together on our behalf and then attended the meetings, sitting just in front of the platform each night with their faces full of expectant faith that God was about to work again.

The increasing media exposure brought a never-ending stream of requests for special appearances that often had me speaking three or four additional times each day: civic gatherings, churches, evangelism parties in the mansions of the rich and famous, school assemblies, and one-on-one interviews by the score.

When newsreels of the Campaign started up in theaters, people began to recognize us on the streets. Of course, we had no staff to handle all the calls, letters, and telegrams that overwhelmed us in a daily avalanche. The word *burnout* was not in the popular vocabulary yet, but I was getting perilously close to that condition.

Before the end of that sixth week, I did not need to put out another fleece to find out whether I could continue the pace. That colorful writer for *Time* magazine had described me earlier as "trumpet-lunged" and having a "cavernous voice." In the final weeks, though, I often felt too weak to stand at the pulpit, and some of my platform-pacing was necessary to keep myself from toppling over when I stood still. I had lost a lot of weight thus far in the Campaign; dark rings circled my eyes. Cliff and Bev (who had to commute back to Chicago one day each week for his radio broadcast) felt the strain too, as did our long-suffering wives. Billie Barrows at the piano worked as hard as any of us, and Lorin Whitney tirelessly played the organ. Ruth herself stayed up long hours each night counseling people. None of us would leave the little counseling tent until every person had been personally talked to.

Drained as I was, physically, mentally, and emotionally, I experienced God's unfailing grace in perpetual spiritual renewal. I wanted the Campaign to close, but I was convinced that God wanted it to continue. All my personal reserves were used up; I had to put my entire dependence on the Lord for the messages to preach and the strength to preach them. "[God's] strength is made perfect in weakness," Paul wrote, "for when I am weak, then am I strong" (2 Corinthians 12:9, 10, KJV). It seemed that the weaker my body became, the more powerfully God used my simple words.

There was another concern. My job was to be president of Northwestern Schools, and all of this Los Angeles ministry coincided with the first term of the academic year. Back in Minneapolis, students were wondering if their president was ever going to come home. Newspaper clippings were pasted up on a board to keep them informed, and they were praying for the Campaign, of course, thrilled at each report of what the Lord was accomplishing. Nevertheless, a few board members were murmuring about the school's absent president. Dr. Riley's widow, Marie, had reason to question her late husband's wisdom in appointing me his successor as president.

And there was still another concern: my family and the personal price they were paying while I was in Los Angeles. Ruth's sister and brother-in-law, Rosa and Don Montgomery, came from New Mexico to join us for the closing week, bringing Anne, who had been staying with them. "Whose baby is this?" I asked when I saw the child in Rosa's arms, not recognizing my own daughter. And the baby went to sleep crying for her aunt, not her mother.

But as the eighth week approached in Los Angeles, we all knew that the end had to come. Not that the blessings were diminishing. It was then that Louis Zamperini was converted. He was the U.S. track star who had pulled a flag bearing the Nazi swastika down from the Reichstag during the 1936 Berlin Olympic Games. Later, in the Second World War, he was shot down in the Pacific and drifted on a liferaft for forty-seven days. He survived attacks by Japanese pilots who swooped down on him for target practice. Finally, the Japanese captured him and put him in prison for two years. Although he was a famous athlete and war hero, he came home feeling unhappy, disillusioned, and broken in spirit. One night he wandered into our tent in Los Angeles with his wife and accepted Christ, and his life was transformed.

Finally, a closing day came for the 1949 Los Angeles Campaign, a month late. In anticipation, a pastors' breakfast on Wednesday of the final week at the Alexandria Hotel drew 500 ministers and other Christian workers. They planned to spend one hour together but stayed for four, listening to testimonies by Hamblen, Vaus, Zamperini, and Harvey Fritts, who starred in a popular television show as "Colonel Zack." In his report on the events, Claude Jenkins indicated that some people thought the breakfast was the spiritual highlight of the Campaign.

On Sunday afternoon, November 20, two hours before the start of the final meeting, 11,000 people packed the tent to standing room only. Thousands milled about in the streets, unable to get in. Hundreds left because they couldn't hear. On the platform with me were 450 fellow ministers, to whom now fell the awesome challenge of shepherding those who had come forward through the weeks.

For that time, the statistics were overwhelming. In eight weeks, hundreds of thousands had heard, and thousands had responded to accept Christ as Savior; 82 percent of them had never been church members. Thousands more, already Christians, had come forward to register various fresh commitments to the Lord. Someone calculated that we had held seventy-two meetings. I had preached sixty-five full sermons, and given hundreds of evangelistic talks to small groups, in addition to talks on the radio.

That evening, exhausted after the final meeting, T.W., Ruth, and I got on the Santa Fe *Super Chief* train, hoping to get a couple of days of rest traveling back to Minneapolis. We were greeted by the conductor and the porter as though we were some kind of celebrities. A strange experience, believe me.

As we knelt together to pray before climbing into our berths, we were both grateful and afraid. We could hardly find words to express to the Lord our thanks for His many mercies to us personally, and for His blessing on the Los Angeles Campaign. But we feared that we did not have the capacity to live up to our responsibilities. People were expecting so much from us now.

When the train stopped briefly in Kansas City, we were met by a couple of reporters. When we got to Minneapolis, the press was again there to interview us, along with some Twin Cities pastors and faculty and students from Northwestern Schools. Until then it had not fully registered with me how far-reaching the impact of the Los Angeles Campaign had been. I would learn over the next few weeks that the phenomenon of that Los Angeles tent Campaign at Washington and Hill

Streets would forever change the face of my ministry and my life. Overnight we had gone from being a little evangelistic team, whose speaker also served with Youth for Christ and Northwestern Schools, to what appeared to many to be the hope for national and international revival. Everywhere we turned, someone wanted us to come and do for them what had been done in Los Angeles. What they didn't know, however, was that *we* had not done it. I was still a country preacher with too much on my plate. Whatever this could be called and whatever it would become, it was *God's* doing.

In the middle of all the press hoopla in Minneapolis, one of George Wilson's little girls came up and handed me a rose.

"Uncle Billy," she said, "we prayed for you."

And of course I had my own two little daughters praying for me every night. That put it all in perspective. That was the whole secret of everything that had happened: God had answered prayer.

THE PRESIDENT

Jimmy Carter

(1924-   )

When Jimmy Carter was elected president in November 1976, and people heard that he was a "born-again" Christian, many were dumbfounded. What kind of a religious fanatic or mindless fundamentalist was that? The northeast quadrant of the country generally feared the worst; the southeast quadrant generally hoped for the best; the rest of the nation generally adopted a wait-and-see stance. In the course of his four-year presidency, Carter managed to modify both the fears and the hopes. But it may be fair to say that he gave "born-again" a good name, just as years later he gave "ex-president" a good name.

Born in the tiny town of Plains, Georgia, Carter left home when barely twenty to attend the U.S. Naval Academy in Annapolis, Maryland. Some years after graduation, he entered the navy's nuclear submarine program in 1952. But his father died in 1953, and this necessitated cutting short his naval career in order to return to Plains and take over the family's peanut business. But he hungered for a wider role than that of peanut farmer. In 1962 he ran for and won a seat in the state senate, and in 1970 he won the governorship of the state of Georgia. Four years later, virtually unknown on the national scene, he astounded his mother (and the nation) when he announced to her that he planned to run for president. "Of what?" she wonderingly replied. To the nation, the unknown candidate regularly introduced himself in this way: "My name is Jimmy Carter, and I am running for president of the United States." Later, as his confidence grew, he added, "And I do not intend to lose."

He did not lose that race, defeating Gerald Ford who as vice president had succeeded to the presidency when Richard Nixon resigned. Carter did lose, however, in the next race against a popular opponent, Ronald Reagan, "the great communicator." Though deeply hurt by his defeat (as was his wife, Rosalynn), Carter threw himself with amazing energy into social, political, and humanitarian reform. He monitored elections around the world, built houses for those unable to afford them, and brokered diplomatic breakthroughs — sometimes with White House blessing, sometimes not. And he wrote books on subjects ranging from his early political campaigns in Georgia to his labors in the Middle East and his memoirs as president. He even wrote a book of poetry and, with his daughter, a book for children.

But he also wrote, frankly and fully, about his religious faith — the only twentieth-century American president, with the possible exception of Woodrow Wilson, capable of so doing and willing to do so. Of course, he taught Sunday school in Plains and even on occasion in Washington; of course, he could be seen regularly attending church, wherever he was; and, of course, he was openly identified as "religious" — whatever that might be understood to mean. But the faith was deep, not shirtsleeve. In the excerpt below, he begins on a note of the simplest Protestant piety with which no evangelical could find fault. But in his book, one sees his journey as that of "faith seeking knowledge." He never settles for a faith more interested in clichés and bumper stickers than in insight and understanding. His was, and is, truly a "living faith."

[See Peter G. Bourne, *Jimmy Carter: A Comprehensive Biography from Plains to Post-Presidency* (New York: Simon & Schuster, 1977).]

The Search for Faith

Religious faith has always been at the core of my existence. It has been a changing and evolving experience, beginning when I was a child of three, memorizing Bible verses in Sunday school. When I was nine years old, I was promoted to the Sunday school class taught by my father, so I had the double influence of the church environment and my own father as my teacher. My faith at first was simple and unequivocal; there was no doubt in my mind about the truth of what I learned in church.

Yet even as a child, I was dismayed to find myself becoming skeptical about some aspects of my inherited faith. We learned in church that Jesus had risen from the dead three days after his crucifixion, and that all believers would someday enjoy a similar resurrection. As I grew older, I began to wonder whether this could be so. I became quite concerned about it, worried not so much about the prospect of my own death as about the possibility that I might be separated from my mother and father. These two people were the core of my existence, and I couldn't bear the idea that I wouldn't be with them forever.

By the time I was twelve or thirteen years old, my anxiety about

Source: Jimmy Carter, *Living Faith* (New York: Times Books, 1996), pp. 16-29; 32-38.

this became so intense that at the end of every prayer, until after I was an adult, before "Amen" I added the words "And, God, please help me believe in the resurrection." What made it worse was that I thought I was the only person with such concerns. I felt guilty that I doubted what the preacher said and what my father taught me in Sunday school.

This was not the kind of thing we would have talked about at home. Although my father was at ease teaching the lessons in church, I think he would have been embarrassed to bring up Christian subjects with me while we were at work in the fields or sitting together at the dinner table. In a way, I saw a different father in Sunday school. I admired Daddy greatly as a man who excelled in many things: he was an unbeatable tennis player, an outstanding baseball pitcher, and a fine hunter and fisherman; he knew how to raise bird dogs so they could find and point quail, and he was a successful farmer and businessman. I took his faith and his Sunday school teaching for granted, and I kept my doubts to myself. It would have been inconceivable to express doubts to him about anything in the Bible.

So even at an early age, I was developing a kind of dual approach to biblical teachings. My sense of faith was preeminent: I *knew* that there was a God who was our creator and that I was being observed and judged in all I did; I knew that Jesus Christ had accepted the punishment for my sins and that through faith in him I could be saved. But I had a nagging degree of skepticism about the relationship between my faith and the scientific point of view I was already developing through my schoolwork and my reading.

Of course, church was much more to me than a source of knowledge about God. It was the center of social life for our family and for the whole community. For example, we had no Boy Scout troop in Plains then, so my father would take his Sunday school class into the woods to camp out all night or go fishing, teaching the town boys something about the outdoors.

Beginning when I was ten or twelve, church was also the place where we became acquainted with our female classmates in a social setting. The church would sponsor closely chaperoned "prom parties" for the young people on Friday nights. Each of us would bring a pound of food — a pound of fried chicken, pork barbecue, bread, potato salad, or cake. Then we'd stroll, talk, and dance. The chaperones made sure there were no wallflowers at these parties, and we had to check back in with them frequently enough to minimize opportunities for "improper" conduct. Prom cards were used to keep track of partners for dances, and no one could dance more than three times, or spend more than fifteen consecutive minutes, with the same partner. These parties were fun, and as I grew older I came to realize that they were also the way our parents arranged for us to explore the field for possible future spouses.

Every summer, our Baptist church held a revival week, designed to heighten the religious commitment of the church members and to convince nonmembers to join. (The Methodist church held its own revival at a different time of year, and the more devout Christians in town would attend both.) The visiting preachers who conducted the ten revival services offered a two-part message. They preached what we called "hellfire and damnation" sermons to convince us that anyone who didn't accept Christ as a personal savior was going to hell. Interspersed was a description of the glorious alternative of redemption and heaven offered by Jesus. Their eloquence and the power of their message were often overwhelming.

Practically everyone in Plains would come to some of these services. There was a morning sermon at ten o'clock, attended by the women while their children were in school and their husbands worked in the stores and fields, and a nighttime service, which entire families could attend. The climax of each sermon was when nonmembers were asked to come forward and declare their intention of accepting Christ as savior. This was the most important step in life, marking the moment at which a person became a member of the Christian community. It was much more important for us Baptists than the rite of baptism, which came soon afterward and symbolized a burial of our old selves with immersion, rebirth into a new life with Christ, and membership in our church.

We didn't believe in what we called "child conversions," although I understand that in some Baptist churches children as young as eight might make the step of accepting Christ and becoming church members. We were encouraged to wait until we were older, and I decided to accept Christ during a revival service when I was eleven. I was then baptized with other new converts on the Sunday following revival week.

What does it mean when I say that I "decided to accept Christ"? Jesus was the Messiah, the long-awaited savior, who came both to reveal God to us and to heal the division between God and humankind. As Jesus told his disciples, "If you have seen me, you have seen God" (John 14:9). Furthermore, the Gospels recount how Jesus, having lived a perfect and blameless life, accepted a death of horrible suffering on the cross on our behalf, as an atonement for the sins we have committed.

Accepting Christ as my savior means believing all these things and entering into a relationship with God through him, so that my past and future sins no longer alienate me from my Creator.

Putting our total faith in these concepts is what is meant by being "born again." It's when there is an intimate melding of my life with that of Jesus: I become a brother with him, and God is our mutual parent. This frees me from the strings that previously limited my relationship with my creator.

Being born again is a new life, not of perfection but of striving, stretching, and searching — a life of intimacy with God through the Holy Spirit. There must first be an emptying, and then a refilling. To the extent that we want to know, understand, and experience God, we can find all this in Jesus. It is a highly personal and subjective experience, possible only if we are watching for greater truths about ourselves and God.

This experience is challenging, even painful at times, but ultimately deeply rewarding. It provides answers to the most disturbing questions about our existence, the purpose of life, and how to deal with sorrow, failure, loneliness, guilt, and fear. In it, we come to know that our gifts from God are not earned by our own acts but are given to us through his grace. As Paul says, "Therefore, since we have been justified through faith, we have peace with God through our Lord Jesus Christ, through whom we have gained access by faith into this grace in which we now stand" (Romans 5:1-2).

The love of Christ lets us feel the fullness of God. Ephesians 3:16-19 describes this experience well:

> I pray that, according to the riches of his glory, he may grant that you may be strengthened in your inner being with power through his Spirit, and that Christ may dwell in your heart through faith, as you are being rooted and grounded in love. I pray that you may have the power to comprehend, with all the saints, what is the breadth and length and height and depth, and to know the love of Christ that surpasses knowledge, so that you may be filled with all the fullness of God.

Being born again didn't happen to me when I was eleven. For me, it has been an evolutionary thing. Rather than a flash of light or a sudden vision of God speaking, it involved a series of steps that have brought me steadily closer to Christ. My conversion at eleven was just one of these steps.

Through it all, my worry over the doubts I felt about some Christian teachings continued, and my skepticism was somewhat heightened when I went away to college. I took part in the usual all-night discussions with my freshman and sophomore classmates about big philosophical topics: Why was I created? What is the purpose of life? Who or what is God? We questioned everything, and we thought we were quite profound.

Then I went to the U.S. Naval Academy, and I became an engineer and later studied advanced science. This was also the first time that I got to know significant numbers of people who were not Protestant Christians. (There were a handful of Jews in our nearby county seat of Americus — respected community members — but their religion was never discussed.) At the Naval Academy, there were many students who attended Protestant religious services, a substantial number who attended Roman Catholic services, and a relatively small number who attended Jewish services. (We also had a few who claimed to be Moslems, Hindus, or atheists, but the rest of us all figured that this was so they wouldn't have to go to the mandatory chapel services.) So for the first time, I had the opportunity to learn something about other faiths.

Worshiping God remained an important part of my life. During my three years at the academy, I attended chapel regularly, and I got to know the chaplain pretty well. I also taught Sunday school; my students were the nine-to-twelve-year-old daughters of the enlisted men and officers who were assigned permanently to the naval base at Annapolis. Out of 3,500 midshipmen, only a handful were equally active in chapel activities, so this was a significant religious commitment on my part.

When I graduated from Annapolis, Rosalynn and I were married, and she moved from the Methodist church in which she'd grown up to join me as a Baptist. However, the following seven years I spent in the navy were a relatively dormant phase in my religious life. With me assigned to various ships at naval bases in Virginia, Hawaii, California, and Connecticut, it wasn't convenient for Rosalynn and me to be part of a single nurturing church community.

Nonetheless, I sought out opportunities to worship when and where I could. For instance, when I got off duty on Sunday mornings after several days at sea, I would almost invariably find a Christian church service to attend on the naval base, despite the fact that I was eager to get home to my young bride. It didn't matter to me what kind of service I went to — I attended either Protestant or Roman Catholic services, and took communion at the Catholic masses; I just went to whichever service was earliest, so I could get home sooner.

Seven years after Annapolis, I was enjoying a burgeoning navy career when I was called home to my father's deathbed. This proved to be a turning point in my spiritual life.

During the weeks before and after my father's death, my family's immersion in the Christian community of Plains was an overwhelming experience for me. I felt that we had a family with not five people in it but several hundred. This was something I had almost forgotten since I'd left home as a teenager. My appreciation for the warmth and power of this Christian fellowship was a major factor in my decision to leave the navy and return to live in Plains.

As soon as we'd moved home, I volunteered to teach Sunday school at the Plains Baptist Church again, taking over my father's own class (the juniors, aged nine to twelve). After a year, Rosalynn joined me as a teacher of the junior girls, while I taught the boys. Soon I became head of the junior department, and also a deacon, one of the important lay ministries in the Baptist church.

My religious questions persisted, however, made more intense, in a way, by my father's death. This was the first real tragedy in my life. (I had lost my grandparents earlier, but they had lived in another community and I was not very close to them.) I found my father's death hard to understand. How could a good man, not nearly as old as many others in Plains, be deprived by God of his productive life? It seemed to me a harsh act, one I could only attribute to what I thought of as the God of the Old Testament, a stern, judgmental figure, very different from the loving, forgiving Jesus I knew from the Gospels.

This is when I began to explore in some depth the writings of theologians. I had never taken a course in religion or theology, but now I bought a large number of books by authors like Dietrich Bonhoeffer, Karl Barth, Martin Buber, Paul Tillich, Hans Küng, and particularly Reinhold Niebuhr, and I began to read and examine their ideas.

I explored more deeply what religion is, considering how my scientific outlook and knowledge, my continuing doubts about the biblical accounts of miracles, and my uneasiness about the relationship between God the Creator and God in Christ could be accommodated to the traditional faith I'd inherited. A torturous time of searching followed. I struggled to understand and differentiate the varying definitions of religion and the nature of God that I found in the works of theologians and philosophers, looking for a point of view with which I could feel comfortable.

I was fascinated by the outlooks of these thinkers, but my own relationship to faith remained an open question. An important part of the answer came to me from the writings of Paul Tillich. One of his themes is that doubt is an acceptable, even necessary aspect of faith — that faith implies a continuing search, not necessarily a final answer.

I found myself turning repeatedly to the story in the Gospel of Mark when a father comes to Jesus in search of a cure for his son, who is suffering seizures. The father asks Jesus to heal his son, saying, "If you can do anything, have pity on us and help us." Jesus replies, "If you can believe! All things are possible to him who believes." And the father responds, "I believe; help my unbelief!" Jesus rebukes the spirit and drives it away from the son, healing him completely (Mark 9:17-27).

The assurance Jesus offers in this story — that we will not be turned away on account of our doubts or skepticism but that he will "help our unbelief" — has meant a great deal to me, especially in times of pain or trouble. At such times, I've felt strongly the need of something more permanent and profound than a successful career, being president, or even my relationship with Rosalynn. Jesus' acceptance has given me this.

Maybe some Christians never lack faith — they are the lucky ones. However, I don't know of anybody who has never had doubts about any aspect of the Christian faith.

We would like to have an absolutely certain base on which to build our lives — unquestioned faith in everything that the Bible tells us about God, about Jesus, about a quality life, about life after death, about God's love for us. Perhaps we are afraid that opening the door to a little questioning might shake the foundation of our faith or anger God. But I came to realize that it is a mistake not to face our doubts courageously. We should be willing to ask questions, always searching for a closer relationship with God, a more profound faith in Christ. It is foolish to think that our own doubts can change the truth.

When I contemplated abandoning my naval career, I prayed fervently that God would guide me to the right decision. Later, when I lost the 1966 governor's election and was tempted to abandon my faith altogether, my search for God's will sustained me through my anger and disillusionment. I have seen many people with broken lives, some on the verge of alcoholism or even suicide, turn and construct new and vibrant lives based on religious faith. The combined testimonies of countless people with similar experiences have helped to perpetuate religious faith as an integral part of the lives of billions of believers.

Yet the acquiring of faith is not an easy or frivolous thing. How can we prove that God created the universe, that the prophets communicated with God, that Jesus was the Messiah, or that the resurrection occurred? How can we prove that our lives are meaningful, that truth exists, or that we love or are loved? When I become absorbed in these questions, it helps me to fall back on my faith as a Christian.

The Danish existentialist Søren Kierkegaard said, "Faith means the betting of one's life upon the God in Jesus Christ, . . . the giving or commitment of one's whole life." My faith — my life commitment — has been instilled in me since childhood. Despite periods of doubt, it has been confirmed and strengthened by the tangible spiritual benefits I have received from the "assurance of things hoped for, the conviction of things not seen" (Hebrews 11:1). It is only through faith that I can maintain a relationship with the omnipotent Creator and my personal savior. Without this, I would feel destitute.

My reading of theology, which helped to open these new ideas about faith for me, was an illuminating experience in which I began to feel at ease with my religion for the first time since I was a little child.

I also began to see that my Christian faith and my scientific outlook could be compatible, not conflicting. One of the Bible passages that has helped me understand this is found in Paul's letter to the Romans. Speaking about the pagan peoples of the day, Paul wrote, "That which is known about God is evident within them, for God made it evident to them. For since the creation of the world His invisible attributes, His eternal power and divine nature, have been clearly seen, being understood through what has been made, so that they are without excuse" (Romans 1:19-20). Paul's point was that the glories of the world around us prove God's existence.

Like Paul, I see the glory of God around me, in the unfathomable mysteries of the universe and the diversity and intricacies of creation. We stand in wonder at how a tree grows from an acorn, how a flower blooms, or how DNA can shape the appearance and character of a living creature. It is almost humanly incomprehensible that in our Milky Way galaxy there are billions of stars equivalent to our own, and then billions of other galaxies equivalent to our own. At the other end of the scale, I marvel that the inseparable atom I learned about in high school is really a collection of remarkable components, matter and anti-matter, rotating in different directions yet held together by forces of immense power, and some particles able to pass through the entire earth without being deflected.

Even more miraculous is the human form, in which the trillions of neuron connections in a single human brain exceed the total number of celestial bodies in the known heavens! Scientific knowledge only enhances my sense of God's glory filling the universe. Over the centuries, scientists have discovered more and more about these truths — truths that have always existed. None of these discoveries contradicts my belief in an ultimate and superior being; they simply confirm the reverence and awe generated by what becomes known and what remains unexplained.

As a believer, I have no problem with discoveries in astronomy, geology, and paleontology: that the universe is enormous and expanding, the earth is ancient, and human beings have evolved from primitive ancestors. It is not difficult for me to accept the "big bang" theory of the origin of the universe, at least until it is refuted by further exploration of the heavens and a new explanation is evolved to explain what God has done. Nor does it shake my religious faith to realize that the early authors of the Scriptures thought that the earth was flat, that stars were little things like Christmas tree ornaments that could fall on us, that the entire process of creation occurred during six earthly days, and that the first woman came from the rib of the first man, both Adam and Eve created in modern human form. The gap between their understanding and ours just indicates that knowledge was revealed later to Galileo, Newton, Darwin, Einstein, and Hubble — and to most of us.

~

In addition to the intellectual realization of a supreme being, we have a purely subjective need to meet a personal yearning. We have an innate desire to relate to the all-knowing, the all-powerful, and the ever-present — to some entity that transcends ourselves. I am grateful and happy when I feel the presence of God within me, as a tangible influence on my thoughts and on the ultimate standards of my life. It is reassuring to me to know that God will always be with me and cares for me. I think of the words of Isaiah: "When you pass through the waters, I will be with you; and through the rivers, they shall not overwhelm you; when you walk through fire you shall not be burned, and the flame shall not consume you. For I am the Lord your God. . . . You are precious in my sight, and honored, and I love you" (Isaiah 43:2-4).

Our Sunday school class often becomes involved in a discussion about how to achieve this closeness to God. Except in moments of crisis, when we reach desperately for some sustaining force, the relationship requires some effort on our part, some reaching out. I remind my class of the man in terrible trouble who prayed, "God, if you'll just get me out of this mess, I promise never to bother you with my prayers again." We need God's presence at all times — not just when life is at its most difficult.

This desire for a personal relationship with God cannot be abolished, even under pressure. A basic reason for disintegration of the once-powerful Soviet Union is that the government required its citizens to put all their faith in the central authority. The communist apparatus — including the army, the party, and the government — was declared to be sufficient to meet all human needs. As Karl Marx said, religion was considered merely "the opium of the people." Eventually, this entire system collapsed, a hollow shell. Eighty years after the Soviet government officially declared atheism dominant and prohibited religion, the seeds of faith still exist, and there is now an explosion of religious fervor in Russia.

There are other elements in our lives that make us turn to Christ, to seek God's will, to excel in our own standards of morality or belief. We want to prove that our lives are meaningful. At the same time, faith has to be predicated on a *desire* to believe. The Leonard Cohen song about Christ's walking on the water says that Jesus knew that "only drowning men could see him." Faced with death, in a storm, the disciples wanted to believe.

I've been disconcerted to find my own religious beliefs incompatible with those of many prominent Baptists. In 1976, during my first campaign for the presidency, I was taken aback when the evangelist Jerry Falwell condemned me because I "claimed" to be a Christian. At the time, I discounted the importance of this criticism, especially since few people then knew who Jerry Falwell was, but before the end of my term in office, he and his organization, the Moral Majority, became quite famous. This was the first national emergence of the so-called Christian Right, later joined by Pat Robertson, the Christian Coalition, and others.

In 1979, this conservative wing of Christianity was strong enough to take over leadership of the Southern Baptist Convention (SBC), which had always been my church "home." I was a longtime, stalwart supporter of the SBC, which represented Baptist congregations totaling 14 million members. I'd served on the fifteen-man board of the Convention's Brotherhood Commission, which sets policy for all the men's affairs and programs, and had even conducted the wedding ceremony for the commission's executive director while I was governor of Georgia (the only wedding I've ever performed). So I was dismayed when the fundamentalists took control of the convention's organization and began purging the more moderate leaders and defining narrowly the criteria for seminary professors and curricula.

In the United States today, there seems to be a growing split between two ways of practicing the Christian faith. On the one hand, there are those who believe that Christianity gives its adherents material benefits. Such churches promise their members comfort, security, financial wealth, and prestige, and they often display an evangelistic zeal that is quite impressive. Many of these churches are very active in public affairs and have become powerful political forces. On the other hand, there are those who consider ministering to the poor, the despised, and the homeless as important elements of Christianity. The first group often looks upon the second as less than truly Christian, sometimes using the phrase "secular humanist" to describe them.

I have been faced with this charge. A high official of the Southern Baptist Convention came into the Oval Office to visit me when I was president. As he and his wife were leaving, he said, "We are praying, Mr. President, that you will abandon secular humanism as your religion." This was a shock to me. I didn't know what he meant, and I am still not sure. He may have said this became I was against a constitutional amendment to authorize mandatory prayer in public schools and had been working on some things opposed by the "religious right," such as the Panama Canal treaties, a Department of Education, and the SALT II treaty with the Soviets.

These differences among Christian groups sap a tremendous portion of our ability, time, money, and influence. Much of our energy is spent in internecine warfare, in arguments and debates that not only are divisive but incapacitate us for our work in the name of Christ.

Our faith should be a guide for us in deciding between the permanent and the transient, the important and the insignificant, the gratifying and the troubling, the joyful and the depressing. We must study the principles on which our faith is founded, but we can't become obsessed with the belief that we have a special ordination from God to interpret the Scriptures and to consider anyone who disagrees with us wrong and inferior. The tendency of fundamentalists, in Christianity and other religions, to condemn those who differ from them is perhaps the most disturbing aspect of their current ascendancy.

Of course, the fellowship of faith is even larger than the Christian world. The first great Christian theologian, Paul, repeatedly emphasized the fundamental importance of faith as a unifying force between Christians and Jews. A burning question in the early church was whether God's covenant with Abraham was exclusively for the Jews. Some feared that if they became Christians they would forgo God's blessing. Paul made it clear that it was the patriarch's faith and not his ethnicity that was significant. He relied on the Scripture: "For the promise that he should be the heir of the world was not to Abraham or to his seed, through the law, but through the righteousness of faith" (Romans 4:13). The covenant with God is shared by Jews and Christians, with faith in one God as the unifying element.

Although the word *faith* is used only twice in the King James Version of the Old Testament (245 times in the New Testament), the writer of Hebrews relates faith directly and by name to a large number of biblical heroes of earlier times whose actions were determined by it. Through faith, Noah built his ark and became the heir of righteousness. Abraham and his wife, Sarah, although "as good as dead," had descendants as numerous as the stars because of their faith. Joseph, near death, had faith enough to call for the exodus of the Israelites from Egypt. Moses gave up the "pleasures of sin" to lead the Jews to freedom, depending on his faith to sustain him through forty years in the wilderness. And through faith, Gideon, Samson, David, Samuel, and the prophets conquered kingdoms, administered justice, shut the mouths of lions, quenched flames, escaped the edges of swords, and had weaknesses turned to strengths. The power of faith is a unifying bond between Christian and Jew and between the heroes of ancient Israel and those of New Testament times.

When people become alienated from one another, it is important to search for a healing force. A husband and wife may have a child who can hold them together. Members of an athletic team who don't really like one another will cooperate in the heat of a game. Our faith in God should play such a unifying role among believers. This may seem obvious, but all too often we forget or ignore it.

Christians of various denominations and shades of practice should emphasize shared concepts that are so great and so important that, compared with them, other differences fade into relative insignificance. Our faith should transcend all merely human issues, such as whether we are immersed or sprinkled in baptism, have few or many ordinances, have servant pastors or a hierarchical church with bishops and maybe a pope. We can rise above all this when we come together as common believers, but doing so requires both an elevation in spirit and a degree of personal humility.

The closest fellowship Rosalynn and I have with those outside our family is through the Maranatha Baptist Church. But *church* does not mean just "Maranatha" or "Baptist" or "Protestant"; it is the totality of those united in the love of Christ. The ultimate vision of the church should be as a worldwide community in which all believers are joined. As I have come to know, reaching out to others in the name of God can be one of the most deeply rewarding experiences any person can enjoy.

THE MARINER

William F. Buckley Jr.
(1925-   )

With an unusually cosmopolitan background as a child and young man — it included years in Mexico City, months in Paris, two separate stays in England, and three years in the U.S. Army — William Buckley in 1946 entered Yale University. Though his earliest schooling had been in Catholic institutions, as one reads in the excerpt below, young Buckley did attend a prep school (Millbrook) that was not Catholic, but nonetheless recognizably religious. Yale, founded by devout Congregationalists in 1707, was not recognizably religious in 1946 — at least not to this Catholic undergraduate. After four years at Yale (1946-1950), William Buckley resolved to write a book about his college. He published it in 1951 under the title, *God and Man at Yale.*

It created a sensation — to indulge in understatement. Buckley had two major complaints against Yale: first, it treated religion with indifference, if not hostility; second, it veered strongly in the direction of big government and a managed economy. With respect to the first point, the twenty-six-year-old student examined the departments of religion, philosophy, sociology, and psychology: their courses, their teachers, their textbooks. On the basis of all this, he concluded that Yale more often shattered than it fortified one's Christian faith. In exploring his second concern, he looked closely at the disciplines of history, political science, and — with special emphasis — economics. The teaching here, he found, supported the thesis that "increased governmental control of the economy is both inevitable and desirable." On the other hand, individualism and free enterprise hardly received a fair hearing.

Buckley thought that the alumni generally and the trustees specifically should know that their values were not widely shared or reflected in the current curricular scene at Yale. And, he wrote, "alumni and friends cannot support an institution that encourages values they consider inimical to the public welfare if they wish to be honest in their convictions and faithful to the democratic tradition." A gauntlet, no, several gauntlets, had been thrown down. And Yale administrators, as well as many of Yale's friends, responded to the book with force, even anger. But the book had made its mark, even as it elevated its author to the rank of a public person.

For nearly half a century since, William Buckley has been in the public eye: on the radio, on television, in the press, and in the publishing world (with nearly forty books). In his "Autobiography of Faith," written some forty-six years after the "Yale book," one detects a more mellow mood, a more searching spirit, a larger sprinkling of humor. It is, of course, brilliant. And it still has an edge: Vatican II was responsible for many "daffy innovations," the daffiest of which was the abandonment of Latin. A Roman Catholic all his life, not a convert like Brownson or Merton or Day, Buckley can still surprise; one of those surprises, described below, is his happy marriage to a Protestant.

[See William F. Buckley Jr., *God and Man at Yale* (Chicago: Henry Regnery, 1951); and for Buckley as mariner, see his *Atlantic High: A Celebration* (Garden City, N.Y.: Doubleday, 1982).]

It was during the summer of 1938 that we were given the dreadful news. I forget from whose hands it came. Probably from "Mademoiselle," our governess. She was the authority in residence at Great Elm, given that my mother, father, and three of my older siblings were traveling in Europe. That left six children to romp happily through one more summer in my father's large house in Sharon, the small village designated by the Garden Club of America two years before as the most beautiful town in Connecticut after Litchfield. The six of us left behind ranged in age from Jim (fifteen) to Maureen (five). We were superintended by Mademoiselle Jeanne Bouchex and by three Mexican nurses; fed and looked after by a cook, a butler, and two maids; trained and entertained in equestrian sport by a groom and an assistant, making use of Father's eight horses; instructed in piano by a twenty-three-year-old New Yorker who came and stayed with us three days of every week, giving us each a lesson every day on one of the five pianos in the house; and in the guitar or banjo or mandolin (we were allowed our pick) by a Spanish-born violinist who traveled once a week from Poughkeepsie.

It might have been Mademoiselle who told us what Father had decided, or it might have been "Miss Hembdt," Father's secretary. She lived in Yorktown Heights, New York, and regularly relayed to us bulletins from Father, transcriptions of letters he would mail her, mostly to do with his business affairs but now and then something directed to

Source: William F. Buckley Jr., *Nearer, My God: An Autobiography of Faith* (New York: Doubleday, 1997), pp. 1-14; 49-52.

one or more of his absent children, supplementing what we would learn from letters received from Mother or from one of our siblings traveling with them. With these notes came our monthly allowances, a directive or so touching on this or that subject, references to a book Father had just read which we should know about, or read ourselves . . . That dreadful day in August the directive, however transmitted, was as horrifying an edict — my two afflicted sisters and I agreed — as had ever been sent to three healthy and happy children from their father. The directive was to the effect that the next school year we would pass in boarding schools near London, the girls at St. Mary's in Ascot, I at St. John's, Beaumont, in Old Windsor.

The news fractured the arcadian spirit of our summer. We had got used to quite another routine, where summer variations evolved almost seamlessly into a return to school where academic life required no radical departures from our way of life and none at all from our surroundings, because we were taught by tutors right there in the same rooms in which we played when indoors during the summer. When school began for us at the end of September, we continued to ride on horseback every afternoon, we swam two or three times every day until the water got too cold, our musical tutors continued to come to us just as they had done during the summer, some of us would rise early and hunt pheasant at our farm before school; our classes began at 8:30, ended at noon, and there would be study hall and music appreciation between 4:00 and 6:00. Three or four neighborhood children joined our school, and though we sorely regretted the summer's end, the academic regimen was light, and at our age — Jane had turned fourteen that summer, Trish was eleven — the schooling we got was as tolerable as schoolwork could be. Now, suddenly, we were to go to boarding schools in England.

Why?

We fled to Aunt Priscilla. She lived with her maiden sister in a house nearby, returning home to Austin, Texas, in the fall. We went to her: *Why? Why? Why?* Aunt Priscilla was infinitely affectionate, sublimely humorous, but also absolutely self-disciplined. After hearing out our outrage, she agreed to write to Father in Europe to put our case before him: What really was the point in going to England to school? We had all already *been* to England to school . . . only five years ago — it was there that Trish and I had first learned English. Jane, Trish, and I had gone to Catholic day schools in London, the oldest four to boarding schools, the two girls to that same St. Mary's, Ascot, where now Jane and Trish would go.

They hadn't liked St. Mary's, hadn't liked it one bit. Aloïse, the oldest, was fourteen, possibly the most spirited girl the dear nuns at St. Mary's had ever come across, with her singular, provocative independence. They had got on at Ascot because by nature Aloïse and Priscilla were irrepressible; but they had never pretended to "like" their school. John (thirteen) and Jim (ten) had gone to the Oratory Preparatory School in Reading. John had kept a diary at the school and was manifestly amused by his foreign experiences, which he depicted in words and in drawings. But the entire family had been shocked and infuriated to learn that not once but t-w-i-c-e, our brother Jim had been — caned! Called into the headmaster's study and told to lean over. The first time, he had received one "swipe." The second time, two swipes. Not quite the stuff of Nicholas Nickleby's Dotheboys Hall, but news of the punishment was received as such in the family corridors, and the rumor spread about the nursery in our house in London that Father and Mother even considered withdrawing the boys. It did not come to that, but Jim was for at least a year after the event regarded by his brothers and sisters as a mutilated object. He, being sunny by nature and serenely preoccupied with his interest in animals and with flora and fauna, actually hadn't thought very much about the episode. For the rest of us, it was the mark of Cain, discoloring our year of English schooling.

And now we were headed back for more of the same kind of thing? We needed to know — why? Surely Aunt Priscilla would set things right.

The Word came, about two weeks later. A letter from Father. She didn't read it to us, but she explained that Father "and your mother" — this was a blatant invention, we knew; it would never have occurred to Mother to impose any such ordeal on us — believed it would be a very fine educational experience for us. "Besides" — Aunt Priscilla winked — "as you know, your father has complained that five years have gone by since he understood *'a single word'*" — Aunt Priscilla did a light imitation of Father, elongating a word or phrase, to give it emphasis — "uttered by any one of his children." In England we would learn to *open our mouths* when we spoke. We moaned our dismay at one of Father's *typical* exaggerations. It is true that Father was a nut on elocution, and true that his nine children, on returning from five years in Europe, had quickly adapted to lazy vocalisms which Father, then sixty, had a progressively difficult time deciphering in the din of the three-tiered dining room, the main table for the older children and the adults, the middle table for those roughly nine to thirteen, the third little table for the incumbent baby(ies).

We felt certain that his objective wasn't merely to put us into

Catholic schools. Such a thing, in our household, would have been supererogatory. Mother was a daily communicant. Father's faith was not extrovert, but if you happened on him just before he left his bedroom in the morning, you would find him on his knees, praying. Our eldest brothers and sisters, here in the States, were not at Catholic schools. So we ruled that out as one of Father's objectives.

We dimly understood that Father had always stressed the value of cosmopolitan experience — we lived now in Connecticut, rather than in Mexico City, where, bilingual, he had gone to practice law after graduating from the University of Texas, intending to raise his family there. But he had been exiled from Mexico in 1921, pronounced by the President of Mexico an *extranjero pernicioso* — a pernicious foreigner. Which indeed he was, having backed a revolution against President Obregón which, among other things, sought to restore religious freedom to Mexican Catholics. He bought the house in Connecticut, but soon, pursuing business concerns, he moved the family to France, Switzerland, and England. We lived abroad for four years. It was in Paris that I first went to school, speaking only Spanish. Was Father simply seeking out further exposure to another culture?

It was much, much later, after World War II, that we learned the hidden reason Father thought it prudent to have three of his children of sensitive age away from home. It was why Aunt Priscilla hadn't read to us out loud the explanatory letter she had received from him: Mother had become pregnant again, against her doctor's advice. It was not known if she would survive the birth of her eleventh child (one baby had died at childbirth, ten years earlier). At the time, we knew only enough to be vaguely apprehensive about Mother. We did not know how dangerous the doctors thought the birth, due the following November, could be.

But whatever speculation we engaged in, however horrified at the very thought of the ordeal ahead, there was never any doubt, in my father's house, what his children would be doing at any given time, i.e., what Father said we would be doing at any given time. So that, on September 18, 1938, after an indulgent twenty-four hours in New York City shepherded about by our beloved young piano teacher to movies, a concert, and Horn & Hardart Automats, we — Mademoiselle, Jane, Trish, and I — boarded the S.S. *Europa* for Southampton.

There was much political tension. We couldn't fail to note it immediately on landing in Southampton. British sentiment was divided between those who favored standing up to Hitler, who had just occupied the Sudetenland in Czechoslovakia, and those who opposed any move that might threaten war. Prime Minister Neville Chamberlain was scheduled to return from his meeting with Adolf Hitler in Munich the next day. Before boarding the train for London we were fitted out with gas masks.

In London we were greeted with Mother's distinctive affection and Father's firm embraces. Little was said, that I can remember, about where we would be taken the next day, but Father did tell me that he had found Fr. Sharkey, the headmaster of St. John's, a "fine" person, and Jane and Trish were told that the mother superior at Ascot was someone other than the mother superior, so disliked by my older sisters, who had presided five years earlier.

Mother drove in one car with Jane and Trish and their bags to Ascot, Father and I in another car, to St. John's.

It was late on a cold English afternoon (Father instructed the driver to detour to the landing field and we saw Neville Chamberlain descend from the airplane that had flown him from Munich to announce that he was bringing "peace in our time"). An hour later, we turned into the long driveway that took us to the pillared entrance to the school, the whole of it contained in one large square brick three-story building.

We were taken by a maid to a primly decorated salon, and Fr. Sharkey, short, stubby, his hair gray-white, came in, took my hand, and chatted with Father for a few minutes about the international situation. Tearfully I bid good-bye to my father and was led up with my two bags to a cubicle, halfway along a line of identical cubicles on either side of a long hallway that held about thirty. To enter you needed to slide open a white curtain that hung down from a rod going across the cubicle's width, about eight feet up from the floor. The rooms had no ceiling of their own — looking straight up, you saw the ceiling of the large hallway, perhaps ten feet up. To your right and to your left were white wooden partitions. On the right, a dresser — two or three drawers and a hanging locker. To the left, your bed. A small table of sorts stood near the bed and on it I quickly placed pictures of my family. On the window ledge I could reach only by standing on my bed I placed one end of a huge Old Glory I had bought that last day in New York, holding it down with two weights I contrived from something or other so that the United States flag could hang down behind my bed, all five feet of it. The dormitory master, Fr. Ferguson, knocked on the wooden partition, drew the curtain to one side, introduced himself, and told me he would lead me to the refectory, as it was time for supper.

The dining hall was crowded with the eighty boys who boarded at St. John's. The youngest were aged nine, the oldest, fourteen. After supper, we went to the study hall. I was three weeks late in arriving for the fall term and so without any homework to do, pending my introduction the next day to my form master.

I don't remember how I passed the two hours. In due course we were summoned to evening prayers. We knelt along two of the quadrangular corridors in the building, a priest at the corner, boys to his left. He led us in prayers, to which we gave the responses. Fr. Sharkey then materialized, and the boys filed by him. He shook hands with each of us and said good night. When it was my turn, he said, "Good night, Billy. You are very welcome at St. John's." We walked up the circular staircase to our cubicles and were given fifteen minutes before Lights Out. Just before the light was switched off, the dormitory master read the Psalm (#130) "De Profundis," to which we gave the responses in Latin. These were thumbtacked behind one of the dresser doors. The first two verses exactly echoed my thought. "Out of the depths have I cried onto thee, O Lord. Lord, hear my voice: let thine ears be attentive to the voice of my supplications."

I don't remember very much about the period of acclimation. I do remember the quite awful homesickness (I had never before spent a night away from my family). It lasted about ten evenings during which, smothering my face with the collar of my pajamas so that I would not be heard by my neighbors, I wept.

I think I remember praying for war, confident that if war came, Father would take us home. Mother had warned us that we would be homesick, that this would go away after a while, and that until then we should offer up our pain to God in return for any private intentions. In a closed conference, back in London, Jane and Trish and I had decided we would offer up our forthcoming torment for the safe and happy birth of Mother's baby in November.

The routine was extremely severe, up against what I had been used to. Rising in the morning always came as a wrenchingly disagreeable surprise. I remember ten years later reading C. S. Lewis's *Surprised by Joy* in which he told that throughout his early school days in England he remembered primarily how tired he always was. I assume Mr. Lewis had a special problem because once awake I was all right, but getting up was for me — for some reason — more difficult than rising, six years later, at 5:30 in the infantry, or, a few years after that, at 4:00 A.M. to do watch duty racing my sailboats. Once or twice every month the school matron, as she was called, would ordain that this boy or that should have a "late sleep," which meant we would sleep an extra forty-five minutes, rejoining our classmates at breakfast, after Mass. In those preconciliar days Catholics could not take Communion unless they had fasted since midnight. For that reason alone, breakfast could not have preceded Mass.

The pews were stacked along the sides of the chapel. Twenty boys sat and kneeled on the top right pew, looking down on the heads of twenty boys a foot beneath them. Then across the little aisle, to the faces of twenty boys at the lower level, and another twenty above them. To view the altar one needed to turn one's head. There was no sermon, except a brief one on Sundays. The Mass lasted about twenty-five minutes. School announcements were given in the refectory.

I have always been impatient, and so it was I suppose surprising that I came so quickly to feel at ease with the daily Mass and then became gradually engrossed in the words and the ritual. We were studying second-year Latin and I was dreadful at it, incapable of understanding why, while they were at it, the Romans hadn't simply settled for Spanish. But I paid increasing attention to the Ordinary of the Mass, which is to say that part of it that doesn't change from Sunday to Sunday. It was easy to follow — the right-hand column of the missals carried the English translation. The liturgy took hold of me and I suppose that this means nothing more than that liturgy has theatrical properties. Yes, but something more, I reasonably supposed, and suppose so now. Twenty-five years later I would write a scorching denunciation of the changes authorized by Vatican II and of the heartbreakingly awful English translations that accompanied the jettisoning of the Latin. The Mass, in Latin, had got to me.

I had of course attended Mass every Sunday for as long as I could remember and thought myself something of a pro in the business inasmuch as I had been trained, in Sharon, to do duty as an altar boy. I very nearly became a godfather — I remember the thrill, followed by the humiliation. Our devout black butler, Ben Whittaker (he was a first cousin of Fats Waller), became a special friend of mine at Great Elm. After his wife gave birth to quadruplets, he told me excitedly that he wished me to serve as godfather. It transpired that I could not act as godfather, not having yet been confirmed. The honor fell to my older brother John, though by the time the formal event took place, only one of Ben's poor babies was still alive.

It was then that I was told about emergency baptisms, extemporaneously given to anyone in danger of dying. I had once improvised on this privilege. Mother had a friend who visited often at Great Elm, sometimes bringing along her two daughters, one in her late twenties, a second a few years older. On overhearing a conversation between Mother and Mademoiselle, I learned that the two ladies had never been baptized. I thought this shocking, talked the matter over with my sister

Trish, we devised our strategy, and knocked at their guest room door early one morning, after establishing that they had both been brought breakfast, in bed, on trays. I knocked and told them that Trish and I were looking for my dog. They welcomed us in to search the room. I knelt down to see if he was under the first bed and, a drop of water on my forefinger, touched it on Arlie's forehead as if reaching to maintain my balance, silently inducting her into the Christian community, while Trish, emerging from under the other bed in search of the dog, did as much for her older sister.

My mother was solemnly attentive when I whispered to her the happy consummation of our Christian evangelism. She did not betray her amusement: that was a part of her magic as a mother. She would never permit herself anything that might suggest belittlement — whatever her child's fancy. And then, too, she was as devoted a child of God as I have ever known and perhaps she permitted herself to believe that her friend's two grown-up daughters, neither one of them at death's door, had in fact been baptized. When in England I found myself going to Mass every day and offering every Mass for the health of my mother, I felt a closeness to her that helped diminish the pain of separation.

In those days I remember a special reverence for Our Lady, to whom I appealed as a mother herself. I hadn't the capacity (even now, I am not comfortable with the abstraction) to imagine infinity. I accepted it as a gospel truth that the Mother of God was "infinitely" wonderful, which meant to me that she was many times as wonderful as my own mother, but this hypothesis I had difficulty with: How was it possible to be many times more wonderful than my mother? I never asked any of the priests for help with that one. After all, I reasoned, they did not know Mother, so they might find the question surprising, impudent even. I knew that would not be the case, if they had *known* Mother. But Our Lady became in my mind an indispensable character of the heavenly cloister. A long time after that I learned that a thing called Mariolatry had been especially contemned by noisy iconoclasts like Charles Kingsley. My first instincts were not combative, but sad: that someone so much like my mother should be disdained was incomprehensible.

No doubt my religious ardor was stimulated by the circumstances we lived in. St. John's was run by Jesuit priests. They were, as members of the Society of Jesus tend to be, thoroughly educated. It required thirteen years to become a member of the Jesuit order and the training was exacting, the regimen spare. Fr. Manning was our form master. At the end of the hour, at every other school I would ever encounter, a fresh master moves in to teach the class his specialty. Fr. Manning did not teach us French, for which purpose a layman was brought in whose British accent, when speaking in French, I would ostentatiously mock, my own being so superior, as anyone's would be who learned French at age six in Paris. But excepting French, Fr. Manning taught every other subject in "Figures IIA" — the equivalent, roughly, of first year junior high. Geography, History, Math, Latin, Doctrine. Each of the six school years at St. John's (grades three to eight) had a single form master. Two of these were pre-ordination Jesuits, climbing up the long ladder to priesthood serving now, so to speak, as field instructors at a boys' boarding school. They were addressed as "Mr." But they met with the priests at faculty conferences, which were conducted in Latin, and I often wondered when did they sleep, since they were always up and around before we rose, and never appeared ready to retire when our lights went out.

I remember once being handed a corrected paper from Fr. Manning in his study. I leaned over to retrieve it and accidentally overturned the can of pipe tobacco. I heard the slightest whinny of alarm and then the majestic Fr. Manning was on his hands and knees, picking up each tobacco grain, one after another, replacing them in his can. "That is my month's allowance, Billy. I cannot afford to let any go unsmoked!" I thought this extraordinary. That this . . . seer should have less than all the tobacco he wanted.

On those rare afternoons when we did not do school sports, we would be taken for long walks in that historic countryside. We were within a few hundred meters of Runnymede, where King John had signed the Magna Carta. Striding alongside Fr. Paine, a tall, angular priest, about thirty-five years old, I'd guess — he was the administrative coordinator at the school and also its disciplinarian — I asked about Fr. Manning's tobacco and he told me that Jesuits took a vow of poverty and that therefore they were given a monthly allowance which had to suffice for all their needs. I asked whether it would be permitted for a friend to give tobacco to a Jesuit priest and he said no, this was only permitted in the case of food, when it was in short supply. (After the war, for several years, meat was very scarce, and Father sent meat every month to the fathers.) Ten years later, at the wedding of my sister Trish, the Jesuit priest who officiated, a lifetime friend of the groom, told my father not to make the mistake of offering him a stipend in return for his services "because under Jesuit rules, we cannot turn down a donation, which in any event goes to the order, not to the priest to whom it is offered." Fr. Paine told me that Jesuit priests needed frequently to check themselves, to guard against the sin of pride, because Jesuits were in fact very proud of the Jesuit order and very happy in it. One inevitably wonders whether that pride is quite whole after the strains of the 1960s.

Fr. Paine would regularly check individual cubicles at night to say good night to each of the boys. When November came, I confided to him that my mother was soon to bear a child, her eleventh, and that I was anxiously awaiting a telegram confirming that the baby had come and that my mother was well. He leaned over and embraced me warmly and did so again extemporaneously after the baby came, and once finally seven months later when my father wrote to say that because of the lowering clouds of war, my sisters and I would be withdrawn from our schools after the winter term.

Fr. Paine's warmth did not affect what I judged the extremity of the punishment I was twice sentenced to, for whatever social infraction. The first time it was a single ferule stroke, smacked down on my open hand, the second, two ferules, one on each hand, the cumulative experience with corporal punishment in my lifetime, if you leave out an unsuccessful fistfight with the strongest and biggest boy at St. John's, a rite of passage for any potential new-boy challenger (his name was Burns — I forget his first name, though first names were universally used, among the boys).

Many years later when as a magazine editor I contracted for the services of European Correspondent Erik von Kuehnelt-Leddihn, I learned from him that while I was a student at St. John's, he was teaching the senior boys down the hill at Beaumont College and that on learning, soon after arriving from Austria, that the ferule was the regular instrument of discipline, he had gone to the priest-executioner and demanded to receive six ferules, the conventional ration for grave infractions, exactly as they were inflicted on student miscreants. He made his demand even after being reassured that, at his age, with adult, callused hands, he would hardly feel my smart. But he persisted, and after receiving the blows reported clinically that far from negligible, six ferule strokes, even for a husky Austrian in his twenties, were a singularly painful experience. I heard that for extreme acts of misbehavior the birch rod was used on the buttocks, but I never knew any boy who received this punishment at St. John's.

Fr. Paine and I exchanged a half dozen letters in the ensuing thirty years, and we spoke once in London over the telephone in the seventies — he was retired and had difficulty in breathing. He told me among other things that the young rowdies in London who were disturbing the peace should be given a good beating.

When Lent came, we were given a retreat by the brother of Fr. Sharkey, also a Jesuit. He was short, like his older brother, irradiating a singular charm on this thirteen-year-old (I had had a birthday soon after my sister Carol was born, and Father had redeemed his promise to make me the godfather). I thought back to this retreat twenty years later when I went to Washington with my brother-in-law for a retreat conducted by the president emeritus of Fordham University, Jesuit Father Robert Gannon, whose short, electrifying sermons I begged him to put on tape, eliciting an assurance that one day he would certainly do this (R.I.P., he never did). They were cognate skills, Fr. Sharkey's and Fr. Gannon's: dramatic, but never melodramatic; persuasive; poignant; inspiriting. I recall only a single parable, if that is the right word for it, from that retreat at St. John's, six months before the world war. I put it in an essay I wrote on my boat during a transatlantic sail. *Esquire* had asked me to write about where, that I had never been, would I most wish to visit? I wrote, on that sunny, breezy day in the mid-Atlantic, that I would most like to visit Heaven because it was there I would be made most happy. I gave Fr. Sharkey's exegesis: He had been approached some weeks earlier, he told us, by a devout elderly woman who asked him whether dogs would be admitted into Heaven. No, he had replied, there was no scriptural authority for animals getting into Heaven. "In that case," the lady had said to him, "I can never be happy in Heaven. I can only be happy if Brownie is also there."

"I told her" — Fr. Sharkey spoke with mesmerizing authority — "that if that were the case — that she could not be happy without Brownie — why then Brownie would in fact go to Heaven. Because what is absolutely certain is that, in Heaven, you will be happy." That answer, I am sure, sophisticated readers of *Esquire* dismissed, however indulgently, as jesuitical. Yes. But I have never found the fault in the syllogism.

❧

I had some satisfaction from Newman on the evolution of doctrine and hoped now to review some of the great controversies over Christianity, some of these continuously at war, some resting in the DMZ. I don't remember ever seeking out Catholic company at Yale, or after Yale, as a

315

matter of fact, primarily for the sake of theological exchanges or religious camaraderie. The most influential professor at Yale — on me — was Willmoore Kendall. Although he was the son of a Methodist preacher, when I met him he was a religious agnostic. We became very close friends. And then a few years after I graduated he told me that he intended to convert to Catholicism and asked me to stand in as his godfather.

But although we spent many hours together (he moonlighted for two years as a senior editor of *National Review*) and corresponded regularly up until he precipitated an estrangement in 1961 ("Willmoore makes it a point not to have more than one friend at a time," was the commonly heard wisecrack about him), there was little grist in our exchanges to fuel religious curiosity or to bring on talk about religious questions. He taught me a great deal by his discursive reflections (Willmoore thought out loud and was a very great teacher) on how to view Catholicism from the eyes of an outsider.

In a vague kind of way I always thought of myself as surrounded by Catholics, though, as related, I went to other than Catholic schools after my year in England. I wooed and married an Episcopalian. In later years, Mrs. Kathleen "Babe" Taylor — my wife Pat's mother — became an intimate friend. She had been civil and attentive on learning that her popular, beauteous daughter (who was Miss Vancouver back then) had become engaged to me. It hurt her pride that Pat would be marrying a Catholic. Babe Taylor was born in Manitoba of parents who were Irish Protestants from Kilkenny, in the Irish Republic. Her parents were dead when I became engaged but they had left with their daughter a heavy deposit of Protestant pride. Babe now faced the second of her two daughters marrying a Catholic. Before World War II, Pat's older sister had married a Catholic Californian. That had been the first religious affront to Mrs. Taylor, who was in those days perhaps the premier hostess in British Columbia. I would learn that the first wedding, in Vancouver, had been performed by a Protestant minister. The bride and groom then traveled to Los Angeles (his home) on a Pullman sleeper and did not consummate their marriage until after a priest had performed a second ceremony. It is worth noting that a "priest" does not marry a bride and groom; he witnesses their exchange of vows.

The negotiations between Babe and me were pretty strenuous, as I thought it wrong to be even ostensibly married by a minister not of my own faith. The negotiations, in hindsight, were amusing. Vancouver's Catholics were presided over by a crusty old bishop who devoted much of his energy to alienating non-Catholics, and in doing so managed to alienate a great many Catholics. The bishop had decreed that any Catholic marrying outside the faith could do so only in the sacristy of a Catholic church, not in the church itself. The idea of excluding from the ceremony Babe and Pat's one thousand best friends was simply inconceivable, and for a little while, owing to these complications, our wedding date was in abeyance. My father came up with an impish plan, which was to import from Camden, South Carolina, the parish priest there, a beloved and humorous man. Ask *him,* unbound by the Vancouver bishop's jurisdiction, to do the wedding. Fr. Burke looked into that possibility and of course learned that it was a violation of diocesan rules for any priest to perform a marriage without the consent of the bishop.

"What would happen if you went ahead and performed the marriage?" Father asked him.

"Well, I guess I'd be reprimanded."

"Well," said my resourceful father, "couldn't you just tell the bishop that you're sorry — and will never again perform a marriage in Vancouver without permission?"

It was too neat, of course; and subjectively deceitful, and so the stratagem was abandoned. At about then, thanks to the good offices of someone — I can't remember who — the Vancouver bishop relented, authorizing a full-scale church wedding. After it, at the wedding reception at Babe's splendid mansion, the Protestant minister pronounced a blessing on the bride and groom, an intercredal civility entirely in order and welcome.

We raised our son as a Catholic, but I never exerted pressure on my wife to join the Church, which she has not done. Perhaps it was owing to my background that I never felt religious loneliness. Perhaps, too, I have been sustained over the years by steadfast temperamental inclinations, in matters religious and ideological. When I wrote *God and Man at Yale,* among other things singling out the antireligious bias there, I had been careful, as suggested above, to define Christianity in language used by an undeniable Protestant theologian, addressing an organization at Yale only months before I wrote. Reinhold Niebuhr had said, "Christian faith stands or falls on the proposition that a character named Jesus, in a particular place at a particular time in history, is more than a man in history but is a revelation of the mystery of self and of the ultimate mystery of existence." Niebuhr had not gone on, in that paper/sermon, to engage in apologetics, i.e., in a formal defense of Christian dogma. I did not hear this done, while at Yale, other than at my own church, in Sunday homilies.

THE POET

Maya Angelou

(1928-   )

Maya Angelou is indeed a poet, but she is much, much more. She has been a producer, director, and actor in the live theater, and has written for television and the movies. She has been honored by Presidents Ford, Carter, and Clinton, has been recognized with many honorary degrees, and has had bestowed upon her a host of literary awards. And she holds a lifetime appointment as the Reynolds Professor at Wake Forest University in Winston-Salem, North Carolina. A poet, yes, but one must surely not stop there.

Growing up in Stamps, Arkansas (about twenty-five miles east of Texarkana, Texas), Angelou knew firsthand the deprivation of the Depression and the trauma of sexual abuse. She also knew the oppressive atmosphere of unyielding segregation and unblinking prejudice. Everyone in authority — in the town, in the state, in the nation — was white. So, young Maya concluded, "Of course, I knew God was white too, but no one could have made me believe that He was prejudiced." She left Arkansas "for good" at age thirteen, to live with her real mother in San Francisco. (The "Momma" in the selection chosen here is really her grandmother, of whom the granddaughter draws a fine and loving portrait.)

In *I Know Why the Caged Bird Sings* (the title is taken from a poem by Paul Laurence Dunbar), one sees the human spirit as indomitable. James Baldwin comments that "Her portrait is a biblical study of life in the midst of death." Maya Angelou survives; she conquers; she redeems.

319

She writes near the end of her book that "The Black Female is assaulted in her tender years by all those common forces of nature at the same time that she is caught in the tripartite crossfire of masculine prejudice, white illogical hate and Black lack of power." She then adds, in a line that speaks to her own life, "The fact that the adult American Negro female emerges a formidable character is often met with amazement, distaste and even belligerence. It is seldom accepted as an inevitable outcome of the struggle won by survivors and deserves respect if not enthusiastic acceptance."

The excerpt below takes us inside the African American religious community in the rural South in the 1930s. We join in a tent revival that includes Baptists, Methodists, and Pentecostals. This revival among blacks shares many features of southern revivalism among whites, but with a clear difference. These worshipers knew that "even if they were society's pariahs, they were going to be angels in a marble white heaven and sit on the right hand of Jesus, the Son of God."

[See Maya Angelou, *Wouldn't Take Nothing for My Journey Now* (Higham, Mass.: Wheeler Pub., 1993).]

Another day was over. In the soft dark the cotton truck spilled the pickers out and roared out of the yard with a sound like a giant's fart. The workers stepped around in circles for a few seconds as if they had found themselves unexpectedly in an unfamiliar place. Their minds sagged.

In the Store the men's faces were the most painful to watch, but I seemed to have no choice. When they tried to smile to carry off their tiredness as if it was nothing, the body did nothing to help the mind's attempt at disguise. Their shoulders drooped even as they laughed, and when they put their hands on their hips in a show of jauntiness, the palms slipped the thighs as if the pants were waxed.

"Evening, Sister Henderson. Well, back where we started, huh?"

"Yes, sir, Brother Stewart. Back where you started, bless the Lord." Momma could not take the smallest achievement for granted. People whose history and future were threatened each day by extinction considered that it was only by divine intervention that they were able to live at all. I find it interesting that the meanest life, the poorest existence, is attributed to God's will, but as human beings become more affluent, as their living standard and style begin to ascend the material

Source: Maya Angelou, *I Know Why the Caged Bird Sings* (New York: Random House, 1970), pp. 120-32.

scale, God descends the scale of responsibility at a commensurate speed.

"That's just who get the credit. Yes, ma'am. The blessed Lord." Their overalls and shirts seemed to be torn on purpose and the cotton lint and dust in their hair gave them the appearance of people who had turned gray in the past few hours.

The women's feet had swollen to fill the discarded men's shoes they wore, and they washed their arms at the well to dislodge dirt and splinters that had accrued to them as part of the day's pickings.

I thought them all hateful to have allowed themselves to be worked like oxen, and even more shameful to try to pretend that things were not as bad as they were. When they leaned too hard on the partly glass candy counter, I wanted to tell them shortly to stand up and "assume the posture of a man," but Momma would have beaten me if I'd opened my mouth. She ignored the creaks of the counter under their weight and moved around filling their orders and keeping up a conversation. "Going to put your dinner on, Sister Williams?" Bailey and I helped Momma, while Uncle Willie sat on the porch and heard the day's account.

"Praise the Lord, no, ma'am. Got enough left over from last night to do us. We going home and get cleaned up to go to the revival meeting."

Go to church in that cloud of weariness? Not go home and lay those tortured bones in a feather bed? The idea came to me that my people may be a race of masochists and that not only was it our fate to live the poorest, roughest life but that we liked it like that.

"I know what you mean, Sister Williams. Got to feed the soul just like you feed the body. I'm taking the children too, the Lord willing. Good Book say, 'Raise a child in the way he should go and he will not depart from it.'"

"That's what it say. Sure is what it say."

The cloth tent had been set on the flatlands in the middle of a field near the railroad tracks. The earth was carpeted with a silky layer of dried grass and cotton stalks. Collapsible chairs were poked into the still-soft ground and a large wooden cross was hung from the center beam at the rear of the tent. Electric lights had been strung from behind the pulpit to the entrance flap and continued outside on poles made of rough two-by-fours.

Approached in the dark the swaying bulbs looked lonely and purposeless. Not as if they were there to provide light or anything meaningful. And the tent, that blurry bright three-dimensional A, was so foreign to the cotton field, that it might just get up and fly away before my eyes.

People, suddenly visible in the lamplight, streamed toward the temporary church. The adults' voices relayed the serious intent of their mission. Greetings were exchanged, hushed.

"Evening, sister, how you?"

"Bless the Lord, just trying to make it in."

Their minds were concentrated on the coming meeting, soul to soul, with God. This was no time to indulge in human concerns or personal questions.

"The good Lord give me another day, and I'm thankful." Nothing personal in that. The credit was God's, and there was no illusion about the Central Position's shifting or becoming less than Itself.

Teenagers enjoyed revivals as much as adults. They used the night outside meetings to play at courting. The impermanence of a collapsible church added to the frivolity, and their eyes flashed and winked and the girls giggled little silver drops in the dusk while the boys postured and swaggered and pretended not to notice. The nearly grown girls wore skirts as tight as the custom allowed and the young men slicked their hair down with Moroline Hairdressing and water.

To small children, though, the idea of praising God in a tent was confusing to say the least. It seemed somehow blasphemous. The lights hanging slack overhead, the soft ground underneath and the canvas wall that faintly blew in and out, like cheeks puffed with air, made for the feeling of a country fair. The nudgings and jerks and winks of the bigger children surely didn't belong in a church. But the tension of the elders — their expectation, which weighted like a thick blanket over the crowd — was the most perplexing of all.

Would the gentle Jesus care to enter into that transitory setting? The altar wobbled and threatened to overturn and the collection table sat at a rakish angle. One leg had yielded itself to the loose dirt. Would God the Father allow His only Son to mix with this crowd of cotton pickers and maids, washerwomen and handymen? I knew He sent His spirit on Sundays to the church, but after all, that was a church and the people had had all day Saturday to shuffle off the cloak of work and the skin of despair.

Everyone attended the revival meetings. Members of the hoity-toity Mount Zion Baptist Church mingled with the intellectual members of the African Methodist Episcopal and African Methodist Episcopal Zion, and the plain working people of the Christian Methodist Episcopal. These gatherings provided the one time in the year when all of those good village people associated with the followers of the Church of God in Christ. The latter were looked upon with some suspicion because they were so loud and raucous in their services. Their explanation that "the Good Book say, 'Make a joyful noise unto the Lord, and be exceedingly glad'" did not in the least minimize the condescension of their fellow Christians. Their church was far from the others, but they could be heard on Sunday, a half mile away, singing and dancing until they sometimes fell down in a dead faint. Members of the other churches wondered if the Holy Rollers were going to heaven after all their shouting. The suggestion was that they were having their heaven right here on earth.

This was their annual revival.

Mrs. Duncan, a little woman with a bird face, started the service. "I know I'm a witness for my Lord . . . I know I'm a witness for my Lord, I know I'm a witness . . ."

Her voice, a skinny finger, stabbed high up in the air and the church responded. From somewhere down front came the jangling sound of a tambourine. Two beats on "know," two beats on "I'm a" and two beats on the end of "witness."

Other voices joined the near shriek of Mrs. Duncan. They crowded around and tenderized the tone. Hand-claps snapped in the roof and solidified the beat. When the song reached its peak in sound and passion, a tall, thin man who had been kneeling behind the altar all the while stood up and sang with the audience for a few bars. He stretched out his long arms and grasped the platform. It took some time for the singers to come off their level of exultation, but the minister stood resolute until the song unwound like a child's playtoy and lay quieted in the aisles.

"Amen." He looked at the audience.

"Yes, sir, amen." Nearly everyone seconded him.

"I say, Let the church say 'Amen.'"

Everyone said, "Amen."

"Thank the Lord. Thank the Lord."

"That's right, thank the Lord. Yes, Lord. Amen."

"We will have prayer, led by Brother Bishop."

Another tall, brown-skinned man wearing square glasses walked up to the altar from the front row. The minister knelt at the right and Brother Bishop at the left.

"Our Father" — he was singing — "You who took my feet out the mire and clay — "

The church moaned, "Amen."

"You who saved my soul. One day. Look, sweet Jesus. Look down, on these your suffering children — "

The church begged, "Look down, Lord."

"Build us up where we're torn down . . . Bless the sick and the afflicted . . ."

It was the usual prayer. Only his voice gave it something new. After every two words he gasped and dragged the air over his vocal chords, making a sound like an inverted grunt. "You who" — grunt — "saved my" — gasp — "soul one" — inhalation — "day" — humph.

Then the congregation, led again by Mrs. Duncan, flew into "Precious Lord, take my hand, lead me on, let me stand." It was sung at a faster clip than the usual one in the C.M.E. Church, but at that tempo it worked. There was a joy about the tune that changed the meaning of its sad lyrics. "When the darkness appears, and the night draweth near and my life is almost gone . . ." There seemed to be an abandon which suggested that with all those things it should be a time for great rejoicing.

The serious shouters had already made themselves known, and their fans (cardboard advertisements from Texarkana's largest Negro funeral home) and lacy white handkerchiefs waved high in the air. In their dark hands they looked like small kites without the wooden frames.

The tall minister stood again at the altar. He waited for the song and the revelry to die.

He said, "Amen. Glory."

The church skidded off the song slowly. "Amen. Glory."

He still waited, as the last notes remained in the air, staircased on top of each other. "At the river I stand — " "I stand, guide my feet — " "Guide my feet, take my hand." Sung like the last circle in a round. Then quiet descended.

The Scripture reading was from Matthew, twenty-fifth chapter, thirtieth verse through the forty-sixth.

His text for the sermon was "The least of these."

After reading the verses to the accompaniment of a few Amens he said, "First Corinthians tells me, 'Even if I have the tongue of men and of angels and have not charity, I am as nothing. Even if I give all my clothes to the poor and have not charity, I am as nothing. Even if I give my body to be burned and have not charity it availeth me nothing. Burned, I say, and have not charity, it availeth nothing.' I have to ask myself, what is this thing called Charity? If good deeds are not charity — "

The church gave in quickly. "That's right, Lord."

" — if giving my flesh and blood is not charity?"

"Yes, Lord."

"I have to ask myself what is this charity they talking so much about."

I had never heard a preacher jump into the muscle of his sermon so quickly. Already the humming pitch had risen in the church, and those who knew had popped their eyes in anticipation of the coming excitement. Momma sat tree-trunk still, but she had balled her handkerchief in her hand and only the corner, which I had embroidered, stuck out.

"As I understand it, charity vaunteth not itself. Is not puffed up." He blew himself up with a deep breath to give us the picture of what Charity was not. "Charity don't go around saying 'I give you food and I give you clothes and by rights you ought to thank me.'"

The congregation knew whom he was talking about and voiced agreement with his analysis. "Tell the truth, Lord."

"Charity don't say, 'Because I give you a job, you got to bend your knee to me.'" The church was rocking with each phrase. "It don't say, 'Because I pays you what you due, you got to call me master.' It don't ask me to humble myself and belittle myself. That ain't what Charity is."

Down front to the right, Mr. and Mrs. Stewart, who only a few hours earlier had crumbled in our front yard, defeated by the cotton rows, now sat on the edges of their rickety-rackety chairs. Their faces shone with the delight of their souls. The mean whitefolks was going to get their comeuppance. Wasn't that what the minister said, and wasn't he quoting from the words of God Himself? They had been refreshed with the hope of revenge and the promise of justice.

"Aaagh. Raagh. I said . . . Charity. Woooooo, a Charity. It don't want nothing for itself. It don't want to be bossman . . . Waah . . . It don't want to be headman . . . Waah . . . It don't want to be foreman . . . Waah . . . It . . . I'm talking about Charity . . . It don't want . . . Oh Lord . . . help me tonight . . . It don't want to be bowed to and scraped at . . ."

America's historic bowers and scrapers shifted easily and happily in the makeshift church. Reassured that although they might be the lowest of the low they were at least not uncharitable, and "in that great Gettin' Up Morning, Jesus was going to separate the sheep (them) from the goats (the whitefolks)."

"Charity is simple." The church agreed, vocally.

"Charity is poor." That was us he was talking about.

"Charity is plain." I thought, that's about right. Plain and simple.

"Charity is . . . Oh. Oh, Oh. Cha-ri-ty. Where are you? Wooo . . . Charity . . . Hump."

One chair gave way and the sound of splintering wood split the air in the rear of the church.

"I call you and you don't answer. Woooh, oh Charity."

Another holler went up in front of me, and a large woman flopped over, her arms above her head like a candidate for baptism. The emotional release was contagious. Little screams burst around the room like Fourth of July firecrackers.

The minister's voice was a pendulum. Swinging left and down and right and down and left and — "How can you claim to be my brother, and hate me? Is that Charity? How can you claim to be my sister and despise me? Is that supposed to be Charity? How can you claim to be my friend and misuse and wrongfully abuse me? Is that Charity? Oh, my children, I stopped by here — "

The church swung on the end of his phrases. Punctuating. Confirming. "Stop by here, Lord."

" — to tell you, to open your heart and let Charity reign. Forgive your enemies for His sake. Show the Charity that Jesus was speaking of to this sick old world. It has need of the charitable giver." His voice was falling and the explosions became fewer and quieter.

"And now I repeat the words of the Apostle Paul, and 'now abideth faith, hope and charity, these three, but the greatest of them is charity.'"

The congregation lowed with satisfaction. Even if they were society's pariahs, they were going to be angels in a marble white heaven and sit on the right hand of Jesus, the Son of God. The Lord loved the poor and hated those cast high in the world. Hadn't He Himself said it would be easier for a camel to go through the eye of a needle than for a rich man to enter heaven? They were assured that they were going to be the only inhabitants of that land of milk and honey, except of course a few whitefolks like John Brown who history books said was crazy anyway. All the Negroes had to do generally, and those at the revival especially, was bear up under this life of toil and cares, because a blessed home awaited them in the far-off bye and bye.

"Bye and bye, when the morning come, when all the saints of God's are gathering home, we will tell the story of how we overcome and we'll understand it better bye and bye."

A few people who had fainted were being revived on the side aisles when the evangelist opened the doors of the church. Over the sounds of "Thank you, Jesus," he started a long-meter hymn:

"I came to Jesus, as I was,
worried, wounded and sad,
I found in Him a resting place,
And He has made me glad."

The old ladies took up the hymn and shared it in tight harmony. The humming crowd began to sound like tired bees, restless and anxious to get home.

"All those under the sound of my voice who have no spiritual home, whose hearts are burdened and heavy-ladened, let them come. Come before it's too late. I don't ask you to join the Church of God in Christ. No. I'm a servant of God, and in this revival, we are out to bring straying souls to Him. So if you join this evening, just say which church you want to be affiliated with, and we will turn you over to a representative of that church body. Will one deacon of the following churches come forward?"

That was revolutionary action. No one had ever heard of a minister taking in members for another church. It was our first look at Charity among preachers. Men from the A.M.E., A.M.E.Z., Baptist and C.M.E. churches went down front and assumed stances a few feet apart. Converted sinners flowed down the aisles to shake hands with the evangelist and stayed at his side or were directed to one of the men in line. Over twenty people were saved that night.

There was nearly as much commotion over the saving of the sinners as there had been during the gratifying melodic sermon.

The Mothers of the Church, old ladies with white lace disks pinned to their thinning hair, had a service all their own. They walked around the new converts singing,

"Before this time another year,
I may be gone,
In some lonesome graveyard,
Oh, Lord, how long?"

When the collection was taken up and the last hymn given to the praise of God, the evangelist asked that everyone in his presence rededicate his soul to God and his life's work to Charity. Then we were dismissed.

Outside and on the way home, the people played in their magic, as children poke in mud pies, reluctant to tell themselves that the game was over.

"The Lord touched him tonight, didn't He?"

"Surely did. Touched him with a mighty fire."

"Bless the Lord. I'm glad I'm saved."

"That's the truth. It make a whole lot of difference."

"I wish them people I works for could of heard that sermon. They don't know what they letting theyselves in for."

"Bible say, 'He who can hear, let him hear. He who can't, shame on 'em.'"

They basked in the righteousness of the poor and the exclusiveness of the downtrodden. Let the whitefolks have their money and power and segregation and sarcasm and big houses and schools and lawns like carpets, and books, and mostly — mostly — let them have their whiteness. It was better to be meek and lowly, spat upon and abused for this little time than to spend eternity frying in the fires of hell. No one would have admitted that the Christian and charitable people were happy to think of their oppressors' turning forever on the Devil's spit over the flames of fire and brimstone.

But that was what the Bible said and it didn't make mistakes. "Ain't it said somewhere in there that 'before one word of this changes, heaven and earth shall fall away?' Folks going to get what they deserved."

When the main crowd of worshipers reached the short bridge spanning the pond, the ragged sound of honky-tonk music assailed them. A barrelhouse blues was being shouted over the stamping of feet on a wooden floor. Miss Grace, the good-time woman, had her usual Saturday-night customers. The big white home blazed with lights and noise. The people inside had forsaken their own distress for a little while.

Passing near the din, the godly people dropped their heads and conversation ceased. Reality began its tedious crawl back into their reasoning. After all, they were needy and hungry and despised and dispossessed, and sinners the world over were in the driver's seat. How long, merciful Father? How long?

A stranger to the music could not have made a distinction between the songs sung a few minutes before and those being danced to in the gay house by the railroad tracks. All asked the same questions. How long, oh God? How long?

THE WITNESS

Barbara G. Harrison

(1934-   )

Widely published author (five books of nonfiction, one novel, and countless essays in such outlets as the *New York Times, Harper's, Esquire,* and *The New Republic*) and world traveler (Libya, India, Guatemala, and Italy), Barbara Grizzuti Harrison long before that had another kind of fame: she was a door-to-door, Bible-quoting Jehovah's Witness missionary. From the age of nine to twenty-one, she and her mother proselytized as best they could their Brooklyn neighbors on behalf of a stirring message of apocalyptic doom.

The Jehovah's Witnesses comprise another of those many made-in-America religious bodies: in the company of Christian Scientists, Seventh-day Adventists, Mormons, followers of Alexander Campbell, and a host of Pentecostal bodies, both black and white. Originating in Allegheny, Pennsylvania, in 1872, the small group of Bible students, under the leadership of Charles Taze Russell, in 1884 incorporated themselves as "The Zion's Watch Tower Tract Society." "As an adolescent," Harrison writes, "Russell had written Bible texts in chalk in front of whorehouses and saloons, warning men against courting eternal damnation." In 1909, after a litigious divorce, Russell led his followers from Pennsylvania to Brooklyn, New York, where he purchased Henry Ward Beecher's Plymouth Church as well as his four-story brownstone parsonage in Columbia Heights. Harrison would later spend three years cleaning the seventeen double bedrooms in the Beecher parsonage.

Meanwhile, the Witnesses continued to flourish both in the United States and abroad. From a few hundred at the end of the nineteenth century, Witness numbers worldwide approach one million at the end of the twentieth. Growth comes through every member serving as an evangelist and through the effective dissemination of printed propaganda. By the mid-1970s printing plants had been established in Australia, Brazil, Canada, England, Finland, France, Germany, Ghana, Japan, Nigeria, the Philippines, South Africa, Sweden, and Switzerland. Well before that time, however, Harrison had fled the fold.

In the Beecher parsonage, now the Witnesses' headquarters, Barbara Harrison describes the routine that no doubt proved deadly to a restless, brilliant adolescent. Bells rang at 6:00 A.M., showers in the communal bathrooms followed, then breakfast with Bible discussion at 6:30, and all to work by 7:30. "We worked six days a week. On Monday nights we had a 'family' reading of *The Watchtower;* on Tuesday nights we were expected to attend a local Bible study group; on Wednesday nights we were supposed to make 'back-calls' or return visits to people with whom we had placed Witness literature on Sundays; on Thursday nights we went to something called the Theocratic Ministry School, where we learned to be more perfect; and on Sunday nights we studied *The Watchtower* again, with a Brooklyn congregation." In 1956, she left.

In addition to learning of a bloody battle of Armageddon not too distant in the future, Barbara Harrison with the Witnesses also learned that the Roman Catholic Church was the "scarlet whore of Babylon," the "abomination of abominations." She now lists her religious affiliation as Roman Catholic.

[See Barbara Grizzuti Harrison, *An Accidental Biography* (Boston: Houghton Mifflin, 1996).]

I have an uncle who created a scandal once by asking for three fried eggs for breakfast. He became a family legend. He was often offered to me as an object lesson in extravagance and selfishness. I come from a frugal family. In my childhood, everything was carefully measured out — love, food, words, approval (even toilet tissue: when I got married, my mother's advice to me was "Don't buy two-ply. People will use as much as if you'd bought one-ply; they won't be able to tell the difference"). Everything was carefully measured out — except tears. We are a family that cries a lot. The women in my family were not ascetic and not, after the Depression, poor; but they had a strong conviction that there were invisible boundaries you didn't step over unless you wanted to join the company of the wasteful (who were also slothful, bad), that everything had its appointed limits ("*decent* limits," they would have said); and goodness was equated with restraint. It was always too cold in the houses I grew up in, and too dark. Conservation was regarded not as deprivation or as dreary self-denial, but as a way to enrich oneself. Love didn't, in their view, multiply and expand; it curled in on itself, fed itself, was kept within "decent limits."

I once got a beating for telling "the Jews next door" what we were having for dinner. That was the kind of information you didn't give

Source: Barbara G. Harrison, *Visions of Glory: A History and Memory of Jehovah's Witnesses* (New York: Simon and Schuster, 1970), pp. 344-50; 355-56; 365-66.

333

away; you hugged it to yourself, you didn't give anything away. And if that was meanness, it wasn't calculated meanness: it was like an Arab's not wanting to have his picture taken for fear that his soul would be stolen away. We hoarded everything, so that we could remain inviolate, so that nobody could steal our souls away, or know our souls; we kept everything locked and secret and hidden. Maybe it was the centuries of Moorish blood in our Southern Italian veins, and our second-generation fears that *they* ("the Americans") would find us out — find us wanting.

Frugal and insular and suspicious; the outside world was full of menace. And when I became a Witness, it was the same story all over again, frugality and insularity and suspicion; the outside world was full of menace, and a niggardly Jehovah kept us safe by keeping us from the light and the heat of the world. He was a chilly and genteel God who didn't like ardent or extravagant gestures (and I got Him and my mother all mixed up).

He was the kind of God who regarded both Oxford and the Cathedral at Chartres as extravagances, the adoration of the saints and the "pursuit of worldly knowledge" as vulgar excesses, show-offy and flamboyant, self-aggrandizing and uncircumspect, wicked. (I asked Him to forgive me for loving stained glass and incense; I kept a copy of *Letter to a Young Poet* in my laundry bag.) Once someone gave me a kaleidoscope. It was my favorite present.

One Sunday summer morning, as I left Watchtower headquarters to go out preaching from door to door, a member of a tightly huddled-together little group of fellow Witnesses, I saw two young women and two men piling into a yellow convertible. They were all laughing. They carried picnic hampers covered with red-and-white-checked cloths, very full. One of the young men turned on the car radio — a Mozart quintet. I wanted to be with them. I wanted to *be* them. I longed for their world of color and light and sound. My longing was so acute it was like a physical pain; and it was followed by an intolerable ennui: I didn't know what I was doing holding a satchel of *Watchtower* magazines, or why I was going to preach, or what I had to do with the Witnesses or they with me. I wanted to run away. I didn't, but I knew at that moment that someday I would.

The four young men and women had come out of a house on Pineapple Street, an old wooden house, white, with a forest-green door and forest-green shutters and dimity curtains and chandeliers that seemed to be lit even in the daytime. The garden of the house, with its cherry tree that had blossoms like crepe paper, was surrounded by a high white wooden fence, and set in the garden fence was a lime-green door with no doorknob on the outside. For days I imagined that if I knocked at that door, they would recognize me and let me in and we would sit in the garden under the cherry tree and I would never have to go back to the Watchtower Building again.

Later that same week, on an impulse, I went alone to Birdland. Basie was playing, and Joe Williams was singing the blues. I had two rye-and-gingers, and felt scared and exhilarated. I came back with my hair smelling of cigarette smoke: "Dirty," my roommate said. It was the first time I had trouble falling asleep.

On the Saturday of that week, a Witness I knew and loved died. And the circumstances surrounding his dying made me understand that when I left (as I knew I would), it wouldn't be because I preferred yellow sports cars and summer picnics and Mozart or jazz to God; it would be because God didn't live in my religion. If He lived at all, He lived somewhere else (not in my heart).

Mike died at a party at a Witness' house. Unlike most Witnesses, he never seemed to give a damn what impression he created on other people. He was funky and loving and flamboyant. He was an iceman; he drove an ice truck. When I was younger, I'd had a temporary job at the UN bank. Mike used to drive me up to the Secretariat building in his truck. We laughed at the incongruity of driving to the UN in a Sicilian-decorated ice truck, and he never used the occasion to preach about the evils of the "beastly United Nations" (which ranked second, in the Witnesses' chamber of Satanic horrors, only to the Vatican). He may have accepted the Witnesses' belief that the UN was the "desolation of desolations," but that didn't deter him from driving up gaily and irreverently to its portals. The fear and loathing such "devilish" places inspired in the Witnesses' hearts, and the repulsion and fascination, seemed entirely lacking in his.

But it was his heart that killed him. He'd had two heart attacks; on the morning of that party, he'd been out preaching for the first time since his convalescence. He was talking about his delight in being able to go from door to door again, talking with gusto about his pleasure in "sharing" (other Witnesses might "give the truth"; Mike shared), when he clutched his chest and began to gasp for air. He took the diamond ring he wore off his finger and gave it and his wallet to his wife (he knew he was dying; his last thoughts were for someone else). A few Witnesses went, spontaneously and generously and compassionately, to his wife to support her. A respected elder from Watchtower headquarters launched — as Mike's gasps began to sound, horribly, more like the final rattle of death — into an interminable story about the people he'd known who'd been taken unaware by death ("I knew someone else who died like that," he said, looking at Mike). Three-quarters of the Witnesses present set themselves to clean up the room in order to "give a good witness" to the police when they arrived. Mike was pronounced DOA. The cops were given a speech about our hope in the resurrection. Mike himself was ignored (except by the police, whose attempts to resuscitate him were heroic); grief was shelved (Mike's wife was sedated). The Witnesses congratulated themselves on the way the police had seemed to be impressed by their decorum and their calm; in their zeal to "give a witness," the actual fact of Mike's death seemed almost forgotten. I can't remember anyone crying out in love or horror — or praying.

The task of telling Mike's young daughter that he had died was delegated to me. As an elder drove me to her house, he recited all the Scriptures I might use to comfort her. He might have been reciting the *Guinness Book of World Records.* (The rest of the Witnesses stayed behind; when I left, Mike's heavily sedated wife lay on a couch while, around her, Witnesses talked about what a pleasant change it must make for the cops to come into a "decent" house, how much nicer than having to break up a drunken fight.) I looked at the elder in a vain attempt to find some trace of sorrow or anger on his face as he continued to offer memorized words of comfort. He had already buried Mike in some recess of his mind; his concern was how to keep Mike's daughter from "going overboard with immoderate grief" (his words — she was 12 years old). I have hated very few people as much as I hated that man, then. "See if you can take Mike's daughter out preaching with you tomorrow morning," he said. "It'll keep her mind from selfishness."

Nobody had cried. Mike's daughter cried, and I couldn't find it in my heart to read a single Scripture to her.

I came to live and work at Bethel — Watchtower headquarters — in 1953, when I was 19. I left early in 1956.

I had had over the years, since my baptism in 1944, little niggles of doubt (and a constant conviction of sin). My doubts terrified me.

Nobody ever told me that all believers doubt, or that the logical consequence of the possession of free will is to question, or that even mystics have at times felt abandoned by the God they adore; what a lot of misery it would have saved me if someone had told me. But the Witnesses couldn't tell me that, because they themselves didn't acknowledge that it was true. To them, faith is total, unquestioning, uncritical, unwavering, and undemanding.

I regarded my irritable intelligence as a kind of predatory animal which, if not firmly reined, would spring on me, attack me, and destroy me.

Since to doubt at all was intolerable, the only solution that seemed possible was to submerge my doubts (to submerge myself) completely. I wanted to be eaten alive, devoured by Jehovah, to spend so much time in his service that my peevish spirit, humbled and exhausted, would no longer have time for querulous doubts. Women are good at turning their desolation to their advantage (or to what they think is their advantage); and what I was doing by entering Bethel was making spiritual capital out of spiritual despair, quelling my restlessness by giving it a death in a new life.

And I had other (baser) motives too: There was, for a woman, great spiritual prestige in being admitted to Bethel. It was both glamorous and holy. Men outnumbered women 10 to 1 at Bethel (although, among rank-and-file Witnesses, women outnumbered men 3 to 1). I had nothing against being surrounded by men. Part of the inner circle, circled about by men; I thought that part would be nice.

And I wanted to please my mother, whose standards I knew I never lived up to (I was never sure what they were) and whose ambition for me was boundless, at the same time that her competition with me was fierce. Simone Weil's mother is reported to have said once, with a mixture of exasperation and tenderness, "Thank God you don't have a daughter who's a saint." I had a mother who was thought to be a kind of saint — the Bible Lady of Brooklyn, they called her. It was a foregone conclusion that all my boyfriends would be more charmed by her than they would by me, by her sacrificial gravity, her seductive saintly gaiety, which were all the more alluring because she was beautiful, with wide blue eyes, a mouth that turned down just slightly — just enough to suggest ineradicable sadness (which everybody tried to eradicate). Viewing me as a spiritual extension of herself, she would be pleased, I knew, if I went to Bethel; she would feel validated and enhanced by my choice. And I would be making up to her for having failed to make her happy. I believed, at that time, that I held the power to make her happy. It was not a good thing, I know better in retrospect, to feel. I wanted to make things good for her, to make up to her for all the things she didn't have, for whatever it was she wept for in my bedroom every night. I wanted to get away from that weeping, and from the acrimony that bound her and my unbelieving father together more closely than the most enduring affection.

I wanted to allay her pain, and I wanted her to stop passing her pain on to me. I really did believe that I was the agent of her happiness; I don't know through what subtle instruction or self-delusion I came to believe that. (But I do know that when, years later, I read, in one of the works of the saints, that God wants us, *obliges* us, to be happy, my first angry reaction was followed immediately by understanding: of course He does; because if you're unhappy, all you can do is make someone else responsible for your unhappiness and pass along your terrible pain. It makes perfect sense to me that God forbids us to despair.)

And I wanted to get away from my father, whose bewilderment took the form of rage, who wept for me (not for himself), and whose tears I rejected and despised. I was in an alliance with my mother against him — an unnatural alliance: my inclination, till my mother and I joined forces against him, was to find him irresistible. It was an unholy bonding; and while, at the time, I dismissed my father as negligible or feared him as a monstrous "Opposer of The Truth," there must, I think, have been part of my nature that recoiled against the pitiless, hard person I was when I was with him. I wanted to get away from all of it — the fights, the yelling, the tears, the recriminations, and the whispered secrets. I didn't want to hear my mother's whispered secrets; I didn't want to be her girlfriend, her "sister." (She signed her notes to me *Connie*. And when she was mad at me, she mailed her notes to me — though we shared not only the same apartment, but the same bedroom — and then handed them to me when the mailman came, with a hard suffering face that I feared more than I feared the judgment of God.) If my mother insisted on going out preaching Christmas Eve, I didn't want to be around to entertain my father's rages and then to defend her when she returned. I didn't want to fight with my father with her holding my hand, urging me on; I knew there was something sick and unholy about what we were doing. (When she introduced herself to my friends, she said, "I am Barbara's relative." She never called herself my mother.)

I took the only escape route I knew. But if you had asked me then I would have said, "I came to Bethel to serve the Lord." And I would have meant it. Many of my motives were obscure to me. But I did want to love God. (I didn't understand that the will to believe is not quite the same as the belief itself.)

I thought I loved God. I loved the idea of loving Him. I *knew* I loved Arnold; I had loved him since I was 15, when he was my high school English teacher who had held my hand in school assembly when I didn't salute the flag. Being at Bethel prevented me from walking down his street every day, hoping for an "accidental" meeting. But it didn't prevent me from fantasizing about him — from dreaming that he would be converted and that we would live together happily ever after in the New World.

I told Nathan H. Knorr, then the Watchtower Society's president, about Arnold — which was pretty stupid, because I must have known what he'd tell me, and I must have guessed I'd disregard it. He told me never to see Arnold again. If he had told me that I could never see my mother and father again, I might have obeyed him; but Arnold was my mother and father, and I couldn't not see him.

There were three public telephone booths at Bethel, unventilated and airless and smelling of the sweat of 500 bodies; like all the doors at Bethel, these had no locks; and I'd call Arnold from one of the booths when my craving couldn't be denied, and we'd arrange to meet. Once I got to his living room and I heard his beloved Schubert *Trout Quintet* or one of the Beethoven quartets he always played for me, there was only joy. A guilt hangover the next day took the form of headaches, a steel vise around my head. (And the guilt had nothing to do with sex — there was no sex; I was guilty for loving him.)

So I carried all this baggage to Bethel with me — my love for Arnold and my doubts; but I went, nevertheless (I really believe this), in good faith. I meant to stay forever. Before I had been there two years, I knew I would have to leave.

One afternoon, as I sat working in the proofreading department of the Watchtower plant at 117 Adams Street, a sudden black storm blew up, and two of the men with whom I shared proofreading tasks raced to the plate-glass windows and said, "Oh, boy! Maybe it's Armageddon. Wouldn't it be wonderful if it was Armageddon? Do you think it's Armageddon? Wow!" I laughed and laughed and laughed, because they sounded so much more like Batman and Robin anticipating a caper with the Joker than like decently awed men awaiting God's final judgment. And of course, my laughter infuriated them. Their little-boy glee gave way to sententiousness and censoriousness, and they silenced my hysterical laughter with glares, demanding to know what, exactly, I found so funny. Perhaps my laughter had made them aware of their own foolishness; I doubt it, though, because they took both Armageddon and themselves very seriously (never for a moment doubting that the Storm of Storms would leave 117 Adams Street, and them, unscathed). I quailed — anything male and angry had the power to subdue me — and said in a voice I didn't recognize as my own (it sounded like the voice of a petulant 9-year-old), "I don't *want* Armageddon to come."

It was the first visible crack in my defenses.

I covered myself very quickly, and very transparently (that was the kind of remark, I knew from experience, that was not likely to go unreported to higher authorities): "I don't think enough people are saved yet," I said. It must have sounded as hollow to them as it did to me; and I felt hollow, as if the storm outside had blown through me, leaving my soul as dry as a whistle.

Then I began to cry.

⌇

I'm talking about my life at Bethel as if it were one of unrelieved gloom; and that isn't true. There were times when I felt absolutely high — stoned on God-talk (which, as it happens, can be a powerful aphrodisiac, among other things). Walking across the Brooklyn Bridge with my friend Walter, holding hands and talking about God; learning to dance the tango with Walter and Peggy and Walter's roommate, Norman; dancing all night on the Society's missionary yacht in New York harbor; picnicking under the George Washington Bridge — there were easy, good times. And the best times were when we were in other people's homes, teaching them the Bible, and they offered us the intimate details of their lives and we felt enhanced and enriched and part of a loving community serving a higher cause.

But in the end, none of that was enough. In the end, my decision to leave had very little to do with people who loved me and people who didn't, with good times and bad times. In the end, it had everything to do with my feelings about the world, which I had been taught was reserved for destruction and which I nevertheless obdurately loved, though my ignorance of it was profound. It had to do with my feeling cramped and lonely and frightened; leaving was survival.

All of this is in the diary I kept the last six months I was at Bethel. When I read these diary notes now, they seem to me grossly self-conscious, not to say narcissistic (but I was, after all, writing as if God were peering over my shoulder — and it's hard to know how to play to that Audience); and they are full of Nichols-and-May 1950s joke words, like "evolve" and "aware" (I was reading Camus, and I was feeling like Columbus, discovering new continents of thought and hoping against hope that the way West was the way East — and that I would blunder my way out to the riches of the world). They sound like the writings of arrested adolescence (I was an arrested adolescent).

When I read these diary notes now, they seem not only florid and naive, but coy as well: I was afraid of revealing myself even to myself; I played mind tricks. Words that were too heavily charged for me to commit to paper — words like *leaving religion* — I wrote in shorthand (under the assumption, I suppose, that neither my roommate nor Jehovah knew Pittman).

The diaries abound in sentences, I'm sorry to say, like "I believe" — or, "I don't believe" — "in happiness"; "I think I can love spring again." I'm leaving them out; as, for the sake of this record, I'm leaving out all sentences of the "I-feel-I-can-stand-on-tiptoe-and-embrace-the-sun" variety. They were, at the time, deeply felt — which is, unfortunately, no guarantee that they sound authentic twenty years later. (*Authentic* is another 1950s word; I suppose that if I had left the Witnesses in the '60s, I would have fallen in love with geodesic domes or used a political vocabulary in which to couch my despair. As it was, I borrowed from the existentialists — which may not have been a bad thing. I still love Camus, Salinger, Brando-the-wild-one, and the rakish skinny Sinatra who faced the world, or so it seemed, with showy grit more than I love Abby, Jerry, Tom, Rennie.)

⌒

Now this is when the fairy Godmother (God/Father?) steps in. In the guise of a balding optometrist (charlatan or scientist or saint, he may have saved my life), in Greenwich Village, across the street from St. Joseph's Church (where now I sometimes go to Mass). Why did I go to Greenwich Village, to which I had never been, for eyeglasses? The Lord knows. (I assume, so much have I changed, that He does.) I don't remember the name of that eye doctor; his shop is no longer there.

He took an inordinately long time examining my eyes. He said: "I don't know your life or who you are or what you're doing. But whatever you're doing, you have to stop it. I've never seen anybody so rigidly controlled, and I've never seen so much strain. You're seeing things that aren't there, and you're not seeing things that are there. You may last six days or six weeks or six months, but you're headed for a breakdown, and it won't be pretty when it comes." Then he said, with a flash of insight that frightened me with its acuity, "I sometimes have to tell priests to take six months off. I'm telling you to take the rest of your life off, if that's what you have to do. If you want to live."

It was all I needed.

I ran down the subway steps. No terror. Somebody had finally told me I was crazy, or as close to it as made no difference. I told my roommate not to wake me up for breakfast, overriding her protests almost gaily (the release!): "The doctor says I'm killing myself." Also slyly (and merrily): "He thinks I'm cracked."

All I'd needed was someone to *tell* me. Another voice, a voice outside my own head.

I slept, on and off, for three days. The resident chiropractor stuck his head in once in a while and offered me cans of soup. (I was not particularly enchanted with the resident chiropractor: his main approach to all physical ailments was a vibrator, which he applied to body parts we weren't even supposed to know the names of.) He sat there with his lap full of Campbell's, urging me to get out of bed to receive it. I nodded my thanks. I didn't want to get out of bed. I didn't want soup or voices or vibrators or sympathy.

My roommate looked frightened and didn't ask any questions. She prayed ostentatiously. The only complete sentence I can remember saying in those three days is "Mary, for God's sake, stop *flopping!*" Margarita came in once to ask me if I wanted anything. "An apple turnover," I said.

When the three days were over, I made an appointment to see Brother Knorr. I was taking in great greedy drafts of air; I felt buoyant.

Brother Knorr thought I needed a rest. He suggested that I transfer to the Society's farm in upstate New York; manual work to bludgeon my brain cells into acquiescence. He addressed all his remarks to the Statue of Liberty. Or so it seemed: he sat with his broad back toward me, facing New York Harbor. His enormous desk between us. More than that between us. Worlds (the world) between us.

I said No, no rest. I didn't trust myself to say anything more.

He swiveled around in his chair (made to order in the carpentry shop).

"Weren't you high school valedictorian?"

"No."

"But you were smart."

"Yes."

"That's your trouble."

I was dismissed.

(I was glad he didn't offer to shake my sweaty hand. I thought, on the way down in the elevator, how long it had been since anybody had held me or touched me.)

I packed my suitcase. I called my mother. She came with a friend to collect me, my suitcase, and a driftwood lamp (my only possessions). I dropped off my key at the front desk. It was snowing. We drove back to Bensonhurst in silence. Back to the bedroom I shared with my mother, and to a silence that has remained unbroken between us: she has never asked me why I left.

THE "MINORITY STUDENT"

Richard Rodriguez

(1944-   )

"Minority Student" is in quotation marks, because it is a phrase applied to Richard Rodriguez, but never adopted by him. He did not care for it, and indeed the use of the term helped drive him away from an academic career. After receiving his bachelor's degree from Stanford in 1967 and his master's from Columbia two years later, Rodriguez returned to California for additional graduate work in English at the University of California, Berkeley. He also spent a year of research and writing at the British Museum in London. The academic life loomed promisingly ahead.

But Rodriguez grew increasingly uneasy about being the beneficiary of affirmative action. He knew many nonwhites with far less privileged background than his; he even knew whites with less preparation than he had received in parochial schools and at Stanford. In some sense, he was a minority, he recognized, but only if one talked in terms of a large class of people, not if one considered the individual. In the late 60s and early 70s, "slowly, slowly the term *minority* became a source of unease. It would remind me of those boyhood years when I had felt myself alienated from the public (majority) society — *los gringos*." By graduate school days, he recognized that in any true cultural sense he was no longer a "minority student." To put it very simply, "The reason I was no longer a minority was because I had become a student."

When the time came to look for a position in the groves of academe, Rodriguez found the discomfort greatly increased. He received

345

job offers without applying; fellow graduate students sent out letter after letter, often without even the courtesy of a reply. "One student,
among the best in the department [at Berkeley], did not get so much as
a request for his dossier. He and I met outside a classroom one day, and
he asked about my prospects. He seemed happy for me. Faculty members beamed at the news. They said they were not surprised. "After all,
not many schools are going to pass up the chance to get a Chicano with
a Ph.D. in Renaissance literature." Once again, the "minority student."
Rodriguez could not make up his mind which of many offers to accept.
He finally decided to accept none. "No, I would say to them all. Finally,
simply, no."

In the excerpt below, we read of an earlier stage in the author's
life: a time in his parochial education where he was conscious not only
of the tension between Mexican-American and majority American, but
also between his private (home) Catholicism and the gringo Catholicism
all around. "Only now do I trouble to notice what intricate differences
separated home Catholicism from school Catholicism." Twelve years of
Catholic schooling clearly prepared Richard Rodriguez to be a student,
but not necessarily a minority student.

[See Richard Rodriguez, *Days of Obligation* (New York: Viking,
1992).]

The steps of the church defined the eternal square where children played and adults talked after dinner. He remembers the way the church building was at the center of town life. She remembers the way one could hear the bell throughout the day, telling time. And the way the town completely closed down for certain feastdays. He remembers that the church spire was the first thing he'd see walking back into town. Both my parents have tried to describe something of what it was like for them to have grown up Catholic in small Mexican towns. They remember towns where everyone was a Catholic.

With their move to America, my mother and father left behind that Mexican Church to find themselves (she praying in whispered Spanish) in an Irish-American parish. In a way, they found themselves at ease in such a church. My parents had much in common with the Irish-born priests and nuns. Like my parents, the priests remembered what it was like to have been Catholic in villages and cities where everyone else was a Catholic. In their American classrooms, the nuns worked very hard to approximate that other place, that earlier kind of religious experience. For a time they succeeded. For a time I too enjoyed a Catholicism something like that enjoyed a generation before me by my parents.

Source: Richard Rodriguez, *Hunger of Memory* (Boston: David R. Godine, Inc., 1982), pp. 77-90.

I grew up a Catholic at home and at school, in private and in public. My mother and father were deeply pious *católicos;* all my relatives were Catholics. At home, there were holy pictures on a wall of nearly every room, and a crucifix hung over my bed. My first twelve years as a student were spent in Catholic schools where I could look up to the front of the room and see a crucifix hanging over the clock.

When I was a boy, anyone not a Catholic was defined by that fact and the term *non-Catholic.* The expression suggests the parochialism of the Catholicism in which I was raised. In those years I could have told you the names of persons in public life who were Catholics. I knew that Ed Sullivan was a Catholic. And Mrs. Bob Hope. And Senator John F. Kennedy. As the neighborhood newspaper boy, I knew all the names on my route. As a Catholic, I noted which open doors, which front room windows disclosed a crucifix. At quarter to eight Sunday mornings, I saw the O'Briens and the Van Hoyts walking down the empty sidewalk past our house and I knew. Catholics were mysteriously lucky, 'chosen' by God to be nurtured a special way. Non-Catholics had souls, too, of course, and somehow could get to heaven. But on Sundays they got all dressed up only to go to a church where there was no incense, no sacred body and blood, and no confessional box. Or else they slept late and didn't go to church at all. For non-Catholics, it seemed there was all white and no yolk.

In twelve years of Catholic schooling, I learned, in fact, very little about the beliefs of non-Catholics, though the little I learned was conveyed by my teachers without hostility and with fair accuracy. All that I knew about Protestants was that they differed from Catholics. But what precisely distinguished a Baptist from a Methodist from an Episcopalian I could not have said. I surmised the clearest notion of Protestant theology from discussions of the Reformation. At that, Protestantism emerged only as deviance from Catholic practice and thought. Judaism was different. Before the Christian era Judaism was *my* religion, the nuns said. ('We are all Jews because of Christ.') But what happened to Judaism after Christ's death to the time the modern state of Israel was founded, I could not have said. Nor did I know a thing about Hinduism, or Buddhism or Islam. I knew nothing about modern secular ideologies. In civics class a great deal was said about oppressive Soviet policies; but at no time did I hear classical Marxism explained. In church, at the close of mass, the congregation prayed for 'the conversion of Russia.'

It is not enough to say that I grew up a ghetto Catholic. As a Catholic schoolboy, I was educated a middle-class American. Even while grammar school nuns reminded me of my spiritual separateness from non-Catholics, they provided excellent *public* schooling. A school day began with prayer — the Morning Offering. Then there was the Pledge of Allegiance to the American flag. Religion class followed immediately. But afterward, for the rest of the day, I was taught well those skills of numbers and words crucial to my Americanization. Soon I became as Americanized as my classmates — most of whom were two or three generations removed from their immigrant ancestors, and all of whom were children of middle-class parents.

When we were eleven years old, the nuns would warn us about the dangers of mixed marriage (between a Catholic and a non-Catholic). And we heard a priest say that it was a mortal sin to read newspaper accounts of a Billy Graham sermon. But the ghetto Catholic Church, so defensive, so fearful of contact with non-Catholics, was already outdated when I entered the classroom. My classmates and I were destined to live in a world very different from that which the nuns remembered in Ireland or my parents remembered in Mexico. We were destined to live on unhallowed ground, beyond the gated city of God.

I was in high school when Kennedy's picture went up on the wall. And I remember feeling that he was 'one of us.' His election to the presidency, however, did not surprise me as it did my father. Nor was I encouraged by it. I did not take it as evidence that Catholics could, after all, participate fully in American public life. (I assumed that to be true.) When I was a senior in high school, consequently, I did not hesitate to apply to secular colleges.

It was to be in college, at Stanford, that my religious faith would seen to me suddenly pared. I would remain a Catholic, but a Catholic defined by a non-Catholic world. This is how I think of myself now. I remember my early Catholic schooling and recall an experience of religion very different from anything I have known since. Never since have I felt so much at home in the Church, so easy at mass. My grammar school years especially were the years when the great Church doors opened to enclose me, filling my day as I was certain the Church filled all time. Living in a community of shared faith, I enjoyed much more than mere social reinforcement of religious belief. Experienced continuously in public and private, Catholicism shaped my whole day. It framed my experience of eating and sleeping and washing; it named the season and the hour.

The sky was full then and the coming of spring was a religious event. I would awaken to the sound of garage doors creaking open and know without thinking that it was Friday and that my father was on his way to six-thirty mass. I saw, without bothering to notice, statues at home and at school of the Virgin and of Christ. I would write at the top of my arithmetic or history homework the initials *Jesus, Mary,* and *Joseph.* (All my homework was thus dedicated.) I felt the air was different, somehow still and more silent on Sundays and high feastdays. I felt lightened, transparent as sky, after confessing my sins to a priest. Schooldays were routinely divided by prayers said with classmates. I would not have forgotten to say grace before eating. And I would not have turned off the light next to my bed or fallen asleep without praying to God.

The institution of the Church stood an extraordinarily physical presence in my world. One block from the house was Sacred Heart Church. In the opposite direction, another block away, was Sacred Heart Grammar School, run by the Sisters of Mercy. And from our backyard, I could see Mercy Hospital, Sacramento's only Catholic hospital. All day I would hear the sirens of death. Well before I was a student myself, I would watch the Catholic school kids walk by the front of the house dressed in gray and red uniforms. From the front lawn I could see people on the steps of the church, coming out, dressed in black after funerals, or standing, the ladies in bright-colored dresses in front of the church after a wedding. When I first went to stores on errands for my mother, I could be seen by the golden-red statue of Christ, where it hovered over the main door of the church.

I was *un católico* before I was a Catholic. That is, I acquired my earliest sense of the Church — and my membership in it — through my parents' Mexican Catholicism. It was in Spanish that I first learned to pray. I recited family prayers — not from any book. And in those years when we felt alienated from *los gringos,* my family went across town every week to the wooden church of Our Lady of Guadalupe, which was decorated with yellow Christmas tree lights all year long.

Very early, however, the *gringo* church in our neighborhood began to superimpose itself on our family life, The first English-speaking dinner guest at our house was a priest from Sacred Heart Church. I was about four years old at the time so I retain only random details with which to remember the evening. But the visit was too important an event for me to forget. I remember how my mother dressed her four children in outfits it had taken her weeks to sew. I wore a white shirt and blue woolen shorts. (It was the first time I had been dressed up for a stranger.) I remember hearing the priest's English laughter. (It was the first time I had heard such sounds in the house.) I remember that my mother served a *gringo* meat loaf and that I was too nervous or shy to look up more than two or three times to study the priest's jiggling layers of face. (Smoothly, he made believe that there was conversation.) After dinner we all went to the front room where the priest took a small book from his jacket to recite some prayers, consecrating our home and our family. He left a large picture of a sad-eyed Christ, exposing his punctured heart. (A caption below records the date of his visit and the imprimatur of Francis Cardinal Spellman.) That picture survives. Hanging prominently over the radio or, later, the television set in the front room, it has retained a position of prominence in all the houses my parents have lived in since. It has been one of the few permanent fixtures in the environment of my life. Visitors to our house doubtlessly noticed it when they entered the door — saw it immediately as the sign we were Catholics. But I saw the picture too often to pay it much heed.

I saw a picture of the Sacred Heart in the grammar school classroom I entered two years after the priest's visit. The picture drew an important continuity between home and the classroom. When all else was different for me (as a scholarship boy) between the two worlds of my life, the Church provided an essential link. During my first months in school, I remember being struck by the fact that — although they worshipped in English — the nuns and my classmates shared my family's religion. The *gringos* were, in some way, like me, *católicos*. Gradually, however, with my assimilation in the schoolroom, I began to think of myself and my family as Catholics. The distinction blurred. At home and in class I heard about sin and Christ and Satan and the consoling presence of Mary the Virgin. It became one Catholic faith for me.

Only now do I trouble to notice what intricate differences separated home Catholicism from classroom Catholicism. In school, religious instruction stressed that man was a sinner. Influenced, I suspect, by a bleak melancholic strain in Irish Catholicism, the nuns portrayed God as a judge. I was carefully taught the demands He placed upon me. In the third grade I could distinguish between venial and mortal sin. I knew — and was terrified to know — that there was one unforgivable sin (against the Holy Ghost): the sin of despair. I knew the crucial distinction between perfect and imperfect contrition. I could distinguish sins of commission from sins of omission. And I learned how important it was to be in a state of grace at the moment of death.

Death. (How much nearer it seemed to the boy than it seems to me now.) Again and again the nuns would pull out the old stories of death-bed conversions; of Roman martyrdoms; of murdered African missionaries; of pious children dying of cancer to become tiny saints; of souls going immediately to heaven. We were taught how to baptize in case of emergency. I knew why some souls went to Limbo after the death of the body, and others went for a time to Purgatory, and why others went to heaven or hell — 'forever and ever.'

Among the assortment of possible sins to commit, sexual sins — the cherries — were certainly mentioned. With the first year of puberty, the last years of grammar school, we began hearing about 'sins of the flesh.' There were those special mornings when the priest would come over from church to take the boys to the cafeteria, while the nun remained with the girls — 'the young ladies' — in the classroom. For fifty minutes the priest would talk about the dangers of masturbation or petting, and some friend of mine would turn carefully in his chair to smirk in my direction or somebody else would jab me in the back with a pencil.

Unlike others who have described their Catholic schooling, I do not remember the nuns or the priests to have been obsessed with sexual sins. Perhaps that says more about me or my Mexican Catholicism than it says about what actually went on in the classroom. I remember, in any case, that I would sometimes hear with irony warnings about sins of the flesh. When we were in eighth grade the priest told us how dangerous it was to look at our naked bodies, even while taking a bath — and I noticed that he made the remark directly under a near-naked figure of Christ on the Cross.

The church, in fact, excited more sexual wonderment than it repressed. I regarded with awe the 'wedding ring' on a nun's finger, her black 'wedding veil' — symbols of marriage to God. I would study pictures of martyrs — white-robed virgins fallen in death and the young, almost smiling, St. Sebastian, transfigured in pain. At Easter high mass, I was dizzied by the mucous perfume of white flowers at the celebration of rebirth. At such moments, the Church touched alive some very private sexual excitement; it pronounced my sexuality important.

Sin remained, nevertheless. Confession was a regular part of my grammar school years. (One sought forgiveness through the ritual plea: 'Bless me, father, for I have sinned. . . .') Sin — the distance separating man from God — sin that burdened a sorrowful Christ; sin remained. ('I have disobeyed my parents fourteen times . . . I have lied eight times . . . I am heartily sorry for having offended Thee. . . .') God the Father judged. But Christ the Son had interceded. I was forgiven each time I sought forgiveness. The priest murmured Latin words of forgiveness in the confessional box. And I would leave the dark.

In contrast to the Catholicism of school, the Mexican Catholicism of home was less concerned with man the sinner than with man the supplicant. God the Father was not so much a stern judge as One with the power to change our lives. My family turned to God not in guilt so much as in need. We prayed for favors and at desperate times. I prayed for help in finding a quarter I had lost on my way home. I prayed with my family at times of illness and when my father was temporarily out of a job. And when there was death in the family, we prayed.

I remember my family's religion, and I hear the whispering voices of women. For although men in my family went to church, women prayed most audibly. Whether by man or woman, however, God the Father was rarely addressed directly. There were intermediaries to carry one's petition to Him. My mother had her group of Mexican and South American saints and near-saints (persons moving toward canonization). She favored a black Brazilian priest who, she claimed, was especially efficacious. Above all mediators was Mary, *Santa María,* the Mother. Whereas at school the primary mediator was Christ, at home that role was assumed by the Mexican Virgin, *Nuestra Señora de Guadalupe,* the focus of devotion and pride for Mexican Catholics. The Mexican Mary 'honored our people,' my mother would say. 'She could have appeared to anyone in the whole world, but she appeared to a Mexican.' Someone like us. And she appeared, I could see from her picture, as a young Indian maiden — dark just like me.

On her feastday in early December my family would go to the Mexican church for a predawn high mass. The celebration would begin in the cold dark with a blare of trumpets imitating the cries of a cock. The Virgin's wavering statue on the shoulders of men would lead a procession into the warm yellow church. Often an usher would roughly separate me from my parents and pull me into a line of young children. (My mother nodded calmly when I looked back.)

Sometimes alone, sometimes with my brother and sisters, I would find myself near the altar amid two or three hundred children, many of them dressed like Mexican cowboys and cowgirls. Sitting on the floor it was easier to see the congregation than the altar. So, as the mass progressed, my eye would wander through the crowd. Invariably, my attention settled on old women — mysterious supplicants in black —

bent deep, their hands clasped tight to hold steady the attention of the Mexican Virgin, who was pictured high over the altar, astride a black moon.

The *gringo* Catholic church, a block from our house, was a very different place. In the *gringo* church Mary's statue was relegated to a side altar, imaged there as a serene white lady who matter-of-factly squashed the Genesis serpent with her bare feet. (Very early I knew that I was supposed to believe that the shy Mexican Mary was the same as this European Mary triumphant.) In the *gringo* church the floors were made not of squeaky wood but of marble. And there was not the devotional clutter of so many pictures and statues and candle racks. 'It doesn't feel like a church' my mother complained. But as it became our regular church, I grew to love its elegant simplicity: the formal march of its eight black pillars toward the altar; the Easter-egg-shaped sanctuary that arched high over the tabernacle; and the dim pink light suffused throughout on summer afternoons when I came in not to pray but to marvel at the cool calm.

The holy darkness of church never frightened me. It was never nighttime darkness. Religion at school and at church was never nighttime religion like religion at home. Catholicism at home was shaped by the sounds of the 'family rosary': tired voices repeating the syllables of the Hail Mary; our fingers inching forward on beads toward the point of beginning; my knees aching; the coming of sleep.

Religion at home was a religion of bedtime. Prayers before sleeping spoke of death coming during the night. It was then a religion of shadows. The last thing I'd see before closing my eyes would be the cheap statue of Mary aglow next to my bed.

But the dark at the foot of my bed billowed with malevolent shapes. Those nights when I'd shudder awake from a nightmare, I'd remember my grandmother's instruction to make a sign of the cross in the direction of my window. (That way Satan would find his way barred.) Sitting up in bed, I'd aim the sign of the cross against the dim rectangle of light. Quickly, then, I'd say the Prayer to My Guardian Angel, which would enable me to fall back to sleep.

In time dawn came.

A child whose parents could not introduce him to books like *Grimm's Fairy Tales*, I was introduced to the sphere of enchantment by the nighttime Catholicism of demons and angels. The superstitious Catholicism of home provided a kind of proletarian fairy-tale world.

Satan was mentioned in the classroom. And depicted on the

nuns' cartoon placards, as bringing all his evil to bear on the temptation of nicely dressed boys and girls. In the morning's bright light and in the safe company of classmates, Satan never aroused very much terror. Around the time I was in fourth grade, moreover, religion classes became increasingly academic. I was introduced to that text familiar to generations of Catholic students, *The Baltimore Catechism*. It is a text organized by questions about the Catholic faith. (Who is God? What is Penance? What is Hope?)

Today's Catholic elementary schools attempt a less mechanical approach to religious instruction. Students are taught — what I never had to be taught — that religion is not simply a matter of dogmas or theological truths; that religion involves a person's whole way of life. To make the point, emphasis has shifted from the theological to the ethical. Students are encouraged to consider social problems and responses to 'practical' dilemmas in a modern world through which angels and devils no longer dance.

My schooling belonged to another time. *The Baltimore Catechism* taught me to trust the authority of the Church. That was the central lesson conveyed through the experience of memorizing hundreds of questions and answers. I learned an answer like, God made us to know, love, and serve Him in this life, and to be happy with Him in the next. The answer was memorized *along with* the question (it belonged with the question), Why did God make us? I learned, in other words, question and answer together. Beyond what the answer literally stated, two things were thus communicated. First, the existence of a question implies the existence of an answer. (There are no stray questions.) And second, that my questions about religion had answers. (The Church knows.)

Not only in religion class was memory exercised. During those years when I was memorizing the questions and answers of *The Baltimore Catechism*, I was also impressing on my memory the spelling of hundreds of words, grammar rules, division and multiplication tables. The nuns deeply trusted the role of memorization in learning. Not coincidentally, they were excellent teachers of basics. They would stand in front of us for hours, drilling us over and over (5 times 5 . . . 5 times 9; *i* before *e* except after *c*; God made us to know, love and serve Him in this world . . .). Stressing memorization, my teachers implied that education is largely a matter of acquiring knowledge already discovered. And they were right. For contrary to more progressive notions of learning, much that is learned in a classroom must be the already known; and much that is already known must be learned before a student can achieve truly independent thought.

Stressing memorization, the nuns assumed an important Catholic bias. Stated positively, they believed that learning is a social activity; learning is a rite of passage into the group. (Remembrance is itself an activity that establishes a student's dependence upon and union with others.) Less defensibly, the nuns distrusted intellectual challenges to authority. In religion class especially, they would grow impatient with the relentlessly questioning student. When one nun told my parents that their youngest daughter had a 'mind of her own,' she meant the remark to be a negative criticism. And even though I was urged to read all that I could, several teachers were dismayed that I had read the novels of Victor Hugo and Flaubert. ('Those writers are on the Index, Richard.') With classmates I would hear the nuns' warning about non-Catholic colleges, stories of Faustian Catholics falling victim to the foolish sin of intellectual pride.

Trust the Church. It was the institution established by the instruction of Christ to his disciple: 'Thou art Peter and upon this rock I will build. . . .' (How could Protestants not hear?) The nun drew her pointer to the chart in front of the classroom where the line of popes connected the name of St. Peter to that of Pope Pius XII. Trust the Church, the nun said. It was through the Church that God was best known. I came to believe: 'I am a Catholic.' (My faith in the Christian God was enclosed by my faith in the Church.)

I never read the Bible alone. In fifth grade, when I told a teacher that I intended to read the New Testament over the summer, I did not get the praise I expected. Instead, the nun looked worried and said I should delay my plan for a while. ('Wait until we read it in class.') In the seventh and eighth grades, my class finally did read portions of the Bible. We read together. And our readings were guided by the teachings of Tradition — the continuous interpretation of the Word passing through generations of Catholics. Thus, as a reader I never forgot the ancient Catholic faith — that the Church serves to help solitary man comprehend God's Word.